The Pleasures of Seafood

THE
Pleasures
of
Seafood

RIMA AND RICHARD COLLIN

Galahad Books • New York

We wish to express our very special thanks for his unfailing judgment and taste to our editor, Donald Hutter.

The New Orleans recipes in this book are based on recipes that originally appeared in slightly different form, in *The New Orleans Cookbook* (Alfred A. Knopf, 1975).

First Galahad Books edition published in 1995.

Galahad Books
A division of Budget Book Service, Inc.
386 Park Avenue South
New York, NY 10016

Galahad Books is a registered trademark of Budget Book Service, Inc.

Published by arrangement with Richard Collin.

Library of Congress Catalog Card Number: 95-78589

ISBN: 0-88365-917-4

Printed in the United States of America.

For
Nikki and Web

CONTENTS

Contents viii

Introduction

Cooking fish and shellfish is a joyous and simple art accessible to all home cooks, whatever their technical skill, wherever they live in America. We are inveterate seafood lovers who want to share with others our personal knowledge of seafood cooking and to communicate its delights. This is a personal cookbook which aims to make fish and shellfish cooking as irresistible to others as it is to us. After years of poring over the existing literature on seafood cooking we are convinced that neither a scholarly compendium of every possible species of fish and shellfish nor a classification by characteristics (firm flesh, oily flesh, etc.) will ever attract people either unfamiliar with seafood preparation or limited in their knowledge of its possibilities.

Cooking seafood is and should be pleasurable and easy, and this book is intended as a genial practical guide, a guide to enjoying seafood cooking. Our approach emphasizes personal encounters with fish and shellfish dishes we have eaten and enjoyed in America and abroad; we try to evoke the visual and sensual appeal of these dishes; we explain the basic principles used in the preparation of each dish and suggest carefully tested substitute fish or shellfish from various regions of America to enable any reader, no matter where he lives, to prepare and enjoy

these dishes or excellent versions of them. The specific dishes are ones we selected to entice readers and cooks into this domain so long unexplored by many Americans, to entice them in the one way we are convinced can make seafood cooks out of persons simply interested in good food—by providing excellent, clear recipes for truly enjoyable and attractive dishes and by teaching the art of seafood cookery through the way the recipes are presented.

Fishing is probably the most widespread sport in the country. Unfortunately, most sport fishermen and their wives cook what they catch in a very limited number of ways, not by choice but because cookbooks and cooking columns suggest few alternatives. Lovers of fish and shellfish who purchase their seafood at fish markets are frequently handicapped by the lack of useful and imaginative cooking information. There is an immense gray area surrounding local and regional fish and the range of dishes applicable to each variety. We want to make fish and shellfish cooking less of a mystery and more of a pleasure, and feel that a book such as this one will be a standard reference work for many years to come. We explain in meaningful cooking terms the differences between regional fish and make it possible for an émigré from the West Coast to find an enjoyable replacement for his beloved rex sole, for a Floridian to find a fish similar to his yellowtail, for a New Orleanian to discover ample supplies of his beloved Lake

Pontchartrain trout in the Midwest. This book will be as useful to the urban fish market shopper as to the fisherman's wife.

We work together, and the narrative voice in this book reflects our collaboration. This book in its totality is the sum of our work together, and also of some separate experiences and reactions.

Choosing dishes for this book was one of our simpler tasks. We cooked what we liked, tried new dishes we thought we might like, adapted techniques and styles of cooking from various regions of America and from many foreign cuisines to fish we thought would work in these preparations. We had many American regional fish flown fresh to New Orleans by air freight and worked with them first hand in our own kitchen, to see what we could and couldn't do with them. We discovered, to our horror, that many standard instructions for handling and preparing certain specific fish and shellfish simply don't work. They appear to have been repeated from one book to the next without anyone really finding out first hand that this mode of skinning or filleting or that mode of cooking something will give you dreadful results or, in many instances, no results at all.

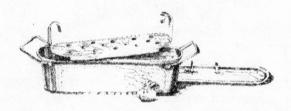

We came to better understand why so many people we know are honestly convinced that preparing seafood at home is immensely difficult. Most people cook from cookbooks and must rely on the instructions they are given. If the instructions are garbled or inadequate or just plain wrong, most home cooks tend to blame themselves. We began to realize that our guiding assumption when we conceived and wrote *The New Orleans Cookbook*—that if the food were clearly explained and accurate reliable recipes provided, anyone who likes to cook could cook first rate Creole food—applied just as much to the realm of seafood cooking.

We have organized this book by styles and techniques of cooking, rather than by types of fish and shellfish. Our reasons were simple and practical. When you begin to get the hang of frying, or of preparing curries, it's natural and logical to want to continue in that vein for a while, to become more adept and to broaden your repertoire of dishes that work in the same way. And the basic utensils and seasonings for any given style are essentially the same. You learn to work with frying oil and to use a long-handled skimmer with ease, and keep getting better at it. Or you become conversant with and bewitched by the rhythms of Indian cooking and, like any budding virtuoso, can't resist a bit more practice and the prospect of a lot more applause. For us the pleasures of seafood are as much to be found in the amazing range of cooking styles, in the immense variety of regional and ethnic experiences it affords, as in the enjoyment of any specific fish or shellfish.

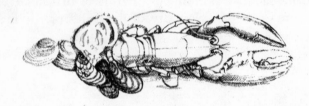

It has always seemed to us far too limiting, and too stifling to the cook's pleasure and imagination, to have the recipes of a seafood cookbook arranged by specific fish or, even less appealing, by the physical characteristics of types of fish ("oily fish," "dry fish," etc.). There's something inescapably clinical and unaesthetic about such a presentation. It's true that mackerel is oily, but it's far more useful to the cook to have some first class recipes for preparing it. There are natural and practical groupings of fish and shellfish, fish that work in precisely the same way in a given dish or with enough similarity that one dish follows logically from the other. Whenever this is the case, we have indicated which regionally available fish are really good substitutes for the one specified in the recipe. There are in fact more similarities than differences in the myriad water creatures of this world. They are far more flexible in cooking terms than is generally admitted. For us, one of the exciting things about planning our next fish or shellfish meal at home is thinking of all the ways it can be prepared.

One of the most troubling parts of our research was the discovery that most cookbooks don't know what they are talking

about when they deal with ethnic or regional food. How dismayed we were to find cookbook entries with Clams à la Creole when we know that New Orleans has no clams to eat, let alone cook. The list is endless. "Bulgarian Fish Pudding": what is Bulgarian about tomato sauce? Or French dishes made with American canned creamed soups? We have tried to avoid such pitfalls. We love to travel, to collect restaurants, and to discover new dishes. We work them out at home from taste memory. When something in our reading strikes us as authentic, we check further. If it is authentic, we then work out our own home version—and identify it as such. We are probably more aware than most eaters of the carelessness and offensiveness of false regional and ethnic scholarship, living as we do in an area so often misrepresented and coming, each of us, from different ethnic backgrounds. In this book you will not find something called Afghanistanian Fried Fish. You will find Greek Fried Fish with Garlic and Almond Sauce and Fried Trout in Pearly Meal. They may not sound as exotic but if you never had really good fried fish before, such dishes will taste exotic. And they are authentic ethnic and regional foods, honestly described.

The Pleasures of Seafood is both a personal record of our encounters with fish and shellfish and a collection of carefully recorded, precise instructions on how to cook the best seafood dishes we have found. We are convinced that great seafood cooking is within the reach of everyone who cooks. We have conceived this book differently from other seafood cookbooks for two reasons. First, we are certain that no dreary catalog of fish and shellfish in alphabetical order, with endlessly repetitive minimal recipes, can convey the true diversity and excitement of seafood cooking. Second, we have deliberately avoided the arcane and "fancy" approach that mainly underscores the author's cleverness and esoteric preferences and makes the reader and would-be cook feel inadequate and discouraged from the outset. We believe that demystifying fish and shellfish, taking their preparation out of the world of snobbery and fashionable cuisine, and making the resources of urban fish markets more accessible and usable are among the most significant aims of this book. Above all, we hope to succeed in communicating to you our love of seafood and some of its boundless pleasures.

1

Some Practical Matters and Prejudices

On Cooking Equipment and Utensils

Most of what you need for cooking seafood you already have. We often muse on the elaborate equipment offered in mail order catalogs for cooking seafood and wonder what we'd do with the fancy $100 or $200 fish poacher or whatever if we had one. Virtually no special equipment is required for seafood preparation. We have two standard electric ovens (18 x 18 inches and 21 x 13 inches) at eye level, both with broiling pans and racks. Before we built our present kitchen we used a prehistoric table model electric broiler. It got hot very quickly and worked beautifully. The heart of any kitchen is the range. Our range has gas burners, but we've worked with electric. Since electric ranges are the most common type we've written the recipe instructions in this book for electric. The only problem with electric burners is forgetting to take the pan off the burner at the right moment. If the cook forgets, the dish is overcooked—and with seafood, overcooked is virtually destroyed.

The most important single piece of seafood cooking equipment is a standard 6 inch ruler. Second is a pair of inexpensive timers with loud bells. Distance from the heat and cooking time are absolutely crucial to good seafood cooking. The most useful general equipment for the seafood cook includes several heavy saucepans, a large pot for stews and chowders, some baking and serving dishes, several large heavy sauté pans or skillets, the usual assortment of wooden spoons, a long-handled fork, whisks, some sharp knives, and two large slotted or perforated spatulas. We also use a simple electric blender (with low, high, and off settings only) and an electric or hand rotary beater.

Several special cooking techniques require some additional equipment. For grilling, an inexpensive hinged grill available in hardware stores is indispensable. Good frying requires an electric deep fryer with a thermostatic control. For mousses you will need an assortment of molds; for smoking, a smoker or a barbecue grill with a cover; for soufflés, some decent soufflé dishes; and for quenelles, a meat grinder or food processor. If necessary, you can improvise in a number of ways. You can grill over a stove burner using a hinged grill; you can deep fry in a saucepan with a frying thermometer attached; you can hand chop, strain, and chop again if you have no grinder; you can whip and fluff by hand if you have no blender. Heavy baking pans lined with cake racks will do if you have no broiling pan and rack, and are always needed if you are broiling for more than the usual number. However, if you plan to cook dishes using any of these techniques regularly, the convenience of the modern tools is well worth their modest price. We have an unusually complete array of pots and pans and lids, but there are still times when the pan we choose has no lid of its own. Then out comes the indispensable heavy-duty aluminum foil.

The nuts and bolts of the seafood cook's kitchen are simple. We eat seafood at home most of the time and yet have never bought a single piece of equipment specifically for cooking seafood. For consistent results, check the thermostats on your ovens at regular intervals. To broil well in a home oven make sure to preheat the oven for at least 20 minutes with the oven door slightly ajar so

---

that the broiler will be very hot when you begin cooking. Seafood cooking presents few problems you cannot solve with a little improvisation and plain common sense. And if you come to enjoy cooking seafood as much as we do, you can acquire a few additional conveniences to make the process simpler and even more enjoyable.

On Plain and Fancy Fish

We really have nothing against sauces or *haute cuisine* fish dishes. We love them. But our favorite fish and the most difficult to find are those that are cooked simply. What can beat a fine broiled fish or one grilled over hot coals? How many times have food writers warned you that a restaurant can't be trusted with fancy fish, so order the plainest ones available? If the restaurant can't hide its ineptitude with a sauce, what are they going to do with a naked fish? Cover it with paprika most likely.

There is such a thing as a plain fish. Before stoves were invented the staple of eighteenth and early nineteenth century cooking was boiled fish. Now that's plain fish. Not much imagination or variation. The old cookbooks might vary the cooking time by 10 or 20 minutes, but only once in a while did the old cooks even season the water or the fish. One of the great events of the French culinary revolution was the end of the boiled fish. Carême in the 1840s inveighed mightily against this primitive practice. In spite of a nostalgic desire for the simple old times with *truite au bleu,* we have gone on to better things. (We think that most of the attraction of *truite au bleu* is not how it is cooked but the fact that the fish is so fresh.)

But we seem to have come perhaps too far. Some eaters are not happy unless the fish is buried under sauces, made into fancy set pieces, or otherwise obscured by fancy menu terms. We've always been puzzled by people who feel they have to "fancy up" the best of nature's bounty. When we are fortunate enough to get an absolutely fresh fish we like to prepare it simply by broiling or grilling it. Simple, yes, but not plain. Simple and beautiful like a great work of art or a sunset. So here's to both ways of enjoying seafood—simple and fancy, but never plain.

_____

On the Joys of Dover Sole
and American Flounder

Why, we ask ourselves, do the good restaurants of San Francisco fly in Dover sole from England when just outside of the city are to be found such seafood delights as petrale, rex sole, sand dab, and just a little way up the coast fresh salmon? We are not trying to single out San Francisco. The restaurants of many American cities do it. They do it because their customers ask them to. Why, when nothing tastes better than the freshest local fish, freshly caught and beautifully cooked?

What probably happened to these diners was the unforgettable experience of great fresh fish. Unfortunately the shock of recognition struck them when they were on a tour of Europe. At home they eat steak; abroad they might just try fish. And what happens? Dover sole in London is delicious. Well, then it must be the Dover sole and not the freshness of the fish or the art of its preparation. The same with the lovely turbot in France. So tourists come back to America having tasted those fish and now plague their restaurants and their fish markets for real sole and turbot. These fish are probably never again as good as they were the first time, since they've had to make a transoceanic journey to get to the newly born fish enthusiasts, who never realized that fish just as good and as unusual, and fresher, are right there in New York, in Minneapolis, Detroit, all over America.

What can compete with Gulf pompano, Lake Superior whitefish, Lake Michigan smelt, Atlantic flounder, New England scrod, West Coast salmon? All great fish are equal. Different, thankfully, but equal. The common striped bass or sea bass is as delicious in its way as Dover sole. Perhaps, more. A. J. Liebling was convinced that the popularity of sole and turbot lay in their delicacy, in the fact that the fish were so mild that the eater took no chances on fishy taste or a taste of any kind. Liebling was, in a way, accurate. The French specifically use turbot so as not to upstage the sauce, which for them is the heart of the dish. But there's probably more whimsy in Liebling than truth. Sole is a delicious fish. It's less delicious when it has had to fly more than a day to reach the eager diner. And that eager diner may be better served, if he's in San Francisco, by the lovely petrale caught just a few hours back.

But then grand restaurants don't make much of a fuss over petrale; they save their best sauces for visiting fish from abroad. It's not that way in all countries. The English could just as easily fly in scrod, the French could truck in Dutch herring. Instead, the French and the English pay their greatest respect to their local fish and are repaid in kind. In New Orleans a local speckled trout, which is actually a weakfish and scorned in many parts of the country, becomes king for a day in dishes as exalted as Trout Amandine. The moral of all this: support your local fish.

On Sherries for Drinking and Cooking

One of the tastes that the nineteenth century epicures on both sides of the Atlantic had in common was a sweet tooth where drinks were concerned. Americans liked their Madeira, Englishmen their rum, and just about everyone except the Spanish their sweet sherries. The Spanish now prize their dry sherries and indeed many so-called dry sherries are marketed in America. But so great is the pull of tradition that many Americans have never tasted a really dry sherry. There is only one widely available in America. It is called Manzanilla. (Any of the many brands is suitable.) And it is delicious.

Neither of us is prejudiced against sweetness in wine. We both love dessert wines, good French Sauternes, fine Portuguese and even some California ports, great German white wines. But in sherry the great taste is not in the sweetness but in the fine nutty flavor, usually masked or overwhelmed in sweet sherry.

Manzanilla is no more expensive than most sherries. It is much cheaper than Bristol Cream, and it will make all the difference in the world in your cooking. But forget the sweet sherries. Like the cooking sherries which came into popularity during Prohibition and which are both undrinkable and uncookable, the sweet sherries are a holdover from a time when drinking a cocktail was socially or otherwise unacceptable. If you must drink them, they're no worse than the sweet French aperitifs like Kir. But unless you have a nineteenth century Englishman's palate, keep them out of the food.

On the Differences Between Home Cooking and Restaurant Cooking

Whenever we read in the papers or magazines a request by a home cook for a restaurant recipe, we wonder how this odd culinary confrontation will turn out. The two styles of cooking are worlds apart. Things that restaurants do easily are virtually impossible in a home kitchen and vice versa. Restaurants can have on hand large batches of sauces, quantities of salads and salad dressings, and accompaniments that are ready to serve. The home cook must work on each preparation as painstakingly as on the main course. Home cooks, however, do not have to turn out 70 different dishes; they can concentrate on making one perfect dish in just the right proportions to feed a family or a set number of guests.

Neither home cooking nor restaurant cooking is inherently superior. Some of the fun of dining out is the multiplicity of courses, the chance for everyone to make a different selection, and the amenities of being waited on by professionals. There is no way the gifted home cook can compete with the best restaurants on matters of choice and service. But offer a professional waiter or chef a home cooked meal and he will leap at the chance. It is a different kind of eating and a different kind of cooking.

We have steered clear of most of the more elaborate restaurant combinations and set pieces, since we feel there is no sense in putting the home cook into competition with an entire restaurant staff. Besides, we suspect that she and her husband are probably more impressed with the decor and service anyway. All of the recipes in this book are designed for the good home cook. Of course, if a restaurant chef wanted to try them out, he might very well like them. But he would also find out that simply multiplying by 50 or 100 doesn't work. The entire dish would have to be rebalanced. And when you cajole the chef at your favorite restaurant and get the house special recipe, the odds are that for one reason or another it just won't work at home.

On the Fishy Taste of Fish

If every time someone had a bad piece of steak he called it meaty, we could see some justification for calling over-the-hill seafood fishy. At one time or another we have all had food that is stale or on the verge of spoiling. Fruit frequently gets overripe, but is a rotten tomato more tomatoey than a good one, or a soggy peach more peachy? No. Then why should a less-than-perfect fish be termed fishy?

Fresh fish taste and smell of the sea, the lake, the river. Properly frozen fish, well preserved, when thawed smell just like fresh ones. On behalf of the Trout Lovers Association of America we are considering suing for libel the next person who demeans the good name of fresh fish. The best way to be assured of fresh fish is to find a reputable fish market and let them know that you insist on the freshest of the catch rather than on a specific variety that may not be as fresh. And when you buy frozen fish or shellfish buy it at a place that is careful with all its frozen food. Freshly caught fish always taste delicious. Let's put the blame where it belongs—with the fisherman or trucker who dawdles on the way to the market. Before he was caught the fish smelled as good as the water he was in.

On Herbs and Spices:
A Checklist and Some Suggestions

Herbs and spices indicated *by name only* in the recipes are those commonly available in groceries and supermarkets in one form only. They include the following:

GROUND FORM	DRIED LEAF FORM
allspice	*basil*
cardamom	*chervil*
cinnamon	*coriander leaf* (cilantro)
cloves	*dill weed*
coriander	*marjoram*
cumin	*oregano*
fenugreek	*tarragon*
ginger	*thyme*
mace	
nutmeg	
sage	
turmeric	

In some regions of the country herbs frequently used in local dishes are marketed in less usual forms—for example, ground thyme, ground bay leaf, ground marjoram. These are difficult to find and often, when found, rather stale. When the recipe calls for them, we suggest reducing the dried leaf forms to powders with a mortar and pestle.

Unless otherwise indicated, the salt listed in the recipes is ordinary table salt. It is not advisable to substitute coarse salt or sea salt, both of which have a less pronounced salinity if used in the indicated quantities.

Black, white, and cayenne pepper work differently in cooked dishes. Black pepper has a stronger taste than white and is often visible in the finished dish; white pepper has a subtler taste and adds aroma. The age and pungency of preground black and white pepper are difficult to determine. Grinding these peppers fresh is the only sure way to achieve consistent results in cooking. With cayenne pepper, the hottest of the three, absolute freshness is less crucial. Just make sure the cayenne you buy is not stale; sniff it and if it has no aroma, look for another jar. Tabasco sauce is made from the same peppers as cayenne, but is measured differently and has a different taste in the finished dish. Do not substitute Tabasco for cayenne.

We grow fresh herbs and know from using them that their taste in cooking can differ markedly from the dried variety. Fresh herbs can vary considerably from batch to batch and season to season. Since there is no way with fresh herbs to achieve the consistency we believe printed recipes should have, we have specified carefully measured amounts of dried. Fresh herbs are fun to grow, and if you grow them you know how good they taste. You can easily determine the needed amount of a fresh herb once you've prepared a recipe as given with dried. (A safe starting estimate is 2 to 3 teaspoons of fresh to ½ teaspoon of dried.)

On Fish Substitutions

We have experimented with all manner of fish substitution charts, general rules and codes, and have found all of them unnecessarily confusing. Previous fish literature and regional traditions have perpetuated the notion that various fish are in general more different than alike, and any complicated apparatus seemed to us to reinforce that erroneous idea. Instead of supplying a fish substitution chart, by its nature oversimplified, we decided to say a few general things.

All fish are different. All fish taste different. Most fish, however, can be substituted in most fish recipes. Obviously a substitute fish will taste different from the original, but not that different. There will be more similarity than dissimilarity. *Most important, the main difference will be apparent only to those who know well both of the fish in question.* For a New Orleanian the substitution of cod for New Orleans trout is immediately noticeable. For a

Midwesterner the difference is purely theoretical. Petrale from the West Coast is not the same as Lake Superior whitefish, but a Bostonian who has had neither will find the differences irrelevant. We are not trying to suggest an obliteration of all differences in fish. We are simply suggesting that common sense will dictate how important the specific fish is in a particular recipe.

Some fish have no substitutes. Catfish is a unique fish and there is nothing that tastes quite like it. But this causes few problems, since catfish lovers know the fish very well and are not going to be seduced by our prose about flounder—and we doubt that city folk who are put off by the looks of catfish will readily succumb to our blandishments. Our hope in this book is to perhaps induce the catfish lover to try one of our carp recipes or a trout dish or to try a process of cooking previously thought too fancy. And to perhaps get the city fish eater into some other byways of fish preparation and away from the one or two dishes that mark his total familiarity with seafood.

If you have preferences for certain local fish, well and good. If you are curious about other fish, try them. You can easily see from the directions we give what size of fish will work in a given recipe. All trout, bass, bluefish, and cod in the small size range will work equally well in any recipe for the other. Flounder and sole are always interchangeable, as are all the variations within that large family such as dab, lemon sole, yellowtail flounder. Rock cod and cod are more alike than different. And pompano *en*

papillote tastes very much like mackerel *en papillote* if the sauce is as distinctive as it should be, even though those two fish have less in common than most varieties.

In other words, substitute freely unless you have some common sense reservations, such as substituting shark for baby trout. Even here a shark steak would work. If you have no choice then live dangerously and experiment. Catfish Dugléré sounds like a bad joke, and we hope we never have to try it to see how badly off the mark it may be, but if we were in the mood for Dugléré and catfish were the only fish around we would welcome the chance to experiment and look forward to the meal with as much anticipation as for Sole Dugléré or Fried Catfish. Many cookbooks tell you to experiment with *any* aspect of the recipes. We would prefer that you follow our cooking instructions as closely as possible, since we have worked them out carefully and know they work. But please experiment as much as you wish with different fish in the various recipes. You can then join us in the new Fish Liberation Movement. All fish are not equal, but any fresh fish is better than no fish at all.

Broiling Recipes

Broiled Pompano

Broiled Pompano Meunière
New Orleans Style

Broiled Flounder

Broiled Boston Scrod

Broiled Lake Trout

Broiled Spanish Mackerel
with New Potatoes

Broiled Flounder with
Crawfish Dressing

Broiled Redfish Hollandaise

Broiled Redfish with Lump
Crabmeat Hollandaise

Broiled Maine Lobster

Broiled Oysters

Broiled Soft Belly Clams

Broiled Soft Shell Crabs

Broiled Stuffed Florida
Lobster

Broiled Sole Maître d'Hôtel

Broiled Striped Bass with
Lump Crabmeat

Broiled Pompano
Pontchartrain

Broiled Oysters en Brochette

Broiled Eel with Butter
Sauce

Broiled Striped Bass with
Egg and Lemon Sauce

Broiled Shark

2

Broiling

Broiling is the simplest and most basic form of seafood cooking, the method that most clearly allows the natural taste of the fish itself to come through in its best form. Whenever we find a fish we've never tasted before, we broil it first. There's no better way to learn first hand the unique flavor and texture of a fresh fish than through this form of cooking. A properly broiled fish is the equal of the grandest and most complicated *haute cuisine* preparations.

Broiling has increasingly become a rare art. We never fail to be astonished at the countless examples of inept broiling we encounter, and have often speculated about the causes. Perhaps one reason broiling is so often poorly done is precisely because it *is* so simple: few restaurants seem able to believe that less is more, especially when it comes to broiling fish. Very well endowed restaurant kitchens frequently overpower a fish with too much heat at too great a distance, producing a fish that is in fact baked rather than broiled. One restaurant we both love is famous for its perfect broiling and one day we asked one of the owners the secret of its unerring success in this form of cooking. He was surprised by our question and indicated that no one there really gave broiling a second thought; everything was left to the waiters, all of whom used one simple, rather small broiler. Each waited his turn and removed his fish as soon as it was cooked; because of the line, no fish ever stayed under the broiler long enough to be overcooked. The more popular the restaurant's broiled fish dishes were, the less chance there was for overcooking. One cause of poor broiling is the attempt to disguise poorly preserved fish: paprika to hide the lack of a well browned upper surface, overcooking to make deteriorating texture indistinguishable.

The home kitchen is the best stronghold for preserving the simple art of broiling. Any home cook can broil fish well—with an oven broiler, an inexpensive table model electric broiler, a hinged grill over a stove-top burner. All that is necessary is some care, timing, and basic respect for the fish or shellfish whose essential flavor and texture are so easily unlocked by this form of cooking. Naturally, you should use the best specimens of fish for broiling. The fresher the better. Perfectly frozen fish carefully thawed can work just as well. What won't work is fish that has been irregularly iced down over a period of days and then displayed under less than optimal conditions.

The star of the broiled dish is not the sauce or the garnish or the intricacy of preparation—it's the fish itself. With a fine pompano, a sweet white fillet of Boston scrod, a lovely flounder, a Maine lobster, what more is needed than some salt and pepper, some melted butter, and a bit of lemon? Mastering the art of simple broiling as detailed in this chapter will make you one of the best seafood cooks in the country.

Basic Broiling Techniques

Timing, intense heat, and distance are all crucial.

Preheat broiler, broiling pan, and rack for 20 to 30 minutes with oven door slightly ajar.

Brush rack with butter before putting seafood on it.

Baste surface of seafood before broiling for attractive browned crust. Never use paprika.

Surface of seafood should be 3½ to 4 inches from source of heat. Raise level of broiling pan if necessary by placing inverted pie pans under it.

Broil fillets for 6 to 8 minutes, thick pieces or whole fish (¾ inch thick or more) 10 to 12 minutes, large shellfish (such as lobster) 12 to 15 minutes.

Only thick pieces (1 inch thick or more) need be turned over.

For more than 3 or 4 portions use heavy baking pan lined with cake racks in place of broiling pan.

For makeshift broiling use flat hinged grill over a stove burner. (Protect hands with heavy mitt.)

Broiled Pompano

A classic broiled fish. Pompano is a beautiful, delicate Gulf fish, expensive, and for us indispensable. With the smaller pompano, leaving the skin on the fillets makes them easier to handle. If the skin is left on, place the fillets skin side down on the rack during broiling.

FOR TWO

*2 small to medium-sized
  pompano fillets
½ c. (1 stick) salt butter
1 Tbs. finely minced fresh parsley*

*1⅓ Tbs. fresh lemon juice
¼ tsp. salt
salt and freshly ground pepper*

Preheat the broiler, broiling pan, and rack for 15 to 20 minutes. While the broiler is heating, melt the butter in a small saucepan over low heat. Remove the pan from the heat and add the parsley, lemon juice, and salt. Stir to mix thoroughly.

Remove the preheated broiling pan and rack from the oven. Brush the rack with some of the melted seasoned butter and place the fillets on it. Sprinkle the fillets with salt and pepper and baste each fillet evenly with about 2 tablespoons of the melted butter. Set the broiling pan in the oven about 3½ to 4 inches from the source of heat. If necessary, raise the position of the pan by placing a pie pan under it to obtain the suggested distance. Broil for 6 to 7 minutes. The top surface will be medium brown with a few darker areas. Remove the pan from the oven as soon as the fish is cooked and place the fillets on heated serving plates. Pour some of the remaining butter over each fillet and serve immediately, garnished with a lemon wedge if desired.

Broiled Pompano Meunière
New Orleans Style

The classic New Orleans way of serving this great Gulf fish. We were introduced to this dish on a first visit to New Orleans, when a waiter at Galatoire's, noticing our slightly dissipated look after several days of glorious eating, suggested we have a "plain" broiled fish. "Try the pompano," he advised. We did. It was a revelation—even more of a revelation than we knew at the moment. The next evening in Atlanta we happily spotted pompano on the menu and ordered it. It tasted like a different fish. The fish was the same, but the preparation wasn't. Nothing could be simpler than Galatoire's quickly broiled pompano with browned butter sauce, called meunière *in New Orleans. The sauce is prepared separately from the small quantity of lemon-butter used for brushing the rack and basting the fillets.*

FOR TWO

MEUNIÈRE SAUCE

¾ c. (1½ sticks) salt butter
½ tsp. freshly ground black pepper

2 Tbs. fresh lemon juice
2 Tbs. finely minced fresh parsley

BASTING SAUCE

¼ c. (½ stick) salt butter
2 tsp. fresh lemon juice
⅛ tsp. salt

---

2 small to medium-sized pompano fillets
salt and freshly ground white pepper

To prepare the meunière sauce, melt the butter in a small, heavy saucepan over low heat, then continue cooking until the butter begins to turn a hazelnut brown. Remove the pan from the heat and add the

---

pepper, lemon juice, and parsley. Stir. The sauce will foam up a bit. When the foaming subsides, return the pan to low heat for about 1 minute, just until the color deepens a bit. Remove once more from the heat and set on the range surface over the pilot light or on a warming tray while you broil the fish.

Broil the pompano as directed for Broiled Pompano, using all the basting sauce. Place the fillets on heated plates and pour about ⅓ cup meunière sauce over each one. (If the meunière sauce has not stayed hot, warm it over medium heat for 30 seconds before saucing the fish.)

Broiled Flounder

Flounder is one of our favorite fish, extremely delicate, with a distinctive yet mild taste. The best way to broil flounder is whole, with the tail left on and the skin scored. Timing is important; a minute or two of overcooking can mar the marvelous delicate texture. Flounder needs nothing more than a simple lemon-butter sauce. It's a common American fish that we find every bit as delicious as sole, which it closely resembles. Treat the Atlantic, Pacific, or Gulf flounder as you would the expensive sole and you'll be hard pressed to tell the difference. If we had to make a choice, we'd choose the flounder.

FOR TWO

2 small to medium-sized flounder, split and cleaned, left whole, with head removed and tail on	2⅔ Tbs. fresh lemon juice
	¼ tsp. salt
	salt and freshly ground black pepper
¾ c. (1½ sticks) salt butter	
1⅓ Tbs. finely minced fresh parsley	

Preheat broiler, broiling pan, and rack and prepare basting sauce as directed for Broiled Pompano.

Rinse the fish under cold running water and dry thoroughly with paper towels. Using a thin sharp knife, cut 3 or 4 X-shaped slits in the upper, thicker side. Sprinkle lightly with salt and pepper, then baste and broil as for Broiled Pompano. Do not turn the fish over. Broiling time will range from 5 minutes for a very small flounder to 7 to 8 minutes for a medium-sized one. The fish is done when the skin at the edges of the slits turns crisp and brown and begins to curl back a bit, and the flesh showing through the slits is quite white. Place on heated plates and pour several tablespoons of butter sauce over each one. Garnish with lemon wedges and serve immediately.

Broiled Boston Scrod

Scrod is a legendary Boston fish, a small cod generally up to 3 pounds in weight. Its name comes from a contraction of "sacred cod," as it was often referred to in early America. When we first tried it at Boston's Durgin Park restaurant, we were confronted with an unforeseen problem which we still have: whether to order lobster or scrod. We were unprepared for finding anything that could compete with our passion for lobster. Leave the skin on the cod fillets; it keeps the large sweet flakes from separating during broiling. Since scrod has very little oil, several deep diagonal slashes in each fillet will allow the simple butter sauce to penetrate and will give you beautiful and delicious results. One of the indispensable American fish.

FOR TWO

2 small scrod fillets or 1 large one cut in half, skin left on (total weight about 1 lb.)
½ c. (1 stick) salt butter
2½ tsp. fresh lemon juice

¼ tsp. freshly ground white pepper
4 tsp. finely minced fresh parsley
salt and freshly ground white pepper

Preheat the broiler, broiling pan, and rack for at least 20 minutes. Melt the butter in a small saucepan over medium heat. Add the lemon juice, pepper, and parsley, reduce the heat to low, then mix thoroughly and cook for 1 minute longer. Remove the pan from the heat.

Rinse the fillets under cold running water, shake off the excess water, then dry very thoroughly between several layers of paper towels. Make three ⅜-inch deep slashes about 2½ inches apart across each fillet with a thin sharp knife, holding the knife at a 45 degree angle. Sprinkle the fillets lightly with salt and pepper. Remove the broiling pan from the oven and brush the rack evenly with some of the melted butter sauce. (A basting brush is ideal, but if you have none a wadded-up paper towel will do nicely.) Place the fillets skin side down on the rack, then spoon about 1½ tablespoons of butter sauce evenly over each one. Set the pan so that the fish is no more than 3½ to 4 inches from the source of heat, and broil for 8 to 10 minutes or until well browned on top. Remove the fish from the broiler as soon as it is cooked and lift onto preheated plates with a long, wide spatula. Mix the remaining butter sauce well and spoon it over the fillets. Garnish with lemon wedges and serve immediately.

Broiled Lake Trout

No fish better illustrates the confusion of nomenclature than trout. There are the famed Colorado brook trout, Rocky Mountain trout, New Orleans speckled trout (actually a weakfish), as well as farm trout and unspecified frozen trout. Yes, they are all different, and yes, the differences can be substantial. Often overlooked in this maze of names is the fact that all fresh trout and most frozen trout are delicious. The original Rocky Mountain trout, the cutthroat, is exceedingly rare. Even most trout fanciers have never tasted it.

Rather than bemoan the scarcity of "real" trout, we can enjoy what is available. Fresh farm trout has a different flavor from most of the others, but it is delicious. Properly frozen and stored trout can be excellent. Frozen trout often tastes terrible in restaurants, not because it was frozen but because it was not frozen quickly and not stored well to preserve its taste and texture properly. The "fishy" taste comes not from the fish but from the poor way it was handled. The finest and freshest fish will deteriorate if not handled with care. In New Orleans we revere our common speckled trout; we cook it with respect and the taste shows it. (New Orleanians are horrified to learn that their speckled trout are thrown back as rejects in other parts of the country.)

Just leave the skin on, cook as carefully as you would your favorite fish, and enjoy this classic American fish under any of its many names.

FOR TWO

2 small trout, filleted, with the skin left on (about 1½ to 2 lb.)
¾ c. (1½ sticks) melted butter
2 tsp. minced fresh parsley

2 Tbs. dry white wine
⅛ tsp. salt
1/16 tsp. freshly ground black pepper

Preheat the broiler, pan, and rack. Brush the rack with about 3 tablespoons of the melted butter. Mix the parsley, wine, salt, and pepper into the remaining butter. Pour evenly over the fillets. Broil for 6 to 7 minutes. Remove immediately from the broiler and place the fillets on heated plates. Stir the butter, seasonings, and drippings that have collected in the broiling pan and spoon over the fillets. Garnish with lemon wedges and serve immediately.

Broiled Spanish Mackerel with New Potatoes

For a number of years before we began to do the research for our cookbooks we loved broiled mackerel. When we began to examine the printed literature on mackerel, we found it invariably referred to as an oily fish, or a fat one. It's quite likely that if we had encountered those descriptions before we came to love the fish we might well have avoided it altogether. Yes, mackerel is an "oily" fish, but more important it is a delicious one (because of its oiliness? in spite of its oiliness?). Perhaps it would be better to describe it as a rich fish and proceed from there. The very freshest mackerel is good simply broiled. And all mackerel is excellent marinated before broiling; the richer the fish the better it tastes marinated. You can marinate the fillets for several hours or through the day. The extra marinating time will not affect it. In this French dish small boiled new potatoes complement the rich taste of the mackerel.

FOR FOUR

4 Spanish mackerel fillets, skin left on

MARINADE

¼ c. olive oil

3 Tbs. fresh lime juice or ¼ c. bottled

½ tsp. freshly ground black pepper

¼ tsp. salt

½ tsp. freshly ground fennel seed (ground with a mortar and pestle)

½ tsp. basil

---

2 lb. new potatoes

2 c. water

1 tsp. salt

BUTTER SAUCE

½ c. (1 stick) salt butter
¼ tsp. freshly ground white
   pepper

2 Tbs. finely minced fresh
   parsley

---

4 tsp. fresh lemon juice, approximately
4 lemon wedges

Rinse the fillets and dry very thoroughly between several layers of paper towels. Place them skin side down in a shallow oval porcelain gratin dish or pie pan. Pour the olive oil evenly over the fish, then the lime juice. Sprinkle on the seasonings, then gently turn the fillets over 3 or 4 times with tongs to coat them evenly with the marinade. Cover the dish with plastic wrap and refrigerate for an hour or more. Preheat the broiler, broiling pan, and rack.

Rinse the potatoes under running water and place them in a heavy 3 to 4 quart saucepan. Add the water and salt and bring to a boil over high heat. Cover, lower the heat to low, and cook for 12 to 15 minutes or until the potatoes are fork tender, but not soft.

While the potatoes are cooking, prepare the butter sauce. Melt the butter over medium heat, then add the pepper and parsley. Mix and remove the pan from the heat.

When the potatoes are done, drain them in a colander, then rinse briefly under cold running water to cool. Peel them and put back into the saucepan. Spoon about 6 tablespoons of the butter sauce over them, then toss gently with a wooden spoon. Cover the pan and set in a 175°F. oven to keep warm, along with 4 dinner plates.

To broil the fish, lift the fillets out of the marinade with tongs, allowing the marinade to drain off. Discard the marinade. Place the fillets skin side down on the broiling rack and place 3½ to 4 inches from the source of heat. Broil for 5 to 7 minutes. Place a broiled fillet on each plate along with 6 to 8 potatoes. Brush each fillet lightly with some of the remaining butter sauce, using a pastry or basting brush. Sprinkle a teaspoon of lemon juice evenly over each fillet, set a lemon wedge to one side, then serve immediately.

Broiling 27

Broiled Flounder with Crawfish Dressing

We originally evolved this dish as a protest against what seemed to us the indiscriminate and gratuitous stuffing of flounder. Flounder is so delicious simply broiled that we felt stuffing it or putting a gross dressing on top of it was a symptom of foolish "gourmetitis." Aware that many people love stuffed flounder, we wanted to devise a dressing that would complement rather than obliterate the fish. We still prefer our flounder un-dressed, but if you like a more elaborate preparation, this is a good one.

FOR TWO

2 small flounder, split and cleaned, left whole, with heads removed and tails on

¼ c. (½ stick) salt butter

1 tsp. fresh lemon juice

1 Tbs. finely minced fresh parsley

⅛ tsp. freshly ground white pepper

⅛ tsp. salt

CRAWFISH DRESSING

1 c. crawfish dressing left from preparing Nantua sauce (see Poached Red Snapper with Nantua Sauce)

3 Tbs. boiling water mixed with 2 Tbs. dry white wine

⅓ lb. whole crawfish, peeled and cleaned

In a small heavy saucepan melt butter over low heat. Remove pan from burner. Add lemon juice, parsley, pepper, and salt. Preheat broiler and broiling rack. Brush broiling rack with some of the melted butter sauce. Place flounder thick side up on rack. Pour remaining butter sauce evenly over them. Broil 3½ to 4 inches from the source of heat for 7 minutes. Remove immediately from broiler. Keep warm on warming tray or in warm (175°F.) oven.

Warm the crawfish dressing in a heavy saucepan along with the water and white wine mixture. Add the crawfish. Cook covered over low heat for 10 to 12 minutes or until the crawfish are warmed through. Heap on top of the broiled flounder before serving. Spoon any liquid that has collected at the bottom of the saucepan around but not over the fish.

Broiled Redfish Hollandaise

Redfish is a prized New Orleans fish that is really a form of bass (channel bass); this favorite New Orleans dish is a good example of how successfully a fine broiled fish lends itself to good saucing. Just as good with any form of bass—striped bass, sea bass, drum. It is most practical to prepare the hollandaise sauce first, then set the blender container in a basin or bowl of warm water while broiling the fish.

FOR TWO

HOLLANDAISE SAUCE

½ c. (1 stick) salt butter
3 large egg yolks

1 Tbs. fresh lemon juice
scant ⅛ tsp. cayenne

---

2 small to medium-sized redfish fillets, skin removed
½ c. (1 stick) salt butter
1 Tbs. finely minced fresh parsley

1½ Tbs. fresh lemon juice
¼ tsp. salt
salt and freshly ground pepper

Set the broiler, pan, and rack to preheat while you prepare the sauce. To prepare the sauce, melt the butter over medium heat in a small heavy saucepan, then set aside. Combine the egg yolks, lemon juice, and cayenne in a blender container. Cover the container, then switch the blender on for a few seconds, just long enough to break the yolks. Turn the blender on again, on high speed, and remove the cover (or the detachable center section of the cover, if there is one). Gradually pour in the hot melted butter in a steady stream. Turn off the blender and cover securely. Switch the blender to high speed for about 30 seconds, then off. Repeat until the sauce appears quite thick. Check the consistency by dipping a long spoon or a knife into it and lifting it out of the sauce; if the sauce coats the spoon or knife thickly and does not drip easily, it is thick enough. If necessary, continue the on-off blender cycle until the sauce is ready. Set the covered container quite near the pilot on the surface of the range or, better yet, in a basin or bowl filled with warm water.

Prepare the basting sauce and broil the fillets as directed for Broiled Pompano. Pour about 2 teaspoons of basting sauce over each fillet, then cover with ⅓ cup hollandaise. Serve immediately.

Broiled Redfish with Lump Crabmeat Hollandaise

This grand variation was created by Arnaud's in New Orleans. It's a lavish and memorable dish, perfect for entertaining. You can multiply the recipe up to the reasonable capacity of your broiler and broiling facilities. One of the best ways to broil fish for six to eight in a standard home oven is to use a heavy shallow baking sheet (such as one uses to bake free form loaves of bread) lined with several rectangular cake racks. (A sheet pan 17¾ × 12⅞ inches is available in restaurant supply houses and makes maximum use of an 18 inch square oven.) The most practical order of steps: sauté the lump crabmeat first and set it in a warm oven; then prepare the hollandaise and keep it warm; broil the fish last. To assemble the portions, place the fillets on heated plates, cover with sautéed crabmeat, then top each with the golden hollandaise.

FOR TWO

SAUTÉED LUMP CRABMEAT

½ lb. lump crabmeat
1½ Tbs. salt butter

To sauté the crabmeat, melt the butter over low heat in a sauté pan or skillet, then add the crabmeat and cook for about 5 minutes, just to warm through. Stir very gently with a wooden spoon as you cook, taking care not to break up the larger lumps. When the crabmeat is warm, set the pan in a 175°F. oven to keep warm.

Prepare the other elements of the dish as directed for Broiled Redfish Hollandaise, and assemble portions by covering each fillet with ¼ cup sautéed crabmeat, then topping with ⅓ cup hollandaise.

Broiled Maine Lobster

There are many arguments over the relative merits of steaming, boiling, or broiling lobsters. Our first choice would probably be boiled, but a properly broiled lobster is very close in flavor and texture. We suspect that many broiled lobsters taste tough and dried out because they have been overcooked. Broiling is simpler and a fraction less intimidating for the novice, since the lobster

can be killed at the market (but only if it's brought home immediately and cooked) rather than in the cooking process. If you
baste the lobster as soon as it's opened with a bit of melted butter,
broiled and boiled become a toss-up.

FOR TWO

Whether you have the market kill and split the lobster or do it yourself, the cleaning process is the same. Remove the stomach (a kind of
sac close to the head) and the intestinal vein that runs down the tail
section close to the back shell. Everything else can be left, since the
liver and any coral are edible and quite delicious. Preheat the broiler
and broiling pan as directed in the preceding recipes (the rack is
not necessary). Melt about ¾ stick butter for each lobster and baste
the exposed flesh sides thoroughly with butter. When the broiler is
quite hot, place the pan so that the lobsters are the usual 3½ to 4
inches from the source of heat and broil for 12 to 15 minutes. If
desired, baste once or twice during cooking with additional butter.
To serve, sprinkle each lobster with salt and freshly ground pepper
and serve on heated plates accompanied by small cups or ramekins
of hot melted butter and 3 or 4 lemon wedges to be used to season
the butter to taste at the table. Provide nutcrackers for breaking the
claws and seafood forks for extracting smaller pieces of meat.

Broiled Oysters

*One day, after years of skepticism, we discovered that there really
is a way to broil oysters successfully—by dusting them with flour,
then basting with a seasoned butter sauce. Prepare the sauce while
preheating the broiler, and don't overcook the oysters—6 to 7
minutes is all it takes.*

FOR TWO

BASTING SAUCE

1 oz. slab bacon, diced	¼ c. thinly sliced green onion
2 Tbs. salt butter	tops
1 tsp. fresh lemon juice	
¼ tsp. freshly ground black pepper	

---

1 pint shucked oysters, drained
flour in a shaker

Begin preheating the broiler, broiling pan, and rack. In a heavy sauté pan or saucepan fry the slab bacon over high heat until it has rendered all its fat and the solid pieces appear quite dark and dry. Remove the pan from the heat and allow to cool for about 1 minute. Remove the bacon pieces with a slotted spoon and discard. Add the butter to the pan and stir until it is completely melted, then add the lemon juice and pepper. Last of all add the green onion tops. If you use a pan that retains heat well, the onion tops will cook without returning the pan to the heat. (They should turn dark.) If necessary, put the pan back on high heat for about 30 seconds to 1 minute to brown the onion tops, then remove it again.

Remove the broiling pan and rack from the oven and brush the rack lightly and evenly with the fat and butter mixture, using a pastry or basting brush. Place the drained oysters on the rack, then dust them very lightly with flour. Using a long-handled spoon, baste the oysters evenly with the sauce remaining in the pan, including the browned onion tops. Put the pan back under the broiler 3½ to 4 inches from the source of heat and broil for 6 to 7 minutes. The oysters will appear quite dark and make a sizzling sound when sufficiently cooked. Remove immediately from the broiler and serve on preheated plates garnished with lemon wedges.

Broiled Soft Belly Clams

We used to think that soft belly clams, that is, those with the chewier muscle tissue trimmed off, were not as good as the complete ones—until we spent some time cooking clams. Clams harden in cooking much more quickly than oysters and the soft bellies are the most delicate way to go with this dish. Take care not to cook them too long, or even soft bellies will get a bit tough.

FOR TWO

Prepare the clams for broiling and the basting sauce as directed for Broiled Oysters. Brush 2 small ovenproof ramekins or metal pans with some of the basting sauce, then top the clams with the remaining sauce as directed. Broil 3 to 3½ inches from the source of heat for 4 to 5 minutes. Set the ramekins on dinner plates to serve.

Broiled Soft Shell Crabs

Clean the crabs immediately before cooking and be sure to dry them very thoroughly between several layers of paper towels.

FOR TWO

Use 1 large or 2 smaller crabs per portion. Clean as directed for Fried Soft Shell Crabs, then rinse and dry thoroughly. Prepare as directed for Broiled Oysters, doubling the quantities given for the basting sauce.

Broiled Stuffed Florida Lobster

Florida lobsters are a form of spiny, or rock, lobsters found along the Gulf and southern waters of the United States. Pale red, with cream or white spots on the shells covering the tail area, which contains most of the meat, they are more closely related to craw- fish than to Maine lobsters. In place of the large meat-filled claws of their Maine cousins, they have numerous long thin tentacles toward the front, with an occasional thick, knobby front feeler coming directly out of the head area. In France these creatures are known as langoustes *and are cooked in a number of excellent and interesting dishes.*

For many years we were under the mistaken impression that Florida lobsters tended to be tough, with a faintly gamey taste. Only when we at last cooked them ourselves did we discover that they are quite delicious, versatile in their possibilities, and much to be prized. Much seafood literature flatly states that only the smallest ones make good eating. This is not true. In fact, Florida lobsters ranging from 1½ to 2¼ pounds are best for cooking and for eating. This, the first recipe in this book for Florida lobsters, describes the simple cleaning and precooking preparation they require and includes the one essential addition if you wish to broil them—butter for basting. The stuffing is a basic one, in- cluded more for its visual appeal than for any intrinsic function with respect to the lobster meat. Quick, easy to prepare, stuffed Florida lobsters are a fine way to become acquainted with these eminently edible and enjoyable creatures.

FOR TWO

2 small Florida lobsters or 1
large lobster
1 c. (2 sticks) melted salt butter

1 Tbs. fresh lemon juice
1 Tbs. finely minced fresh
parsley

SIMPLE STUFFING

1 c. chopped onions
3 Tbs. salt butter
2 Tbs. thinly sliced green onion
tops
¾ tsp. salt
¼ tsp. freshly ground black
pepper
¼ c. fine bread crumbs

¼ tsp. thyme
⅛ tsp. mace
1 large egg, well beaten
scant 1/16 tsp. cayenne
1½ tsp. lemon juice
3 Tbs. finely chopped blanched
almonds (optional)

DIPPING SAUCE

¾ c. (1½ sticks) salt butter
2 Tbs. lemon juice
¼ tsp. freshly ground white
pepper

1 tsp. minced chives

To split and clean the lobsters, place them back down on a cutting surface. Using a strong sharp knife, cut directly into the undershell just below the head (which takes almost half the length) and continue cutting until you have reached the feathery tail area. Turn the lobster around and in the same manner cut from the midpoint all the way down to the end of the head. Now turn the lobster back shell up and cut through to meet the underside cut. With your fingers, break off the eyes and any tentacles that appear likely to hang off the dinner plate. (There's very little meat in them, but it's fun to try and get at it, so don't overdo.) Once again, turn the lobster halves back side down. Remove the intestine, a small, hard, grayish sac in the head area. Also pull out the intestinal vein which runs the length of the lobster and is located toward the back or hard shell area. (If you can't find it, don't worry too much; it will cook away under high heat and be unnoticeable later.) The vein should be about ⅛ inch across and should come out in one continuous piece.

To make room for the stuffing, remove all the matter above the solid segment of meat contained in the tail. The coral or orange-colored "fat" is quite delicious; if possible, save it and spoon it around the stuffing before broiling. Preheat the broiler and pan. (The rack will not be necessary.)

To prepare the stuffing, sauté the onions in butter until they are soft and just beginning to turn brown. Add the onion tops, salt, pepper, bread crumbs, thyme, and mace. Cook, stirring, for about 3 minutes more, then remove the pan from the heat. Add the beaten egg and toss lightly with a fork. Add the cayenne and lemon juice and toss again to mix very thoroughly. At this point add the almonds, if used, and mix again. Scoop the stuffing out of the pan and shape into balls. Place each ball in the cavity above the tail section of each lobster half and press down gently to spread out. Leave the surface of the stuffing slightly rounded for an attractive effect.

Melt the butter for basting and add the lemon juice and parsley. Remove the broiling pan from the oven and set the lobster halves on it. Pour a generous amount of butter sauce over the exposed meat and about 2 teaspoons over the stuffing. Broil 3½ to 4 inches from the source of heat for 12 to 15 minutes. While the lobsters are broiling, prepare the dipping sauce by melting the butter and stirring in the remaining ingredients. Serve 1 or 2 lobster halves per portion with a small cup or ramekin of dipping sauce placed to one side.

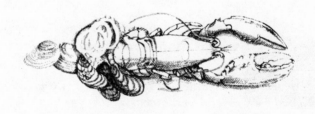

Broiled Sole Maître d'Hôtel

We are always astonished to hear people praise sole because "it doesn't really taste like fish," and are reminded of A.J. Leibling's remark that sole is a fish popular primarily with people who are afraid of fish. Frankly, we're inclined to think that if you prefer chicken you should eat chicken. If you like fish you'll like sole, not because it lacks taste but because it has a distinctive delicate taste. Under all those sauces sole is usually shrouded in, there really is a fine fish. Try this most elegant of sole dishes, broiled with a simple butter sauce—the best demonstration we know of our thesis that the finest fish do taste like fish. That's why they're so good. (Of course, broiled flounder may be better—it's at least as good.)

FOR TWO

2 sole fillets, skin removed	salt and freshly ground white
¾ c. (1½ sticks) salt butter	pepper
2 Tbs. fresh lemon juice	

Preheat the broiler, pan, and rack for 15 to 20 minutes. Melt the butter over low heat, then stir in the lemon juice and set aside. Sprinkle the fillets lightly with salt and pepper. Brush the broiling rack with some of the melted butter, then place the fillets on it. Spoon about 4 teaspoons of butter evenly over each fillet. Broil 3½ to 4 inches from the source of heat for 6 to 7 minutes, then remove immediately from the oven. Place the fillets on heated plates and pour about ⅓ cup butter sauce over each one. (The sauce should cover the fillets and also collect in the bottom of the plate.) Garnish to one side with a lemon wedge and serve immediately.

Broiled Striped Bass with Lump Crabmeat

Two superb seafoods together in one dish. It's impossible to improve on good bass or good crabmeat, so they're not really better together—but what an embarrassment of riches! A marvelous festive dish, very simply prepared.

FOR TWO

Sauté ½ pound lump crabmeat as directed for Broiled Redfish with Lump Crabmeat Hollandaise. Set the sautéed crabmeat in a 175°F. oven while you broil the bass. Using 2 small to medium-sized bass fillets, skin removed, prepare as directed for Broiled Pompano. To serve, place the fillets on heated plates, brush with several teaspoons of the remaining butter sauce, then cover each with ¼ pound of sautéed crabmeat. Top the crabmeat with some additional butter sauce, garnish with lemon wedges, and serve immediately.

Broiled Pompano Pontchartrain

When we in New Orleans feel most moved to demonstrate our love of a particular fish, we top it with one or two very small sautéed soft crabs and call it Pontchartrain, after the lake from which so many of New Orleans' seafood pleasures come.

FOR TWO

Clean 4 very small soft shell crabs as directed for Fried Soft Shell Crabs. Rinse them and dry very thoroughly between several layers of paper towels. In a sauté pan or skillet, melt 4 to 5 tablespoons of butter over medium heat. Sprinkle the crabs lightly with salt and pepper and dust very lightly with flour. Sauté in hot butter for about 2 minutes on each side or until golden brown. Place on a platter lined with paper towels and set in a 175°F. oven or on a warming tray while you broil the fish.

Prepare 2 small to medium-sized pompano fillets as directed for Broiled Pompano. To serve, place each fillet on a heated plate, then place 2 sautéed crabs side by side on top of each one. Spoon about ⅓ cup of the remaining butter sauce over each serving, garnish with lemon wedges, and bring to the table immediately.

Broiled Oysters en Brochette

Plump oysters alternating with pieces of bacon on a long skewer— a kind of oyster shish kebab. Before beginning to cook, check to see in what direction you can place the skewers so that they will remain suspended over the broiling pan by resting on the edges. If the skewers are too short, even for the narrower dimension, try placing them diagonally across opposite corners—that should do the trick. Place the broiling pan at an angle under the heat if you use this method, and reverse the direction of the angle after

2 minutes of broiling to get even browning. Another suggestion: use a large sturdy frying pan rather than the broiling pan; it will support almost any skewers. Be sure to preheat the frying pan as you would the broiler pan.

FOR TWO

20 to 24 freshly shucked oysters, well drained

4 slices lean breakfast bacon, cut into 1 inch squares

salt and freshly ground black pepper

cayenne

a shaker filled with flour

¾ c. (1½ sticks) melted salt butter

7 Tbs. fresh lemon juice

Preheat the broiler and broiling pan. Fry the bacon squares until partially cooked, for 3 to 4 minutes, then place on paper towels to drain. Fill 2 long flat skewers with alternating oysters and bacon squares, with a bacon square at each end. Sprinkle with salt and pepper and with a very small amount of cayenne. Dust lightly and evenly on both sides with flour. Mix the melted butter and lemon juice together and drizzle about 3 tablespoons of the sauce over the skewers as evenly as possible. Place the skewers across the broiling pan so that the ends rest on the rim and the oysters do not touch the bottom of the pan. Broil for 3 to 4 minutes on each side. A golden brown crust will form on the oysters. To serve, slide the oysters and bacon onto heated plates by pushing down from the ring end with a fork. Spoon the remaining butter sauce over the portions.

Broiled Eel with Butter Sauce

We adore eel, but had never eaten them simply broiled. They had always been served to us in rich stews, or smoked, or topped with elaborate sauces. At last one day a long-awaited call came from one of the large seafood houses in the city: some local fishermen from "inland" had just brought in a good catch of fresh eel.

First on the list of eel dishes we had been planning to cook for this book was, of course, the broiled version. Then we'd know what they really taste like unadorned. Delicious. And even a rich fish such as eel works well with a good simple butter sauce.

FOR TWO

1 lb. filleted eel	*5 tsp. fresh lemon juice*
6 Tbs. (¾ stick) salt butter	*salt and freshly ground pepper*
2 Tbs. finely minced fresh parsley	

Preheat the broiler, pan, and rack. Melt the butter in a small saucepan, then stir in the parsley and lemon juice. Brush the rack very lightly with butter sauce, then place the eel on it. (If necessary, cut each eel fillet into 2 even lengths, so the pieces will fit comfortably on the broiling rack.) Sprinkle lightly with salt and pepper. Set no more than 3½ inches from the source of heat and broil for 10 to 12 minutes. To serve, place the fillets on heated plates and spoon several table-spoons of butter sauce over each portion. Garnish with lemon wedges and serve immediately.

Broiled Striped Bass with Egg and Lemon Sauce

One of our favorite restaurateurs, a Greek from Marseilles, com-bined bass with the classic Greek avgolemono sauce for this un-usual and delicious dish.

FOR TWO

EGG AND LEMON SAUCE

1½ Tbs. butter	*2 egg yolks*
1 Tbs. flour	*1½ to 2 Tbs. fresh lemon juice*
1 c. hot fish or chicken stock	

2 small to medium-sized bass fillets, skin removed	1⅓ Tbs. fresh lemon juice
½ c. (1 stick) salt butter	¼ tsp. salt
1 Tbs. finely minced fresh parsley	salt and freshly ground black pepper

To prepare the sauce, melt the butter in a small heavy saucepan over low heat. Stir in the flour, mixing with a whisk to keep the texture smooth and free of lumps. Gradually pour in the hot stock, stirring, and cook over low heat until thickened, about 2 or 3 minutes. Remove the pan from the heat. In a stainless steel or porcelain bowl, beat the egg yolks with a whisk for 2 minutes. Add the lemon juice, a few drops at a time, continuing to beat. Then add the thick liquid, about 1 tablespoon at a time, still beating, until the sauce begins to appear quite thick and stable. At this point you can increase the quantity of liquid added each time. Be sure each addition is thoroughly incorporated before going on to the next. When the sauce is completed, it should be quite thick and fluffy and should evenly coat a spoon dipped into it so that it can be lifted out without dripping. Set the bowl of sauce in a basin of warm water while you broil the fish.

Preheat the broiler, pan, and rack. Prepare the butter sauce and broil the fillets as directed for Broiled Pompano. To serve, spoon about 2 tablespoons of butter sauce over each fillet, then top with about ½ cup egg and lemon sauce. Serve immediately.

Broiled Shark

Our local seafood dealer claimed that shark was plentiful, inexpensive, and delicious. He was right. Reminiscent in some ways of swordfish, shark is a firm fish with very little oil and a fine delicate flavor.

FOR TWO

1 shark fillet, about 13 to 16 oz.	2 Tbs. fresh lemon juice
¾ c. (1½ sticks) salt butter	¼ tsp. salt
2 Tbs. finely minced fresh parsley	salt and freshly ground pepper

Preheat the broiler, pan, and rack. Melt the butter and add the parsley, lemon juice, and salt. Divide the fillet into 2 equal pieces and sprinkle with salt and pepper. Brush the boiling rack generously with butter sauce, then place the fillets on it. Baste each piece with about 2 tablespoons of butter sauce, then broil 3½ to 4 inches from the source of heat for 9 to 10 minutes. To serve, place the fillets on heated plates and pour about ¼ cup butter sauce over each one. Squeeze 3 or 4 additional drops of lemon juice over each one, then garnish with lemon wedges and serve immediately.

Grilling Recipes

Grilled Bass Maître d'Hôtel

Grilled Bass in Foil

Grilled Mackerel

Venetian Style Charcoal
Grilled Whole Fish

Special Sauce for Charcoal
Grilled Whole Fish

Marinated Charcoal Grilled
Shrimp

Marinated Charcoal Grilled
Crabs

Barbecued Charcoal Grilled
Shrimp

Hickory Barbecue Shrimp

Grilled Florida Lobster with
Brandy and Butter Sauce

Grilled Rock Shrimp
(American Langoustines)

Grilled Oysters

Charcoal Grilled Salmon
Steaks

Grilled Bluefish

Bass Grilled with Fennel
(Loup au Fenouil)

3

Grilling

Grilling is one of the most ancient methods of fish cooking. It is still widely practiced in much of Europe and the Far East. In America we seem to reserve our best grilling techniques for meat —steaks and hamburgers—although there is no inherent reason why backyard barbecues cannot do just as well with fish and shellfish. Ironically, it is in the new Japanese steakhouses across the country, with their large open grills, that the avant-garde of grilling seafood is presently found.

The two basic elements of grilling are intense heat and smoke. By controlling and varying the application of heat and smoke we can expand the variety of grilled dishes almost indefinitely. Different types of wood produce different smoked flavors and even an "unseasoned" smoke can be used with distinctive results. By using marinades and seasonings you can enhance or change the flavor of the smoke as it permeates the seafood.

Grilling involves hand-to-hand contact with the ingredients and its primary satisfactions come from its simplicity, from bypassing the complicated, civilized kitchens that we've come to rely on. Serious barbecuers will want to pursue some of the applications of smoking and curing detailed in Chapter 14. Here we explore primarily the basic procedures and pleasures of simple backyard grilling or grilling on the newer indoor kitchen grills similar to those used by the Japanese steakhouses.

Basic Grilling Techniques

Preheat charcoal grill or char-rocks for at least 30 minutes.

Dry rinsed seafood thoroughly.

Drain marinated seafood well.

Time properly: 10 to 12 minutes per side for fillets; 15 minutes per side for thick pieces and large shellfish.

If grilling distance cannot be adjusted, increase or decrease cooking time proportionately.

Add seasoning after grilling has begun or after cooking is completed.

Shell-like containers of heavy aluminum foil permit slower grilling and more smoke flavor. With this method, baste before cooking.

Grilled Bass Maître d'Hôtel

Bass is one of the most plentiful of American fish and one of the most delicious. Sea bass and freshwater bass are both excellent and sturdy fish, ideal for grilling. The extra touch of a simple butter sauce added at serving time sets off the fine smoky flavor.

FOR TWO

2 bass fillets, skin removed	1½ Tbs. fresh lemon juice
salt and freshly ground pepper	2 tsp. finely minced fresh parsley
½ c. (1 stick) salt butter	

Preheat the charcoal grill for at least 20 minutes, until the coals (or char-rocks, if you are using an indoor charcoal grill) are glowing red. Rinse the fillets briefly under cool running water and dry very thoroughly with paper towels. Place the fillets on the grill. If the grill is adjustable, raise the supports about 1 inch higher than the lowest position. If the grilling distance cannot be adjusted, it will be necessary to reduce the grilling time indicated here by 4 to 5 minutes for each side.

To grill the fish, cook for 10 minutes on each side. The side facing the coals will appear well browned. If desired, sprinkle each side lightly with salt and pepper immediately prior to grilling. Or sprinkle after the fish has been removed from the grill.

While the fish is cooking, melt the butter in a small pan over the heat of the grill. Stir in the lemon juice and parsley and mix thoroughly. To serve, pour about ¼ cup of butter sauce over each fillet.

Grilled Bass in Foil

The fish cooks more slowly this way and gradually absorbs more smoke. Best results are obtained by seasoning and basting the fillets prior to putting them into their foil shells. This method is especially practical when you have other things to tend to while the fish is over the coals.

FOR TWO

2 bass fillets, skin removed	salt and freshly ground pepper
½ c. (1 stick) salt butter, melted	¼ c. melted butter, approxi-
2½ tsp. lemon juice	mately, for additional basting

Preheat the grill for at least 20 minutes. Rinse and dry the fillets as directed in Grilled Bass Maître d'Hôtel, then place each one on a rectangle of heavy-duty aluminum foil large enough to extend about 3 to 4 inches on each of the longer sides and about 2 inches at the top and bottom. Mix the ½ cup butter with the lemon juice. Sprinkle the fillets with salt and pepper, then baste each with ¼ cup of the butter and lemon sauce. Fold the foil up around all sides so as to almost totally enclose the fillets. Leave an opening about 1¼ inches wide the length of each fillet. Set the foil boats on the grill and cook for 30 minutes. During the last 10 minutes, open out the foil so that the folded-up edges are at right angles to the grill and baste the fillets with several additional tablespoons of butter. Serve by setting the foil boats directly on plates or by carefully lifting the fillets out of the foil with a wide spatula (so as not to break them), then pour the butter remaining in the foil over them. Garnish with lemon wedges and provide additional salt and pepper to be added to taste.

Grilled Mackerel

American herring is less plentiful than European herring and tends to be less sturdy in texture. After grilling herring, we decided to try mackerel the same way. It worked better; the texture closely approximated that of European herring and the natural richness gave the grilled fish a sweet, moist flavor. Small whole mackerel or filleted larger ones work best here.

FOR TWO

2 small whole mackerel, split and cleaned, heads and tails left on, or 1 large mackerel, filleted, with the skin left on
¼ c. olive oil, approximately

salt and freshly ground black pepper
3 Tbs. fresh lime juice or lemon juice, if limes are not available

Preheat the grill for 15 to 20 minutes. Rinse and dry the fish, then rub lightly on both sides with olive oil. Sprinkle generously with salt and pepper. Place the fish in a hinged grill and fasten securely. Grill for 8 to 10 minutes on each side. Right after placing the fish on the grill, sprinkle the top side with 1½ tablespoons lime juice. Repeat after you turn the fish over. Serve on heated plates, garnished with wedges of lime.

Venetian Style Charcoal Grilled Whole Fish

Small whole fish that have been split and cleaned are particularly attractive prepared this way. They are soaked in a strong salt solution, then placed on a lightly greased hinged grill. When finished, the flavor is marvelously smoky and the flesh remains pleasantly moist. Any additional seasonings should be sprinkled on after cooking. This method of grilling can also be adapted to the home broiler; it requires extensive preheating (at least 25 minutes) and leaving the oven door open at least 4 inches during cooking. Rest the hinged grill on the raised edges of the broiler pan and make sure the fish is no more than 4 inches from the source of heat to get a good dark crust.

FOR TWO

2 whole small fish (speckled trout, croaker, mackerel, mullet, etc.), split, cleaned, heads removed, tails left on

½ c. coarse salt dissolved in 2 c. water in a large bowl

Preheat the charcoal grill for at least 15 to 20 minutes. Dip the fish one at a time in the salt solution so that they are totally immersed. Do not shake off the excess moisture. Simply place the whole fish on a lightly buttered hinged grill, then fasten the grill closed. Charcoal grill for 7 to 9 minutes on each side. Serve plain or with ¼ cup Special Sauce (see following recipe).

Special Sauce for Charcoal Grilled Whole Fish

Excellent with crisp, well browned grilled fish.

FOR TWO

½ c. (1 stick) salt butter
2 Tbs. finely minced fresh parsley
1 tsp. borage

¾ tsp. sage
2½ tsp. fresh lemon juice

In a small heavy saucepan melt the butter over medium heat. Add the parsley, borage, and sage and cook for 2 minutes more. Remove the pan from the heat and stir in the lemon juice. Spoon about 2 tablespoons of sauce over each fish and pour the rest into a small bowl. Set the bowl on the table with a spoon in it and let each person add more sauce if desired.

Marinated Charcoal Grilled Shrimp

Peeled and deveined shrimp with the tails left on, marinated briefly, then grilled over preheated coals. A hinged grill makes it simple to get the shrimp browned on both sides without having to turn each one over individually. Serve plain or with melted butter for dipping.

FOR TWO

2 lb. whole fresh shrimp, peeled and deveined, with tails left on

MARINADE

2 Tbs. fresh lime juice
¾ tsp. freshly ground black pepper
¾ tsp. salt
⅛ tsp. dill weed
⅛ tsp. sugar

½ tsp. cumin
½ tsp. basil
1½ tsp. finely minced fresh garlic
1 Tbs. olive oil
2 tsp. minced chives

Combine the ingredients for the marinade in a wide shallow porcelain dish or pie pan. Mix very thoroughly. Lay the shrimp flat in the marinade and allow them to absorb the ingredients for at least 20 to 30 minutes. Turn them over after 10 to 15 minutes. Preheat the grill for 20 minutes. Lift the shrimp out of the marinade with tongs and place them on the bottom side of a hinged grill. Close the grill securely and grill the shrimp 6 to 7 minutes on each side. Serve with small individual bowls or cups of melted butter for dipping.

Marinated Charcoal Grilled Crabs

Cracked hard shell crabs prepared like shrimp. Increase the marinating time and double the grilling time.

FOR TWO

Crack open 4 hard shell crabs. Remove the gray fibrous matter. (If the crabs are fat, there will be a great deal of a yellow pastelike substance. This is edible, and much prized by hard crab fanciers. Do not remove it before marination.) Remove the claws and crack them without peeling. Marinate as directed for Marinated Charcoal Grilled Shrimp, increasing the marinating time to 2 hours. Preheat the grill for at least 20 minutes, then place the crabs directly on the grill. If desired, use a hinged grill for the claws. Grill for 15 to 18 minutes on each side, then serve with nutcrackers, seafood forks, and melted butter for dipping.

Barbecued Charcoal Grilled Shrimp

Shrimp basted with a good homemade barbecue sauce as they grill—another excellent outdoor preparation. This dish works best with the larger shrimp. Be sure to save some of the sauce for dipping.

FOR TWO

2 lb. whole fresh shrimp, peeled and deveined, tails left on or removed as desired

BARBECUE SAUCE

10 Tbs. salt butter

1 Tbs. fresh lemon juice

1 Tbs. shredded green onion or 1¼ tsp. dried shredded green onion

2¾ tsp. liquid hickory smoke

2¾ tsp. Worcestershire sauce

scant 1/16 tsp. cayenne

Preheat the grill for 20 to 30 minutes. Rinse and dry the shrimp. While the grill is heating, prepare the barbecue sauce. Melt the butter in a small heavy saucepan over low heat, then add the lemon juice and mix. Add the green onion and cook for 4 minutes. Add the liquid smoke and Worcestershire sauce and cook for 2 minutes. Mix very thoroughly, then remove the pan from the heat. Stir in the cayenne, then cover the saucepan. Allow to steep, covered, for 20 to 30 minutes. Reheat, beating vigorously with a whisk, for a minute or two just before using, to baste the shrimp.

Place the shrimp in a hinged grill and set on the preheated grill, or set the shrimp directly on the grids of the grill. Grill for 8 to 10 minutes on each side, basting frequently with barbecue sauce. Serve with additional sauce in small individual ramekins set to one side of each plate.

Hickory Barbecue Shrimp

Marinated shrimp grilled over coals sprinkled with hickory chips have a tantalizing hickory flavor and aroma. If you have an indoor grill with char-rocks, place a layer of pulverized hickory chips directly over the rocks; be sure to set your heat control about 2 numbers lower than you normally would to keep the hickory chips from flaming up.

FOR TWO

2 lb. whole fresh shrimp, peeled and deveined, tails left on

MARINADE

½ c. (1 stick) salt butter
1 tsp. Worcestershire sauce
¼ tsp. Tabasco
1 tsp. sugar
¼ tsp. salt

1 tsp. freshly ground black pepper
⅜ tsp. cayenne
1 tsp. fresh lemon juice
1½ tsp. liquid hickory smoke

¼ c. hot melted butter, approximately

Prepare the marinade by melting the butter, then adding the remaining ingredients. Marinate the shrimp for at least 30 minutes, turning them over after 15 minutes. While the shrimp are marinating, preheat the grill. Add the hickory chips about 10 minutes before you begin to grill. Place the shrimp in a hinged grill and grill for 5 to 6 minutes on each side. Serve with about ¼ cup hot melted butter to which 3 to 4 tablespoons of the marinade have been added.

Grilled Florida Lobster with Brandy and Butter Sauce

An excellent way to enjoy the chewy texture and hearty flavor of Florida lobsters. The lobsters are split open and grilled in the shell, meat side down first. This shrinks the meat a bit and

---

creates space around it, so that when you turn the halves over the fine smoky brandy and butter sauce seeps in around the meat as well as coating the top.

FOR TWO

2 small Florida lobsters or 1 large lobster

BRANDY AND BUTTER SAUCE

½ c. (1 stick) salt butter	¼ tsp. freshly ground black
1½ Tbs. brandy	pepper
2 Tbs. minced chives	

Split and clean the lobsters as directed for Broiled Stuffed Florida Lobster. Scoop out the coral and reserve in a cup. (If left in, it would drip out during the first minutes of grilling, since the lobsters are first placed open side down.) Preheat the grill for 20 minutes, then grill the lobsters for 10 minutes with the open side facing the coals. While the lobsters are grilling, melt the butter in a small saucepan, then add the brandy, chives, and pepper. Cook for 1 to 2 minutes, just until the chives begin to turn dark, then remove from the heat and set aside. After you turn the lobsters over, put the reserved coral back in place, then baste the exposed meat with 2 to 3 tablespoons of the sauce, making sure that some of it seeps down into the spaces between the meat and the shell. Grill for 10 minutes on the second side. Place on plates and pour the remaining sauce into small ramekins. Place the ramekins to one side of the lobsters before serving.

Grilled Rock Shrimp

American Langoustines

Rock shrimp are a recent fishing bounty. These creatures have been present for some time deep in the Gulf of Mexico, but only recently have they been widely fished. They so closely resemble European langoustines that we wonder why they're not marketed under that name. They can't legally be called rock lobsters since lobsters under 1 pound are not legal fishing prey. The "rock shrimp" designation is a bit confusing to most people, since they don't taste like shrimp and have a totally different texture. Avail-

able frozen—peeled or in the shell—they're plentiful, inexpensive, and make great eating. One of the best ways to try them is grilled.

FOR TWO

1 lb. peeled rock shrimp	1 c. melted butter, approximately
salt and freshly ground pepper	lemon wedges

Rinse and dry the rock shrimp. Preheat the grill for 20 minutes. Sprinkle the rock shrimp liberally with salt and pepper and place directly on the grids. Grill for 10 to 12 minutes on each side, basting with melted butter several times. Serve on heated plates with additional melted butter in individual ramekins for dipping and lemon wedges for seasoning the butter if desired.

Grilled Oysters

FOR TWO

2 dozen freshly shucked oysters, thoroughly drained	¼ c. melted butter, approximately
salt and freshly ground black pepper	lemon wedges
flour in a shaker	

Preheat the grill for 15 minutes. Place the oysters in a platter and sprinkle lightly with salt and pepper. Dust lightly and evenly with flour. Turn over carefully and repeat on the other side. Place the oysters in a hinged grill and fasten the grill securely. Drizzle one side with melted butter and place on the grids buttered side down. Grill for 5 minutes. Drizzle the upper side with butter and turn over. Grill for 5 minutes on the second side. Serve with lemon wedges.

Charcoal Grilled Salmon Steaks

Salmon is one of those legendary fish for which there is no substitute. We will never forget our first grilled fresh salmon prepared over an open coal grate in a San Francisco Italian open *kitchen restaurant, cooked slowly in the rising heat and smoke. If you are fortunate enough to get some fresh salmon, this is our favorite way of preparing it. Serve it with the best white wine you can find for a festive grand occasion meal.*

FOR TWO

2 fresh salmon steaks, cut about 1¼ inches thick
salt and freshly ground black pepper

Preheat the grill for at least 25 minutes. Place the salmon steaks at a distance of 6 inches from the coals and grill for 15 minutes on each side. If there is no way you can arrange your grill setup for a 6 inch distance, use whatever is the maximum distance you can manage and reduce the grilling time to the following ratios: 13 minutes each side for a 5 inch distance, 12 minutes each side for a 4 inch distance, 11 minutes each side for a 3 inch distance. To serve, sprinkle the steaks with salt and pepper and garnish with lemon wedges.

Grilled Bluefish

That marvel of American seafood restaurants, Gage & Tollner in Brooklyn, raises the cooking of bluefish to the level of an unforgettable art. As is evident from many of our comments in this book, we regard many restaurant seafood cooking techniques with something less than awe—but the Grilled Bluefish at Gage & Tollner is so good and so unusual that we asked the proprietor how it is done. It turns out that Gage & Tollner uses an open grate set at an angle over very slow-burning anthracite coal, an old fashioned procedure that explains the incredible taste and beauty of the bluefish. The secret is the intense heat, with very little smoke. The subtly smoky flavor is quite unlike the results obtained with simple backyard charcoal grills. In fact, the increasingly popular indoor grills outfitted with permanent charrocks yield results remarkably similar to those produced with slow-burning anthracite coal. These grills are widely used for grill cooking in Japanese steakhouses around the country. The method described here will work very well with any fine fresh fish, but we'll always remember our first taste of that unbelievable bluefish.

FOR TWO

2 bluefish fillets, skin removed or left on as desired

salt and freshly ground black pepper

¼ c. melted butter, approximately

lemon wedges

Preheat the char-rock grill at the highest setting for 15 minutes, then turn the heat control down to 8 or 9 on the heat dial. Allow to run for 6 to 8 minutes at the lower setting. Sprinkle the fillets lightly with melted butter to prevent the fish from sticking. Grill the fillets for 10 to 12 minutes on each side, or until the side facing the heat appears darkly scored with the marks of the grid and is a lighter smoky color between grid marks. To serve, place the fillets (skin side down if the skin was left on) on heated plates and sprinkle lightly with salt and pepper. Baste each portion with about 1 tablespoon of melted butter, then sprinkle with a few drops of lemon juice. Garnish with lemon wedges and serve immediately.

Bass Grilled with Fennel
Loup au Fenouil

In this version, we use crushed fennel seed in place of the traditional fennel stalks and bass in place of loup de mer, a Mediterranean sea bass. The traditional method involves placing the grilled fish over a bed of fennel stalks and setting them aflame

---

with Armagnac. The juices are then strained and served over the fish. The high point is the moment when the stalks are burning and a divine aroma fills the room. Frankly, we prefer this drier version, as much for its taste as for its simplicity: the fish retains a pungent smokiness and the skin stays crisp.

1 medium to large whole striped bass or sea bass, split and cleaned, head and tail left on
1/4 c. olive oil, approximately
1½ tsp. salt
1/4 tsp. freshly ground black pepper
1 Tbs. fennel seed, ground with a mortar and pestle
1 Tbs. brandy

Begin preheating the grill. Rinse the fish under cold running water, then dry very thoroughly with paper towels. Make 3 or 4 crosswise slashes about 1/4 inch deep on each side of the fish. Mix the oil, salt, pepper, ground fennel seed, and brandy together with a whisk for a few minutes to create an even suspension of ingredients. Using a basting or pastry brush, paint the fish evenly all over with the seasoned oil mixture. Using the tip of the brush, put additional seasoned oil into each of the slashes. Place the fish in a hinged grill and grill for 8 to 10 minutes on each side, or until the skin is quite crisp and well browned, and beginning to curl back at the edges of the slashes. Remove the fish from the hinged grill and carefully divide it into 3 or 4 thick slices with the side of a large spatula. (If necessary, cut through the backbone with a thin sharp knife.) Lift each piece carefully onto a heated plate with the spatula, then sprinkle with a few drops of lemon juice. Serve immediately.

Another way to serve: Place the whole grilled fish upright on an oval platter at the center of the table and have the diner break off pieces of the flesh for himself. In order to keep the fish on its belly and upright on the platter, carefully open out the incision to create a kind of stand. If it still wobbles, wedge it into a stable position with some clean attractive twigs, preferably with a few leaves on them.

Frying Recipes

New Orleans Trout
  Amandine

Sole Amandine

Sole Colbert

Pan Fried Trout

Pan Fried Trout in Pork Fat

Fried Trout in Pearly Meal

Fried Catfish

Fried Red Snapper

Philippine Fried Bass with
  Vegetables

Finnish Rye-Fried Fish

Scallops Fried in Batter

Crumb Fried Clams

Fried Shrimp in Corn Flour

Beer Batter Shrimp

Shrimp Tempura

Fried Soft Shell Crabs

Soft Shell Crabs Beurre
  Noisette (New Orleans
  Meunière)

Soft Shell Crabs Amandine

Oysters Fried in Corn Meal

Batter Fried Oysters

Oysters Fried in Cracker
  Meal

Crumb Fried Oysters

Fried Oysters en Brochette

Frogs' Legs Beurre Noisette

Conch Steak

Fried Conch

Clam Fritters

Conch Fritters

Greek Fried Bass with Garlic
  and Almond Sauce

Sole with Apples and Cream
  Sauce

Striped Bass with Apples
  Beurre Noisette

Striped Bass with Bananas
  Beurre Noisette

4

Frying

Frying has such a bad press that we frequently find ourselves in the role of crusaders bent on clearing its good name. All of the charges against frying are true: most American frying *is* greasy; most of the time the food being fried is obliterated and indigestible. But those charges should be brought against bad frying techniques and not against the process itself. In New Orleans, where frying is second nature, most of the seafood restaurants make the finished oyster or crab or shrimp or trout look like the result in one of those television commercials where almost every drop of the frying medium is poured back into the container. What the commercials don't tell us is that this is *not* due to any magical qualities in the shortening, but to the precise and easily learned techniques of good frying. Do it right and frying is one of the driest, healthiest, cleanest, and most satisfying ways of cooking. And it is great for seafood of all kinds.

There is one absolutely basic lesson to learn about deep frying: the correct temperature of the frying medium. A precise and accurate 375°F., for raw or partially precooked seafood. Deep fry your seafood at 375° F. and it will be perfectly dry, digestible, and delicious. Correct frying uses less oil or fat than any other technique including broiling. Oh, how we detest those calorie books that add terrifying quantities of calories to a fried dish on the assumption that half a bottle of shortening and all the bread crumbs in the world will find their way into the 4 ounce portion of fish. And then there are the big city food writers who, never having seen a piece of properly fried fish, object to the very idea. They seem to envision some illiterate man with very dirty hands throwing fish into a cauldron of rancid black fat. The English, who in matters of food know very little, do know their frying, and their use of a newspaper to wrap fried English fish and chips is brilliant. Imagine what greasy frying would do to newsprint. Their wrapping proves to the customer that the finished fried product is as dry as a bone. And if the English can cook something properly then anyone can! (One of us is from an English family.)

Frying is a delightful, creative, infinitely fascinating cooking technique—ideal for more kinds of seafood and for more variations than any other technique we know. From English fish and chips to the *haute cuisine* French Sole Colbert, from New Orleans' legendary Trout Amandine to Japan's ethereal tempura, from pan fried whole American rainbow trout to perfectly fried crisp thin fillets of Channel catfish, the list of treasures belonging to this way of cooking seafood is almost endless.

Basic Frying Techniques

DEEP FRYING

Maintain proper frying temperature, generally 375°F.

Fill fryer no more than halfway with oil to allow for bubbling up.

Fry in small batches to avoid suddenly lowering frying temperature below 375°F.

After each use, strain frying oil, cool, then refrigerate in covered container.

Discard bottom inch of stored oil before each use and replace with fresh oil.

Discard entire batch of oil after 10 uses, or sooner if oil turns black.

SHALLOW FRYING

Fat should be hot but not smoking before food is added.

Test fat temperature with a small cube of bread; it should turn brown in 60 seconds but not get blackened.

Raise burner heat for a minute when adding food, then lower heat again.

If browning is too rapid, lower heat on gas range or remove pan from heat on electric range.

New Orleans Trout Amandine

Visitors to New Orleans have always loved this dish. Because of its delicacy they refuse to believe it is actually fried. Many good eaters are convinced that frying is either unhealthy or bad for their social standing. As Trout Amandine demonstrates, it needn't be. Despite the fact that many cookbooks will instruct the eager cook to sauté the trout, the real secret is deep frying at 375°F. This is what gives the fish its beautiful crust and delicious nutty flavor which so well complement the almonds and the browned butter.

FOR TWO

2 small to medium-sized speckled trout fillets
cold milk
½ c. flour
¾ tsp. salt

⅛ tsp. freshly ground black pepper
1/16 tsp. cayenne
vegetable oil for deep frying

AMANDINE SAUCE

¾ c. (1½ sticks) salt butter
⅔ c. blanched slivered almonds
1 Tbs. fresh lemon juice

½ tsp. freshly ground black pepper

Frying 59

Rinse the fillets and dry thoroughly with paper towels. Place in a shallow dish and pour in sufficient cold milk to just cover them. Combine the flour, salt, pepper, and cayenne in a bowl and mix very thoroughly. Begin heating the oil in a deep fryer to 375°F. Coat the fillets by lifting them out of the milk, letting the excess liquid drain off, then rolling in the seasoned flour to cover evenly. Place on a plate to dry for a few minutes. Fry 1 or 2 at a time until golden brown, about 8 minutes, then lift out of the oil with a long-handled skimmer (or the frying basket, if you use one) and drain over the fryer for about 45 seconds. Place side by side and not touching on a platter covered with several thicknesses of paper towels and set the platter in a 200°F. oven to keep warm while you prepare the sauce.

To prepare the sauce, melt the butter in a heavy 2 to 3 quart sauce-pan over medium heat. Cook until the butter begins to turn slightly brown, then add the almonds. Cook for 1 to 2 minutes more, until the butter turns hazelnut brown, then remove the pan from the heat. Add the lemon juice and pepper and mix with a wooden spoon. The sauce will foam up; wait until the foaming subsides, then return the pan to low heat for 1 minute. Once again remove the pan from the heat. Mix very thoroughly.

To serve, place the fried fillets on heated plates and spoon a bit more than ⅓ cup of the sauce over each one. Arrange the almonds so that most of them cover the fillets, with a few placed to each side. Garnish with lemon wedges and serve immediately.

Sole Amandine

An adaptation of New Orleans Trout Amandine to sole—Dover sole, lemon sole, any sole. Sole Amandine is as delicious as the original trout version with browned butter New Orleans style. In New Orleans when we run out of trout we use redfish; if sole is not available bass will do as well. Sole is a fine fish, but it has no innate magical qualities. It's the style of cooking rather than the specific fish that makes this a spectacular dish.

FOR TWO

Prepare as directed for New Orleans Trout Amandine, substituting 2 sole fillets for the speckled trout.

Sole Colbert

A haute cuisine *dish from the French canon that deserves to be better known in America. The fish is pan fried in butter and peanut oil with a bread crumb crust. The classic restaurant preparation involves cutting back the thicker top fillet, then frying the fish, removing the exposed backbone, and filling the cavity with melted butter. This home version with 2 separate fillets tastes just as good—a sort of butter sandwich between 2 pieces of fish.*

FOR TWO

2 large or 4 small sole fillets (preferably both the thicker top fillet and the thinner bottom one, if your fish market can manage to keep the bottom one intact)

1 large egg

¼ c. cream

⅔ c. fine bread crumbs, approximately

salt and freshly ground pepper

6 Tbs. (¾ stick) salt butter

3 Tbs. peanut oil or corn oil, if you have no peanut oil, but the flavor will be less fine

⅔ c. melted butter for the sauce

1⅔ Tbs. fresh lemon juice

Rinse and dry the fillets. If you are using 2 large ones, divide each in half across. Beat the egg and cream together in a shallow dish or pie pan. Combine the bread crumbs and a small amount of salt and pepper in a bowl. Dip the fillets in the egg and cream mixture, then roll in the bread crumbs until thoroughly and evenly coated. Place side by side on a platter to dry for a few minutes while you heat the butter and oil.

In a heavy sauté pan or skillet, melt the butter over medium heat. When the butter is *almost* melted, add the peanut oil and stir to mix. Continue heating until quite hot, 4 to 5 minutes. (You can test by shaking a drop of water from a fingertip onto the oil. If it dances, the oil is hot enough.) Do not overheat or the oil will begin to turn brown. If this should happen, reduce the heat a bit and add an additional tablespoon of peanut oil. Pan fry the coated fillets until golden brown and crisp, about 4 minutes on each side. Turn them over very carefully with a long wide spatula so as not to break them. While the fillets are frying, melt the butter for the sauce and add about half the lemon juice. Taste; if desired, add the rest. (The butter sauce should have just enough lemon in it to reduce the oily feel of the butter on the tongue, but not enough to make the sauce taste noticeably lemony.)

When the fillets are done, place on paper towels to drain briefly. To serve, place 1 fillet (the thinner ones, if you have them) on each heated plate. Ladle ⅓ cup of the butter sauce over each one, then cover with the second fillet. Serve immediately.

Pan Fried Trout

This technique will work for any fresh lake, brook, or rainbow trout. Small whole fish about 1 pound each are best. If your pan is large enough, leave the heads on. Be sure the oil in the skillet is hot enough, and handle the fish gently when turning it over. If any pieces of the crisp delicious skin fall off, just put them back in place; the patches are barely noticeable. Sometimes, even with the greatest care, the fish breaks in half during turning or while being moved to the plate; this is hard to disguise, but no one really minds—it tastes so good. While the fish are draining briefly, make the lovely browned butter sauce right in the pan.

FOR TWO

2 small whole speckled trout, lake trout, or brook trout, cleaned, heads removed if desired	*salt and freshly ground black pepper* *flour in a shaker* *vegetable oil for pan frying*

BUTTER SAUCE

4 Tbs. (½ stick) salt butter
2 tsp. fresh lemon juice
1½ Tbs. finely minced fresh parsley

Rinse the fish under cold running water and dry very thoroughly with paper towels. Place on a platter and sprinkle generously on both sides with salt and pepper. Dust with an even coating of flour. Heat about ⅛ inch of vegetable oil in a large heavy skillet until quite hot but not smoking. (A drop of water sprinkled into the pan should dance rapidly.) Fry the fish until browned and crisp on the bottom, 4 to 5 minutes, then turn over very carefully with 2 large spoons or a large wide spatula. Fry in the same manner on the second side. Lift the fish carefully out of the pan with a spatula and place on several layers of paper towels to drain. Pour off any oil remaining in the skillet.

To prepare the butter sauce, melt the butter over high heat and cook until lightly browned. Remove the pan from the heat and add the lemon juice. After the foaming subsides, put the pan back on the heat and add the parsley. Brown for about 1 minute more, then once again remove the pan from the heat.

Serve the fish on heated plates. Put the butter sauce in a cup or small ramekin, to be added as desired at the table.

Pan Fried Trout in Pork Fat

We particularly like this method for a very special fish such as a rare rainbow trout or one of our own especially pretty small speckled trout. The fish is lightly coated with seasoned cracker meal and fried in fat rendered from salt pork. The trick is getting the fat hot enough. If you don't, the fish will be greasy; if you do, it will be beautifully crisp and absolutely delicious.

FOR TWO

2 *whole rainbow trout, split and cleaned*
2½ *oz. salt pork, cut into small pieces*
¼ *c. fine cracker meal*

¾ *tsp. salt*
¼ *tsp. freshly ground black pepper*
¼ *tsp. paprika*

Rinse the fish and place on paper towels to dry. Fry the salt pork in a large heavy skillet until all the fat is rendered. Remove the pan from the heat. Remove the solids with a skimmer or slotted spoon and discard. Combine the cracker meal, salt, pepper, and paprika in a pie pan or wide bowl and mix well with a fork. Roll the still damp fish in the meal until evenly coated all over. Place on a flat platter to dry side by side but not touching. Return the pan to the heat and heat until the fat is quite hot. Fry the fish until crisp and browned on each side, about 4 minutes per side. Place on paper towels to drain for a minute or so, then serve on heated plates with lemon wedges. If desired, place a pat of anchovy butter sauce (see Poached Scrod with Anchovy Butter Sauce) rather than the usual tartar sauce at the side of each portion.

Fried Trout in Pearly Meal

A half-and-half mixture of yellow corn meal and yellow corn flour is called pearly meal in New Orleans. It gives fried fish a good crunchy crust that is less heavy than one of pure corn flour. (Corn-starch is more finely ground than corn flour. It should be substituted only if you can't find corn flour anywhere.)

FOR TWO

2 small to medium-sized trout fillets	¾ tsp. salt
cold milk	⅛ tsp. freshly ground black pepper
½ c. yellow corn flour	a few grains of cayenne
½ c. yellow corn meal	vegetable oil for deep frying

Rinse the fillets and dry with paper towels. Soak in cold milk to cover. Combine the corn flour, corn meal, salt, pepper, and cayenne in a bowl and mix thoroughly. Preheat oil in a deep fryer to 375°F. When the oil is sufficiently hot, lift the fillets out of the milk, letting the excess liquid drain off, then roll in the seasoned flour and meal mixture to coat evenly. Place on a platter to dry for several minutes, then fry until golden (this crust rarely turns brown) and quite crisp, 6 to 7 minutes. Remove from the oil, let drain over the fryer for a few seconds, then place on paper towels to complete draining for about 1½ minutes. Serve on heated plates garnished with lemon wedges.

Fried Catfish

One of the major disadvantages of being a sophisticated urbanite in twentieth century America is never having tasted a great cat-fish. And worse still, not knowing what one is missing. Most Americans love the cat; it is the most widely eaten American fish. This is one fish that must come from fresh water—the lower the salinity the better the catfish. The trick in frying great catfish is using thin fillets, less than ¼ inch thick. When you can't get tiny catfish you can get the same results with thicker fillets by slicing them across with a sharp knife into thinner fillets. Use a deep fryer with an accurate temperature control. A simple test for properly fried catfish: you should be able to pick up a fried fillet 3 or 4 inches long by one end and not have it bend or wilt—and it should crunch when you bite into it. This version uses the hearty seasoning the Cajuns of southwestern Louisiana love. You can reduce the cayenne to ¼ to ½ teaspoon if you prefer. A great American fish.

FOR FOUR

1 medium to large-sized freshwater catfish, cleaned and filleted, skin removed, the fillets then sliced across to a thickness of about ⅛ inch

cold milk

1½ c. finely ground yellow corn meal

2¼ tsp. salt

1 tsp. freshly ground black pepper

1½ tsp. cayenne

vegetable oil for deep frying

Rinse the fillets under cold running water and dry very thoroughly with paper towels. Place in a bowl with cold milk to cover. Combine the corn meal and seasonings in another bowl and mix very thoroughly. Also mix again after coating each fillet, to keep the seasonings evenly distributed. Preheat oil in a deep fryer to 375°F. Remove the fillets one at a time from the milk and roll in the seasoned meal to coat evenly. Place on a large flat platter to dry, leaving space between them. Let dry for at least 5 minutes, then fry 4 to 6 pieces at a time. (Don't crowd the fryer; if you do, the oil temperature will drop too much.) Fry until the pieces are a light brownish gold, 6 to 7 minutes per batch. Remove from the oil and place on paper towels to drain for a few minutes, then set on a platter covered with paper towels. Put the platter in a 200°F. oven to keep warm while you fry the rest of the fillets. Place each successive batch in the warm oven. The fillets will remain hot and crisp for as long as 35 minutes.

Fried Red Snapper

A Greek seafood restaurant in Pensacola, Skopelos, convinced us that we had grievously underestimated red snapper. We had eaten too many oversauced, overcooked, and overpraised dishes made with snapper, and we were tired of its apparently fashionable popularity. Skopelos changed our minds. This Fried Red Snapper is an outstanding example of how a local fish treated with respect and taste will respond accordingly.

FOR TWO

2 small red snapper fillets or 1
  medium to large fillet
1 large egg mixed with 3 Tbs.
  cold water
¾ c. white corn meal

1 tsp. salt
½ tsp. freshly ground black
  pepper
scant 1/16 tsp. cayenne
vegetable oil for deep frying

If you are using a single medium or large snapper fillet, divide it into 2 portions. Rinse the fillets under cold running water, then dry very thoroughly with paper towels. Begin preheating the oil in a deep fryer to 375°F. Put the egg and water into a shallow dish or pie pan. Combine the corn meal and seasonings in a bowl and mix very thoroughly. First dip the pieces of fish in the egg mixture on both sides, then roll in the seasoned meal to coat evenly and thoroughly. Place on a flat platter to dry, not touching one another, for a few minutes. Fry until crisp and a medium gray-brown color, 7 to 8 minutes, then drain on paper towels for a minute or so. Serve on heated plates garnished with lemon wedges.

Philippine Fried Bass with Vegetables

An unusual fish dish first prepared for us in New Orleans' only Philippine restaurant, a dish we loved at first taste. The crisp whole fish is served on a large platter surrounded by stir-fried vegetables in a light beef stock sauce.

FOR FOUR TO SIX

1 medium to large bass, split and
  cleaned, head and tail left on
salt and freshly ground black
  pepper

flour in a shaker
3 Tbs. sesame oil combined with
  3 Tbs. vegetable oil

The Pleasures of Seafood 66

VEGETABLE SAUCE

3 qt. fresh vegetables (pea pods, celery, onions, green onions, bean sprouts, Chinese celery cabbage, young green beans, several garlic cloves, broccoli, green peppers, etc.)

additional vegetable oil if needed

¼ c. drained sliced water chestnuts

⅓ c. beef stock

2 Tbs. dry sherry

¼ tsp. ginger

¾ tsp. sugar

½ tsp. salt

Rinse the fish and dry very thoroughly. Sprinkle on both sides with salt and pepper, then dust very lightly with flour. In a large sauté pan or brazier which will hold the fish comfortably (if absolutely necessary, remove the head) heat the sesame and vegetable oil until quite hot. Shallow fry the fish on both sides in the hot oil until crisp and well browned. Shake the pan frequently to keep the fish from sticking; if the oil begins to smoke, reduce the heat a bit. Use 2 large spoons or 2 spatulas for turning the fish over, rather than forks, so as not to break the skin. When the fish is cooked, carefully lift it out of the pan with a long wide spatula and place it on the large serving platter you plan to bring to the table. Remove the pan from the heat. Set the platter in a 175°F. oven while you prepare the vegetables.

Check the amount of oil left in the pan. You will need about 4 tablespoons for stir-frying. If necessary, add vegetable oil to make up the amount. To prepare the vegetables for frying: cut the celery into slivers about 3 inches long; slice the onions ⅜ inch thick; cut the green onions in half across, then cut the bottom halves into thin slivers; cut the celery cabbage into pieces 3 inches long by about ½ inch wide; dice the garlic coarsely; cut the broccoli into slivers after breaking up the florets; slice the green peppers into thin rounds. Put the pan over high heat. When the oil is quite hot, add the fresh vegetables and the water chestnuts. Stir-fry for 4 to 5 minutes, tossing them and turning the mass over constantly. Sprinkle on the beef stock, sherry, ginger, sugar, and salt after the vegetables have cooked for 3 minutes. Test a few pieces of vegetable for doneness. They should be cooked, but still quite crisp. As soon as the vegetables are done, scoop them out of the pan with a large slotted spoon or a skimmer and place in a bowl. Cook the liquid remaining in the pan for 1 minute more, stirring constantly, then remove the pan from the heat. Remove the platter of fish from the oven and carefully arrange the vegetables around the fish, with about ½ cup spread thinly over the top. Pour the liquid from the pan over the vegetables surrounding the fish; do not pour any of it on the fish itself. To serve, place the platter in the center of the table. Allow each diner to help himself to some of the vegetables and to pieces of the fish flesh broken directly off the carcass.

Finnish Rye-Fried Fish

We have always been surprised at how little curiosity food writers and fish lovers have shown in experimenting with different frying batters and procedures. We came across a version of this dish while browsing through our collection of ethnic cookbooks and decided it looked promising. Certainly, a fish dipped in egg and cream and coated with rye flour, then pan fried in butter should taste delicious. It does.

FOR TWO

2 sole or flounder fillets	½ tsp. salt
1 large egg	½ c. (1 stick) salt butter
¼ c. heavy cream	2 lemon wedges
¾ c. light or medium rye flour	
¼ tsp. freshly ground black pepper	

Rinse the fillets under cold running water and dry thoroughly between several layers of paper towels. In a pie dish or wide bowl beat the egg and cream together with a fork. Combine the rye flour, pepper, and salt in another pie dish and mix with a spoon or fork to blend evenly. Dip each fillet first in the egg and cream mixture, then in flour to coat evenly. Place on a platter to dry.

In a heavy skillet or sauté pan melt the butter over medium heat, then continue heating until the butter is sizzling but not brown. Carefully place the coated fillets in the pan and cook until golden brown on the bottom side. (Lift gently with the edge of a spatula to check the color.) Turn the fillets over and brown on the other side. When done, remove to heated plates and spoon several tablespoons of the browned butter from the pan over each serving. Garnish with lemon wedges.

Scallops Fried in Batter

Those of you who have an abundant supply of fresh scallops know how good they are. For those who don't, properly processed frozen scallops are an excellent substitute. We enjoy Dublin Bay as well as Massachusetts scallops here in New Orleans thanks to expert freezing. Here is a simple but classic way to enjoy scallops, fresh or frozen: firmly cooked in a crisp batter puffed up a bit with egg white.

FOR TWO OR THREE

1 lb. small to medium-sized scallops
vegetable oil for deep frying

BATTER

½ c. flour
1½ Tbs. olive oil
¼ tsp. salt
⅛ tsp. freshly ground white pepper

3 to 4 Tbs. tepid water
1 large egg white

---

very finely minced fresh parsley
lemon wedges

Rinse the scallops and roll in several layers of paper towels to dry. Begin preheating oil for deep frying to 375°F. Combine all ingredients for the batter except the egg white. Beat the egg white in a small bowl with a whisk or a hand electric mixer with one beater removed until light and airy. Fold into the batter lightly to mix; do not beat or you will remove all the air. Dip the scallops in the batter and fry, 6 to 8 at a time, until golden brown and crisp; this should take approximately 4 minutes. Remove from the oil and place to drain on paper towels for a minute or so, then put on a platter lined with paper towels and place in a 175°F. oven to keep warm. Continue in the same manner until all the scallops are done. To serve, place on heated plates, sprinkle with minced parsley, and garnish with lemon wedges.

Crumb Fried Clams

An old favorite at that grand old Brooklyn seafood museum, Gage & Tollner. Let the cracker crumb coated clams dry before frying: they'll spatter less and keep their coating while frying. This works equally well with shucked whole clams and with soft belly clams with the hard muscle cut off. Since we don't live in clam country and don't get enough clams to find the chewiness a hardship, we have no sharp preference. But the softness of the soft bellies is awfully pleasant. Maybe half with and half without.

FOR TWO

2 doz. freshly shucked small to medium-sized hard shell clams

1 large egg mixed with 2 Tbs. cold water

1 c. fine bread crumbs

1½ tsp. salt

¼ tsp. freshly ground black pepper

a few grains of cayenne

vegetable oil for deep frying

Drain the clams in a colander, then place on 2 or 3 layers of paper towels. Cover with several more layers and, after a few minutes, turn the towel-enclosed clams over. (This will drain off the remaining moisture.) Put the egg and water mixture into a pie dish or other wide shallow container and beat lightly with a fork. Put the bread crumbs and seasonings into a bowl and mix well. Preheat oil in a deep fryer to 375°F. To coat the clams, dip them one at a time in the egg and water, turning them over to coat evenly, then in the seasoned bread crumbs. Place the breaded clams on a large flat platter to dry in a single layer and with a bit of space between them if possible. Allow to dry for about 5 minutes, then fry in batches of 6 to 8 until crisp and browned, 2 to 3 minutes per batch. As you remove each batch from the fryer, place the clams on paper towels to drain for 1 minute, then on a platter covered with paper towels. Set the platter in a 175°F. oven to keep warm. Continue as directed above until all the clams are fried. Serve on heated plates garnished with lemon wedges.

Fried Shrimp in Corn Flour

Of all the coatings we've tried on fried shrimp, this is our consistent favorite. Seasoned corn flour adheres easily to the rinsed and barely drained shrimp and makes a light, deep gold crust with a crunch you can literally hear across the room.

FOR TWO OR THREE

1 lb. whole fresh shrimp, peeled and deveined, tails left on if desired
1¼ c. yellow corn flour
2½ tsp. salt

¾ tsp. freshly ground black pepper
⅛ tsp. cayenne
vegetable oil for deep frying

Rinse the peeled shrimp under cold running water and place them on paper towels to drain. Preheat oil in a deep fryer to 375°F. Put the corn flour into a large bowl along with the seasonings and mix very thoroughly with a whisk or fork. Roll 8 to 10 shrimp at a time in corn flour and fry until crisp and dark gold in color, 4 to 5 minutes per batch. Drain on paper towels for 1 minute, then place on a platter covered with paper towels and set in a 175°F. oven to keep warm. Continue frying the remainder of the shrimp in batches, taking care to mix the corn flour a bit before coating each batch. (The seasonings tend to settle to the bottom in this type of mixture.) Coat each batch just before frying; do *not* allow the usual drying time or the moisture will seep through and mar the coating. When placing the newly fried shrimp on the warming platter, try as much as possible to keep them in a single layer; this will retain the maximum crispness. To serve, place the shrimp on heated plates.

Beer Batter Shrimp

The best Beer Batter Shrimp we've ever tasted are served at Annie's restaurant in Henderson Point, Mississippi. After a number of versions we at last worked out this recipe. One of the secrets of the distinctive flavor is using flat beer. Another is allowing the batter to marinate for at least 3 hours.

FOR THREE OR FOUR

BATTER

1 c. flat beer	1½ tsp. sugar
1 Tbs. salt	1 c. flour
2 tsp. baking powder	⅛ tsp. cayenne

---

1 to 1¼ lb. peeled, deveined large or medium shrimp
vegetable oil for deep frying
flour in a shaker

Open the beer and pour off into a bowl 2 hours before mixing the batter. Leave uncovered at room temperature. To prepare the batter, combine all the ingredients in a large mixing bowl and whip at medium-high speed with an electric mixer until frothy and rather thin in texture. (Or whip vigorously by hand with a whisk for about 4 minutes.) Cover the bowl with a plastic wrap and let stand at room temperature for at least 3 hours.

Preheat oil in a deep fryer to 375°F. Rinse the peeled shrimp briefly and dry with paper towels. Place flat on a large platter and dust evenly with flour. Turn the shrimp over and dust on the other side. Uncover the batter and mix vigorously with a whisk for about 1 minute. Dip the floured shrimp one at a time in the batter to coat thoroughly, hold for a few seconds over the bowl to let the excess batter drip off, then drop into the hot oil. Fry 8 to 10 shrimp per batch until golden brown, about 3½ minutes. Drain on paper towels for 1 minute, then place on a platter covered with paper towels and set in a 175°F. oven to keep warm. Continue dipping and frying the shrimp in batches as indicated above. Try to place the cooked shrimp as much as possible in a single layer on the warming platter. Serve on heated plates.

Shrimp Tempura

The ethereal batter of lightly fried Japanese style shrimp should be enough to convince skeptics of the enormous delicacy possible in fried seafood.

---

1 to 1½ lb. peeled, deveined shrimp, tails left on

BATTER

2 large eggs, separated
½ c. beer
2 tsp. olive oil
½ c. flour
2 tsp. soy sauce

½ tsp. dry mustard
¼ tsp. salt
⅛ tsp. freshly ground white pepper

---

flour in a bowl, approximately ¾ c.
vegetable oil for deep frying

Begin heating oil in a deep fryer to 375°F. In a large bowl combine the egg yolks, beer, oil, flour, and seasonings and beat vigorously with a whisk until thoroughly blended. In another, smaller bowl beat the egg whites until stiff. Fold them into the batter gently so as not to knock the air out of them. (The batter should still look a bit streaky after folding.) Rinse the shrimp and dry thoroughly with paper towels. Holding them by the tails, dip the shrimp one at a time first in the bowl of flour, then in the batter. Allow each shrimp to drip over the batter bowl for a few seconds, then drop into the hot oil. Repeat until you have a batch of 6 to 8 shrimp. (They will puff up quite a bit and room must be allowed in the fryer for expansion.) Fry until crisp and golden, about 4 minutes, then drain on paper towels for 1 minute. Place on a large platter covered with paper towels and set in a 175°F. oven to keep warm. Continue frying the shrimp in small batches. To serve, place on heated plates and provide small cups or ramekins containing a dipping sauce of 5 parts soy sauce to 1 part sake with a tiny amount of ground ginger mixed in.

Fried Soft Shell Crabs

If you ask someone who has lived in New Orleans what he misses most, odds are the answer will be soft shell crabs. These delicate creatures are scarce in most of the country and abundant in New Orleans, where they are available virtually all year. On days when there are no soft shell crabs New Orleanians act as if the world has come to an end. Understandable. The reason New Orleans

---

*has the best soft shell crabs is not because they grow better in
Lake Pontchartrain (though this may be true), but because we cook
them with love, care, and lots of experience and we're not afraid
to fry them. Because soft shell crabs are rare and expensive in
most parts of the country, there is a tendency to treat them too
gingerly. Nothing gives soft crabs that marvelous nutty flavor except deep frying. If you have very small crabs and you are lucky,
you may get them right some of the time in a sauté pan, but it
won't be consistent. The best way here is also the simplest: perfect frying with a well seasoned batter at the precise temperature
will give you gorgeous crabs every time and a good start on a lifetime of addiction.*

FOR FOUR

4 large or 8 small soft shell crabs	*½ tsp. freshly ground black*
cold milk	*pepper*
2 c. flour	*¼ tsp. cayenne*
1 tsp. salt	*vegetable oil for deep frying*

To clean the crabs, lay them, back down, on paper towels spread
out on a wooden chopping surface. Remove the "apron," or loose
triangular covering on the underside of the crabs, then turn them over.
With a very sharp knife cut off about ⅓ inch of the front of the head.
This will remove the eyes. Then reach into the opening and remove
the small tannish gray sac that is behind the eye cavity. Lift up the
pointed flaps on each side of the top and pull out the fibrous matter
("dead man") with your fingers. Lay the flaps down again. Be careful
not to crush and mutilate the crabs when you handle them.

To fry, rinse the cleaned crabs quickly under cold running water and
gently pat them dry with paper towels. Put them to soak in about
1½ inches of cold milk in a pie dish or bowl for 10 to 15 minutes.

Meanwhile, combine the flour and seasonings in a large bowl, and
preheat the oil for deep frying to 375°F. Carefully remove the crabs
from the milk, let them drain for a few seconds, then roll them gently
in the seasoned flour to coat thoroughly. After coating, place the crabs
on a large platter side by side, taking care not to let them overlap.
Fry 1 or 2 at a time, depending on size, in the preheated oil until
deep golden brown—from 6 to 12 minutes, depending on the size of
the crabs and the condition of the oil. (It takes a bit longer to get
the right color with oil that has not been used before. The surface of
the crabs is sealed as soon as they are put into the oil, so you are not
likely to overcook them if it takes a bit longer to achieve the right

brownness.) Since soft shell crabs tend to float on the surface of the oil, turn them over frequently with tongs during frying to ensure even browning.

As each batch is done, lift the crabs out of the oil with tongs or by raising the frying basket, if you are using one. Let them drain over the pot for about 1 minute, then put them on a platter lined with paper towels and place the platter in a preheated 200°F. oven until all the crabs are fried. Serve hot.

Soft Shell Crabs Beurre Noisette
New Orleans Meunière

A simple extra touch, brown butter sauce on crisply fried soft shell crabs. We can't decide which way we like them better, plain or this way.

FOR FOUR

4 large or 8 small soft shell crabs	½ tsp. freshly ground black
cold milk	pepper
2 c. flour	¼ tsp. cayenne
1 tsp. salt	vegetable oil for deep frying

BEURRE NOISETTE

¾ c. (1½ sticks) salt butter	½ tsp. freshly ground white
2 tsp. fresh lemon juice	pepper

Clean and fry the crabs as directed for Fried Soft Shell Crabs. Keep them in a 200°F. oven while you prepare the sauce.

To prepare the sauce, melt the butter over medium heat in a 2 to 3 quart saucepan. Cook just until the butter begins to brown, then remove the pan from the heat. Add the lemon juice and pepper, and mix with a wooden spoon. The sauce will foam up. When the foaming subsides, return the pan to the heat and cook for 1 to 2 minutes longer, or until the sauce turns a rich hazelnut brown. Remove from the heat. To serve, place the fried crabs on heated plates. Stir the sauce thoroughly and spoon about 3 tablespoons over each portion.

Soft Shell Crabs Amandine

The most lavish way to serve soft shell crabs, with brown butter and almonds browned in the butter sauce. An embarrassment of riches.

FOR FOUR

Prepare 4 large or 8 small soft shell crabs as directed for Soft Shell Crabs Beurre Noisette. Keep the crabs warm as indicated. Add 1 cup slivered blanched almonds to the butter sauce as the butter is melting. When the butter begins to brown, the almonds will turn golden brown. Remove the almonds from the pan with a slotted spoon and reserve in a cup or small bowl while you complete the sauce. To serve, top each portion of crab with ¼ cup browned almonds, then pour the sauce over.

Oysters Fried in Corn Meal

Fried oysters are a way of life in New Orleans. New Orleanians love fried oysters and prepare them several ways. We first tasted corn meal fried oysters in a tiny oyster restaurant, Tom's, in Empire, Louisiana, where freshly shucked oysters were carefully fried in pure corn meal. Simple and delicious, a classic way to fry oysters.

FOR THREE OR FOUR

1½ pt. freshly shucked oysters
vegetable oil for deep frying
1 c. finely ground yellow corn meal
2 tsp. salt
¾ tsp. freshly ground black pepper
⅛ tsp. cayenne

Put the oysters to drain in a colander. Begin heating the oil in a deep fryer to 375°F.

Combine the corn meal, salt, pepper, and cayenne in a bowl and mix thoroughly with a whisk. Scoop 6 to 8 oysters at a time out of the colander and roll them in the seasoned corn meal. The dampness still remaining on the oysters will make the meal adhere. Be sure to get the coating even and to leave no bare spots. Leave them in the meal until the oil reaches the indicated temperature, then drop them into the oil. Fry for 2 to 3 minutes, until crisp and golden brown in color. Remove from the fryer with a long-handled skimmer or slotted spoon and place on several layers of paper towels to drain about 1 minute, then place in a single layer with some space between them on a large platter covered with paper towels. Set the platter in a 200°F. oven to keep warm. Continue frying the oysters in small batches as indicated, then draining and putting them in the oven to keep warm, until all the oysters are fried. If the thermostat on the fryer indicates that the oil temperature has dropped below 375°F. after a batch is fried, wait until it comes back to the proper temperature before adding the next batch. Also, skim off any browned particles that collect on the surface of the oil after each batch is fried. (This will prevent spattering and discoloration of the oil.) Serve on heated plates with lemon wedges.

Batter Fried Oysters

The most common style of frying oysters, hearty and much more filling than those fried in corn meal. These are the oysters most often used in the giant oyster loaves New Orleanians regard as a diet staple.

FOR FOUR OR FIVE

1½ pt. freshly shucked oysters	*1½ c. yellow corn flour*
vegetable oil for deep frying	*1½ tsp. salt*
about 1½ c. flour	*¼ tsp. freshly ground black*
2 large eggs beaten with 2 Tbs.	*pepper*
cold water	*⅛ tsp. cayenne (optional)*

Place the oysters in a colander to drain. Preheat oil in a deep fryer to 375°F.

Put the flour in a bowl or pie dish and the egg and water mixture in a shallow dish. Combine the corn flour, salt, pepper, and cayenne in a large bowl and mix thoroughly with a whisk. Roll the drained oysters briefly in paper towels to dry. Have handy a large flat platter on which to dry the oysters before frying. Dip the oysters one at a time first in the unseasoned flour to coat lightly, then in the egg and water mixture. Last, roll each one in the seasoned corn flour to coat evenly and thoroughly. Place on the platter to dry for a few minutes. Continue until all the oysters are coated and ready for frying. Fry 5 or 6 at a time until crisp and a very deep gold color with occasional flecks of brown, about 3 minutes. Drain briefly on paper towels, then place on a platter covered with paper towels and set in a 175°F. oven to keep warm while you complete the frying. Serve on heated plates with lemon wedges.

Oysters Fried in Cracker Meal

By dipping the oysters in egg and water, then in seasoned cracker meal, you get crisp oysters with a light crust. Be sure the oil is hot enough; at only 20° F. below the correct temperature cracker meal will absorb a lot of oil and you'll have an on-the-spot demonstration of why frying is sometimes held in ill repute.

FOR TWO OR THREE

1 pt. freshly shucked oysters (about 3 doz. small or 1½ doz. large oysters)
vegetable oil for deep frying
2 c. cracker meal

1 tsp. salt
⅜ tsp. freshly ground black pepper
2 large eggs
2 Tbs. cold water

Drain the oysters in a colander. Preheat the oil in a deep fryer to 375°F.

In a large bowl combine the cracker meal, salt, and pepper. Mix well with a spoon. In a small bowl put the eggs and water, then mix thoroughly with a fork or a whisk. Put the oysters into the egg and water, then roll them in the seasoned cracker meal. Fry in batches of 8 to 10 at a time depending on size. (Do not crowd the fryer.) Fry until golden brown, 3 to 4 minutes per batch. Lift the oysters out of the fryer with a skimmer, permitting the oil to drain back into the fryer. Place the oysters on a large platter covered with several layers of paper towels and set in the oven. Repeat, placing each completed batch on the covered platter. Place the oysters on the platter side by side in a single layer. Don't heap them one on the other or they may get soggy. Serve on heated plates with lemon wedges.

Crumb Fried Oysters

Suggested to us by the clams at Brooklyn's Gage & Tollner and tried on our own Louisiana oysters with excellent results. The cracker crumbs lend a sweet and nutty taste to the fried oysters. Allow at least 10 minutes for drying the coating to keep the oil from spattering and the coating from falling off in spots during frying.

FOR TWO OR THREE

1 pt. freshly shucked oysters
1 large egg mixed with 2 Tbs. cold water
1 c. fine bread crumbs
1½ tsp. salt

¼ tsp. freshly ground black pepper
a few grains of cayenne
vegetable oil for deep frying

Prepare as directed for Crumb Fried Clams. Serve on heated plates with lemon wedges.

Fried Oysters en Brochette

A marvelous way to cook oysters, shish kebab style, with the flavor of bacon mingling with the crisp oysters inside the crunchy crust. Heartier and more filling than the broiled version of this dish.

FOR TWO

1 pt. freshly shucked oysters
vegetable oil for shallow frying
3 slices lean breakfast bacon, cut into 1 inch squares

salt and freshly ground black pepper
a few grains of cayenne
a shaker filled with flour

BATTER

1½ c. flour
1 tsp. salt
1 large egg
½ c. cold water

¼ c. cold milk
½ tsp. freshly ground black pepper
¼ tsp. paprika

Preheat the oil in an electric skillet to 365° to 375°F. (If you don't have one, use a heavy frying pan and a frying thermometer.) Drain the oysters in a colander and place on paper towels to finish draining. Fry the bacon squares until partially cooked, 3 to 4 minutes, then drain on paper towels. Fill 2 long flat skewers with alternating oysters and bacon squares, with a bacon square at each end. Sprinkle with salt and pepper and a very small amount of cayenne. Dust lightly and evenly on both sides with flour.

Mix the ingredients for the batter with a whisk or electric mixer in a mixing bowl, then pour into a shallow baking dish or a pie pan. Dip the filled skewers in the batter by placing them over the rim of the dish and turning slowly to form an even coating of batter. If necessary, use a spoon to cover any spots that do not get coated with the turning motion. Coat evenly and fairly thickly, then place over a deep bowl to drip for about 1 minute. Fry on all sides, leaving the ring end of the skewer out of the oil. (Be sure to handle the ring end with tongs or insulated gloves.) When the coating is crisp and nicely browned all around, about 6 or 7 minutes, remove from the oil and drain briefly on paper towels. Serve on heated plates garnished with lemon wedges. Slide off the skewers at the table, or immediately before serving if you prefer.

Frogs' Legs Beurre Noisette

For the best tasting frogs' legs get the tiny tender ones rather than the larger meatier ones—and forget the garlic that seems to plague frogs' leg cooking in America. This is one of the best, and simplest, versions of a delicacy too few people have enjoyed. Many of the prized small frogs' legs come from Japan and are available frozen. Just defrost them, still wrapped, in a basin of cool water, then rinse and dry.

FOR THREE OR FOUR

12 pairs small frogs' legs
2 to 3 c. cold milk, approximately

COATING

1½ c. flour
1½ tsp. salt
½ tsp. freshly ground black
  pepper

⅛ tsp. cayenne
scant ⅛ tsp. mace

*vegetable oil for deep frying (1 part peanut oil combined with
2 parts corn oil is excellent here)*

BEURRE NOISETTE

*1 c. (2 sticks) salt butter
5 tsp. fresh lemon juice
2 tsp. finely minced fresh parsley*

Using a sharp knife, remove the bottom joint of the frogs' legs (which is attached to the feet) and discard. Separate the pairs by cutting through the joint with a clean, strong stroke. Rinse the legs under cool running water and drain on paper towels, then roll in another batch of paper towels to remove the last bit of moisture. Place flat in a pie dish or wide-bottomed shallow bowl. If necessary make a second layer. Pour in cold milk to cover and allow to soak at room temperature for 1 to 1½ hours.

Begin heating the oil in a deep fryer to 375°F. or, if you are using a electric deep skillet with a thermostatic control, to 400°F. Combine the ingredients for the coating in a bowl and mix thoroughly with a whisk. Remove the frogs' legs from the milk about 4 at a time and roll in the seasoned flour to coat thoroughly, then place to dry for about 2 minutes on a platter, with space left between them so that they do not touch. Fry about 4 at a time in the hot oil until golden brown and crisp, 5 to 7 minutes per batch, turning often with tongs to ensure even browning. Place on paper towels to drain briefly, then place on a platter covered with paper towels and set in a 175°F. oven to keep warm while you fry the rest.

To prepare the sauce, melt the butter over medium heat in a small heavy saucepan and cook until it begins to turn light hazelnut brown. Remove the pan from the heat and add the lemon juice and parsley. The sauce will foam up. When the foaming subsides, return the pan to the heat and cook for 1 minute more. Stir thoroughly and remove from the heat again. To serve, place 3 or 4 pairs of frogs' legs in preheated individual gratin dishes or on plates with raised edges. Spoon about ¼ cup of the sauce over each portion, being sure to include some of the browned solid matter that has settled to the bottom of the saucepan. If using gratin dishes, set them on plates. Bring to the table immediately.

Conch Steak

Floridians love conch and this is one of the favorite ways of preparing it. The steak is pounded out and fried in bread crumbs; it has a fine chewy texture and nutty flavor.

FOR TWO

¾ to 1 lb. conch meat, sliced
½ inch thick
salt and freshly ground black
pepper

1 large egg mixed with 2 Tbs.
cold water
1 c. fine bread crumbs
vegetable oil for deep frying

Cut the slices of conch into 2 or more pieces. If the pieces are too large for your fryer after pounding out, cut them up again. Rinse, then dry very thoroughly. Pound out on both sides with the scored side of a mallet until quite thin, about ⅜ inch thick. (If you don't have a mallet, use the underside of a heavy saucer.) Sprinkle generously with salt and pepper. Preheat oil in a deep fryer to 375°F.

Place the egg and water mixture in one pie dish and the bread crumbs in another. Beat the egg and water with a fork to mix thoroughly. Dip each piece of conch in egg and water, then roll in bread crumbs to form an even coating. Place on a platter to dry for 3 to 5 minutes before frying. Fry from 1 to 3 pieces at a time depending on the capacity of your fryer. It is better to underload than to overload it, since too much food at one time will lower the oil temperature and give you unsatisfactory results. Fry until brown and crisp, for 3 to 4 minutes, then place on a platter covered with several layers of paper towels and set in a 200°F. oven to keep warm. Continue as directed until all the conch pieces are fried. Serve on heated plates with lemon wedges.

Fried Conch

One of our favorite seafood restaurants, Vincent's Clam Bar in downtown New York, fries its conch this way, in crisp strips with a hearty batter.

FOR THREE OR FOUR

1 lb. conch meat, cut into slices
¼ inch thick, then into strips
about 2½ inches long by ⅜
inch wide

flour in a shaker
vegetable oil for deep frying

¾ c. flour	2 large eggs, lightly beaten
¼ c. olive oil	7 Tbs. tepid water
1 tsp. salt	
½ tsp. freshly ground black pepper	

Begin preheating the oil in a deep fryer to 375°F. Combine the ingredients for the batter in a mixing bowl and beat vigorously with a whisk or with an electric mixer. Set aside. Lay the conch strips on a large work surface or a very large flat platter and dust lightly but evenly with flour. Turn them over and dust with flour on the other side. Dip the floured strips one at a time into the batter, letting the excess drip back into the bowl for a few seconds, then drop into the frying oil. This can be done very quickly; you should be able to dip about a dozen strips in a minute or so. Fry the strips in batches of a dozen until crisp and light brownish gold in color, about 4 minutes. Lift the strips out of the oil with a long-handled skimmer or large slotted spoon and place on several layers of paper towels to drain briefly, then put on a platter covered with paper towels and place in a 175°F. oven to keep warm. Continue dipping and frying in small batches, then draining and setting to keep warm. Serve in a single large bowl in the center of the table and provide tongs or a large serving spoon so the diners can help themselves.

Clam Fritters

Primarily for New Englanders, who have an abundance of clams. Deep frying gives these fritters a crispy exterior and brings out the natural flavor of the clams. We've added a bit of extra seasoning.

FOR TWO OR THREE

1 c. shucked clams	1 c. milk or ⅔ c. milk and ½ c. clam liquor
1 c. flour	
1 tsp. double-acting baking powder	1 Tbs. grated onion
	1 tsp. fresh lemon juice
1 tsp. salt	1 Tbs. finely minced fresh parsley
¼ tsp. freshly ground black pepper	
1 large egg	vegetable oil for deep frying

Grind the clams in a meat grinder, using the coarse blade, or chop them very fine. Sift the flour, baking powder, salt, and pepper into a large bowl. Add the egg and mix very thoroughly, lifting the mixture to allow air to be incorporated into it. Add the milk (and clam liquor, if used). Stir gently with a whisk until smooth. Add the ground clams to the batter and fold in thoroughly. Add the onion, lemon juice, and parsley. Mix with a tossing motion. Heat oil in a deep fryer to 365°F. When the oil is at the desired frying temperature, drop the batter, about ¼ cup at a time, into the hot oil and fry until brown on both sides. 7 to 8 minutes in all. (If you hold the fritters down under the surface of the oil with the back of a skimmer, there will be no need to turn them over.) Fry in batches that will fit comfortably in your fryer. (The average home fryer will hold 2 or 3 fritters with ease; 4 or more are probably too many.) Place the fried fritters on a large platter covered with several layers of paper towels and place the platter in a 200°F. oven to keep warm while completing the rest. Serve very hot.

Conch Fritters

FOR TWO OR THREE

Prepare as directed for Clam Fritters. Substitute 1½ cups finely diced or ground conch meat for the clams; increase the milk by 3 tablespoons; add 3 tablespoons thinly sliced green onion tops to the batter. Serve with lemon wedges and several teaspoons of prepared horseradish.

Greek Fried Bass with Garlic and Almond Sauce

Greeks do grand things with seafood, especially with bass. The puréed garlic sauce with almonds (skordalia) is one of the headiest you'll ever taste, and if you like garlic, you'll like this sauce. Begin by chopping up the garlic and pounding it into a paste with a mortar and pestle—or use a blender from the very beginning. The sauce should be thick, with a texture like softened peanut butter. This recipe makes about 3 cups of sauce, since it's difficult to work with in smaller quantities; you can save the left-

over sauce in a tightly closed container under refrigeration for several weeks.

GARLIC AND ALMOND SAUCE

6 large or 10 small garlic cloves
½ c. finely chopped almonds
1¾ c. mashed potatoes or cooked, drained, and mashed chick-peas
4 slices white bread, crusts removed, soaked in water, then squeezed dry

¾ c. olive oil, approximately
½ c. white wine vinegar, approximately
½ tsp. salt, more if desired

---

4 small to medium-sized bass fillets, skin removed
vegetable oil for deep frying
salt

freshly ground black pepper
flour or fine cracker meal

To prepare the sauce, chop the garlic very fine, then pound it to a paste with a mortar and pestle or purée in a blender. (If you use a blender, be sure to scrape down the sides of the container several times during puréeing or you will lose too much of the garlic.) Add the almonds and pound them in (or purée them in). Add the potatoes and soaked bread and mix well. Transfer the paste to a mixing bowl and begin adding the oil and vinegar alternately, in very small amounts, beating very thoroughly after each addition, as for a mayonnaise. A whisk used rapidly with a sweeping rotary motion, a handheld electric mixer at low-medium speed, or a standing electric mixer will all give excellent results. After you have added about ½ cup of the oil and ⅓ cup of the vinegar, check the consistency. The sauce should already be fairly smooth and thick. If it appears lumpy and difficult to mix, add a bit more oil and a bit more vinegar and mix at high speed. Check again. If, after adding all the oil and vinegar, you find the sauce beginning to turn a bit thin rather than fluffy and viscous, add a bit more soaked, squeezed dry bread. Add the salt and mix in thoroughly. Taste; if necessary, add a bit more salt and mix in well. Spoon the sauce into a bowl or jar, cover, and refrigerate until you are ready to serve.

To fry the fish, preheat the oil in a deep fryer to 375°F. Rinse the fillets, dry quickly with paper towels, then sprinkle with salt and pepper. Roll in flour or cracker meal to coat thoroughly, then place

Frying 85

on a platter to dry for about 5 minutes. Fry until golden brown and crisp, 5 to 6 minutes, in two batches if necessary. Drain on paper towels and place in a 200°F. oven to keep warm if you have a second batch to fry. To serve, place the fillets on heated plates and heap about 3 tablespoons of the sauce on the plates to one side of the fish. Place a lemon wedge on the other side.

Sole with Apples and Cream Sauce

Fruit and fish go so well together that we are surprised not to find the combination on restaurant menus or in most cooking litera-ture. This is a grand dish with an elegant cream and fruit sauce, ideal with sole or flounder. W find it most practical to prepare the fish first and keep it warm while preparing the sauce.

FOR TWO

2 sole or flounder fillets, skin removed

1 large egg beaten with 1 Tbs. water

about 1 c. fine bread crumbs

¾ tsp. salt

¼ tsp. freshly ground white pepper

3 Tbs. butter plus 3 Tbs. peanut oil for pan frying

APPLE AND CREAM SAUCE

4 Tbs. butter

1 medium-sized apple, cored, pared, and sliced ½ inch thick

2 Tbs. finely minced shallots

2 tsp. flour

½ c. chicken stock

1 c. heavy cream

¼ c. Calvados or applejack

¼ tsp. salt

¼ tsp. freshly ground white pepper

2 tsp. sugar

1 tsp. Dijon mustard

Rinse the fillets and dry very thoroughly. Put the egg and water into one pie dish and the bread crumbs into another. Add the salt and pepper to the bread crumbs and mix thoroughly with a fork or spoon. First dip the fillets in the egg and water mixture, then roll in the bread crumbs to coat evenly and thoroughly. Place on a platter to dry. In a large heavy skillet or sautéing pan, melt the butter over medium heat. Add the peanut oil just before the butter is completely melted and stir with a wooden spoon or spatula to mix. Continue heating until the butter and oil mixture is quite hot. To check, dampen a fingertip with water and sprinkle a drop or two into the pan. If the drop dances merrily, the oil is hot enough. Do not heat until it begins to smoke or the oil will become discolored. About 3 to 5 minutes over medium-high heat should be just about right. Pan fry the fillets until golden brown, 4 to 5 minutes on each side. Turn them over carefully with a wide spatula so as not to break them. When done, place on a platter covered with paper towels and set in a 175°F. oven to keep warm while you prepare the sauce.

Drain off all but about 1 tablespoon of the oil and butter left in the sauté pan and wipe out any solids that cling to the pan with paper towels. Add 3 tablespoons of butter and heat until it sizzles very lightly. Place the apple slices flat in the pan and sauté until browned and soft on the bottom side, about 4 minutes. Turn over and sauté on the other side for about 3 minutes. Remove the apple slices from the pan with a fork, allowing the excess butter to drain back into the pan, and place on a small plate. Set the plate in the warm oven along with the fish. Add the remaining tablespoon of butter to the pan and sauté the shallots until soft and very lightly browned, stirring frequently. Sprinkle in the flower and stir with a whisk until thoroughly mixed in. Add the chicken stock and mix. Heat for about 1 minute, then gradually pour in the cream, stirring constantly. Add the Calvados and stir, then the salt and pepper. Put the apple slices back into the pan and sprinkle with the sugar. Cook in the sauce for 2 minutes, spooning the liquid over the apples as you cook. Add the mustard to the sauce surrounding the apples; do not put it over them. Continue cooking for 1 minute more, stirring very gently to incorporate the mustard into the sauce without disturbing the apple slices, which will be quite tender by this time. To serve, place the fillets on heated plates, top with several apple slices, then spoon the sauce over the top and around the sides. Serve immediately.

Striped Bass with Apples Beurre Noisette

A simple pan fried fish topped with sautéed apples in a rich brown butter sauce.

FOR FOUR

4 small to medium-sized bass
fillets, skin removed
1 large egg mixed with 1 Tbs.
cold milk
1½ c. bread crumbs

1¼ tsp. salt
½ tsp. freshly ground white
pepper
¼ c. (½ stick) salt butter
¼ c. peanut oil

APPLES BEURRE NOISETTE

2 small or 1½ medium-sized
apples, cored, pared, and sliced
½ inch thick
3 Tbs. butter

4 tsp. fresh lemon juice
½ tsp. marjoram
1 tsp. sugar

Pan fry the bass fillets as directed for the sole fillets in Sole with Apples and Cream Sauce. Increase cooking time 1 minute for each side. Keep the fish warm as directed.

To prepare the sauce and topping, first skim any visible brown solids from the pan, then wipe around the inner sides with a paper towel. Add 2 tablespoons of the butter to the pan and melt over medium-high heat. Add 2 teaspoons of the lemon juice and the marjoram. Place the apple slices in the pan and sauté until soft and attractively browned, about 3 minutes on each side. Remove the fried fillets from the warm oven and place several apple slices on top of each one. Raise the heat under the pan, add the remaining tablespoon of butter, 2 teaspoons lemon juice, and the sugar, and cook, stirring rapidly, until the sauce in the pan is the color of toasted hazelnuts. Tip the pan to one side and spoon about 3 tablespoons of sauce, including the browned matter which will have settled to the bottom, over each portion. Serve immediately.

Striped Bass with Bananas Beurre Noisette

Wheeler's restaurant in London makes a version of this dish, often called Sole Capri, with Dover sole. It's just as delicious with bass and looks as good as it tastes, especially on a warm summer evening.

FOR FOUR

Prepare as directed for Striped Bass with Apples Beurre Noisette, substituting 2 bananas sliced in half across, then in half lengthwise, for the apples. Top each portion with 2 pieces of sautéed banana. Decrease the sugar added during the final moments of browning the butter sauce to ¾ teaspoon, then sauce as directed.

Poaching and Saucing Recipes

Poached Red Snapper with
  Nantua Sauce

Sole Dugléré

Sole Véronique Français

Sole Véronique Français
  with Hollandaise

Sole Véronique
  Pontchartrain Hotel,
  New Orleans

Sole Dieppoise

Sole Gismonda

Sole Bercy

Sole Normande

Sole Marguéry

Sole with Almond and
  Coriander Sauce

Poached Bass with Almond
  Curry Sauce

Poached Scrod with Anchovy
  Butter Sauce

Polish Christmas Eve Bass

5

Poaching and Saucing

Poached and sauced fish dishes include many of the grandest classic French seafood preparations as well as dishes from many other cuisines. At the outset we'd like to clear the terrain a bit and dispel some of the mystique that has made many of these dishes appear forbidding and inaccessible.

First, there is the widely held assumption that poached and sauced dishes are the highest expression of culinary skill, far beyond the capacities of home cooks. This is nonsense. Yes, making a really first class sauce requires careful attention to timing, seasoning balance, and texture; yes, properly poaching a fish is not a haphazard business. But no good seafood cooking is the result of carelessness and whim. Home cooks can quickly and easily learn the few simple basics. They will find that poaching is easy and that preparing first class sauces is not at all as difficult as they have been led to believe. Most of the dishes in this chapter take well under an hour to prepare and are ideally suited to the home.

Second, many of the most famous French dishes in this genre use sole and turbot, often leading home cooks to believe that without sole and turbot they cannot prepare anything even approaching the "classic" dishes. This, too, is patently untrue. We have prepared excellent poached and sauced fish dishes with all manner of fish, from commoner and less expensive whiting and haddock and trout to higher priced but still moderate striped bass and flounder. Sole and turbot are delicately flavored fish; they efface themselves under the star attraction, the sauce itself. But they have no magical qualities of their own. It's often fun to put a stronger flavored fish under a grand sauce, or to thumb one's nose at establishment snobbery with Shark Bercy. Although it may sound strange and taste different from Sole Bercy, it tastes very good indeed. And it is just as valid. Enough of seafood snobbery!

We enjoy grand sauces and *haute cuisine* as much as other good eaters—but we also like our fish untrammeled and unsauced. A grand sauce may enhance the fish; it may give us a dish *as good* as the same fish freshly caught and cooked in one of the basic ways outlined in the first three chapters. But nothing—not the grandest or the most delicious sauce in all the world—is going to *improve* the taste of one of our favorite fish.

Variety of preparation is certainly useful for good and plentiful local fish, wherever one lives. Unfortunately, the innate quality of a poached and sauced fish is not as crucial as in one of the basic styles, and many restaurant kitchens are aware that all manner of sins may be hidden under a striking sauce. They also, for purposes of expediency, too often reduce most of the grand sauces to one all-purpose cream sauce with varying additions, giving all the grandly named menu dishes a tired sameness.

In this chapter we have carefully chosen our own favorite grand dishes. We have deliberately omitted the classic dishes that are primarily set pieces and have concentrated on those that use sauces in a dramatic and interesting way, on dishes that really taste good and aren't merely "fancy." And as the Polish and Mexican dishes demonstrate, the French do not have a monopoly on *haute cuisine* seafood cooking.

Bring poaching liquid to full boil, then lower to simmer before adding seafood.

Keep liquid at a simmer while poaching seafood.

Time cooking period carefully.

Remove cooked food from liquid with slotted spoon or spatula.

Keep poached food warm in 175°F. oven or on warming tray while preparing sauce.

Handle poached fish carefully; use long broad spatula to avoid breaking.

Where poaching liquid is to be used in sauce, strain liquid carefully and reserve.

Alternate poaching method:
use buttered skillet or heatproof baking dish;
bring liquid to boil over burner;
add food;
when simmer returns, cover skillet loosely and set in 350°F.;
oven poaching takes approximately twice as long as skillet poaching.

Poached Red Snapper with Nantua Sauce

Poaching is at the heart of much French haute cuisine *seafood cooking. Because the preferred French fish used for the classic preparations are sole or turbot, many people assume it is the fish rather than the preparation that gives the dish its distinction. In a sense, when you poach a fish and put a grand sauce on it you are upstaging the fish. The sauce is above all what you will taste. Sole and turbot are delicate fish and tend to intrude even less than might a richer fish such as mackerel. We always prefer to broil or grill our favorite and freshest fish because we love the taste of the fish themselves. When we are in the mood for a more elaborate preparation we are likely to choose a fish we eat often, one that is not a great novelty, so we can enjoy the saucing without worrying about missing the taste of the fish.*

This dish came into existence when we had a much lower

opinion of snapper than we have now. We were writing another cookbook and we knew how much many persons loved snapper; it was not a fish we liked unadorned so we decided to make it the sacrificial fish that would be lost under the sauce. The sauce, a variation on the famous French crawfish sauce, turned out so well that Red Snapper with Nantua Sauce became one of our favorites. Which is probably the point of French fish cooking and why we decided to lead off this chapter with snapper. It is not only delicious, it is as good as many of the sole dishes that follow.

There are two basic ways of poaching a fish without overcooking it: in a large skillet on top of the stove or in a low oven. The stove is quicker; oven poaching is ideal if you are doing other things like finishing a sauce that needs all of your attention. The Nantua sauce with butter, cream, and brandy is simpler than the usual restaurant procedures. If you have no crawfish, shrimp will work almost as well, giving you a slightly milder sauce. A level teaspoon of tomato paste will attractively deepen the color without changing the flavor.

FOR FOUR

COURT BOUILLON

⅓ c. dry white wine	2 whole cloves
3 c. water	4 whole black peppercorns
1 small white onion, thinly sliced	1 bay leaf, broken in half
	⅛ tsp. thyme
4 parsley sprigs	1 slice fresh lemon about ¼
½ tsp. salt	inch thick

---

4 red snapper steaks, sliced about ½ inch thick
(about 1½ lb. total weight)

NANTUA SAUCE

1 lb. crawfish, peeled, cleaned, parboiled for 2 to 3 minutes	¼ tsp. freshly ground white pepper
6 Tbs. butter	⅛ tsp. cayenne
¾ c. heavy cream	5 Tbs. fish stock or strained
1 Tbs. brandy	poaching liquid
1 tsp. salt	¼ c. flour

Combine all the ingredients for the court bouillon in a large heavy skillet or sauté pan. Bring to a boil and simmer for 8 to 10 minutes. Remove the solids with a fine mesh skimmer or slotted spoon. Keeping the liquid at a low boil, place the snapper steaks flat on the bottom of

---

the pan. Simmer gently, spooning some liquid over the top of the fish from time to time, for 8 to 10 minutes. Immediately remove the fish from the liquid with a large slotted spatula, allowing the excess liquid to drain back into the pan. Handling the fish carefully, place the fish on serving plates and set in a 175°F. oven while you prepare the sauce. If your oven does not have a good tight seal, cover the plates loosely with aluminum foil to keep the fish from drying out.

Purée the parboiled crawfish through a sieve or in an electric blender. Melt butter in a large heavy sauté pan or saucepan and add the puréed crawfish. Mix well. Add the cream, brandy, salt, pepper, and cayenne. Simmer, covered, over low heat for 35 minutes, stirring frequently. Remove from the heat. Add 5 tablespoons strained poaching liquid to the mixture and stir. Strain out all the solids and put the strained liquid into a saucepan over very low heat. Add the flour very gradually in small quantities, stirring constantly, to achieve a smooth texture. To serve, spoon about ¼ cup sauce over each portion of snapper. Save the strained-out solids for making crawfish dressing. (See Broiled Flounder with Crawfish Dressing.)

Sole Dugléré

The most beautiful of the classic French sole dishes and our personal favorite. Like many popular dishes it fares poorly in most restaurant kitchens, perhaps because classic dishes are often taken for granted. The keys to a successful Dugléré are fresh ripe tomatoes, careful layering of the poaching elements, and the extra butter swirled into the dish at the very end. One of the most impressive fish preparations ever conceived, beautiful to look at as well as to taste.

FOR THREE OR FOUR

2 large ripe tomatoes, blanched, then peeled, cored, and coarsely chopped

2 Tbs. salt butter

POACHING BASE

3 or 4 sole fillets, skin removed
about 1⅓ Tbs. softened butter for greasing baking dish
¼ c. finely minced shallots
½ tsp. salt

¼ tsp. freshly ground white pepper
3 Tbs. finely minced parsley
½ c. dry white wine
½ c. light chicken or fish stock

SAUCE

2 Tbs. salt butter	½ tsp. salt
2 Tbs. flour	¼ tsp. chervil
⅓ c. milk	a few grains of cayenne
strained, reduced poaching liquid (see p. 95)	1 tsp. lemon juice
	1 Tbs. cold salt butter
⅓ c. heavy cream	
¼ tsp. freshly ground white pepper	

To pureé the tomatoes, melt the butter in a small sauté pan over medium heat. Add the chopped tomatoes and cook, stirring and mashing with a wooden spoon, until most of the liquid has evaporated and the tomatoes are reduced to a thick purée. Remove from the heat and set aside.

Preheat the oven to 350°F. Butter the inner surface of a baking dish that will hold the fillets comfortably. Scatter the minced shallots evenly over the bottom of the dish, then sprinkle with ½ teaspoon salt and ¼ teaspoon freshly ground white pepper. Spoon half the tomato purée evenly over the bottom, then place the fish fillets flat over the purée. Cover with the remaining tomato purée and sprinkle with the parsley. Add the wine and stock, carefully pouring them into the dish *around* the sides and not *over* the contents. Bring to a simmer over medium heat, cover the dish loosely, then set in the preheated oven for 10 to 12 minutes. Remove the dish from the oven and carefully lift the fillets with a slotted spatula onto serving plates. Cover the plates loosely with foil and set in a warm oven while you prepare the sauce.

Strain the poaching liquid into a small heavy saucepan. Bring to a boil and cook, stirring frequently, until reduced to a bit more than half (about 1 cup). Remove the pan from the heat. In another, slightly larger saucepan prepare the velouté by melting the butter, then stirring in the flour, and last, adding the milk gradually; cook until thickened. Add the reduced poaching stock to the velouté, stirring with a whisk, then stir in the cream. Keep the sauce smooth and the heat at low. Simmer at low for about 5 minutes, then add the pepper, salt, chervil, and cayenne. Remove the pan from the heat and stir in the lemon juice. Swirl in 1 tablespoon cold butter.

Drain off any excess liquid that has collected around the fillets. Spoon the sauce evenly over the fish, then serve at once.

Sole Véronique Français

Not part of the classical French canon, although prepared in the French style, Sole Véronique has a mixed ancestry and probably originated in Middle Europe. We like three versions of it and can't decide among them, so we have included them all. This is the most classic of the three, with a butter sauce and Curaçao, cèpes, lemon juice, and peeled green grapes. For home dining, it is most practical to glaze the sauced fillets in a single large baking dish and then carefully lift each portion onto individual plates.

FOR TWO OR THREE

2 or 3 sole fillets, skin removed
about 1⅓ Tbs. softened butter for greasing baking dish

POACHING BASE

½ c. water
¼ c. chicken or fish stock
¼ c. Curaçao liqueur
6 white peppercorns
½ tsp. marjoram

¼ tsp. salt
3 parsley sprigs
1 bay leaf, broken in half
⅛ tsp. nutmeg

SAUCE

1 tsp. fresh lemon juice
¾ c. peeled green grapes, poached in water and lemon juice for 4 minutes
¼ oz. dried cèpes, soaked in water and drained thoroughly

1 Tbs. butter rubbed together with 1 tsp. flour with your fingers (beurre manié)
2 Tbs. butter for dotting the sauce

Grease the inner surface of a heatproof baking dish or an attractive skillet thoroughly with softened butter. Place the fillets in the dish and add the ingredients for the poaching base. Bring to a boil over medium heat on top of the stove, then cover loosely and set in a preheated 350°F. oven for 12 minutes. Remove from the oven and lift the fillets out of the liquid carefully with a slotted spatula, allowing the liquid to drain back into the dish. Place them on a single large ovenproof platter, cover loosely with aluminum foil, and set in a 175°F. oven to keep warm or set on a warming tray while you prepare the sauce. Also begin preheating the broiler.

To prepare the sauce, strain the poaching base into a 2 to 3 quart heavy saucepan and cook, stirring frequently, until reduced by half. Add the lemon juice, grapes, and *cèpes*. Crumble in the butter and flour mixture with your fingers, stirring constantly with an even motion with a whisk to keep the sauce smooth. Cook for about 2 minutes longer, until the sauce is thickened. Remove the pan from the heat.

Remove the baking dish containing the fish from the oven and uncover. Carefully wipe up any liquid that has collected around the fillets using a paper towel. Arrange the fillets attractively, then carefully spoon the sauce from the pan over them, distributing the grapes and *cèpes* evenly. Dot the surface of the sauce with small pieces of butter, then set the platter under the broiler about 4 inches from the source of heat.

Glaze until the surface of the sauce appears to have formed a smooth skin with medium to dark brown flecks scattered across it, about 4 minutes. Remove from the oven. To serve, carefully lift the fillets from underneath along with their sauce coating onto heated plates and bring to the table immediately.

Sole Véronique Français with Hollandaise

The combination of grapes and the orangy flavor of the Curaçao is so heady, a topping of piquant hollandaise seemed to us an appropriate gilding of the lily.

FOR TWO OR THREE

Prepare ⅔ cup hollandaise sauce as directed for Broiled Redfish Hollandaise. Keep warm in a bowl or basin of warm water. Prepare Sole Véronique Français as directed, omitting the 2 tablespoons butter used for dotting. Instead, cover the surface of the sauce with an even layer of hollandaise sauce just before serving.

Sole Véronique Pontchartrain Hotel, New Orleans

New Orleans cuisine is famous for taking French dishes and sauces and imaginatively changing them into entirely new ones. The Pontchartrain Hotel invented a form of Sole Véronique—Trout

Véronique. Theirs was the version we tasted first and came to love. We became familiar with the others when tracing the origins of the New Orleans dish—the rewards of scholarship. The New Orleans Véronique does not use Curaçao, and the Creole style hollandaise is spicy and glazed under the broiler. All three Véroniques are excellent with flounder, bass, or good New Orleans trout.

FOR FOUR

4 sole fillets, skin removed

POACHING LIQUID

2½ c. water	*3 whole black peppercorns*
¼ c. dry white wine	*1 bay leaf, broken in half*
1 Tbs. salt butter	*⅛ tsp. thyme*
1 tsp. salt	*1 slice fresh lemon, ¼ inch thick*

HOLLANDAISE SAUCE

1½ c. (3 sticks) salt butter	*3 Tbs. fresh lemon juice*
9 large egg yolks	*¼ tsp. cayenne*

1⅓ c. green seedless grapes, peeled and cut in half lengthwise

To poach the fish, combine the ingredients for the poaching liquid in a large heavy skillet or sauté pan. Bring to a boil over high heat, then reduce the heat just enough to keep a low simmer going. Place the sole fillets in the liquid and cook at a low simmer for 5 to 6 minutes. Do not overcook them. Remove the fillets from the poaching liquid carefully using a large slotted spatula, allowing the excess liquid to drain back into the pan. Place in a large ovenproof baking dish or on an ovenproof platter large enough to hold them comfortably side by side. Cover the platter loosely with aluminum foil and set in a 175°F. oven to keep warm or set on a warming tray while you prepare the sauce. Begin preheating the broiler.

Prepare the hollandaise sauce as directed for Broiled Redfish Hollandaise. Add the grapes to the sauce and mix very gently to distribute them evenly. Spoon the sauce, including the grapes, evenly over the fillets in the baking dish. Glaze by placing under the broiler about 4 inches from the source of heat for about 1 minute, or just until the surface of the sauce begins to brown. Remove immediately from the heat. To serve, with a spatula lift the fillets carefully from underneath onto heated plates along with their glazed coating. Bring to the table immediately.

Sole Dieppoise

Heavy cream, white wine, and poaching liquid are the bases of this classic Norman dish. Mussels, boiled shrimp, or clams can be added to the sauce just before glazing. Have the fish market save the fish trimmings for you; they are essential for a flavorful stock.

FOR TWO OR THREE

FISH STOCK

2 carrots, finely chopped	1 bay leaf, broken up
1 medum-sized onion, finely chopped	4 parsley sprigs
2 Tbs. salt butter	1½ c. dry white wine
1 Tbs. olive oil	1½ c. water
fish trimmings or 1 c. chicken stock, reduced to ¼ c.	⅛ tsp. freshly ground white pepper
½ tsp. thyme	¾ tsp. salt

SAUCE

2 Tbs. salt butter	¾ c. heavy cream
2 Tbs. flour	¼ tsp. salt
1½ c. strained fish stock (see above)	¼ tsp. freshly ground white pepper

---

2 or 3 sole fillets, skin removed	¼ c. dry white wine
softened butter for greasing baking dish	1 c. strained fish stock, approximately
salt and freshly ground white pepper	

1½ tsp. butter for dotting

To prepare the fish stock, in a heavy 3 to 4 quart saucepan, sauté the carrots and onions in the butter and olive oil until very soft and just beginning to turn brown. Add the remaining ingredients for the stock and bring to a boil. Reduce the heat and simmer for 20 minutes, stirring occasionally. Strain through a very fine mesh strainer (or a piece of dampened wrung-out cheesecloth placed over a coarse strainer) into a bowl or large heatproof measuring cup.

To prepare the sauce, melt the butter over low heat in a 2 to 3 quart heavy saucepan. Stir in the flour gradually, stirring constantly with a whisk or wooden spoon to keep the mixture smooth. Gradually stir in 1½ cups of the strained fish stock and cook until thickened, 3 to 4 minutes. Add the cream very slowly, stirring constantly until thoroughly blended in, then cook over low heat for about 1 minute. Sprinkle in the salt and pepper and mix. Remove the pan from the heat and set aside while you poach the fish.

To poach the fish, rub the inner surface of a heatproof baking dish or a heavy skillet with butter. Place the fillets in the dish and sprinkle lightly with salt and pepper. Add the wine and enough strained fish stock to just cover the fillets. Place the fish over medium heat until the liquid begins to simmer. Remove from the heat, cover loosely with a piece of aluminum foil, and poach in a preheated 350°F. oven for 10 to 12 minutes. Remove from the oven and uncover. Pour off the poaching liquid into a cup or small bowl. Preheat the broiler.

Put the pan containing the sauce back over low heat and warm very slowly, stirring constantly. If the sauce appears to have thickened noticeably, add 1 or 2 teaspoons of the reserved poaching liquid to thin it out a bit. Stir rapidly to make sure the sauce is perfectly smooth. Pour the sauce evenly over the fillets. Dot the surface with 1½ teaspoons butter, then glaze under the broiler 3½ to 4 inches from the source of heat for about 2 minutes, just until the butter melts and begins to darken slightly. To serve, lift the fillets from underneath with a large spatula and set on heated plates, taking care to disturb the glazed sauce covering as little as possible. Bring to the table immediately.

Sole Gismonda

One of the most unusual of the grand sole dishes. Port wine is the most striking ingredient, accenting the egg yolk and cream-thickened sauce heightened with rosemary. Particularly good served with small boiled potatoes coated with melted butter and sprinkled with freshly minced parsley.

FOR TWO OR THREE

2 or 3 sole fillets, skin removed
softened butter for greasing baking dish

POACHING STOCK

½ c. chicken or fish stock
⅛ tsp. salt
⅛ tsp. freshly ground white pepper

a small bay leaf, broken in half
⅜ tsp. ground rosemary
2 parsley sprigs
½ c. port wine

SAUCE

strained poaching stock (see above)
2 large egg yolks, well beaten

3 Tbs. heavy cream
¼ tsp. salt
⅛ tsp. cayenne

To poach the fish, rub the inner surface of a heatproof baking dish or a heavy skillet with butter. Place the fish fillets in the dish, then add the remaining ingredients for the poaching base. Set the dish over medium heat and bring to a boil. Remove the dish from the heat, cover loosely with aluminum foil, and set in a preheated 350°F. oven for 10 to 12 minutes. Remove from the oven and uncover. Carefully pour off the poaching liquid into a bowl or measuring cup, taking care not to break up the fish fillets. Recover the dish and set the fish in a 175°F. oven to keep warm while you prepare the sauce.

To prepare the sauce, strain the poaching liquid into a heavy 2 to 3 quart saucepan. Cook over medium heat until reduced by one-third, stirring frequently. Remove the pan from the heat and allow the liquid to cool a bit. Ladle about 3 tablespoons of the still warm liquid into the bowl containing the beaten egg yolks, stirring rapidly with a whisk to keep the yolks from lumping up, then gradually stir the contents of the bowl into the saucepan, keeping the whisk in motion as you pour. Return the pan to very low heat and gradually add the cream, always stirring. Sprinkle in the salt and cayenne and mix thoroughly. Cook the sauce over low heat just until warmed through. Do not let it come to a boil. To serve, place the poached fillets on heated plates and spoon the sauce over them. Garnish with small boiled potatoes coated with melted butter and sprinkled with minced parsley.

Sole Bercy

*One of the lightest of the French sole dishes, with a delicate but-
ter, shallot, and white wine sauce. The pale smooth sauce is most
attractive served in colored oval gratin dishes or in faience plates
with decorated rims.*

FOR TWO OR THREE

2 or 3 sole fillets, skin removed

POACHING LIQUID

¼ c. dry white wine	½ tsp. salt
¼ c. water	1/16 tsp. ground thyme
3 white peppercorns	1/16 tsp. ground bay leaf

SAUCE

1½ Tbs. salt butter	¼ tsp. fresh lemon juice
3 Tbs. finely chopped shallots	3 Tbs. cold salt butter
⅓ c. dry white wine	1 Tbs. finely minced fresh parsley
⅓ c. strained poaching liquid (see above)	
about ¾ c. velouté, made with 1½ Tbs. butter, 1 Tbs. flour, ½ c. strained poaching liquid, with water or chicken stock added to make up the quantity	

To poach the fish, place the fillets in a heavy skillet and add the
ingredients for the poaching liquid. Bring to a boil over high heat,
then reduce the heat and simmer very gently for 5 to 6 minutes.
Remove the skillet from the heat immediately and lift the fillets onto
plates or a single large platter with a spatula, allowing the liquid to
drain back into the pan. Cover the fillets loosely with aluminum foil
and set in a 175°F. oven to keep warm while you prepare the sauce.
Strain the poaching liquid.

To prepare the sauce, melt the butter over medium-low heat in a
heavy saucepan and sauté the shallots until soft but not brown. Add
the wine and ⅓ cup of the poaching liquid. Cook over medium heat,
stirring frequently, until reduced by half. In a separate small pan
make the velouté by melting the butter, then gradually stirring in
the flour and mixing until smooth. Gradually pour in ½ cup of
liquid composed of the remaining poaching liquid plus enough
water or chicken stock added to make up the quantity. Cook over
medium-high heat until thickened, then cook at a low boil for

exactly 1 minute. Remove the pan from the heat and stir in the lemon juice. Remove the fish from the warm oven and, if they were kept warm on a large platter, place the fillets on individual heated plates. Add 3 tablespoons cold salt butter to the sauce and swirl in with a wooden spoon or spatula, leaving the sauce looking attractively streaky. Sprinkle in the parsley and stir just once, then spoon the sauce over the fillets. Serve immediately.

Sole Normande

La Couronne in Rouen is the oldest inn in France, founded in 1385. It was there we first experienced the special magic of a Norman sauce dramatically flamed with Calvados, the great French apple brandy. One of our special favorites, this is an ideal dish for a festive dinner.

FOR FOUR

4 sole fillets, skin removed

POACHING LIQUID

2½ c. water	3 whole black peppercorns
¼ c. dry white wine	1 bay leaf, broken up
1 Tbs. salt butter	⅛ tsp. thyme
1 tsp. salt	1 slice fresh lemon, ¼ inch thick

SAUCE NORMANDE

2 Tbs. salt butter	1½ c. strained poaching liquid
2 Tbs. flour	(see above)
¼ tsp. salt	1 c. heavy cream
¼ tsp. freshly ground white pepper	6 Tbs. Calvados or applejack

Poach the fish as directed for Sole Véronique Pontchartrain Hotel, New Orleans, then remove the fillets to a flambé pan or large heavy skillet. Cover loosely with aluminum foil and set in a 175°F. oven to keep warm while you prepare the sauce. Strain the poaching liquid.

To prepare the sauce, melt the butter in a heavy 2 to 3 quart saucepan over low heat. Gradually stir in the flour, stirring with a whisk to keep the mixture smooth. Sprinkle in the salt and pepper, stir to mix, then remove the pan from the heat. Check the temperature of the strained poaching liquid; it should still be warm. If it is not, warm it briefly over low heat. Return the pan containing the butter and flour to low heat and gradually pour in 1½ cups of the poaching liquid, stirring constantly to keep the sauce smooth. Cook over low heat until the sauce begins to thicken, then very gradually add the cream. Continue cooking over low heat, stirring, until the cream is completely blended in, then add 3 tablespoons of the Calvados. Cook over low heat for 2 minutes more, then once again remove the pan from the heat.

To serve, remove the pan containing the poached fillets from the oven. Pour the sauce over them. Set the pan over very low heat. Heat the remaining 3 tablespoons of Calvados in a small skillet until boiling, then pour it over the contents of the pan and ignite immediately. Keep the flame going by tipping the pan with a slow circular motion. When the flame dies out, lift the fillets onto heated plates and pour the sauce from the pan over them. If you wish, the flaming can be accomplished at the table in the following manner: Set the pan containing the fillets and the sauce over an alcohol burner. Heat until very hot, then add the remaining Calvados. When the Calvados begins to bubble around the sides of the pan, ignite immediately. Flame and serve as directed above.

Sole Marguéry

This is the original Marguéry dish from which New Orleans' fabled trout Marguéry originated. It is one of the richest and most dramatic of the classic French poached and sauced sole dishes. Few home kitchens have readily on hand all the seafood ingredients included in the sauce at its most lavish, but the fundamental flavor and texture can readily be duplicated at home. The only shellfish necessary to a fine Marguéry sauce are shrimp; you can use fresh or frozen with equally excellent results.

FOR FOUR

4 sole fillets, skin removed

POACHING LIQUID

2½ c. water	*3 whole black peppercorns*
¼ c. dry white wine	*1 bay leaf, broken in half*
1 Tbs. salt butter	*⅛ tsp. thyme*
1 tsp. salt	*1 slice fresh lemon, ¼ inch thick*

MARGUÉRY SAUCE

½ c. (1 stick) salt butter	*¼ tsp. salt*
¼ c. flour	*1 lb. boiled shrimp, peeled and deveined**
2½ c. hot strained poaching liquid, with boiling water added if necessary to make up the quantity	*½ c. sliced fresh mushrooms or, if fresh are unavailable, good quality canned mushrooms may be substituted; drain them very thoroughly*
2 large egg yolks, lightly beaten	
1 Tbs. fresh lemon juice	

Poach the fish as directed for Sole Véronique Pontchartrain Hotel, New Orleans, then remove the fillets to a single large platter or 4 serving plates. Cover loosely with foil and set in a 175°F. oven to keep warm while you prepare the sauce. Strain the poaching liquid.

To prepare the sauce, melt 3 tablespoons of the butter over low heat in a 2 to 3 quart saucepan. Stir in the flour gradually with a wooden spoon or spatula, keeping the mixture smooth. Slowly add the hot strained poaching liquid, stirring constantly with a whisk or a wooden spoon to keep the sauce perfectly smooth. Cook over low heat until thickened, about 5 minutes, then remove the pan from the heat. Add the egg yolks a bit at a time, stirring rapidly to keep them from cooking. Add the lemon juice and salt and blend thoroughly. Melt the remaining 5 tablespoons of butter in another, smaller saucepan. Return the larger saucepan to low heat and slowly add the melted butter, stirring very gently. When the butter is evenly blended in, add the boiled shrimp and sliced mushrooms. Cook over low heat, stirring gently, until the shrimp and mushrooms are heated

---

* We prefer to use the spicier New Orleans Boiled Shrimp, but the Mild Boiled Shrimp work just as well in this sauce.

---

through, 4 to 5 minutes. Do not allow the sauce to come to a boil. To serve, spoon equal quantities of the sauce over each portion, being sure to place 2 or 3 shrimp on top of each piece of fish.

Sole with Almond and Coriander Sauce

Poached fillets with a handsome golden green sauce containing almonds, green serrano chilies, coriander leaf, and bread fried in olive oil and garlic. This Mexican fish dish is a fascinating example of the way Mexico absorbed French cooking techniques into its indigenous cuisine. If you can't find serrano chilies, widely available in 4 ounce cans, substitute blanched, peeled green pepper and a bit of cayenne. Mix the ingredients for the sauce in a blender with an on-off rhythm, and stop when the sauce looks thick, with small even ripples throughout. Further puréeing will make it too thin.

FOR THREE OR FOUR

1½ lb. sole fillets

COURT BOUILLON

1 c. water	*1 bay leaf, broken in half*
½ c. dry white wine	*1 parsley sprig*
½ small onion	*¼ tsp. thyme*
2 whole cloves	*5 whole black peppercorns*
½ carrot, sliced	*½ tsp. salt*

SAUCE

1½ Tbs. olive oil	*1 Tbs. dried coriander leaf*
2 tsp. minced garlic	*(cilantro) or ⅓ c. fresh*
1½ oz. stale French or white bread	*¾ tsp. lime juice*
⅔ c. blanched slivered almonds	*¼ tsp. sugar*
2 canned green serrano chilies, about ¼ c. or ¼ c. sliced, blanched, and peeled green pepper, plus ⅛ tsp. cayenne	*¼ tsp. salt*
	reserved strained court bouillon (see above)

Combine the ingredients for the court bouillon in a skillet and bring to a boil over high heat. Place the fish fillets flat in the water and allow to come to a boil again. Cover the skillet loosely, lower the heat,

---

and simmer for 5 to 6 minutes, just until the fish flakes easily when poked with a fork. Lift the fillets out of the skillet with a wide slotted spatula, allowing the liquid to drain back into the pan, and place them in a shallow baking dish. Cover the dish with aluminum foil and place in a 175°F. oven to keep warm while you prepare the sauce. Strain the poaching liquid and reserve.

Heat the olive oil in a small skillet along with the garlic. Put the bread in the hot oil and fry until brown on both sides. Lift the bread out of the skillet with a fork and place on a platter to cool for a minute or so, then cut into ¾ inch pieces. Put the bread pieces into a blender container along with the remaining ingredients for the sauce. Add the strained poaching liquid and blend on high speed for a few seconds, then turn the blender off. Repeat until the sauce appears evenly blended and thick, with regular small ripples throughout. Pour the sauce into a saucepan and bring to a simmer over medium heat, stirring constantly. Simmer for 3 minutes, then remove from the heat. Place the fillets on heated plates and top with generous portions of sauce.

Poached Bass with Almond Curry Sauce

Our adaptation of an East African dish using poached fish and a curry sauce. The original sauce used peanuts, but we found that almonds gave a more delicate flavor. And as explained more fully in Chapter 7, we balance individual spices rather than using a prepared curry powder. This is also an excellent way to serve leftover poached fish. It can be reheated in a 400°F. oven in a covered baking dish with about ⅓ cup of the original poaching liquid if you have any, or with ¼ cup of water, 1 tablespoon of dry white wine, and a bit of salt and pepper. Heat just until warmed through, about 12 to 14 minutes if you start with chilled fish.

3 or 4 bass fillets, skin removed

POACHING LIQUID

½ c. water
⅓ c. dry white wine
¾ tsp. salt
2 tsp. butter
1 bay leaf, broken in half
¼ tsp. thyme

3 whole white peppercorns
1 tsp. finely chopped orange rind
¼ tsp. ground fennel seed
(ground with a mortar and pestle)

ALMOND CURRY SAUCE

3 Tbs. salt butter
1 c. chopped onions
one 1-lb. can peeled tomatoes, well drained and mashed (about 1 c.)
⅛ tsp. coriander
½ tsp. turmeric
⅛ tsp. cumin
¼ tsp. chili powder
⅛ tsp. ground cloves
⅛ tsp. cinnamon

1/16 tsp. ginger
⅛ tsp. dry mustard
⅛ tsp. cayenne
1 c. water
¾ c. slivered almonds, pulverized to a coarse texture in a blender
½ tsp. salt
¼ tsp. freshly ground black pepper
¾ tsp. sugar

To poach the fish place the fillets in a large heavy skillet along with all the ingredients for the poaching liquid. Bring to a boil over high heat, then reduce the heat sufficiently to just keep a low simmer going. Cook at a low simmer for 8 to 9 minutes, then remove the fillets from the liquid with a large slotted spatula, allowing the liquid to drain back in the pan. Place the fillets on a single large platter or on 4 serving plates, cover loosely with aluminum foil, and set in a 175°F. oven to keep warm while you prepare the sauce. Strain the poaching liquid and refrigerate, covered, for use as a fish stock in other preparations. (If you plan to keep it longer than 2 days, freeze it.)

To prepare the sauce, melt the butter over low-medium heat in a large sauté pan or skillet. Add the onions and sauté until quite soft but not browned. Add the mashed tomatoes and stir thoroughly. Continue cooking over low heat. Add the remaining ingredients in the order given above, stirring to mix well after each addition. Raise the heat to medium and cook, stirring frequently, for 8 to 10 minutes, until the sauce is completely mixed and even in color and the consistency is thick and pleasantly lumpy, similar to that of cooked tapioca. Taste to check for a thorough integration of seasonings. If any of the elements seems to stand out distinctly from the others, reduce the heat a bit and cook for 3 to 4 minutes longer, stirring gently but constantly. To serve, place the fillets on heated plates and spoon generous quantities of the sauce over each one.

Poached Scrod with Anchovy Butter Sauce

Scrod is one of America's great fish. It poaches beautifully, retaining its fine firm texture and distinctive sweet taste. One evening we decided to try our favorite anchovy butter sauce with freshly poached scrod—they were excellent together. The sauce can easily be prepared ahead of time, spooned into small ramekins or butter molds, then covered and refrigerated. Be sure to cover with several layers of plastic wrap or everything nearby will begin to smell of anchovies. The sauce works well with any poached fish and makes a fine heady dipping sauce for shellfish.

FOR TWO

2 scrod fillets, skin left on

COURT BOUILLON

¾ c. water	2 parsley sprigs
¼ c. dry white wine	¼ tsp. thyme
½ tsp. salt	4 whole black peppercorns
1 bay leaf, broken in half	

ANCHOVY BUTTER SAUCE

4 or 5 anchovy fillets, drained	¼ tsp. freshly ground black pepper
½ c. (1 stick) salt butter, softened	½ tsp. brandy
1 Tbs. fresh lemon juice	½ tsp. tarragon

To poach the fish, place the fillets in a large heavy skillet along with the ingredients for the court bouillon. Bring to a boil, then reduce the heat to the point where the liquid in the skillet is at a low simmer.

Cover the skillet loosely and cook for 8 to 9 minutes. Remove from the heat, uncover, then lift the fillets out of the liquid carefully with a slotted spatula, allowing the excess liquid to drain back into the pan. Place the fillets on serving plates, cover loosely with foil, and set in a 175°F. oven to keep warm while you prepare the sauce.

To prepare the sauce, mash the anchovy fillets in a large mortar with a pestle (or use the back of a wooden spoon and a small sturdy bowl). Mix in about 2 tablespoons of the softened butter at a time with a fork, until well blended. Add the remaining ingredients and mix thoroughly, this time with a spoon, scraping the sides and bottom of the mortar and lifting the mixture from the bottom to the top several times. For immediate use, cover the mortar or bowl with plastic wrap and set in the freezer for 4 to 5 minutes. For later use, spoon the sauce into individual butter molds or small ramekins, cover with several layers of plastic wrap, and place on the top shelf of the refrigerator to chill thoroughly. To serve, spoon about 2 tablespoons of anchovy butter sauce on top of each fillet and garnish with lemon wedges.

Polish Christmas Eve Bass

One of the glories of the poached fish repertoire, this Polish dish boasts a sauce made of honey, raisins, almonds, white wine, lemon, cinnamon, and cloves. And it tastes as good as it sounds. It is so special that the Poles rightly reserve it for special occasions the way we do our Thanksgiving turkey. Originally made with carp, it is equally good with bass or snapper. Like holiday turkey it should be made in large enough portions so that some is left over, since it is as delicious chilled as hot.

VEGETABLE FISH BOUILLON

4 c. cold water	1 medium onion, cut in quarters
6 black peppercorns	1 celery stalk, cut up
1 bay leaf, broken in half	1 carrot, cut up
1 tsp. salt	3 parsley sprigs
fish head and trimmings	

---

2 lb. bass, cut into large pieces
2 c. strained vegetable fish bouillon (see above)

SAUCE

1 c. honey	½ c. dry white wine
2 tsp. flour	¼ c. raisins
1 c. fish broth	¼ c. slivered almonds
⅓ tsp. cloves	¾ tsp. salt
½ tsp. cinnamon	¼ tsp. freshly ground black
2 tsp. grated lemon rind	pepper
juice of 1 lemon	

To prepare the vegetable fish bouillon, combine all the ingredients in a large pot and bring to a boil. Reduce the heat and simmer for 25 to 30 minutes. Allow to cool a bit, then strain.

To poach the fish, put 2 cups of the strained vegetable fish bouillon into a heavy skillet or sauté pan. Add the fish and bring to a boil. Cover the pan loosely and set in a preheated 350°F. oven for 25 minutes. At the end of that time, lift the pieces of fish carefully out of the pan with a slotted spatula and place them on serving plates. Cover loosely with foil and set in a 175°F. oven to keep warm while you prepare the sauce. Or, if you prefer, place all the pieces of fish in a single dish and cover, then transfer the pieces onto heated plates at serving time. Be careful not to break up the pieces during the additional handling.

To prepare the sauce, heat the honey in a large sauté pan or saucepan. When the honey becomes thin and moves freely across the bottom of the pan when you tip it, add the flour, a little bit at a time, stirring rapidly with a whisk. Raise the heat and when bubbles begin to appear in the honey indicating it is boiling, lower the heat again and add all the remaining ingredients except the salt and pepper. The sauce will foam up at this point; to prevent any spillover,

---

reduce the heat a bit more if necessary. Stir to mix thoroughly, then sprinkle in the salt and pepper, and raise the heat just enough to keep the sauce at a very low simmer. Simmer for 10 minutes. To serve, spoon about ⅓ cup of the sauce over each portion, placing some of the raisins and almonds on top of each piece of fish. Serve with 2 or 3 small boiled potatoes or several thick slices of larger potatoes at the side of each dish.

To save leftover fish and sauce for serving chilled the next day, place the drained cooked pieces of fish in a baking dish, then pour the sauce over them. Cover the dish tightly with several layers of plastic wrap and refrigerate.

Boiling, Braising, and Steaming Recipes

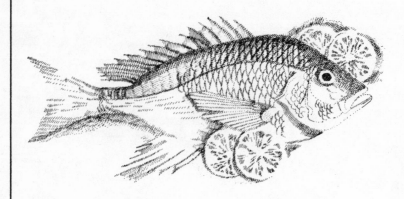

New Orleans Boiled Shrimp

Mild Boiled Shrimp

Baltimore Steamed Shrimp

Boiled Maine Lobster

Steamed Maine Lobster

Boiled Crabs New Orleans
Style

Steamed Crabs Chesapeake
Style

Steamed Soft Shell Clams

Steamed Hard Clams

Boiled Crawfish Cajun Style

Boiled Crawfish New Orleans
Style

Basic Mild Boiled Crawfish

Crawfish in Dill

Crawfish à la Nage

Florida Lobster à la Nage

Boiled Florida Lobster

Rock Shrimp Boiled in the
Shell

Moules Marinière

Clams Marinière

Redfish Courtbouillon

Chinese Braised Carp

Chinese Steamed Carp

6

Boiling, Braising,
and Steaming

Except for the intriguing exotica of several Chinese dishes, boiling and steaming heads us into American seafood country. And into the endless debates on boiled versus steamed Maine lobster, on the seasonings and fatness of New Orleans crabs, on the life-sustaining indispensability of Chesapeake steamed crabs, on New England steamer clams and clam broth. The major issue here is not the techniques, which are all simple and easily learned, but the availability of regional shellfish. The reason boiling and steaming are second nature to people living in New Orleans, Baltimore, and Boston is that in those cities seafood is abundant. You won't find the French steaming lobsters or clams, and you won't find anyone but a New Orleanian able to consume such immense quantities of boiled seafood. The American regional dishes detailed here are already well known to natives of their regions. Those living outside of an area will be hard pressed to secure the ingredients to satisfy their cooking curiosity. In a sense this chapter is the equivalent of carrying coals to Newcastle.

But there are a few things to be accomplished. The Chinese steaming and braising techniques, the French steaming techniques of the *marinière* dishes are unfamiliar to many. And perhaps we can teach expatriates from the seafood areas ways of survival in foreign lands. Nothing is more piercing to the ear than the cry of anguish of a displaced seafood lover. Rather than thanking fate for not having put him down in Des Moines, a New Orleanian in Baltimore loudly proclaims all people around the Chesapeake heathens for not boiling their crabs; Yankees condemned to New Orleans lament the loss of their lobsters and clams; and Baltimoreans hold forth on the irreplaceability of their native seafood, totally unaware that they have been eating Louisiana crabs and Long Island oysters a good part of their lives. Things aren't as bad as these hard-done-by expatriates make them out to be— and if we can save them a year or so of grief this chapter will have served at least one useful purpose. Californians and Floridians tend to adapt more easily—perhaps they are too complaisant. And perhaps after reading this chapter some Californians will decide that not all seafood self-destructs the instant it comes into contact with salt, pepper, herbs, or spices. Any techniques New England, New Orleans, or Baltimore can contribute to the boiled shellfish lexicon of the West Coast will be a step up.

For the rest of you in the middle of the country there is hope if you wish to explore the pleasures of boiled seafood. Fly it in. (See "Air and Ice," Chapter 17.) It's easy, it costs much less than a trip to any of the coasts, and while you may never become as argumentative, as opinionated, or as obnoxious as the marvelous boiled and steamed seafood addicts of America, you also will not simply take for granted one of the most pleasurable ways of eating seafood known to man and, even with air freight, one of the least expensive.

Basic Boiling Techniques

Boil seasoned court bouillons for 5 to 10 minutes before adding shellfish.

Time boiled seafood from moment when court bouillon returns to a boil after seafood has been added.

Remove seafood from water immediately when cooking time is complete. Simplest removal method: empty contents of pot into colander set in sink.

Basic Braising Techniques

Braise fish uncovered in lightly simmering liquid.

Baste frequently.

Cook until two-thirds of liquid has boiled off.

Use seasoned residue in pan as a sauce.

Basic Steaming Techniques

Use small amount of water in large heavy pot with tight lid.

Time from moment pot is covered.

Remove shellfish from liquid or drain off liquid as soon as cooking time is complete.

New Orleans Boiled Shrimp

In New Orleans shrimp are cooked whole—heads, tails, and all— in a spicy court bouillon and served chilled in their full glory from a large bowl in the center of the table. For anyone who assumes boiled seafood is dull or plain, these spicy shrimp eaten out of hand will reveal the joys of the fine art of boiling. And they're just as good served still warm from the pot. Shrimp prepared this way make an excellent and memorable shrimp cocktail, although traditionalists may prefer the milder version which follows for peeling and for cocktails. Boiled shrimp make a fine appetizer; they also make a hearty, informal full meal. A dinner of boiled shrimp requires a table set with plates or bowls for the debris and

plenty of cold beer. The most crucial thing to remember in pre-
paring boiled shrimp is not to overcook them: allow the court
bouillon to boil for 10 minutes before adding the shrimp and they
will have a superb flavor without being soggy.

FOR TWO TO FOUR EATEN OUT OF HAND;
FOR EIGHT IN COCKTAIL OR SALAD FORM

2 lb. whole fresh shrimp, including the heads

COURT BOUILLON

4 qt. cold water	*4 fresh thyme sprigs or 1 tsp.*
1 c. salt	*dried thyme*
juice of 2 large lemons (about	*5 bay leaves, broken in half*
6 Tbs.)	*1 tsp. celery seeds*
¾ tsp. Tabasco	*½ tsp. dry mustard*
1 tsp. allspice	*1½ tsp. freshly ground black*
10 whole cloves	*pepper*

Combine all the ingredients for the court bouillon in a heavy 6 to 8
quart saucepan or kettle. Bring to a boil and boil vigorously for 10
minutes. Add the shrimp; the boiling will slow down or stop. When the
liquid comes to a full boil again, set the timer: 5 minutes for small
shrimp, 6 minutes for medium, 7 for large. Reduce the heat a bit
if necessary to keep the pot from boiling over. As soon as the
shrimp are done, dump them into a large colander set in the sink.
Allow to drain thoroughly, then cool at room temperature for 5 to 8
minutes. Serve still warm, or place in a large bowl, cover with several
layers of plastic wrap, and refrigerate. If desired, provide ketchup, hot
prepared horseradish, lemon wedges, and Tabasco along with small
cups or ramekins so that the diners can mix their own dipping sauce.

Mild Boiled Shrimp

Whole shrimp cooked in a court bouillon designed to set off the
natural flavor of the shrimp without adding a peppery-salty di-
mension. A pleasant change from the spicier versions, and an
excellent basic way to cook shrimp that will be used in other
dishes. If you cannot locate ground bay leaf and ground thyme,
make your own with a mortar and pestle.

---

2 lb. whole fresh shrimp, with or without heads

COURT BOUILLON

3 qt. cold water	1/16 tsp. cayenne
2½ tsp. salt	½ tsp. fresh lemon juice
¼ tsp. freshly ground black pepper	1/16 tsp. ground bay leaf
	1/16 tsp. ground thyme
⅛ tsp. freshly ground white pepper	1/16 tsp. mace

Combine the ingredients for the court bouillon in a 5 to 7 quart saucepan or kettle and bring to a boil. Lower the heat and simmer for 5 minutes, then add the shrimp. Raise the heat. When the water boils up again cook 5 minutes for small shrimp, 6 for medium, 7 for large. Remove the pan from the heat and dump the contents into a large colander set in the sink. Allow to drain and cool for at least 5 to 8 minutes before handling.

Baltimore Steamed Shrimp

The Baltimore style of cooking shrimp in the shell. The heads are removed and the shrimp steamed in a small amount of water and vinegar with an enormous amount of seasoning. They are spicier than New Orleans Boiled Shrimp—we found that out one morning at a seafood stand in Baltimore's Lexington Market, where locals were eating huge quantities of these shrimp and washing them down with beer and clams and oysters on the half shell.

FOR FIVE OR SIX AS AN APPETIZER

2 lb. whole fresh shrimp, heads removed

STEAMING LIQUID AND SEASONINGS

½ c. cold water	¼ tsp. cloves
½ c. vinegar	¼ tsp. ground bay leaf
1½ tsp. salt	¼ tsp. mace
½ tsp. freshly ground black pepper	¼ tsp. ground celery seeds
	⅛ tsp. cardamom
⅜ tsp. dry mustard	⅛ tsp. ginger
⅜ tsp. paprika	⅛ tsp. cinnamon

Combine the liquid and seasonings in a 4 to 5 quart saucepan for which you have a well-fitting lid. (If desired, set a rack on the bottom of the pan. It's not really necessary, since 1 cup of liquid will give a depth of a scant ¼ inch at the bottom of a pan this size.) Bring to a boil. Add the shrimp and stir gently, then cover the pan. Reduce the heat a bit, then steam until tender, 10 to 15 minutes depending on the size of the shrimp. Remove the pan from the heat and drain off the liquid. Allow the shrimp to cool to room temperature before serving.

Boiled Maine Lobster

One of the great American seafood dishes and, to our minds, the best way to eat the luxurious Maine lobster. Maine or North American lobsters have a unique flavor and texture, unmatched even by the superb French spiny or rock lobsters such as the demoiselles de Cherbourg *or* Britanny *lobsters. The single most essential trick in cooking Maine lobster is to add as little as possible to them, to give their natural flavor the center of the stage. The standing arguments over whether to boil, steam, or broil them are basically beside the point. Properly carried out, all 3 methods will do justice to this delicate creature. One tends to prefer whichever style one grew up with. For those who have never had a Maine lobster respectfully cooked, any of the 3 basic methods will make a fine introduction. For both boiling and steaming, the lobster should be live and the court bouillon mild. The only pitfall to avoid in all methods is overcooking.*

FOR TWO

2 live Maine lobsters, each 1 to 1½ lb.

6 qt. cold water

5 Tbs. salt

Have the lobsters ready to be plunged into the water as soon as it comes to a boil. It's most practical to leave the wooden pegs inserted in the huge claws in place until the very last minute. (The lobsters should be moving a bit, but they don't go very far and are unlikely to get off the edge of the counter in the time it takes to bring the water to a boil.) If there's a bit of seaweed clinging to them, leave it in place; it will simply add a bit more flavor to the court bouillon.

Put the water and salt into a very large pot or kettle (10 to 12 quarts is ideal) and bring to a rolling boil over high heat. Remove the claw pegs with tongs, grasp the lobster firmly from behind the head, and plunge head first into the water. Cover the pot loosely and when the water comes to a boil again, cook 7 to 8 minutes for a 1 pound lobster, 10 to 12 minutes for a 1½ pound lobster. (If the lobsters are larger, add 2 minutes for each additional ½ pound.) When done, remove from the water with tongs, allowing the excess liquid to drain back into the pot.

To open and clean the lobsters, place them on their backs on a roomy work surface. Slit the undershell lengthwise with a large sharp knife, or sturdy kitchen shears, or both. Pry the split shell open and remove and discard the dark vein, the intestinal sac near the head, and the feathery spongy tissue located toward the sides. Do not discard the green liver (tomalley) or any lobster coral (the roe); these are delicious and should be eaten along with the meat. Using a sharp knife and if necessary a mallet, finish splitting the lobster in half through the hard upper shell which is resting on your work surface. Serve both halves of each lobster on a single large plate. Provide nutcrackers for breaking open the claws, seafood forks or picks if you have them for extracting the meat from smaller areas, and a small cup or ramekin of hot melted butter to the side of each plate along with several lemon wedges for flavoring the butter.

Steamed Maine Lobster

As simple and as good a way of cooking live Maine lobster as boiling. Steamed lobsters often come out a bit soggier than boiled, although they shouldn't. Steaming aficionados, the most vocal of the lobster cooking factions, often cook their lobsters a bit too long and neglect to drain them thoroughly.

FOR TWO

2 live Maine lobsters, each 1 to 1½ lb.

1½ qt. cold water

2½ Tbs. salt

You will need a large steamer, such as is used for steaming clams, or a very large pot and a steaming rack or basket (or a round cake rack raised off the bottom of the pot about 3 to 4 inches by placing a small metal bowl upside down on the bottom of the pot with the rack resting on it). Put the water and salt into the pot, bring to a boil over high heat, then handle the lobsters as directed for Boiled Maine Lobster, placing them side by side on the rack. Cover the pot loosely and steam 8 to 9 minutes for a 1 pound lobster, 11 to 13 minutes for a 1½ pound lobster.

Open, clean, and serve as directed for Boiled Maine Lobster.

Boiled Crabs New Orleans Style

From the arguments that arise over boiling crabs, particularly between crab lovers from New Orleans and those from Baltimore, it would be easy to believe the crabs enjoyed in those two cities are of entirely different species, when in fact they are identical and interchangeable. Because of the climate and the water conditions in the New Orleans area, Louisiana blue claw crabs are more abundant and therefore cheaper; many Chesapeake area wholesalers and restaurants make use of this bounty to supplement the blue claws in such high demand among their customers. New Orleanians, used to eating their boiled crabs in huge quantities, are outraged at the prices they must pay in Baltimore, where hard crabs cost about three times what they cost back home.

The real differences between cooked hard shell crabs in New Orleans and Baltimore, the two American cities where these shellfish are considered a diet staple, are in the cooking techniques. In New Orleans we boil them in a very spicy, peppery court bouillon loaded with salt and cayenne. We eat them out of hand, usually chilled, but also occasionally still warm from the pot. A newcomer to a New Orleans seafood restaurant faces several major problems of logistics and etiquette when his boiled crabs arrive: along with his beer tray full of crabs he is given a single implement, a knife. He becomes a true New Orleanian when he at last figures out what his next move is. The best way to open a boiled crab is to crack the apron on the underside until it can be pried off, then split the crab open and dig out the golden fat (the best part) and the meat from the body, then the more difficult meat from the claws. Well seasoned fat lake crabs are a way of life in New Orleans.

2 doz. live hard shell crabs
6 qt. cold water
3 Tbs. liquid Crab and Shrimp Boil*

2 c. salt
juice of 4 large lemons (about ¾ c.)
10 drops Tabasco

In a 10 to 12 quart pot or kettle, combine the water and seasonings. Bring to a vigorous boil and boil for 10 minutes. Add the live crabs. When the water boils up again, boil for 15 to 20 minutes, depending on size. When cooked, remove the crabs from the water and drain thoroughly. Allow to cool at room temperature for 8 to 10 minutes, then serve warm, or place in large bowls covered with several layers of plastic wrap and refrigerate, to be served chilled.

* Where Crab Boil is not available, use: 2 tsp. allspice; 20 whole cloves; 2 tsp. thyme; 10 bay leaves, broken in half; 2 tsp. celery seeds; 1 tsp. dry mustard; 1 Tbs. freshly ground black pepper.

Steamed Crabs Chesapeake Style

The Baltimore style of cooking crabs is ingenious—it makes the eater an integral part of the seasoning process. The seasoning is sprinkled on the crab shells and the crabs are then steamed. Most of the seasoning remains on the shells. When you eat, armed with a knife and a mallet, the spices cover your fingers and coat your hands, as well as your lips, ensuring that each piece of crabmeat will be heartily seasoned by the time you swallow it. The Chesapeake crabs are not as salty as the New Orleans ones, but they're a good deal hotter.

FOR FOUR OR MORE

1 dozen live hard shell crabs
1 c. cold water, approximately
1 c. vinegar, approximately

6 Tbs. Baltimore Seafood Seasoning*
6 Tbs. salt

* Where Baltimore Seafood Seasoning is unavailable, substitute: 1 Tbs. freshly ground black pepper; 2¼ tsp. dry mustard; 2 tsp. paprika; 1½ tsp. cloves; 1½ tsp. ground bay leaf; 1½ tsp. mace, 1½ tsp. ground celery seeds; ¾ tsp. cardamom; ¾ tsp. ginger; ¾ tsp. cinnamon.

Set a rack raised at least 2 inches off the bottom of a very large kettle. Add equal quantities of water and vinegar to just below the level of the rack. Mix the seafood seasoning and salt together thoroughly. Place a layer of crabs on the rack, then sprinkle each layer with the seasoning and salt mixture. Make another layer of crabs and season in the same way. (If necessary, make a third layer.) Bring the liquid to a boil over high heat, then cover the pot and steam the crabs for 18 to 20 minutes. When done, remove from the pot, allow to cool at room temperature for about 5 minutes, then serve with knives and mallets.

Steamed Soft Shell Clams

Steamers are an old American tradition, simple to prepare and serve. The final clearing out of sand is accomplished at the table by dipping the clams in the strained steaming liquid with which they are served. And when all the clams are eaten, you are left with the best part, according to steamer enthusiasts, the broth, which is drunk or spooned out of its serving bowl. Handle the broth carefully and leave the sandy dregs undisturbed.

FOR FOUR

2 qt. steamer clams
½ c. water
pepper for sprinkling

1¼ c. (2½ sticks) hot melted
butter
lemon wedges

Rinse the clams thoroughly. Change the washing water several times until no more sand appears to settle to the bottom of the water. Put the clams into a large heavy kettle. Add the water and sprinkle with pepper. Cover the kettle loosely and set over high heat. Steam the clams until the shells are partially open, about 10 minutes. Remove the cooked clams to large individual soup bowls. Strain the liquor from the kettle and serve it in separate bowls, along with small cups of hot melted butter and lemon wedges, for dipping. Provide soup spoons for the shells and seafood forks for the clams.

Steamed Hard Clams

The smaller hard shell clams are best for this dish, since the larger ones tend to get quite tough during the steaming process.

FOR FOUR

2 qt. small hard shell clams   hot melted butter
½ c. water, approximately   lemon wedges
salt and pepper for sprinkling

Scrub the clams very thoroughly with a brush under cold running water. Discard any that are obviously open. (This indicates they are not using their muscles to close their shells and protect themselves, and are dead.) Tap any clams that appear to be very slightly open or attempt to wedge the tip of a knife into the space between the shells. If the shells shut up tight, the clams are alive and safe to eat. If not, discard them.

Place the clams in the bottom of a large heavy kettle. Add the water and a small amount of salt and pepper. Bring to a boil over high heat, cover the pot, and steam until all the clams are open, normally about 7 to 10 minutes. Decrease the heat a bit during the steaming and cover the pot loosely to prevent boiling over. When most of the clams are open, uncover the pot and remove them, using tongs, to individual bowls. Steam any clams that haven't opened a few minutes longer. If they still remain closed, discard them. Strain the steaming broth and save for flavoring other dishes. Serve the bowls of clams with small ramekins of hot melted butter and provide lemon wedges for seasoning the butter as desired. Put a deep bowl in the center of the table for discarded shells.

Boiled Crawfish Cajun Style

Crawfish are small crustaceans that look like miniature spiny lobsters; they grow in the murky, muddy waters of swamps. Louisiana has lots of bayous, swamps, and other assorted basins of standing moisture—and an enormous quantity of crawfish. (The fancy spelling—and pronunciation—is crayfish. Crawfish with a w is standard in southwestern Louisiana.) The Houma Indians were the first to discover the delightful edibility of craw-

fish. *Their passion is now shared by Louisiana Frenchmen, French Frenchmen, and Scandinavians. Crawfish grow all over the United States, but in the largest numbers in Louisiana, where 90 percent are consumed locally. Some are exported to France, where they are much scarcer. Crawfish keep and ship better already cooked, but the Cajun style of cooking them is far too spicy for the French; many a promising crawfish deal has fallen through because of cultural and gastronomic differences. In Louisiana crawfish are cooked in a peppery court bouillon and eaten in enormous quantities, quantities literally unimaginable to the French.*

FOR FOUR

5 lb. live crawfish
cold salted water for purging

COURT BOUILLON

1¼ c. salt
8 lemons, cut into quarters
2 celery stalks, chopped
4 onions, cut into quarters
2 Irish potatoes, cut into quarters
6 whole bay leaves

3 to 4 sprigs of fresh thyme or
1 tsp. dried thyme
4 bags Crab Boil
1 tsp. cayenne
4 to 5 qt. plus 1½ c. cold water

Purge the crawfish by soaking them in cold salted water. Drain, rinse, and repeat the soaking process until the soaking water no longer becomes muddy. In a 10 to 12 quart pot or kettle, combine about 4 to 5 quarts of cold water with the vegetables and seasoning and bring to a boil. Boil for 10 minutes, then add the live crawfish. Also add a bit more water if necessary; the water should just cover the crawfish. Bring to a boil again and cook for 10 to 12 minutes, depending on the size of the crawfish.

At the end of cooking time, remove the pot from the heat, add 1½ cups cold water, and allow to stand at room temperature for 10 minutes. Drain the crawfish in a colander, reserving the solids (lemons, celery, onions, potatoes) to be fished out and served on plates along with the crawfish. Serve warm.

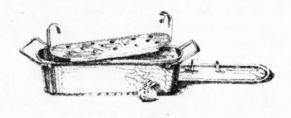

The Pleasures of Seafood 126

Boiled Crawfish New Orleans Style

Identical with Cajun crawfish, except that they are served chilled. The crawfish season is generally late November to mid-June, and it's easy to tell when the season is at its height: when New Orleanians can buy 3 pounds of boiled crawfish for under $2.00. Three pounds per hungry crawfish eater is a conservative estimate. Boiled crawfish are eaten out of hand, with no implements, off beer trays or newspapers spread on a table. The meat is in the tail; the highly prized fat and the spicy court bouillon are in the head and are sucked out. Eating boiled crawfish in Louisiana is a joyous and somewhat noisy art. The thoroughly demolished crustaceans are then thrown onto an enormous pile of debris. One gets very thirsty eating boiled crawfish; many pitchers of beer are easily consumed. And with each sip of beer, one has the urge for more boiled crawfish—and so it goes. After all, the season is a short one, only 6 months of the year.

FOR FOUR

Prepare as directed for Boiled Crawfish Cajun Style. Allow the drained crawfish to cool to room temperature, along with the reserved solids. Place in large bowls, cover with several layers of plastic wrap, and refrigerate until chilled.

Basic Mild Boiled Crawfish

A pleasantly balanced, delicate court bouillon makes this way of boiling crawfish ideal for tasting them as they really are, without other flavors overwhelming them. Also indispensable for cooking crawfish to be used in other dishes.

FOR 3 TO 5 LB. CRAWFISH

4 to 5 lb. live crawfish or 2 to 3 lb. frozen peeled crawfish

COURT BOUILLON

3 qt. cold water	½ tsp. fresh lemon juice
2½ tsp. salt	1/16 tsp. ground bay leaf
¼ tsp. freshly ground black pepper	1/16 tsp. mace
⅛ tsp. cayenne	1/16 tsp. ground thyme

Boiling, Braising, and Steaming 127

If you are using live crawfish, clean and purge them in salted water as directed for Boiled Crawfish Cajun Style. Frozen peeled crawfish can be added to the steeped court bouillon directly. (They will defrost within less than a minute in the pot.) Combine the ingredients for the court bouillon in a large pot or kettle and bring to a boil over high heat. Boil for 5 minutes, then add the live or frozen peeled crawfish. Cook for 12 to 13 minutes for whole crawfish, precisely 8 minutes for frozen. Drain immediately in a colander. Allow to cool for about 10 minutes at room temperature, then refrigerate in a tightly covered bowl for later use.

Crawfish in Dill

The Scandinavian style of boiled crawfish, much more delicately seasoned than the Louisiana version and served in far smaller quantities. Probably the most accessible of the boiled crawfish dishes to newcomers. Equally good served at room temperature or chilled and marinated for a day or two.

FOR THREE OR FOUR

30 live crawfish

COURT BOUILLON

3 qt. cold water	*¼ c. dill seeds*
¼ c. salt	*3 Tbs. dried dill weed*

several bunches fresh dill (can be omitted if unavailable)

Wash the crawfish very thoroughly under cold running water, then place them to soak in a large bowl or basin of water while you prepare the court bouillon. Put the ingredients for the court bouillon, along with 1 bunch of fresh dill if you have it, into a 7 to 10 quart pot or kettle. Bring to a boil over high heat. Reduce the heat slightly and boil for 7 to 8 minutes or until the liquid has a noticeable dill flavor. Remove the fresh dill with a spoon, then drop the crawfish, several at a time, into the boiling water. Turn the heat to maximum if necessary to keep the boil going. When all the crawfish have been added, cover the pot, reduce the heat to medium, and cook for 7 minutes. Immediately remove the crawfish from the liquid with a large slotted spoon and place them in a large bowl lined with fresh dill, if available. Strain the court bouillon and pour it over the crawfish in the bowl. Allow to stand at room temperature until cooled, then serve at room temperature or refrigerate to be served chilled. Cover the bowl with several layers of plastic wrap before refrigerating and allow at least 8 hours for sufficient chilling. If desired, refrigerate for 24 to 48 hours; this will marinate the crawfish and give them a very interesting flavor. To serve chilled, drain the crawfish and heap on a platter covered with a generous layer of fresh dill. Provide melted butter for dipping.

Crawfish à la Nage

The classic French boiled crawfish dish, served in soup bowls swimming in their delicately seasoned court bouillon, in portions of 8 to 10 at most. The French love of crawfish is no better illustrated than by the sight of splendidly dressed diners in grand restaurants peeling their crawfish by hand in the court bouillon.

FOR FOUR

32 live crawfish

COURT BOUILLON

4 carrots, peeled and thinly sliced	*1½ c. dry white wine*
2 medium-sized onions, chopped	*2 c. cold water*
3 shallots, finely chopped	*2 tsp. salt, approximately*
½ tsp. thyme	*6 black peppercorns, cracked*
3 parsley sprigs	*with a mallet or the back of*
2 small bay leaves, broken up	*a heavy saucer*

1/16 tsp. cayenne

Clean and purge the crawfish as directed for Boiled Crawfish Cajun Style. Combine the ingredients for the court bouillon in a very large pot or kettle and bring to a boil over high heat. Reduce the heat and simmer uncovered for 25 to 30 minutes. Raise the heat to bring the bouillon back to a rolling boil, then quickly add the crawfish. Sprinkle in the cayenne and stir once. Cover the pot, reduce the heat a bit, and simmer for 6 to 8 minutes, until the crawfish turn bright red. Remove the crawfish to large soup bowls with a mesh skimmer or slotted spoon. Spoon equal quantities of the vegetables from the pot over and around the crawfish, then ladle the cooking liquid from the pot generously over each portion. Serve hot.

Florida Lobster à la Nage

Florida lobster doesn't taste like Maine lobster and although it looks like a giant crawfish, its flavor is unlike crawfish. But we have found a few similarities between the two clawless cousins. One of them is that Florida lobster is delicious prepared as the French prepare crawfish, à la nage, *with the wine and water court bouillon and the colorful vegetables surrounding it in the bowl.*

FOR TWO

*2 Florida lobsters, each 1 to 1¾ lb., fresh or frozen**

COURT BOUILLON

5 carrots, peeled and thinly sliced
2 medium-sized onions, chopped
4 shallots, finely chopped
¾ tsp. thyme
4 parsley sprigs
3 small bay leaves, broken up

1½ c. dry white wine
2 c. cold water
2 to 3 tsp. salt, approximately
7 black peppercorns, cracked with a mallet or the back of a heavy saucer

---

1/16 tsp. cayenne
1 tsp. brandy

Rinse the lobsters under cold running water and allow to drain. Combine the ingredients for the court bouillon in a large pot or

---

* The best quality Florida lobsters are marketed parboiled and flash frozen. They have been immersed in boiling water for just a minute or two to suspend their texture and flavor at peak. Treat them as you would fresh, that is, boil them in the frozen state or defrost first for other preparations.

---

kettle and bring to a boil over high heat. Reduce the heat and simmer uncovered for 20 to 25 minutes. Raise the heat again and when the water reaches a rolling boil, add the lobsters. Add the cayenne and brandy and stir. When the water comes to a boil again, reduce the heat and simmer for 15 to 18 minutes. Remove the lobsters from the liquid with tongs and set aside to cool a bit. Continue simmering the court bouillon until it is reduced by about one-third, approximately 10 minutes. Split and clean the lobsters as directed for Broiled Stuffed Florida Lobster. Place both halves of each split and cleaned lobster in a large, wide soup bowl and ladle about ¾ cup of the reduced court bouillon, along with the vegetables, over each portion. Serve immediately, along with seafood forks and small ramekins of melted butter for dipping if desired. Place a small bowl of lemon wedges at the center of the table.

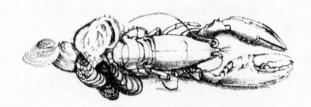

Boiled Florida Lobster

Our favorite way of cooking whole Florida lobsters, with just enough seasoning to highlight their natural flavor. We also use this basic style in preparing Florida lobsters to be used in more complex dishes. If you have a large enough pot, leave the long feelers on or break them off and throw them into the pot. There's good usable meat in the larger ones, and it's fun to suck the meat out of the smaller ones as a kind of cook's reward.

2 or 3 Florida lobsters	*1 Tbs. fresh lemon juice*
4 to 6 qt. cold water	*7 drops Tabasco*
¼ c. salt	

Bring the water and seasonings to a boil over high heat, then boil for 6 to 8 minutes. Add the lobsters. When the water comes to a boil again, cook for 15 minutes. Remove immediately from the water and allow to drain thoroughly. Cool for 12 to 15 minutes at room temperature before peeling or refrigerating for later use.

To split and clean the lobsters, place them on a cutting surface. With a strong sharp knife, cut into the undershell just below the head and continue cutting down to the tail. Turn the lobster around and cut down through the head. Turn the lobster over and cut through to meet the underside cut. Break off the eyes and the thin tentacles. Turn the lobster halves shell side down and remove the intestines, a small gray sac in the head area. Also pull out the intestinal vein which runs the length of the lobster and is located near the back shell.

Rock Shrimp Boiled in the Shell

Rock shrimp from the Gulf of Mexico are plentiful and delicious. Similar to Adriatic scampi, Dublin Bay prawns, and French langoustines, they can be prepared in ways much like shrimp, which they most resemble. However, their taste and texture are closer to those of rock lobsters. One of the commonest forms in which they are marketed is frozen in the shell, with the heads removed. Some of the frozen varieties have been very briefly parboiled; these can be treated just as you would those that have been frozen raw. This recipe for rock shrimp boiled in a basic mild court bouillon is useful for preserving the meat for chilled dishes and for use in a number of other preparations. It is not necessary to defrost the rock shrimp before adding them to the boiling liquid. They take a few minutes longer than shrimp to cook, but don't overcook them or they'll lose their pleasant chewy texture.

FOR 1 TO 2 LB. ROCK SHRIMP IN THE SHELL

1 to 2 lb. frozen rock shrimp in the shell

COURT BOUILLON

2 qt. cold water
5 tsp. salt
¼ tsp. freshly ground black pepper
¼ tsp. freshly ground white pepper

⅛ tsp. cayenne
2 tsp. fresh lemon juice
⅛ tsp. ground bay leaf
⅛ tsp. ground thyme
⅛ tsp. mace

Rinse the frozen shrimp very quickly under cold running water, then place in a colander to drain while you prepare the court bouillon.

Combine the ingredients for the court bouillon in a 4 to 6 quart heavy saucepan. Bring to a boil. Lower the heat slightly and simmer for 10 minutes. Add the rock shrimp and when the water boils up again, cook for 10 minutes. Immediately dump into a colander, then allow to cool at room temperaure for 8 to 10 minutes. Place in a stainless steel or porcelain bowl, cover with several layers of plastic wrap, then refrigerate. Use within 3 to 4 days. Peel the rock shrimp just before you plan to use them.

Moules Marinière

The traditional French mussel dish, enriched a bit by the addition of cream to the broth. Mussels are often scarce, but if you can get them, this is a simple and excellent way to prepare them. Discard any mussels that have opened before cooking, take care not to overcook them (they get tough and rubbery), and serve as the French do with a bowl for les déchets, *the debris or empty shells.*

FOR THREE OR FOUR

4 lb. fresh mussels
1 c. cold water
¾ c. dry white wine

BROTH

3 Tbs. finely minced shallots
6 Tbs. (¾ stick) salt butter
½ tsp. freshly ground white pepper
¼ tsp. salt

½ c. heavy cream
1 Tbs. minced fresh parsley
½ c. water
1/16 tsp. mace

Discard any mussels that are open. Rinse the remaining ones thoroughly under cold running water to remove excess sand. Put the mussels into a 4 to 6 quart saucepan and add the water and wine.

Boiling, Braising, and Steaming 133

Bring to a boil, reduce the heat a bit, and cover the pan loosely. Steam for 8 to 10 minutes or until all the mussels are open. (Discard any that do not open after 12 minutes of steaming; they are either spoiled or will be too tough to make good eating.) Remove the opened mussels one at a time with tongs, allowing the liquid in them to drain back into the pan, and place in a large bowl. Set aside.

Strain the liquid from the large pan into a smaller one through 2 layers of dampened and wrung-out paper towels laid over a fine mesh strainer. Add the shallots, butter, pepper, and salt and simmer over low heat until the butter melts. Remove the pan from the heat. Add the cream very gradually, stirring as you pour, then add the parsley. Return the pan to low heat and slowly add the water. Sprinkle in the mace. Raise the heat a bit and bring the broth to a very slight boil. Once again remove the pan from the heat and stir to mix thoroughly. Check the temperature of the broth. It should be hot, but not too hot to taste comfortably. If not hot enough, return to low heat for 30 seconds to 1 minute, then remove from the heat again. Place the opened mussels in their shells in wide shallow soup bowls (Italian spaghetti bowls are perfect in size and shape) and ladle the broth over the portions. Stir with each dip of the ladle to distribute the elements evenly. Serve immediately.

Clams Marinière

The smaller hard shell clams are delicious prepared the same way as mussels.

FOR TWO OR THREE

Using 2 to 3 dozen fresh small hard shell clams, prepare and serve as directed for Moules Marinière.

Redfish Courtbouillon

The traditional New Orleans boiled fish dish, spicy, colorful, and delicious. It works well with bass, whiting, haddock, just about any firm fresh fish with a medium to large flake. The main feature, the glorious sauce, penetrates and transforms the fish.

FOR FOUR

ROUX-BASED COURT BOUILLON

⅓ c. vegetable oil

½ c. flour

1¾ c. chopped onions

1 c. thinly sliced green onion tops

¾ c. chopped green pepper

1 Tbs. finely minced garlic

⅓ c. chopped celery

one 1-lb. can peeled whole tomatoes, coarsely chopped (about 2¼ c. after chopping)

1 Tbs. finely minced fresh parsley

3 whole bay leaves, broken into quarters

½ tsp. thyme

¼ tsp. marjoram

6 whole allspice

2 tsp. salt

½ tsp. freshly ground black pepper

⅛ tsp. cayenne

½ tsp. basil

2½ Tbs. fresh lemon juice

¾ c. dry red wine

2½ c. water

---

1 medium-sized redfish, cleaned and cut into 2 inch slices across
8 slices fresh lemon, each about ⅛ inch thick

In a heavy 4 to 5 quart pot or kettle, heat the oil. Add the flour, stir, lower the heat, and cook over low heat, stirring constantly, until a roux the color of rich peanut butter is formed, about 25 minutes. Add the onions, green onion tops, green pepper, garlic, and celery and brown for another 8 to 10 minutes, stirring constantly. Add the chopped tomatoes, parsley, bay leaves, thyme, marjoram, allspice, salt, pepper, cayenne, basil, lemon juice, and red wine. Stir to mix thoroughly, then slowly add the water, mixing well. Bring to a boil, then lower the heat and simmer uncovered for 35 minutes. Stir frequently and scrape the sides and bottom of the pot with a wooden spoon or spatula to prevent scorching and to allow the sauce to thicken evenly.

Rinse the redfish steaks under cold running water and shake them dry. Add them to the court bouillon along with the lemon slices. Cook at a low simmer for exactly 10 minutes, then remove the pot from the heat. Serve 2 slices of redfish per person with about 1 cup of sauce poured over.

Chinese Braised Carp

Freshwater carp is one of the world's most delicious fish. The Chinese and Middle Europeans prepare it with love and genius, while other cuisines frequently ignore it. This Chinese haute cuisine dish makes full use of the visual beauty of the carp, which is marinated whole, fried briefly in hot sesame oil, and then braised in a sauce containing ginger root, green onions, dried black mushrooms, and bamboo shoots. The only tricky part of the preparation is transferring the fish from the pan to a serving plate without breaking it. Using an attractive oval skillet which can be brought to the table gets around the problem nicely. If the fish you select simply will not fit into your largest skillet, remove the head and if necessary the tail before cooking; most of the drama of the whole fish presentation will still be preserved. To break up dried ginger root, which can resist even the strongest hands and sharpest knives, place it in a towel and pound with a mallet. Buffalo, which looks, tastes, and cooks like carp, is an excellent substitute.

FOR FOUR

1 carp or buffalo, 4 to 5 lb., split and cleaned, and left whole

MARINADE

½ c. soy sauce
2 tsp. salt
½ cup dry sherry (Manzanilla)

¾ c. sesame oil for frying the fish

SAUCE FOR BRAISING

3 Tbs. sesame oil	*½ c. marinade*
1 tsp. salt	*1 Tbs. sugar*
1 c. green onion tops, cut into 2 to 3 inch lengths, then slivered	*1 c. water*
	1 oz. dried black mushrooms
1 Tbs. broken-up ginger root, plus 4 large pieces	*one 8-oz. can bamboo shoots, thoroughly drained*

Rinse the fish under cool running water inside and out, then dry thoroughly. Place in a shallow stainless steel pan or porcelain baking dish. Make a series of ⅛ inch deep slashes across the fish on both sides at intervals of about 1½ inches, using a thin sharp knife. Add the ingredients for the marinade, pouring them carefully over the entire

---

The Pleasures of Seafood 136

surface of the fish. Spoon some of the marinade over the fish every 5 minutes, and turn it over after 15 minutes. Marinate for another 10 minutes, basting with marinade several times. Carefully pour off the marinade and reserve.

In the large heavy skillet you will use for both cooking and serving the fish, heat ¾ cup sesame oil until very hot. Fry the fish for 2 to 3 minutes on each side in the hot oil, shaking the skillet to keep the skin from sticking and turning the fish over very carefully to keep the skin and flesh intact. (If some of the skin breaks off, scoop it out of the pan with the tip of a knife and press it back in place on the fish.)

Prepare the sauce while frying the fish or, if you prefer, remove the skillet from the heat and set aside briefly while you prepare the sauce. In a separate small saucepan heat 3 tablespoons sesame oil until very hot, then reduce the heat a bit and stir in the salt, green onion tops, and ginger root. Stir quickly, then add the marinade, sugar, and water. Bring to a boil, then add the mushrooms and bamboo shoots. Stir again. Return the skillet containing the fish to high heat, then pour the sauce from the small pan into the skillet around the fish. As soon as the sauce begins to simmer in the skillet, reduce the heat to medium and simmer the fish, uncovered, until very little liquid remains in the skillet, about 25 to 30 minutes. Spoon a small amount of the liquid over the fish several times during braising. To serve, bring the skillet to the table, then cut off pieces of the fish, including the crisp skin, and place on heated plates. Spoon the solids from the bottom and sides of the skillet around each serving along with several teaspoons of the liquid.

Chinese Steamed Carp

A very delicate whole fish dish, characteristic of the superb balance of flavor elements and attention to visual appeal found in Chinese cooking. There is no need for special fish poaching equipment; all you really need is a heavy saucepan or brazier that will hold the fish comfortably. Very little liquid and a tight-fitting cover are the keys to successful steaming. All the delicious flavors of the sauce—slab bacon, green onions, ginger root, and sherry—slowly permeate the fish. Serve any solids that remain in the pot around the portions.

FOR THREE OR FOUR

1 carp or buffalo, 3 to 4 lb., split and cleaned, head, tail, and fins removed
4 oz. slab bacon, rind trimmed off, diced ¼ inch thick
1½ Tbs. broken-up ginger root
5 green onions, cut into lengths, then into slivers

¼ c. dry sherry (Manzanilla)
1 tsp. sugar
½ tsp. salt
¾ c. chicken stock
½ c. water

Rinse the fish under cold running water, then shake dry. Cut slashes ½ inch deep across both sides at 1 inch intervals and place to drain on paper towels. In a heavy 2 to 3 quart saucepan cook the bacon over high heat until sizzling, then add the ginger and green onions. Stir-fry for 1½ minutes, then reduce the heat slightly. Add the remaing ingredients and mix very thoroughly. Place the fish in a brazier or saucepan wide enough to hold it comfortably. Pour the sauce over the fish. Using a long wooden spoon, push the solids off the top of the fish and down into the spaces at the sides of the pan. Turn the heat to high and bring the liquid in the brazier to a boil. Cover tightly and reduce the heat to medium-low. Steam for 30 minutes, uncovering once to turn the fish over very carefully, after 10 to 12 minutes. Serve on heated plates with any solids that remain in the bottom of the pot arranged around the pieces of fish.

Curry Recipes

7

Curries

Curry powder has as much to do with Indian, Pakistani, or any other curry cooking as ketchup with the flavor of aged beef. Curry is a style of cooking and one of the most pleasurable we know. In its immense range of taste possibilities and its careful attention to balance and texture, curry cooking at its best is infinitely complex, the equal of the finest French or Chinese *haute cuisine*. It may well be the *most* beautiful in the aesthetic configuration of the cooking process. The various elements in a classic Indian curry dish are magically transformed, and as you watch the colors change in the pan, the entire house is suffused with delicate, sensual aromas, and the finished dish produces an almost musical harmony and counterpoint of flavors and textures.

Curry is a process, not a powder. It is a wide range of cooking using many spices and calling for techniques that have their own special logic and sequence. The techniques are unusually simple to master and great fun to put into practice in a home kitchen. As for the spices, the first thing you must do is throw out whatever curry powder you already have—and along with it all the misconceptions it connotes. Curries depend on serial blendings of spices, blendings more varied than any pre-prepared curry powder can possibly suggest. You need only a small group of out-of-the-ordinary spices. Once you've acquired them, it's simple to create the blends that best suit each dish in the curry repertoire. And you'll find that they all taste *different* from one another and that the harsh monotony many people associate with curries is in fact simply the taste of commercial curry powder.

With the basic spice shelf you will be free to concentrate on the simple but unique techniques involved in preparing curry dishes. Seasonings are added in stages, with a special rhythm and a logic that can become a new art form for the cook. The finest curries are a result of the successive vaporizations of several groups of seasonings, abetted by enormous quantities of chopped onions which mysteriously leave no onion flavor at all when the dish is completed.

Reading most printed literature on curry that blandly assumes curry powder to be the indispensable mysterious secret to Indian cooking, we are reminded of the story of a Caribbean island that tried to gain the friendship of visiting Americans by proudly serving each American who came a meal of cornflakes, milk, and ketchup, which they took to be characteristic of all American cooking. The art of making curry is not difficult. Why so many food writers think that most Americans are afraid of all spices, or of complex spices, or of understanding difficult or unusual cuisines is beyond us. Any people who could figure out a way of combining scrawny cattle with a surplus of corn and coming up with prime beef can solve any gastronomic problem.

Ironically, with the universal familiarity of ketchup in America we are more than halfway there when it comes to curry. Ketchup is a fair example of one part of the curry process—adding a mixture of flavorings to a seemingly pedestrian element—and indeed the original form of ketchup came from the Far East. The notion that spiciness is abhorrent to most Americans is utter nonsense. When Americans taste food that is "too hot," they are actually tasting pepper in its raw and uncooked state. In that form, pepper is unpleasant and indigestible (except for Texans, who will eat anything peppery, no matter the form). In properly cooked spicy dishes, the hotness lingers in the mouth and on the palate; it does *not* descend into the throat. If you find your throat raw and constricted from pepper, be assured the dish you are eating has been poorly cooked. In curries, be they wet, dry, or medium, the guiding principle is not hotness but balance. Many curries are sweet, some are hotter than others, but very few are as hot as Texas chili, New Orleans or Baltimore crabs, or even country sausage.

We have simplified a few of the indigenous techniques used in preparing these dishes. For example, while in India *all* the spices are ground by hand, one can get excellent results with purchased ground spices—as long as they are pungent when you buy them and discarded from your shelf when they lose their aroma (your nose will tell you when that is). A few rare ones are not available in ground form; these are quickly ground with a mortar and pestle. Also, some curries are placed "on dum" after cooking; that is, the cooking vessels are covered and sealed with wax, then placed in the dying ashes of a wood fire for several hours. We have found that placing good heavy pots with snugly fitting lids in a low oven for about 15 minutes accomplishes the same steeping process.

For those who already love curry, this chapter may suggest some new ideas and some unusual ways of cooking seafood. For those who are unfamiliar with curry or who haven't liked the curries they've tasted, we offer these recipes as an invitation to embark on one of the most enthralling cooking experiences you will ever have.

Basic Curry Techniques

Do not use packaged "curry powder."

Do not begin cooking until all chopping, crushing, puréeing is complete and all seasonings are at hand.

Controlled heat at several different levels will be needed. On electric ranges use three burners, one set at medium high, one at low, the third unlit.

Use a large heavy sauté pan.

For covered stages use tight-fitting lids or makeshift lids of heavy aluminum foil.

Time the addition of seasonings carefully; stir in each new element when it is added, shaking pan to incorporate thoroughly.

Basic Shrimp Curry

A fine rich curry ideally suited to peeled fresh shrimp. The sauce gets its hefty texture from lots of chopped onions cooked down into the base and yogurt added in the final stage. Frequently used in Indian cooking, yogurt provides thickness and creaminess while having no discernible taste in the completed dish. The addition of the seasonings in several stages is characteristic of the best Indian cooking.

FOR TWO

BASE

3 Tbs. salt butter
2 c. finely chopped white onions

FIRST SEASONING

1 tsp. turmeric	*½ tsp. cumin*
2 tsp. coriander	*¼ tsp. cayenne*
⅛ tsp. fenugreek	*¼ tsp. freshly ground black*
¼ tsp. ginger	*pepper*

---

1 lb. peeled and deveined raw shrimp (about 2 lb. in the shell)

SECOND SEASONING

½ tsp. salt
1¼ tsp. sugar

LIQUID

5 Tbs. yogurt
½ c. water
1 Tbs. fresh lemon juice

Melt the butter in a heavy sauté pan and add the onions. Cook, stirring frequently, until the onions are a light brown color and begin

---

to stick to the bottom of the pan. Sprinkle in the elements for the first seasoning and mix thoroughly. Cook over medium-low heat for 1 minute, then add the shrimp. Raise the heat slightly and cook for about 3 minutes, tossing gently to turn the shrimp over, until they begin to appear lightly glazed. Sprinkle in the salt and sugar and cook for 30 seconds more. Add the yogurt 1 tablespoon at a time, stirring after each addition to blend thoroughly. Add the water gradually, stirring constantly. Continue to cook over medium heat. Add the lemon juice after all the water has been incorporated. Cook for 3 to 4 minutes after adding the lemon juice, then stir very thoroughly, turn off the heat, and cover the pan tightly. Allow to stand covered for 10 to 12 minutes. Just before serving, uncover and reheat over high heat, stirring constantly, for 1½ minutes.

Fish Curry with Almonds, Cream, and Raisins

A delicate, aromatic curry with one of the most striking sauces we know, containing crushed almonds, raisins, and heavy cream. Crush the almonds with a mortar and pestle to get a paste of the proper texture. Whirling them in a blender gives you a purée instead and thins the sauce out too much. We like to enjoy the sauce with tablespoons or with bread, but it's also excellent with rice—just put the rice to one side.

FOR FOUR

BASE

2½ Tbs. butter
2 c. finely chopped white onions
½ tsp. cinnamon

———————

1½ lb. firm fresh fish, cut into large pieces (redfish, bass, red snapper, etc.)

SEASONINGS

½ tsp. turmeric
½ tsp. coriander
½ tsp. cumin
⅛ tsp. cloves
½ tsp. ground bay leaf
¼ tsp. cayenne

½ tsp. freshly ground black pepper
½ tsp. salt
¾ c. seedless raisins
½ c. milk

———————

4 oz. blanched almonds,   *½ c. yogurt*
crushed with a mortar and   *½ c. heavy cream*
pestle

Melt the butter in a heavy sauté pan. Add the onions and cinnamon, and toss to mix. Cook over medium-high heat, stirring and scraping the bottom of the pan, until the onions are browned, about 10 minutes. Place the pieces of fish over the onions, then sprinkle with the seasonings in the order given above. Toss the fish very lightly after each addition. Add the raisins and milk, and mix gently. Raise the heat a bit until the liquid in the pan begins to simmer, then lower the heat again just enough to keep a simmer going. Shake the pan from side to side every few minutes. Cook for about 5 minutes or until the fish is almost done, then raise the heat again to cook off all the remaining liquid.

Mix the crushed almonds, yogurt, and cream together thoroughly, then add to the pan. Cook, covered, over very low heat for 8 minutes, uncovering to stir several times. Then remove the cover, raise the heat to high, and cook for 1½ minutes, stirring constantly. Serve immediately.

Indian Shrimp Braised with Honey

Our favorite curried shrimp dish, festive and beautiful. We adapted shikar korma, *an Indian dish with pork, and came up with a winner. We prefer to serve this without rice—the medium-thick sauce is delicious scooped up with a spoon or some fresh home-made bread. The trick to getting a perfect sauce and not over-cooking the shrimp is simple: the shrimp are braised for a few minutes, then removed from the pan; they go back in again at the very end. Be sure to peel and refrigerate the shrimp and to have* all the seasonings measured out, chopped, etc., before beginning to cook—the timing of steps is important. If you use frozen shrimp, defrost them thoroughly and dry between paper towels before cooking.

FOR TWO OR THREE

1 to 1¼ lb. peeled and deveined raw shrimp (2 lb. whole in the shell)

5 tsp. honey

2 Tbs. salt butter, cut up

¼ tsp. salt

FIRST SEASONING

2 Tbs. finely chopped shallots

¼ tsp. turmeric

¼ tsp. freshly ground black pepper

½ tsp. finely chopped orange rind, zest only

½ tsp. finely chopped lemon rind, zest only

2 Tbs. water

¾ c. yogurt, whipped until fluffy

SECOND SEASONING

½ tsp. finely minced fresh garlic

¼ tsp. cardamom

¼ tsp. cinnamon

¼ tsp. sugar

1/16 tsp. cayenne

⅛ tsp. mace

¼ tsp. salt

---

5 Tbs. water, more if necessary

TOPPING

shredded, dried unsweetened coconut
thinly sliced green onion tops

Heat the honey in a sauté pan over medium heat until it is melted. Tip the pan with a circular motion as the honey begins to melt to coat the bottom evenly. When small bubbles begin to appear in the honey, add the pieces of butter. When the butter is completely melted, stir to mix, then add the shrimp. Raise the heat to high and cook for 4 minutes, tossing the shrimp gently with a wooden spoon to braise and coat them evenly. Sprinkle in the salt as you toss. Remove the shrimp from the pan with a slotted spoon and put them into a bowl. Reserve.

Keeping the heat at medium-high, add all the ingredients for the first seasoning except the yogurt, stirring after each addition. Cook, scraping the sides and bottom of the pan, until most of the water has evaporated, then add the yogurt, about 2 tablespoons at a time,

---

mixing it in thoroughly as you add. Cook until you can begin to see the butter separate around the edges of the mixture, 3 to 4 minutes. Add the ingredients for the second seasoning, cook for 2 minutes more, then add the water. Mix very thoroughly to form a smooth, even-textured sauce; cook for about 3 minutes, then add the reserved shrimp. Raise the heat to high; when the sauce begins to boil, reduce the heat to medium and simmer the shrimp, stirring frequently, for 4 minutes. Cover the pan and remove immediately from the heat. Set in a preheated 200°F. oven for 12 to 15 minutes before serving. To serve, sprinkle each portion with about 1 tablespoon of coconut and 1½ tablespoons of green onion slices. Provide bowls of additional coconut and green onion slices to be added at the table.

Shrimp Malai

An Indian shrimp dish with coconut oil, shredded unsweetened coconut, and a delicate blend of spices added in carefully orchestrated stages—a true curry. The large amount of chopped onions is characteristic: the onion taste completely disappears but the cooked-down solids give the sauce its handsome texture. (A far cry from flour-thickened curries seasoned with prepared curry powders!) Black mustard seeds are available in the better spice shops in large cities, and by mail; if you can't find any, omit them; yellow mustard seeds are stronger and also add too much unwanted color. All the other spices are sold in supermarkets everywhere.

This has been a favorite company dish in the homes of friends for several years now, ever since they ate it with us and carried off copies of the recipe. The sauce is medium-thick and best served over the shrimp with no rice on the plate. You can multiply the recipe to suit your needs with no changes or rebalancing; use suitably larger cooking vessels.

FOR TWO

BASE

3 Tbs. coconut oil
2 c. finely chopped white onions
1½ tsp. finely minced fresh garlic

FIRST SEASONING

¾ tsp. turmeric	⅛ tsp. cayenne
½ tsp. freshly ground black mustard seeds	⅛ tsp. freshly ground black pepper
¼ tsp. ginger	⅛ tsp. cumin
¼ tsp. cinnamon	⅛ tsp. fenugreek

1 lb. peeled and deveined raw shrimp (2 lb. whole in the shell), well drained

LIQUID

¼ c. shredded, dried unsweetened coconut soaked in ¼ c. milk
¾ c. milk

FINAL SEASONING

¼ tsp. freshly ground black mustard seeds	½ tsp. salt
¼ tsp. cayenne	⅛ tsp. cinnamon

Heat the oil in a heavy sauté pan, then add the onions and garlic. Cook over medium heat, stirring frequently, until browned. Keeping the pan over low heat, sprinkle in the ingredients listed for the first seasoning in the order given above. Stir to mix after each spice is added and scrape across the bottom of the pan to mix in all the browned matter. When all the first seasoning spices have been added, cook for about 1 minute, then add the shrimp. Place them flat in the pan, then cook over high heat for 3 to 4 minutes, turning the shrimp gently but frequently so that they become seared and coated with the seasonings. When the shrimp are coated, gradually add the soaked coconut, stirring continually. Add the milk a bit at a time, stirring to keep the sauce that is beginning to form quite smooth. Keep the heat at medium-low and stir every few minutes. Add the final seasoning in the order given above, mixing gently after each ingredient is added. Cook the shrimp gently for a total of 10 minutes from the time you add the last of the milk. Then raise the heat to high and cook, stirring constantly, for 1½ minutes. Serve immediately.

Oyster Curry

A delicate curry made with sesame oil, dried coconut, coconut milk, and chicken stock, ideal for setting off the flavor of freshly shucked oysters. Add the oysters at the very end and cook them for only a few minutes, just until they begin to curl around the edges. Good with boiled rice or by itself.

FOR TWO

BASE

1 Tbs. salt butter
1 Tbs. sesame oil
1 c. finely chopped white onions

FIRST SEASONING

½ tsp. black mustard seeds, crushed with a mortar and pestle

½ tsp. turmeric
¼ c. shredded, dried unsweetened coconut

LIQUID FOR BASE

1 c. chicken stock

SECOND SEASONING

2 small bay leaves, broken into quarters
¼ tsp. freshly ground black pepper
¼ tsp. crushed red pepper

⅜ tsp. cinnamon
¼ tsp. coriander
⅛ tsp. cloves
¼ tsp. cumin

---

5 Tbs. coconut milk (6 Tbs. shredded, dried unsweetened coconut soaked in ½ c. whole milk for 30 minutes, liquid then strained)

1½ doz. freshly shucked oysters, drained, liquor reserved
¼ c. oyster liquor
½ tsp. salt, less if chicken stock is very salty

In a large heavy sauté pan melt the butter over medium heat. Add the sesame oil as the last bit of butter is melting and stir to mix. Add the onions, raise the heat a bit, and sauté, stirring frequently, until the onions are darkly browned. Be sure to scrape across the bottom of the pan with a spatula to keep the onions from sticking. Add the elements for the first seasoning, mix, and fry at high heat, stirring very rapidly, for 1 minute. Add the chicken stock and as soon as the liquid in the pan comes to a boil, reduce the heat just enough

---

to keep a noticeable simmer going. Simmer, stirring, for 2 minutes, then add the elements for the second seasoning. Mix very thoroughly and simmer for 12 minutes. Add the coconut milk, bring to a boil, then boil, stirring, for 2 minutes. Reduce the heat a bit and add the oysters, oyster liquor, and salt. Simmer for 4 to 5 minutes, mixing very gently from time to time, just until the oysters curl around the edges. Serve in plates with a raised rim and provide bowls of chutney and additional dried coconut to be added at the table. Boiled rice or bread, served separately, can be used to soak up the gravy. Do not put rice on the plate with the curry, since this dish does not have a great deal of liquid.

Crab Curry

Prepared like Basic Shrimp Curry, this is excellent with saffron or plain boiled rice.

FOR TWO

Prepare as directed for Basic Shrimp Curry, substituting 1 pound of lump crabmeat for the shrimp.

Crabmeat Kerala

A rare Indian crabmeat curry, with roasted coconut, ginger, tomato, tamarind, and lots of minced fresh garlic. Have the vegetables chopped, the coconut roasted, and the liquids measured out before beginning to cook. And top each serving with 3 to 4 tablespoons of Major Grey chutney before serving: we've found this dish really reaches its flavor potential with the chutney mixed in. Provide additional chutney to be added as desired.

FOR THREE OR FOUR

BASE

3 Tbs. salt butter
2 c. chopped white onions

SEASONINGS AND LIQUID

¾ tsp. ginger   ¼ tsp. cayenne
1 tsp. turmeric   ⅛ tsp. freshly ground black
1 Tbs. coriander   pepper
2 Tbs. finely minced fresh garlic   8 oz. tomato sauce
½ c. roasted, shredded, dried   1 tsp. salt
    unsweetened coconut*   1 c. water
2½ Tbs. tamarind paste†

---

1 lb. lump crabmeat
Major Grey chutney

Melt the butter over medium heat in a large heavy sauté pan or skillet. Add the onions and cook, stirring frequently, until the onions are golden brown with some darker flecks, 8 to 9 minutes. Sprinkle in the ginger, turmeric, and coriander, tossing to mix. Add 4 teaspoons of the garlic and mix again. Reduce the heat to very low and add the coconut, tamarind paste, cayenne, and black pepper. Toss and cook for 1 minute longer, then remove the pan from the heat. Add the tomato sauce, salt, and water and mix very thoroughly. Return the pan to the heat and raise the heat to high. Cook, stirring, until the sauce begins to boil. Add the remaining 2 teaspoons garlic, reduce the heat to medium, then cook, stirring and scraping the sides and bottom of the pan, for 4 minutes. Add the crabmeat, stir very gently to mix, then cover the pan loosely and cook over medium-low heat just until the crabmeat is warmed through; this should take about 6 minutes. Spoon the portions onto heated plates and top each portion with 3 generous tablespoons of Major Grey chutney before serving.

---

* To roast the coconut, place it in a small heavy skillet and keep over high heat for 4 to 5 minutes, tossing constantly with a spoon or fork to keep the browning even. Once the coconut is browned, spoon it into a small bowl. (If left in the skillet, it will continue to brown and get a burned taste.)

† Dried tamarind is available in 1 pound chunks at specialty shops and spice stores. To make tamarind paste, put 2 ounces of dried tamarind in a small saucepan with 3 tablespoons water. Cook over high heat, stirring and mashing the tamarind with the back of a spoon, until it is completely dissolved in the water and a kind of thick syrupy paste has formed. Then push the paste through a conical passoire or coarse sieve to strain out the solids. Scrape any paste that clings to the underside of the sieve into a bowl with a spoon. (If you cannot obtain tamarind, use dried unsweetened prunes with a bit of vinegar or lemon added. Make a paste as directed for tamarind.)

King Crab Curry

In this and the following recipe it is essential to defrost the shell-fish thoroughly and to remove all excess moisture completely before cooking.

FOR TWO

Prepare as directed for Basic Shrimp Curry, substituting 1 pound king crabmeat for the shrimp. Cut the crabmeat into ½ inch cubes before adding to the base. If fresh limes are available, substitute 4 teaspoons fresh lime juice for the lemon juice specified in the final stage of preparation.

Lobster Malai

A variation of Shrimp Malai, for leftover lobster meat or as an unusual way to prepare Florida or Danish lobster. In fact, the chewier the lobster the better the results.

FOR TWO

Prepare as directed for Shrimp Malai, substituting 1 pound lobster meat for the shrimp. Be sure to defrost frozen lobster thoroughly and to drain it well before adding to the sauce. A simple way to remove the last bit of excess moisture is to roll the meat gently in several layers of paper towels after draining.

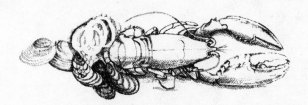

Lobster Curry

Not really for Maine lobsters unless you happen to have extra large ones that no one can finish. For some time we've been convinced that the standard preparation of American Gulf lobsters lacked imagination. Chinese restaurants are almost alone in being willing to experiment with non-Maine lobsters. We found that in curries, where the sauce is the main attraction, the chewy Florida lobster works beautifully.

FOR TWO

Prepare as directed for Basic Shrimp Curry, substituting 1 pound of lobster meat for the shrimp.

Turtle Vindaloo

Vindaloos are among the hottest of the Indian curries. We find this type of highly seasoned purée in which the basic element is marinated for at least 24 hours perfect for turtle meat. Prepare the marinade in a blender set at high speed, then cover the turtle meat with it. Use a porcelain or stainless steel bowl; other metals tend to impart a metallic taste in contact with strong marinades. Serve Turtle Vindaloo with boiled rice to soak up the rich, strong sauce.

FOR FOUR

2 lb. turtle meat, cut into 1½ to 2 inch chunks

MARINADE

2 Tbs. coriander	*8 small whole cloves*
1½ tsp. cayenne	*2 medium-sized white onions, cut up*
2 tsp. turmeric	
1 Tbs. cumin	*3 Tbs. olive oil*
¾ tsp. ginger	*1½ c. white wine vinegar*

---

4 Tbs. butter	*½ tsp. cardamom*
8 small bay leaves, broken up	*4 tsp. coriander*
1 tsp. salt	*½ tsp. nutmeg*
1½ inches stick cinnamon, crushed with a mortar and pestle	*½ tsp. mace*
	½ tsp. ginger
½ tsp. cloves	*¼ tsp. cayenne*
½ tsp. freshly ground black pepper	*3 Tbs. honey*

Rinse, dry, and cut up the turtle meat, trimming off any fat or muscle. Prepare the marinade by putting all the ingredients in an

---

electric blender. Spin at high speed for a few seconds, then turn off. Repeat until the marinade appears even in color and rather thin. Place the turtle meat in a porcelain or stainless steel bowl, then pour the marinade over. (Be sure to spoon out any marinade that clings to the sides or inside cover of the blender.) Mix well with a spoon, then pack the turtle meat down if necessary so that it is completely covered by the marinade. Cover the bowl with several layers of plastic wrap and refrigerate for 24 hours.

To cook, melt the butter over medium heat in a large heavy sauté pan or saucepan. Add the contents of the bowl. Be sure to scrape out and include all the marinade. Keeping the heat at medium, add the remaining ingredients in the order given. Stir to mix after each addition. Bring the mixture to a boil, then lower the heat just enough to keep a low simmer going. Partially cover the pan and cook, stirring from time to time, for 1 hour or until the turtle meat is tender. Serve with boiled rice.

Conch Vindaloo

A variation of Turtle Vindaloo that works in the same way. Don't let the "hotness" of vindaloo frighten you. The principal characteristic of the finished dish is in fact a kind of aromatic tartness that goes very well with chewier seafood.

FOR FOUR

Prepare as directed for Turtle Vindaloo, substituting 2 pounds conch meat for the turtle meat. Pound out the conch to a thickness of ½ to ¾ inch, then cut into 1 inch squares before marinating and reduce the marinating time to 6 to 8 hours.

Crab Malai

A variation of Shrimp and Lobster Malai that works very well with the frozen snow crab or king crab pieces available in supermarket freezer cases.

FOR TWO

Prepare as directed for Lobster Malai, substituting 1 pound crabmeat for the lobster. Defrost, drain, and dry frozen crabmeat as directed for lobster.

Soft Belly Clam Curry

An unusual dish, an Indian curry made with shucked hard shell clams with the tougher muscle tissue cut away. Freshly shucked clams are best here, but if opening them in the raw state is a task you find difficult, clams that have been steamed open also work quite well. Two things to remember: use the smaller hard clams—they don't get as tough during cooking—and add them toward the end of preparation since they require very little cooking.

FOR TWO

Prepare as directed for Oyster Curry, substituting 1½ dozen shucked clams for the oysters. Strain the steaming broth or the clam liquor very thoroughly to remove the sand. See Steamed Hard Clams for directions on steaming the clams open.

Curried Red Snapper

A fish curry made with red snapper, just as good with a number of large firm fish. Have the fish cut into steaks at the market, then cut the steaks into large cubes.

FOR TWO

Prepare as directed for Basic Shrimp Curry, substituting 1 pound red snapper steaks about 1 inch thick for the shrimp. Remove the skin and, if necessary, the center bone, then cut into 1 inch cubes. Serve with boiled rice (see Creole Turtle Stew).

Green Onion and Melon Chutney

A delightful homemade chutney, fun to make in the summer melon season. It will keep under refrigeration for a week or more.

MAKES ABOUT 1⅓ CUPS

1¾ c. green onions, cut into 2½ inch lengths

two ⅛-inch slices of fresh cantaloupe, rind pared, cut into 2 inch pieces

¾ c. cold water

2 Tbs. beef tea or beef concentrate

1½ Tbs. Chinese Plum Sauce or currant jelly with ¼ tsp. lemon juice added

1⅓ Tbs. rice vinegar

½ tsp. coarse salt

⅛ tsp. white pepper

⅛ tsp. black pepper

1/16 tsp. cayenne

3/16 tsp. cumin

1/16 tsp. ginger

1/16 tsp. cloves

⅛ tsp. coriander

1 Tbs. sugar

⅓ c. buttermilk

Combine all the ingredients except the buttermilk in a sauté pan. Simmer over low heat, stirring frequently, for about 15 minutes, until the green onions are soft. Add the buttermilk, stir, and cook for 5 minutes longer. Remove the pan from the heat and pour into a stainless steel or porcelain bowl. Allow to cool to room temperature, then cover with plastic wrap and refrigerate.

Peach and Onion Chutney

A great way to make use of fresh peaches that have gotten overripe.

MAKES ABOUT 1⅓ CUPS

Prepare as directed for Green Onion and Melon Chutney, substituting 1¼ cups finely chopped white onions for the green onions and 1½ cups peeled fresh peaches cut into 1½ inch chunks for the melon.

Sautéing Recipes

Eel in Green Sauce
  (Anguilles au Vert)

Biscayan Squid

Greek Stuffed Squid
  (Kalamaria Yemista)

Lump Crabmeat Amandine

Sautéed Snow Crabs with
  Ginger and Figs

Crabmeat Dewey

Crabmeat with Pea Pods

Crabmeat Stuffing or
  Dressing

Shrimp à l'Américaine

Lobster à l'Américaine

Lobster Newburg

Lobster Norfolk

Crab Norfolk

Shrimp Norfolk

Sautéed Shrimp with Sour
  Cream and Dill Sauce

Sautéed Barbecue Shrimp

Sautéed Rock Shrimp
  (American Langoustines)

Scallops with Saffron and
  Cream

Frogs' Legs Provençale

Green Turtle Steak

Sautéed Dolphin (Mahi
  Mahi) with Lemon-Butter
  Sauce

Sautéed Sand Dabs

8

Sautéing

The sautéing process is as common to some of the most complex of *haute cuisine* dishes, such as Belgian Eel in Green Sauce, as it is to the most basic such as Lobster Norfolk. It ranges from a quick form of shallow frying done in a small amount of butter and oil to a gentle glazing of the basic ingredients. One of the fundamental aims of sautéing is to add part of the cooking medium to the dish being cooked. Butter is most often the cooking medium—it gives sautéing its lovely taste and richness.

Because it is one of the best ways in which to fuse various elements, sautéing is frequently used in combination with other cooking techniques. Possibly more than any other cooking method in this book, sautéing triumphs most in its undertones: not in what is heard but in what is overheard. Timing is important in sautéing—the right ingredient at the right moment can be the key to the delicate balance of a dish. Careful timing and careful handling are eminently well suited to home kitchens as well as to careful small restaurant kitchens.

You may find the enormous range of dishes in this chapter surprising. They are some of our favorites. And you will notice that in this chapter shellfish are much more predominant than fish. Shellfish are sturdier in texture and will not fall apart in the longer and slower sautéing dishes; many shellfish are ideal main elements here, absorbing flavors during cooking without getting overcooked. Larger or thicker fish sauté well, and delicate fish such as tiny California sand dabs can be sautéed in just over a minute. Butter, olive oil, vegetables, and seasonings are the flavor keys to this lovely form of seafood cooking.

Basic Sautéing Techniques

Use heavy sauté pan or skillet and monitor heat level carefully.

Stir seafood gently while cooking.

Time carefully.

Keep liquid at a minimum and, when covering is indicated, use tight-fitting lids or makeshift heavy foil lids.

If stove burners cannot be set at very low, remove pan from heat for brief periods.

When multiplying sautéing recipes, do not directly multiply liquids; increase liquids gradually until desired texture appears.

When stir-frying precedes sautéing, test oil temperature by sprinkling drop of water on heated surface; when drop dances on the surface oil is sufficiently hot.

Eel in Green Sauce
Anguilles au Vert

The most delicious French and Belgian eel dish we know. The eel are sautéed in butter and white wine with an abundance of herbs. The herbs give the dish its rich subtle flavor and its splendid color. Parboiling the skinned eel with salt and vinegar keeps them firm during sautéing and also removes the excess fat; this technique works well with any sauced eel dish. If you can get fresh chervil, tarragon, or sorrel, use 2 tablespoons of the fresh herb

---

for each teaspoon of dried. The Belgians consider this one of their unique national dishes; the French claim to have originated it. Once you have it, you'll see why everyone wants to take credit for inventing Eel in Green Sauce.

FOR FOUR

2 lb. small eel, skinned, cleaned, and cut into 1½ inch pieces

2 to 3 qt. water, with 1 tsp. salt and 1½ tsp. vinegar added

flour for dredging

salt and freshly ground black pepper

GREEN SAUCE

4 Tbs. (½ stick) salt butter

⅓ c. chopped green onion tops

¼ c. chopped parsley (leaves only; discard the stems)

2 tsp. chervil

½ c. chopped uncooked spinach (fresh or frozen)

¼ tsp. sage

½ tsp. tarragon

¼ c. chopped fresh sorrel (optional)

¾ c. dry white wine

¾ tsp. salt

a few grains of cayenne

2 large egg yolks

¼ c. heavy cream

Bring the seasoned water to a boil over high heat in a 3 to 4 quart saucepan. Add the eel and cook for 2½ to 3 minutes. Immediately remove the eel from the water by lifting them out quickly with a mesh skimmer or dumping the contents of the pan into a colander set in the sink. Allow to drain well. Combine the greens in a bowl, mix briefly, then set aside.

Dredge the eel evenly with flour. Melt the butter over medium heat in a sauté pan, then place the flour-coated eel in the hot butter. Sprinkle the top side lightly with salt and pepper. Cook, shaking the pan to keep the eel from sticking, for 1½ to 2 minutes, then turn them over. Again sprinkle the upper side with salt and pepper. Cook for 1½ to 2 minutes, then add the greens. Cook, stirring, for 3 minutes longer. Add the wine and stir to mix. Cover the pan loosely and cook over medium-low heat for 8 to 10 minutes, until the greens are soft and look well blended. Remove the pan from the heat and stir in the salt and cayenne. Check the thickness and amount of sauce. There should be about ½ inch in the pan or approximately 1¼ cups of sauce. If necessary, add ¼ to ½ cup of water, stir, and heat a bit, then once again remove the pan from the heat.

Combine the egg yolks and cream in a small bowl and beat with a fork or whisk until well blended. Spoon about 3 to 4 tablespoons of the hot sauce from the pan into the egg and cream mixture and beat for a few seconds, then add the mixture gradually to the sauce in the pan, stirring gently but constantly. When all the egg and cream mixture has been blended into the sauce, return the pan to low heat just until the sauce is slightly thickened, from 4 to 8 minutes depending on the size and thickness of the sauté pan. Do not let the sauce come to a boil. Serve several pieces of eel topped and surrounded with a generous quantity of sauce for each portion. Use heated plates, preferably plates with raised rims.

Biscayan Squid

A marvelous squid dish from the Spanish Basque Provinces. Flaming the pan juices with brandy halfway through the cooking process gives the sauce its fine smoky undertone. The green pepper, charred in the oven to give it a special taste and texture, blends well with the hearty Basque flavors of onions, garlic, and tomatoes. Generally prepared with young small squid, this dish works just as well with medium-sized squid, which are more readily available and much easier to clean.

FOR TWO OR THREE

2 lb. small or medium-sized squid, cleaned	1 c. chopped onions
4 Tbs. salt butter	¾ chopped carrot
5 Tbs. olive oil	1 green pepper, charred, scraped, seeded, and chopped*
1 tsp. salt	1½ tsp. finely minced garlic
½ tsp. freshly ground black pepper	one 16-oz. can peeled Italian tomatoes, cut up and drained
⅛ tsp. cayenne	1 Tbs. minced parsley
¼ c. brandy plus 1 Tbs.	2 small bay leaves, crushed
2 Tbs. finely minced shallots	½ tsp. thyme

To clean the squid, rinse each one under cool running water. Have on hand a platter lined with paper towels on which to place the squid after cleaning. Grasp each one firmly around the body with one hand and pull the head and tentacle section away from the body sharply with the other hand. If you plan to use the tentacles, cut them away

* Rub the pepper with olive oil, place in a small ramekin, and bake in a preheated 500°F. oven until browned and blistery, 8 to 10 minutes. Rinse under cold running water, then peel off the skin. Pull the pepper open. Remove the seeds and membrane and discard them. Chop.

from the rest of the head just above the eyes with a sharp knife, and reserve. Some of the inner matter from the body will have been removed during this first phase. Now push one finger down into the cavity of the body and ease out the remainder of the inner matter. Also pull out the thin translucent cartiledge that runs along the inside of the body to one side. (It looks like a thin wedge of plastic.) Check to make sure the body is cleaned by squeezing gently, beginning at the tail end, all the way up. With very small squid, it is simplest to turn them inside out to complete the cleaning. Holding the body under the running water, rub the outer covering off with your fingers, exposing the clean white meat. Also pull off the finlike projections near the tail end and discard. Shake off the excess water and place the cleaned squid on the platter to drain. If desired, cut larger squid into rectangles about 1 $\times$ 2 inches, or into 1 inch rounds.

Melt 2 tablespoons of the butter over medium heat in a heavy 3 to 4 quart saucepan. Add 2 tablespoons of the olive oil and mix. Heat for a minute more, then add the squid, salt, pepper, and cayenne. Cook, stirring frequently, until the squid are golden, about 5 minutes. Add ¼ cup of the brandy, raise the heat for about 1 minute to get the brandy quite hot, then ignite. Lower the heat a bit and flame the contents of the pan, tipping it with a rotating motion to prolong the flaming, until the flame dies out. Pour the contents of the pan into a bowl and reserve.

Put the remaining 2 tablespoons butter and 3 tablespoons olive oil into the pan and warm over low heat until the butter is completely melted. Stir to mix thoroughly, then add the shallots, onions, carrot, green pepper, and garlic. Cook over very low heat until the vegetables are soft and glazed, stirring frequently. Do not allow them to brown. Add the tomatoes, parsley, bay leaves, thyme, the remaining tablespoon of brandy, and the squid and pan juices reserved earlier. Raise the heat and bring to a simmer, then cover the pan and turn the heat down to low. Cook for 20 to 25 minutes, until the squid are tender. Uncover to stir every 5 minutes or so.

While the squid are cooking, prepare 2 cups boiled rice. To serve, ladle the portions of squid, vegetables, and pan juices onto heated plates and spoon about ⅔ cup rice onto each plate to one side, just touching but not mixed in with the squid.

Greek Stuffed Squid
Kalamaria Yemista

We never liked stuffed squid as much as unstuffed until we worked out this marvelous Greek dish. Spectacularly beautiful with its rice, currants, tomatoes, parsley, and pine nuts, it tastes even better than it looks. It's a good idea to prepare a large quantity—it is even better chilled. This recipe will feed at least four and can be doubled or even tripled with no problems as long as you have a large enough skillet or sauté pan with a cover. In lieu of a cover, you can make one using heavy-duty aluminum foil. You'll need a lot of patience to stuff the squid and close each one with a toothpick, but splits and flaws won't show in the finished dish, since the sauce and the stuffing are the same.

FOR FOUR

1½ lb. medium-sized squid (about 12 to 16, with 4 to 6 inch bodies)
½ c. olive oil
1½ c. chopped onions
2 tsp. finely minced garlic
¾ tsp. salt
½ tsp. freshly ground black pepper

½ c. uncooked rice
1 c. tomato sauce
1 bay leaf, crushed
½ c. dried currants or dark raisins
¼ c. coarsely chopped parsley
¼ c. pine nuts
¾ to 1 c. water

Clean the squid as directed for Biscayan Squid, leaving the bodies whole and reserving the tentacles to be used in the stuffing. Sauté the onions and garlic in olive oil until lightly browned, then add the salt, pepper, and rice. Cook over medium-high heat for about 3 minutes, stirring, to seal the rice. Chop the tentacles and add them along with all remaining ingredients except the water. Stir and cook over medium heat for 6 minutes, gradually adding ½ cup of the water. Remove the pan from the heat. Stuff the squid with the pan mixture, then close with a toothpick. Rub a large heavy skillet with a wadded-up paper towel on which you've poured several tablespoons of olive oil to coat. Place the squid in the skillet and add ¼ to ½ cup of water to the mixture in the saucepan, then pour over the squid in the skillet. Bring to a simmer, then cover, lower the heat, and cook for 25 minutes. Uncover and spoon the sauce over the squid several times during cooking. After 25 minutes, remove the cover, raise the heat a bit, and cook for 2 minutes more. Serve on heated plates with 3 or 4 squid covered with and surrounded by the sauce from the pan. The toothpicks are generally removed at the table, but you can take them out just before serving if you take care to pull gently so as not to open the stuffed squid and spoil the visual appeal of the presentation.

Lump Crabmeat Amandine

The simplest amandine *preparation we know and one of the most attractive to serve. Stir the crabmeat very gently when warming it, then set the pan in a warm oven while making the sauce. You can multiply this recipe indefinitely; just use a larger pan, or sauté the crabmeat in batches, set in the warm oven, then sauce all the portions just before serving.*

FOR TWO

¾ *lb. lump crabmeat*
2½ *Tbs. salt butter*

AMANDINE SAUCE

6 *Tbs.* (¾ *stick*) *salt butter*	2 *Tbs. fresh lemon juice*
¼ *tsp. freshly ground white pepper*	1 *tsp. finely minced fresh parsley*
	½ *c. slivered, blanched almonds*

Preheat the oven to 200°F. and put the serving plates in it. In a small sauté pan melt the butter over low heat, then add the crabmeat. Sauté over low heat, stirring very gently with a wooden spoon, just until warmed through, 5 to 6 minutes. Cover the sauté pan and place it in the warm oven while you prepare the sauce.

To prepare the sauce, melt the butter in a heavy saucepan over medium heat, then add the pepper. Cook the butter just until it gets foamy and slightly brown at the edges. Lower the heat and add the lemon juice and parsley. Stir to mix, then add the almonds. Cook over low heat until the almonds and butter are nicely browned. Remove the pan from the heat.

To serve, place the portions of sautéed crabmeat on the warmed dinner plates, then top with equal quantities of almonds and browned butter.

Sautéed Snow Crabs with
Ginger and Figs

The Chinese are fond of crabs cooked with ginger and figs. Fresh figs or well drained figs from jars work beautifully with the frozen snow crabs available in most markets.

FOR TWO OR THREE

8 oz. frozen snow crabs, defrosted, drained, and patted dry with paper towels, then cut into large pieces

1½ Tbs. salt butter

1½ Tbs. sesame oil

¾ tsp. crushed dried ginger root (see Chinese Braised Carp for instructions)

¼ c. very finely chopped green onion tops

2 Tbs. dry sherry (Manzanilla)

½ tsp. white wine vinegar

1 tsp. coriander

¼ tsp. salt

½ tsp. freshly ground white pepper

½ tsp. sugar

½ c. chicken stock

½ c. mashed ripe figs

1 tsp. soy sauce

¾ c. whole figs, stems removed

In a heavy sauté pan melt the butter, then add the sesame oil. Continue to heat until very hot but not smoking. (Test by sprinkling a drop of water into the oil with a fingertip. If the drop dances on the surface of the oil, the oil is hot enough.) Add the crabs, ginger, and 3 tablespoons of the green onion tops and stir-fry for 1½ to 2 minutes, just until the pieces of crab appear glossy, indicating they have been sealed in a coating of hot oil. Be sure to keep the contents of the pan in constant motion during the stir-frying to keep them from burning. Reduce the heat to low and add the sherry and vinegar. Toss with a wooden spoon to moisten the crabs and pieces of ginger, then sprinkle in the coriander, salt, pepper, and sugar. Toss again, raise the heat to medium-high, and add the chicken stock. Cook for 4 to 5 minutes, stirring gently from time to time, then add the mashed figs. Stir them into the sauce and mash any larger pieces against the sides of the pan with the back of a wooden spoon. Add the remaining green onion tops. Cook until the sauce is well blended and thick, then sprinkle in the soy sauce. Stir to mix, then add the whole figs very gently so as not to crush them. Continue cooking just long enough to warm the whole figs, about 2 to 3 minutes, then remove the pan from the heat. To serve, use a large serving spoon to lift the contents of the pan from the bottom upward onto heated plates, so as to preserve the layers into which the dish has settled. Spoon any liquid and solids remaining in the bottom of the pan carefully over the portions. Serve immediately.

Crabmeat Dewey

Our version of the only Crabmeat Dewey we find totally irresistible, the one served at Brooklyn's venerable Gage & Tollner. Ed Dewey, the proprietor, says the dish was not named after his father, who first introduced it, but after Admiral Dewey because the colors in the sauce suggested the Spanish flag. It is quite simple to make and requires very little time. Watch the timing and the stirring and the sherry. Most poorly prepared Crabmeat Dewey uses too much sherry, and the wrong kind. Use Manzanilla, the driest and palest of Spanish sherries. Any other sherry will sweeten the flavor and discolor the sauce.

FOR TWO

½ lb. lump crabmeat	1 Tbs. dry sherry
2 Tbs. salt butter	(Manzanilla)
¼ c. sliced mushrooms	¾ c. heavy cream
6 Tbs. drained sliced pimientos	1 large egg yolk
⅜ tsp. salt	
⅛ tsp. freshly ground white pepper	

In a medium-sized heavy sauté pan melt the butter over low heat. Add the mushrooms and pimientos and cook over low heat, stirring gently with a wooden spoon for 2 minutes. Add the crabmeat, salt, and pepper. Continue cooking over low heat, stirring *very* carefully so as not to break up the crabmeat lumps, until warmed through, about 4 minutes. Mix the sherry, cream, and egg yolk together in a small bowl with a fork, then add to the contents of the sauté pan. Continue cooking over low heat until the sauce thickens to the consistency of light sour cream. Serve in preheated individual ramekins. If you wish to duplicate the original three-color dish as served years ago, you can garnish each portion with several thin strips of peeled sautéed green pepper.

When multiplying the recipe it may be necessary to use about one-fourth to one-third less cream than direct multiplication would indicate, due to the proportionately greater depth of liquid. (Few persons have large enough sauté pans to accommodate the quantity for 6 or 8 with no change at all in the amount of liquid.) Add one-third less cream than your total to the egg yolks and sherry, then proceed as indicated above. If the sauce becomes too thick during the final stage of cooking, stir in the remaining cream 2 tablespoons at a time until the desired texture is achieved.

Crabmeat with Pea Pods

A dish we invented one evening when we were about to move and found only some Chinese snow peas in the refrigerator to go with our crabmeat. It's been a favorite ever since. Prepare it in an attractive skillet that can be brought to the table.

FOR TWO

12 oz. lump crabmeat

4 Tbs. (½ stick) salt butter

1 lb. 4 oz. Chinese pea pods
(fresh or frozen)

2 Tbs. water (eliminate if
frozen pea pods are used)

1 Tbs. minced chives

¾ tsp. finely minced garlic

¾ tsp. fresh coarsely ground
black pepper

⅓ tsp. salt

1½ Tbs. white wine

1 Tbs. Worcestershire sauce

Melt the butter slowly over low heat in a heavy skillet. Lower the heat and add the crabmeat, pea pods,* and water. Warm slowly, stirring with a wooden spoon, until the pea pods are warm. Add the remaining ingredients. Mix thoroughly and cook over medium heat for 1 minute. Cover the skillet and cook for 2 minutes longer. Remove the skillet from the burner and place, loosely covered, in a 175°F. oven until served.

* Frozen pea pods may be added without defrosting. Just break up the chunks a bit to eliminate some of the ice.

Crabmeat Stuffing or Dressing

Used as a dressing on broiled lobster, a stuffing for fish and shrimp, and in New Orleans where we have lots of crabmeat as a dish called stuffed crab, which are crab shells filled with crabmeat stuffing. The crabmeat is mixed with vegetables, soaked white bread, seasonings, and a bit of white wine. We deliberately omit the usual garlic, which tends to overpower the delicate flavor of the crabmeat.

¼ lb. lump crabmeat

2 Tbs. salt butter

1 c. coarsely chopped white
onions

¼ c. soaked, crumbled white
bread, excess moisture
squeezed out

2 Tbs. Worcestershire sauce

3 Tbs. finely minced fresh
parsley

¾ tsp. salt

½ tsp. freshly ground black
pepper

2 Tbs. dry white wine

In a sauté pan melt the butter over medium-low heat. Add the onions and sauté until soft and lightly browned. Add the crabmeat and the remaining ingredients. Stir very gently to mix and cook over low heat for 5 to 6 minutes. Remove the pan from the heat and allow to cool to room temperature. Shape as needed for filling or stuffing. Or put into a stainless steel or porcelain bowl, cover with several layers of plastic wrap, and refrigerate.

Shrimp à l'Américaine

A splendid French dish with a name of uncertain origin and a flavor that indicates its Provençal origins. Whole shrimp are sautéed in the shell in butter and olive oil, giving the base its rich color and hearty shrimp flavor, then removed. Fresh ripe tomatoes, Armagnac, and white wine add layers of flavor, and when the sauce is done, the peeled shrimp are returned to cook for just a few minutes. A triumph of timing, balance, and gusto, this dish is exciting to cook and a pleasure to serve.

FOR THREE OR FOUR

2 lb. whole shrimp in shells

7 Tbs. salt butter

2 Tbs. olive oil

½ tsp. freshly ground black
pepper

SAUCE

⅓ c. minced shallots

4 tsp. finely minced fresh garlic

¼ c. Armagnac or brandy

1 to 1¼ lb. ripe tomatoes,
chopped

½ c. dry white wine

¾ tsp. salt

¼ tsp. freshly ground black
pepper

⅛ tsp. cayenne

¼ tsp. thyme

⅛ tsp. ground bay leaf

Place the shrimp in a colander and rinse under cold running water. Allow to drain very thoroughly. In a large heavy sauté pan melt the butter over medium heat, then add the olive oil. Mix thoroughly with a wooden spoon or fork, then add the whole shrimp. Sprinkle in the pepper. Raise the heat a bit and cook the shrimp, tossing them constantly with the spoon, until the shells turn pink. (This should take from 3 to 4 minutes.) Immediately remove the pan from the heat. Remove the shrimp from the pan with a slotted spoon, allowing the juices to drain back into the pan, and place them in a wide bowl to cool. When the shrimp are cool enough to peel, remove the shells and place the peeled shrimp in a smaller bowl. Cover the bowl and refrigerate until the sauce is completed. Pour any additional juices that may have collected in the large bowl back into the pan. Remove any pieces of shell or tentacle carefully with a spoon.

To prepare the sauce, heat the butter and oil remaining in the pan over medium heat, then add the shallots and garlic. Cook, stirring frequently, until soft, about 6 to 8 minutes, then add 2 tablespoons of the Armagnac. Stir to mix thoroughly, then add the tomatoes. Mix with a wooden spoon and cook over medium heat for 4 minutes, mashing the tomatoes down with the back of the spoon. Add the wine and the seasonings, and cook at a simmer until the tomato pieces are very soft and the skin has come off most of them. This should take from 10 to 15 minutes, depending on the ripeness of the tomatoes. Place a coarse sieve or conical-shaped *passoire* over a large bowl and empty the contents of the pan into it. Purée the solids remaining in the sieve with a wooden spoon or pestle, scraping the puréed matter off the underside of the sieve and into the bowl with a knife or spoon. Return the strained sauce to the pan and discard the solids remaining in the sieve. Add the remaining 2 tablespoons of Armagnac and mix thoroughly. Cook the sauce over medium-high heat until it is reduced by about one-third or until you have approximately 1 cup of sauce in the pan. Return the peeled shrimp to the sauce and cook them for 4 to 5 minutes, spooning the sauce over them frequently to ensure that they are heated through. Serve on preheated plates with plenty of sauce spooned over each portion.

Lobster à l'Américaine

A classic French dish prepared with live langoustes *or spiny lobsters. It works beautifully with the American equivalent of* langoustes, *Florida lobsters, as well as with Danish or South African rock lobsters. We don't feel it's necessary to begin the dish with live lobsters, as most French recipes specify, but it is essential to use the shells, as in the preceding recipe for Shrimp à l'Américaine, for both color and flavor. You can discard the lobster shells before serving or serve French style with everyone picking the meat out of the shell in the midst of all the sauce. With some dishes it's fun to be messy and this is one of them.*

FOR FOUR

Prepare as directed for Shrimp à l'Américaine, substituting 2 Florida lobsters, 1 to 1½ pounds each, or 4 Danish rock lobster tails for the shrimp. If you use Florida lobsters, split and clean them as directed for Broiled Stuffed Florida Lobster, then divide each half into 3 or 4 pieces. For Danish rock lobsters, split them open, then break each tail into 4 pieces. Cook as directed for the shrimp, increasing the final reimmersion period in the last stage to 6 to 8 minutes.

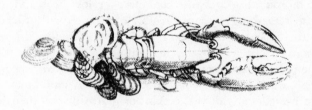

Lobster Newburg

First introduced at Delmonico's in New York before the turn of the century, this lobster dish with a cream and egg yolk thickened sauce and wine has become immensely popular and, like many dishes whose accessibility is broad, one of the most carelessly prepared seafood dishes we know. With brandy and dry white wine

*rather than the usual overdose of sweetish sherry, and freshly
cooked lobster rather than the standard shreds of stale leftovers
or watery chunks of canned lobster, it's easier to understand how
the fuss began.*

*1½ c. cooked lobster meat, cut
into ¾ inch pieces (average
yield of a 1¾ lb. cooked
Florida lobster; see Boiled
Florida Lobster for cooking
and cleaning directions)*

4 Tbs. (½ stick) salt butter

¼ tsp. salt

1/16 tsp. cayenne

¼ c. brandy

¼ c. dry white wine

1 large egg yolk

1 c. heavy cream

scant ⅛ tsp. nutmeg

½ tsp. fresh lemon juice

¾ tsp. sugar

Melt the butter over medium heat in a sauté pan, then add the
lobster meat. Cook for 2 minutes, stirring gently. Sprinkle in the salt
and cayenne and mix. Add the brandy and cook for 1 minute, then
add the wine and mix thoroughly. Remove the pan from the heat.
Beat the egg yolk in a small bowl with ½ cup of the cream, then
spoon about ¼ cup of the sauce from the pan into the egg and cream
mixture, stirring rapidly with a whisk. Pour the contents of the bowl
into the sauté pan and return to low-medium heat. Cook until
the sauce begins to thicken, stirring gently with a wooden spoon,
then reduce the heat to low. Add the nutmeg, lemon juice, and sugar
and mix thoroughly. Continue cooking over low heat and gradually
stir in the remaining ½ cup cream. The sauce will thicken a bit
more, until it has the consistency of thick buttermilk; this will take
approximately 4 to 6 minutes depending on the size of the sauté
pan. When the desired consistency is reached, remove the pan from
the heat. To serve, spoon the sauce and equal amounts of lobster
meat into heated individual ramekins or gratin dishes, then place the
ramekins on dinner plates and bring to the table. (The sauce will
continue to thicken just a bit more from the time the pan is removed
from the heat to the moment it is served. This is normal.)

Lobster Norfolk

It's difficult to call the Norfolk style of cooking shellfish an American classic, since it has barely spread from its point of origin in the Chesapeake area, and even there it is increasingly rare. We first encountered Lobster Norfolk not in Norfolk but in a marvelous Washington, D.C., seafood restaurant, O'Donnell's. There the Norfolk dishes are sautéed in individual round-bottomed ramekins set into the open wells of gas burner grills. The gas range is at the front of the restaurant and one can watch the high flames leap up around the ramekins and into the pans. Very simple. All it takes is butter and lobster and a cooking utensil that can maintain very high heat, such as a cast iron or copper skillet. The lobster is our favorite of all the Norfolks.

FOR TWO

1 lb. uncooked lobster meat, cut into large pieces
1 c. (2 sticks) salt butter

Place 2 serving ramekins in a 200°F. oven to warm while you prepare the lobster. Melt the butter over low heat in a medium-sized, heavy cast iron or copper skillet and add the lobster as soon as the melting is complete. Raise the heat to high and cook, tossing the lobster gently and continuously with a fork, for 7 to 9 minutes. After the first 4 minutes, turn the heat down to medium to keep the butter from burning. During the last minute or two, tilt the pan with a circular motion to distribute the butter as you toss. To serve, heap the lobster in the preheated ramekins and pour any butter remaining in the skillet over the portions. Set the ramekins on plates and serve immediately.

Crab Norfolk

Best with the larger lumps of crabmeat or the sturdier snow crab pieces available frozen in many supermarkets. Defrost frozen crabs by setting them, in their wrapping, in a basin or bowl of cool water; dry them thoroughly with paper towels before cooking.

FOR TWO

Prepare as directed for Lobster Norfolk, substituting 1 pound crabmeat for the lobster. Reduce the cooking time to 5 to 6 minutes.

Shrimp Norfolk

Prepare as directed for Lobster Norfolk, substituting 1 pound large peeled and deveined Gulf shrimp for the lobster. Reduce the cooking time to 6 to 7 minutes and add ⅛ teaspoon freshly ground white pepper during the final minutes of preparation.

Sautéed Shrimp with Sour Cream and Dill Sauce

A Scandinavian idea, combining good sautéed shrimp and a rich sour cream sauce with the characteristic dill flavor.

FOR TWO

SOUR CREAM AND DILL SAUCE

1 c. heavy sour cream	¼ tsp. dry mustard
2 tsp. dried dill weed or ⅓ c. torn-up fresh dill	¼ tsp. sugar
¾ tsp. salt	⅛ tsp. freshly ground white pepper

1 lb. fresh whole shrimp, peeled and deveined	¼ tsp. freshly ground white pepper
3 Tbs. salt butter	½ tsp. fresh lemon juice

Soak the dried dill weed in 1½ tablespoons of water for 5 minutes, then drain; or if you use fresh dill, tear it into small pieces. Put the sour cream into a small heavy saucepan and warm very slowly over low heat. Add the dill after 3 minutes and stir to mix. Add the salt, dry mustard, sugar, and pepper and mix again. Warm for 1 minute more, then remove the pan from the heat and reserve.

To sauté the shrimp, melt the butter over medium heat in a heavy sauté pan or skillet, then add the shrimp. Raise the heat a bit and cook, stirring frequently, for 3 minutes. Add the pepper and lemon juice and toss to mix. Cook for 2 minutes longer, then remove the pan from the heat. Add the reserved sauce to the pan containing the shrimp and stir once, then return the pan to low heat for a minute or two. Do not allow the sauce to come to a boil. To serve, spoon the shrimp onto heated plates and cover with the sauce.

Sautéed Barbecue Shrimp

Two great restaurants in New Orleans make versions of this Italian barbecue shrimp dish and locals constantly and happily argue the merits of Mosca's, made with garlic and oil, and Manale's, made with a peppery buttery sauce. Our own version uses butter, oil, lots of pepper, garlic, herbs, and headless shrimp. (One of the dramatic moments at Manale's is the arrival of a heap of whole shrimp, heads, tails, and all, in their bowl of sauce.) We find that simmering the sauce first, then letting it steep for a while before adding the shrimp gives the richest possible flavor. After being simmered briefly in the sauce, they're then baked for a short time to get even more of the seasoning inside the shell. At certain times of the year, when the shrimp are not too large and their shells are relatively soft, it's fun to cook them with their heads on—and eat them shells and all. Be sure to serve barbecue shrimp in bowls, with lots of sauce, and to include the solids from the bottom of the pan. Knives and forks are fine, and so are fingers, for enjoying what's become a classic New Orleans dish.

FOR FOUR

2 lb. fresh shrimp in the shells, heads removed	½ tsp. basil
1 c. (2 sticks) salt butter	½ tsp. oregano
1 c. vegetable oil	½ tsp. salt
2 tsp. finely minced garlic	½ tsp. cayenne
4 bay leaves, finely crushed	1 Tbs. paprika
2 tsp. rosemary, crushed with a mortar and pestle	¾ tsp. freshly ground black pepper
	1 tsp. fresh lemon juice

Melt the butter over medium heat in a 3 to 4 quart heavy saucepan or sauté pan, then add the oil and stir to mix. Add all the remaining ingredients except the shrimp and cook, stirring constantly, until the sauce comes to a boil. Reduce the heat a bit and simmer for 8 minutes, stirring frequently. Remove the pan from the heat and allow to stand, uncovered, at room temperature for about 30 minutes, stirring once or twice.

To cook the shrimp, return the pan of sauce to medium heat and when the sauce is well heated, about 3 minutes, stir once and add the shrimp. Cook for 5 to 7 minutes, just until the shrimp turn pink, stirring frequently but gently with a wooden spoon. Remove the pan from the heat and place in a preheated 450°F. oven for 10 minutes.

To serve, ladle the shrimp into heated bowls and cover each portion with ½ cup sauce. Stir the sauce thoroughly each time you ladle some out, and at the end, scoop out the solids that have settled to the bottom of the pan with a spoon and put them on top of the shrimp. Bring to the table immediately. Provide a bowl for disposing of the empty shells.

Sautéed Rock Shrimp
American Langoustines

Peeled and deveined rock shrimp sautéed in butter, white wine, and chives.

FOR TWO

1 lb. peeled and deveined rock shrimp	*⅜ tsp. freshly ground white pepper*
3 Tbs. salt butter	*½ tsp. salt*
1⅓ Tbs. minced chives	*⅛ tsp. sugar*
¼ c. dry white wine	*1/16 tsp. cayenne*

Rinse the peeled and deveined rock shrimp under cool running water and roll in several layers of paper towels to remove any excess moisture. In a large heavy sauté pan melt the butter over medium heat. Add the shrimp and the remaining ingredients. Sauté, stirring frequently, until the shrimp are cooked through but not mushy, about 10 to 12 minutes. Serve in preheated individual ramekins or gratin dishes set on dinner plates. Be sure to spoon all the sauce from the pan over the portions.

Scallops with Saffron and Cream

An unusual southern French scallop dish using saffron, white wine, and heavy cream glazed with freshly grated Swiss cheese. Serve it in individual ramekins or a single gratin dish attractive enough to bring to the table. Frozen scallops work perfectly; just be sure to defrost and dry them thoroughly before cooking.

2 to 2½ lb. scallops, cut in half, or in quarters if they are medium to large size

¼ c. finely minced shallots

½ tsp. ground saffron (saffron threads should be broken up and ground with a mortar and pestle for accurate measuring)

1 c. dry white wine

½ c. water

3½ tsp. fresh lemon juice

½ tsp. salt

½ tsp. freshly ground white pepper

2 Tbs. salt butter kneaded with 4 tsp. flour (beurre manié)

6 Tbs. heavy cream

½ c. freshly grated American Swiss, French Gruyère, or Swiss Emmenthal cheese

Place the scallops in a large sauté pan with the shallots, saffron, wine, water, lemon juice, salt, and pepper. Bring to a boil over medium-high heat, then reduce the heat and simmer, loosely covered, for 8 minutes. Remove the pan from the heat, uncover, and remove the scallops from the pan with a slotted spoon, allowing the liquid to drain back into the pan. Reserve the scallops in a bowl covered with a piece of foil.

Put the pan back on the burner and reduce the liquid by half over high heat, stirring frequently and scraping down the sides of the pan. Stir the butter kneaded with flour into the liquid, reduce the heat slightly, and cook for about 1 minute. Reduce the heat to low and add the cream, 1 tablespoon at a time, mixing in gently after each addition. Return the scallops to the sauce in the pan and cook over low heat (just below a simmer) for 6 to 8 minutes, just until the sauce thickens. Remove the pan from the heat and spoon the portions into individual baking ramekins or into a single large gratin platter. Be sure to spoon some of the sauce *over* each scallop. Sprinkle evenly with the grated cheese and set under a preheated broiler about 4 inches from the source of heat until the cheese is browned, about 1½ to 3 minutes. To serve, place individual ramekins on dinner plates, or, if you use a single gratin platter, bring it to the table along with 4 heated plates and carefully lift the portions from the platter onto the plates using a large wide spatula so as to keep the browned cheese crust intact. Spoon any sauce that remains in the gratin platter around the portions.

Frogs' Legs Provençale

In theory this is a delightful dish; in general practice it is simply wretched, tough frogs' legs swimming in too much tomato paste and too much garlic. In this version the frogs' legs are sautéed in butter and olive oil, then sauced with the pan juices simmered with a small amount of garlic and some fresh ripe tomatoes. In this form it is once again a delicious and delicate dish.

FOR FOUR

12 to 14 pairs small frogs' legs	¼ c. olive oil
1½ c. cold milk, approximately	1½ Tbs. fresh lemon juice
flour in a shaker	1½ Tbs. finely minced parsley
salt and freshly ground black pepper	2 large or 3 medium-sized fresh ripe tomatoes
¼ c. (½ stick) salt butter	1½ tsp. finely minced fresh garlic

Clean and separate the frogs' legs as directed for Frogs' Legs Beurre Noisette. Place in a wide-bottomed bowl and cover with cold milk. Soak for 1½ to 2 hours. Lift out of the milk with tongs, allowing the liquid to drain off, then place on a large flat platter. Sprinkle evenly with flour on the top side, then sprinkle lightly with salt and pepper. Turn the frogs' legs over and flour and season on the other side. If necessary, lift them up individually and dust with flour the spots that have remained bare.

In a large heavy sauté pan, melt the butter over medium heat and add the olive oil. Mix. Sauté the frogs' legs, 4 to 6 at a time, in the hot butter and oil until golden brown, about 3 to 4 minutes on each side. As each batch is done, remove with tongs to a large platter. Remove the pan from the heat. Set the platter in a 200°F. oven to keep warm and add the newly sautéed frogs' legs as they are completed. When the last batch is added, sprinkle all of them with the lemon juice and minced parsley, then return the platter to the warm oven.

Blanch the tomatoes in boiling water for about 1 minute, then rinse under cool water. Peel off the skin and cut up over a bowl, discarding the tougher inner core and any large seeds you find. Return the sauté pan to medium heat and add the tomatoes and garlic to the oil, butter, and pan juices. Mix thoroughly. Raise the heat a bit more and cook for 5 to 7 minutes, stirring frequently and breaking up the larger tomato pieces with the back of a wooden spoon. Remove the pan from the heat. To serve, place the sautéed frogs' legs on heated plates and ladle the sauce from the pan over each portion. Serve immediately.

Green Turtle Steak

Green turtle is a Florida favorite and one of the best green turtle steaks we've had is served at the Port of Call, a Miami seafood restaurant. The secret to preparing this dish successfully is first pounding out the steaks, which are cut from huge 200 to 300 pound sea turtles. Pounding out tenderizes the meat and allows it to absorb the seasonings from the flour coating and some of the oil and butter in which it's sautéed. The dish is finished in a hot oven and sprinkled with lemon juice just before serving.

FOR TWO

2 turtle steaks, about ½ lb. each
2 large eggs
½ c. milk
1½ c. flour
1 Tbs. salt
½ tsp. freshly ground black pepper

¼ tsp. nutmeg
½ c. olive oil
½ c. (1 stick) salt butter
4 tsp. fresh lemon juice

Using first the scored, then the flat side of a mallet, pound the steaks out until they are about ⅓ inch thick. In a pie dish or bowl beat the eggs and milk together with a fork. Combine the flour, salt, pepper, and nutmeg in a bowl and mix thoroughly with a whisk. First dip the steaks in the egg and milk mixture, then roll in the seasoned flour to coat evenly. Place on a platter to dry for about 5 minutes before sautéing.

In a large heavy sauté pan or skillet, heat the olive oil and add the butter. Mix, and continue heating until fairly hot, but not at all smoking. Fry the coated steaks (one at a time if necessary) in the oil and butter until golden brown and crisp, about 5 minutes on each side. Remove to a large ovenproof platter. Heat the oven to 425°F. and place the platter in the oven for 12 to 15 minutes. Remove from the oven, place on heated serving plates, and sprinkle each steak with 2 teaspoons of fresh lemon juice. Serve immediately.

Sautéed Dolphin (Mahi Mahi)
with Lemon-Butter Sauce

As Floridians and Hawaiians know, dolphin is a lovely fish to eat. We like it best simply sautéed and topped with a classic lemon-butter sauce.

FOR TWO

2 fresh dolphin fillets, skin removed

BATTER

1 c. milk	*¼ tsp. freshly ground white*
½ c. flour	*pepper*
1 tsp. salt	*2 large eggs*

½ c. vegetable oil
¼ c. (½ stick) salt butter

LEMON-BUTTER SAUCE

½ c. (1 stick) salt butter
¼ tsp. freshly ground white pepper
1⅓ Tbs. fresh lemon juice

Rinse the fillets under cool running water and dry very thoroughly with paper towels. Combine the ingredients for the batter in a bowl and mix thoroughly with a whisk. Dip the fillets in the batter and place on a wire rack (a cake rack works very well) over a large platter or a surface which can be easily wiped clean later. Allow to dry while you prepare the oil and butter for frying. In a heavy sauté pan heat the oil, then add the butter. Continue heating until the butter is melted, then stir and heat for 1 to 2 minutes longer. Sauté the fillets until light golden brown, about 3 to 4 minutes on the first side and 2 to 3 minutes on the second side. Place on heatproof serving plates and set in a 175°F. oven to keep warm while you prepare the lemon-butter sauce. To prepare the sauce, melt the butter in a small sauce-pan over low heat. Stir in the pepper and lemon juice and heat for 30 seconds longer. Stir again, and remove the pan from the heat. Remove the platters of fillets from the warm oven and spoon about ¼ cup lemon-butter sauce over each plate. Place 1 or 2 lemon wedges to the side of each plate and bring to the table immediately.

Sautéed Sand Dabs

These small, delicate West Coast fish are excellent just sautéed for a minute or two and served hot with the butter from the pan and a small amount of lemon juice.

FOR TWO

6 sand dab fillets, skin removed
½ c. (1 stick) salt butter

⅛ tsp. freshly ground white pepper
1 Tbs. fresh lemon juice

In a sauté pan or skillet melt the butter over medium heat. Add the sand dab fillets and sprinkle with the pepper. Cook over medium heat for 1 to 1½ minutes on each side, then remove to heated plates. Sprinkle about 1½ teaspoons lemon juice over each portion and serve immediately.

Baking Recipes

Oysters Mornay

Oysters Rockefeller

Oysters Bienville

Italian Baked Oysters

Clams Casino

Oysters Casino

Coquilles Saint-Jacques
(Scallops with White Wine
and Mushrooms)

Snails Bourguignonne

Italian Snails with Cheese
(Lumache al Formaggio)

Stuffed Snails
(Escargots Farcis)

Lobster Thermidor

Stuffed Baked Lobster with
Crabmeat

Crabmeat Imperial

Crabmeat au Gratin

Crabmeat Ravigote (Hot)

Lump Crabmeat Hollandaise

Savannah Baked Deviled
Crab

Charleston Shrimp Pie

Norwegian Steamed Fish
Pudding with Dill and
Tomato Sauce

Alsatian Fish and Potato Pie

Marinated Baked King
Mackerel

Florida Red Snapper with
Orange

Mexican Whole Striped Bass
with Adobo Sauce

Roast Eel with Fruit Mustard

9

Baking

The range of baked seafood dishes is spectacular. From the familiar *haute cuisine* snail and oyster dishes, through the hearty Scandinavian fish puddings and French fish pies, and a number of exotic regional dishes, we have included baked seafood dishes and dishes finished in the oven we particularly enjoy.

Baking is one of the best ways to entertain, since almost all baked and oven-finished dishes can be prepared ahead of time just short of the final phase. Indeed, most of the time-consuming work is in the pre-preparation—chopping, puréeing, simmering, or sautéing the ingredients before the final baking. Except for a nice collection of attractive serving dishes, no special equipment besides a standard home oven is needed. Once the dish is in the oven with the temperature and the timer set, the cook can relax; the main work is over.

Some simple cautions about baking should be observed. The temperature of your oven should be checked every month or so with a mercury-type oven thermometer for any wide fluctuations from the indicated temperature. A 10° to 20°F. difference is not serious since different parts of the same oven vary by that much, but 40°F. can be catastrophic with a houseful of guests coming or with one of your own favorite home dishes planned for the evening. Consistency of preparation is also essential in baking since there is no chance to rebalance the ingredients once they are in the oven.

One of the most fascinating aspects of baking is the complete transformation of the separate elements once the baking process begins. The finished baked dish is not the simple sum of the parts you have put in, but a new entity combined under oven heat to form entirely new flavors and aromas. Certain spices change radically according to the liquidity and heat of their surroundings. You cannot adjust the spices in a baked fish as you can in a sautéed one. But once you have worked out a baked dish you love, you can be sure of consistent results every time. These are some of the most remarkable and marvelous dishes of the seafood repertoire, both familiar and exotic.

Basic Baking Techniques

Check oven thermostats periodically with oven thermometer.

For high temperatures preheat oven for 20 minutes.

Unnecessary opening of oven door reduces heat and retards cooking time.

For dishes that are browned on top, check for color no sooner than 5 minutes before minimum time indicated in recipe.

Place aluminum foil under baked dishes that may bubble over.

When baking several dishes at once, increase oven heat by 25°F. or increase baking time by 10 to 15 minutes.

Time carefully.

Use attractive baking dishes that can be brought to the table.

The Pleasures of Seafood 184

Oysters Mornay

French haute cuisine *sauces are seldom used with oysters, reflecting the fact that in France oysters are scarce and expensive. The French are pragmatic in matters of food; if you can't improve on oysters in their natural state, why try? In New Orleans, where oysters are abundant, the repertoire of cooked oyster dishes is enormous. This is our version of one of the few classic French baked oyster dishes, and while nothing in fact surpasses raw oysters on the half shell, this preparation comes close to equaling them. The liquid saved from poaching the oysters is reduced and then becomes part of the sauce along with freshly grated Parmesan cheese. Large scallop shells or ramekins about 5 inches across are ideal for both baking and serving this dish. For those whose only acquaintance with Mornay sauce is in American French restaurants, where it is too often merely a pasty floury paste topped with cheese, this Mornay sauce will be a revelation.*

FOR TWO

1 pint oysters (approximately 18 to 24 oysters) and their liquor
2 Tbs. salt butter
2 Tbs. flour
½ c. hot milk
¼ tsp. salt
⅛ tsp. freshly ground white pepper

1/16 tsp. cayenne
1 Tbs. heavy cream
¼ c. freshly grated Parmesan cheese
2 tsp. butter, cut into small pieces

In a heavy 2 to 3 quart saucepan melt the butter over low heat. Stir in the flour gradually and mix with a whisk or a wooden spoon until smoothly blended. Add the hot milk in a slow steady stream while stirring with a whisk. Cook until the sauce becomes quite thick, always stirring. The sauce will reach its maximum thickness within 3 to 5 minutes. Remove the pan from the heat and add the salt, pepper, and cayenne. Mix once, then add the cream. Return the pan to low heat and cook for about 45 seconds as you mix in the cream, then add the cheese. Stir briskly to blend the cheese into the sauce. When the cheese is fully blended in, the sauce will appear smooth and have no noticeable lumps in it. Remove the pan from the heat once again and set aside while you poach the oysters.

To poach the oysters, put them into a small saucepan along with their liquor. Bring to a simmer over medium-high heat, then reduce the heat and simmer for precisely 1 minute. Place a strainer over a bowl and dump the contents of the pan into it. Allow the oysters to drain thoroughly.

Return the pan containing the sauce to low heat and stir in 2 table-spoons of the hot oyster liquor collected in the bowl. Cook for 4 to 5 minutes, stirring to reduce the sauce a bit. Spoon a thin layer of sauce over the bottom of each ramekin, then place the oysters in scallop shells or ramekins about 5 inches in diameter and spoon the sauce over them evenly. Dot the surface of each portion with 1 tea-spoon of butter cut into small pieces. Set the ramekins on a baking sheet or pan and bake on the middle rack of a preheated 500°F. oven until the sauce bubbles and turns a light golden brown with a few darker spots, about 10 minutes. To serve, set the ramekins on dinner plates.

Oysters Rockefeller

Few seafood creations have been more successful than Oysters Rockefeller. The legend is enormous, the reality even more im-pressive. Antoine's in New Orleans still makes the best Rocke-fellers to be found anywhere, and they are as much loved by natives as by visitors. The dish originated as an alternative to Snails Bourguignonne; snails were scarce in New Orleans and oysters were not, giving the French Creole chefs at Antoine's a chance to go one better on a cherished Old World traditional dish. In many ways Oysters Rockefeller symbolize the very spirit of Creole settlement in the "New France" which was New Orleans—characterized by a willingness to go beyond tradition, and a breathtaking originality. To this day, almost every New Orleans seafood restaurant at least attempts to make Rockefellers. The naming of the dish has two equally convincing explanations: because they were so rich and/or because they were so green. De-licious, easy to prepare at home, and most successful when the sauce is made in large batches and chilled. It improves with a little age.

ROCKEFELLER SAUCE

2 c. (1 lb.) salt butter, softened

2¼ c. very finely chopped cooked spinach (frozen or canned will work as well as fresh)

½ c. very finely chopped fresh parsley

1 c. very finely chopped green onion tops

¼ c. very finely chopped celery (do not use the tougher, thicker outer stalks—they tend to be too watery)

1½ tsp. salt

1 tsp. freshly ground white pepper

1 tsp. marjoram

1 tsp. basil

1 tsp. cayenne

1 tsp. freshly ground anise seed

½ c. Pernod or Herbsaint

---

4 doz. oysters on the half shell, drained
8 pans rock salt or ice cream salt

Cream the butter lightly in a mixing bowl with a wooden spoon or a pastry blender. Purée the spinach, parsley, green onion tops, and celery in an electric blender on high speed for 1 minute. (If necessary, purée in small batches, then mix the puréed greens together.) Add the puréed greens to the softened butter. Add the remaining ingredients and blend very thoroughly. Place a large piece of wax paper on a flat surface and heap the mixture from the bowl onto it. Roll out to a thickness of ¼ inch. Cover with another piece of wax paper. Roll up and refrigerate for at least 3 hours before using. Preheat the oven to 500°F. When ready to cook the oysters, take them out of their shells. Remove any remaining pieces of shell with your fingers and place the oysters on paper towels to remove the last bit of moisture. Wash the shells thoroughly and dry well. Place a drained oyster on each shell and set them 6 to a pan on rock salt. Unroll the chilled roll of Rockefeller sauce and cut 4 dozen rectangles about 2 inches by 1¼ inches. Roll up and return the remaining sauce to the refrigerator. Place a rectangle of sauce over each oyster and bake in a 500°F. oven for 14 to 16 minutes, until the sauce bubbles and becomes lightly browned on top. Set the pans on dinner plates and allow to cool for 3 to 5 minutes before serving.

Baking 187

Oysters Bienville

Another cherished New Orleans baked oyster dish, more difficult to prepare than the Rockefellers. In their original form, Bienvilles require the spicy boiled shrimp many New Orleans restaurants normally have on hand in the course of an evening's cooking. At times, some shredded lump crabmeat is added as well. We worked out this version which retains the spirit and flavor of the original Bienvilles in the spicy béchamel thickened with fresh egg yolks but does not require the shrimp. It's ironic that as grand a dish as Oysters Bienville probably originated as a way of using leftover shellfish.

FOR FOUR

BIENVILLE SAUCE

½ c. (1 stick) salt butter

1 c. finely chopped green onions

¼ c. finely minced parsley

1½ tsp. finely minced garlic

½ c. flour

½ c. heavy cream

1½ c. milk

4 large egg yolks, well beaten

¼ c. dry sherry

1 tsp. salt

1 tsp. freshly ground white pepper

½ tsp. cayenne

⅔ c. finely chopped mushrooms (if canned are used, drain very thoroughly)

3 Tbs. finely crumbled fried lean bacon (optional)

---

2 doz. oysters on the half shell, drained

4 pans rock salt

To prepare the sauce, melt the butter in a large heavy saucepan over low heat. Add the green onions, parsley, and garlic and cook, stirring frequently, until quite soft, about 10 minutes. Gradually stir in the flour and mix with a wooden spoon until smooth. Add the cream and milk slowly, stirring constantly until the mixture is quite smooth, then add the egg yolks, sherry, salt, pepper, and cayenne. Blend thoroughly, then continue cooking over low heat until the mixture begins to thicken. Stir in the mushrooms and, if used, the bacon, then cook over low heat for about 4 to 6 minutes, until the sauce is quite thick. Spoon the sauce into a large, shallow porcelain or glass dish, to a depth of 1½ to 2 inches. Let cool for a few minutes at room temperature, then cover with plastic wrap and refrigerate for at least 1½ hours.

Half an hour before you plan to bake the oysters, preheat the oven to 500°F.

To prepare the oysters for baking, wash the shells well and dry them. Put an oyster on each shell and set them 6 to a pan on the rock salt. Spoon 1 heaping tablespoon of sauce evenly over each oyster. Bake for 15 to 18 minutes or until well browned on top. To serve, set the pans on dinner plates.

Italian Baked Oysters

One of New Orleans' legendary Italian restaurants is located in a roadside shack about 17 miles from the city. Mosca's restaurant combines New Orleans seafood with Roman cooking genius and their oysters Mosca is a prized local dish. This is a version of that simple and completely addictive baked oyster dish.

FOR FOUR

1½ pt. freshly shucked oysters (about 2½ doz. medium-sized oysters), drained
¼ c. (½ stick) salt butter
¼ c. olive oil
⅔ c. Italian bread crumbs
½ tsp. salt
½ tsp. freshly ground black pepper

⅛ tsp. cayenne
½ tsp. tarragon
½ tsp. oregano
2 Tbs. finely minced fresh parsley
2 tsp. finely minced garlic
2 Tbs. finely chopped green onion tops

In a heavy saucepan, melt the butter over low heat. Mix in the olive oil and heat for a few minutes longer. Add all the other ingredients except the oysters and mix well, then remove the pan from the heat. Place the well-drained oysters in individual ramekins or gratin dishes and spoon equal portions of the sauce over each. Bake in a preheated 450°F. oven until the topping is well browned, about 18 minutes. Set the ramekins on dinner plates and serve immediately.

Clams Casino

We remember fondly many trips to Locke-Ober in Boston for Clams Casino, the classic dish of the baked clam canon. Clams are much harder (literally) to cook than oysters, something we didn't fully appreciate until we began experimenting with clams in some of our favorite oyster dishes. Most of them didn't work because clams get tougher as they cook and are not as juicy as oysters. Which simply makes us admire even more this rare haute cuisine American classic.

FOR TWO

1 doz. freshly opened hard shell clams, drained

1 doz. well-scrubbed clam shells

2 pie pans filled with rock salt to a depth of about ½ inch

SAUCE

2 oz. lean breakfast bacon (about 3 slices), cut into 1 inch pieces

⅓ c. finely minced green onion tops

6 Tbs. (¾ stick) salt butter

¼ tsp. freshly ground black pepper

¼ tsp. ground thyme

1 tsp. fresh lemon juice

1 Tbs. bread crumbs

TOPPING

½ c. bread crumbs

Begin preheating the oven to 475°F. Place the drained clams on half shells and set them 6 to a pan on the rock salt. To prepare the sauce, cook the bacon over medium heat in a heavy sauté pan until the lean portions are lightly browned and most of the fat has been rendered in the pan. Add the green onions and stir. Add the butter and continue cooking until melted. Stir thoroughly, then add the pepper, thyme, lemon juice, and 1 tablespoon bread crumbs. Toss to mix very thoroughly, then remove the pan from the heat. Spoon the sauce evenly over the clams, then sprinkle each one with 2 teaspoons of bread crumbs. Bake in the preheated 475°F. oven until browned, about 13 to 15 minutes. To serve, set the pans on dinner plates.

The Pleasures of Seafood 190

Oysters Casino

Somewhat different because oysters do not have the nutty flavor of clams, but a delicious variation nonetheless.

FOR TWO

Prepare as directed for Clams Casino, substituting 1 dozen freshly opened and drained oysters for the clams and the deeper half of the oyster shells for the clam shells. Add ¼ teaspoon mace to the sauce along with the ground thyme.

Coquilles Saint-Jacques
Scallops with White Wine and Mushrooms

This classic French scallop dish has suffered the fate of many famous French preparations. Listed de rigueur *on many fancy restaurant menus, it is known to many only through versions containing leftover scallops, shrimp, or fish embedded in a tasteless flour and water paste. The real dish is a work of genius, more suited in most instances to the care and attention lavished on it by the home cook than to the unfortunate shortcuts and overly large batch sizes of restaurant kitchens. The fine heady sauce is made from the reduced poaching liquid, heavy cream, and freshly grated Parmesan cheese. Expertly frozen scallops work perfectly; defrost them quickly, still wrapped, in a basin of cool water and dry very thoroughly before cooking. Coquilles Saint-Jacques is traditionally served in scallop shells; it is also attractive in individual baking ramekins.*

FOR FOUR AS A FIRST COURSE; FOR TWO AS A MAIN DISH

COURT BOUILLON

¾ c. dry white wine	¼ tsp. marjoram
¼ c. water	¼ tsp. salt
1½ Tbs. salt butter	⅛ tsp. freshly ground black pepper
2 parsley sprigs	
½ small white onion	3 white peppercorns
1 small bay leaf, broken up	

---

1 lb. scallops, rinsed and thoroughly drained

Baking 191

SAUCE

6 Tbs. chopped mushrooms
(if canned are used, drain very
thoroughly)
2 Tbs. salt butter
2 Tbs. flour
¾ c. scalded milk
⅛ tsp. freshly ground white
pepper

¼ tsp. salt
¼ tsp. nutmeg
4 tsp. grated Parmesan cheese
6 Tbs. heavy cream
1 tsp. fresh lemon juice

Combine the ingredients for the court bouillon in a heavy 2½ to 3 quart saucepan. Bring to a boil over high heat, then add the scallops. Cook just until tender, 4 to 5 minutes for medium to large ones, 1½ to 2 minutes for tiny bay scallops. Place a fine mesh strainer over a large bowl and empty the contents of the pan into it. Place the scallops in a loosely covered dish or bowl and set in a 200°F. oven to keep warm while you complete the sauce.

Return the strained court bouillon to the pan and cook until reduced to about ⅓ cup. Add the chopped mushrooms, stir, then remove the pan from the heat and set aside. In a heavy 2 to 3 quart saucepan melt the butter over medium heat, then reduce the heat to low and gradually add the flour, stirring evenly and quickly with a wooden spoon to keep the roux smooth. Remove the pan from the heat and add the milk. Stir briskly with a whisk and return the pan to the heat, still stirring. Cook until the béchamel thickens, about 2 minutes. Remove the pan from the heat again. Add the reduced court bouillon and the mushrooms. Cut the cooked scallops in half if they are small, into cubes approximately ¾ inch across if they are large. Add the cut-up scallops to the sauce, along with the pepper, salt, and nutmeg. Return the pan to low heat and cook, stirring frequently. After 3 to 4 minutes add the grated cheese and cook for 2 minutes more. Add the cream 1 tablespoon at a time, stirring gently, to thin the sauce out a bit. Cook until completely warmed through, 2 to 3 minutes longer, then remove the pan from the heat. Add the lemon juice and stir to mix.

Preheat the broiler to very hot and set 4 scallop shells, each 4½ to 5 inches in diameter, on a shallow baking pan. Place the fluted wide edges of the scallop shells on the rim of the pan, if the rim is no higher than ½ to ¾ inch. If the rim is too high, wedge the fluted edges against the inner sides of the pan at a height of about ½ inch, using some gravel or rock salt as a support. (This will prevent the shells from tipping over and spilling their contents when you fill them.)

Spoon the mixture evenly into the shells, then set the pan about 4 inches from the source of heat and glaze until lightly browned on top, about 4 minutes.

Snails Bourguignonne

On the name of this classic dish: the snails rather than the wine come from Burgundy. In America we are delighted to get good quality snails and haven't the luxury of arguing, as the French do, over regional differences in snails. In France as well as America the majority of snail dishes are prepared with canned snails. We have experimented with a wide variety of canned snails and found some noticeable differences in flavor as well as size. The best snails are the smallest ones, packed 2 dozen to the can. Unfortunately, they are almost impossible to find, even in gourmet food stores. More widely available are the giant and the large sizes, 12 and 18 to the can respectively. The best way to overcome the less desirable characteristics of these overfed farm snails is to poach them first; this removes most of the unpleasant fat and the "canned" flavor.

There are several ways to serve snails properly. The elaborate classic method with shells, metal snail plates, and tongs makes for an agreeable ceremony. The newer ovenproof snail dishes from France with depressions for 4 to 6 snails simplify the stuffing while preserving the flavorful concentration of snail butter around each individual snail. You can also use small baking ramekins and put 4 to 6 snails in each one; increase the quantity of minced shallots by half to keep the snail butter from becoming too liquid. One last tip: we've found that cutting the giant or large-sized snails in half before poaching gives you the perfect size for all baked snail dishes.

2 DOZEN SNAILS, FOR FOUR TO SIX

24 small or 12 giant or large canned snails
(cut each of the giant or large snails in half)

POACHING LIQUID

1 c. dry white wine   *8 white peppercorns*
1 c. water   *½ tsp. salt*

SNAIL BUTTER

6 Tbs. salt butter, softened
8 tsp. finely minced parsley
2 tsp. finely minced garlic
4 tsp. finely minced shallots

1 tsp. freshly ground white pepper
¼ tsp. salt
⅛ tsp. nutmeg

Drain the snails thoroughly. Cut in half if using giant or large snails. Place in a small saucepan along with the ingredients for the poaching liquid. Bring to a boil, cover loosely, reduce the heat to low, and cook for 5 minutes. Drain the snails and dry very thoroughly between several layers of paper towels.

To prepare the snail butter, cream the softened butter in a bowl with the back of a wooden spoon or a pastry blender. Add the remaining ingredients and continue creaming until the ingredients are evenly blended. Finish the creaming with a wooden spatula or spoon, testing for even distribution of ingredients by spreading some of the butter across the inner side of the bowl: the color should be distributed in even flecks and there should be no large areas without green in them. If necessary, mix for a minute longer.

To prepare the snails for baking, place a small ball or "nut" of snail butter (about the size of a hazelnut) inside each snail shell or at the bottom of each depression in an ovenproof snail plate. Put a snail or half a snail inside each shell or in each depression of the snail plate. Close each shell or top each depression with another "nut" of snail butter. Pack the butter into the shells with the tip of your finger; gently press the butter flat over each depression with the tip of a spatula or the back of a small spoon.

To bake, set the filled snail shells on metal snail plates; place the filled snail dishes on a flat baking sheet. Bake in a preheated 425°F. oven for 10 to 12 minutes, until the snail butter is bubbling visibly and beginning to brown slightly where it is exposed to the heat. Set the metal dishes or snail plates on dinner plates to serve. Supply snail forks (or seafood forks) for both. Supply snail tongs for holding the stuffed shells. Serve hot French bread for soaking up the sauce.

The Pleasures of Seafood 194

Italian Snails with Cheese
Lumache al Formaggio

The French may seem to have a monopoly on the great snail dishes—until you first taste this masterful Italian creation. The sauce, made with butter, olive oil, fresh ripe tomatoes, Parmesan cheese, and white wine is the equal of the classic French snail butter. Serve in any of the three ways described in Snails Bourguignonne.

FOR FOUR

2 Tbs. salt butter

2 Tbs. olive oil plus 2 tsp.

2 tsp. finely minced garlic

1 Tbs. finely minced parsley

2 large ripe tomatoes, parboiled and peeled

1 tsp. dried basil or 2 Tbs. fresh

½ tsp. nutmeg

1 c. freshly grated Parmesan cheese plus an additional ½ c. for the final topping

1 tsp. salt

1¼ tsp. freshly ground black pepper

2⅔ Tbs. dry white wine

2 Tbs. tomato paste

---

24 small or 12 giant or large canned snails
(cut each of the giant or large snails in half)

POACHING LIQUID

1 c. dry white wine

1 c. water

8 white peppercorns

½ tsp. salt

Melt the butter in a saucepan. Add 2 tablespoons olive oil and mix. Sauté the garlic and parsley over low heat until soft, then chop the peeled tomatoes and add them to the pan. Cook until very soft, stirring with a wooden spoon, about 12 minutes. Add the basil and nutmeg and mix. Sprinkle in 1 cup of the grated cheese and stir to mix evenly. Add the salt, pepper, white wine, tomato paste, and 2 teaspoons olive oil. Mix very thoroughly and cook over low heat, stirring frequently, for 3 to 4 minutes. Remove the pan from the heat. Allow to cool at room temperature for about 5 minutes. Prepare the snails for baking as directed for Snails Bourguignonne. Cover the opening of each shell or the top of each depression with the remaining ½ cup grated cheese. Bake in a preheated 425°F. oven for 10 to 12 minutes, until the cheese is bubbly and lightly browned.

Stuffed Snails
Escargots Farcis

An unusal country dish from the south of France, snails topped ("stuffed") with a butter, bread crumb, and white wine sauce containing dried cèpes, French mushrooms with a marvelous nutty flavor. The cèpes are available dried in 1 ounce packages at better markets throughout America. Rather than being reconstituted with water, in this dish they are briefly sautéed in their dried state, giving the topping a crunchy texture which sets off the delicately spicy flavor. Serve Stuffed Snails in individual oven-proof ramekins.

FOR FOUR

2 doz. small or 1 doz. giant or large snails (cut the larger ones in half)

6 Tbs. salt butter

½ oz. dried cèpes, broken up, or other dark dried mushrooms

4 tsp. finely minced parsley

1 tsp. finely minced garlic

½ tsp. freshly ground white pepper

2 Tbs. bread crumbs

2 tsp. dry white wine

Poach the snails as directed for Snails Bourguignonne, then drain and place in small ramekins. Melt the butter over medium heat in a small saucepan and sauté the *cèpes* for about 3 minutes, then add the parsley, garlic, and pepper. Stir, reduce the heat to low, and cook for 2 minutes, then sprinkle in the bread crumbs. Stir to distribute the crumbs, then add the white wine. Remove the pan from the heat. Stir again, then spoon evenly over the portions of snails. Bake in a preheated 425°F. oven for 7 to 8 minutes. To serve, set the ramekins on plates.

Lobster Thermidor

A dish that has unfortunately become a way of stretching leftover lobster meat in most restaurants. The original dish, a version of which is given here, has a rich delicate sauce that sets off freshly and carefully cooked lobster meat to considerable advantage.

2 Florida lobsters, each 1¼ to 1¾ lb.

6 Tbs. (¾ stick) salt butter

½ c. sliced mushrooms (if canned are used, drain very thoroughly)

½ tsp. salt

¼ tsp. freshly ground black pepper

½ c. bread crumbs

2 large egg yolks, lightly beaten

⅜ tsp. dry mustard

¼ tsp. nutmeg

1/16 tsp. cayenne

1 Tbs. finely minced fresh parsley

2 Tbs. finely chopped, drained pimiento

2 tsp. Worcestershire sauce

⅓ c. dry white wine

1 Tbs. Cognac or brandy

1 c. heavy cream

⅓ c. freshly grated Parmesan cheese

Cook and clean the lobsters as directed for Boiled Florida Lobster. Remove the small and large tentacles and extract whatever usable meat you find in them. Remove the meat from the bodies and the greenish-gold liver from the head. If you are planning to use the shells for baking the dish, rinse and clean them thoroughly, then dry and set aside. Begin preheating the oven to 375°F.

Melt ¼ cup of the butter over low heat in a heavy 3 to 4 quart saucepan. Add the mushrooms, salt, and pepper and sauté for 2 minutes. Add the bread crumbs and egg yolks and toss with a fork. Remove the pan from the heat. Stir in the mustard and nutmeg. Mix thoroughly. Add the reserved lobster meat, cayenne, parsley, pimiento, and Worcestershire. Mix again and return the pan to low heat. Cook for 1 minute, then stir in the wine and Cognac. Heat for a few seconds, then gradually stir in the cream with a folding motion, lifting the mixture from the bottom with a wooden spoon. Do not beat or you will remove too much air and reduce the fluffiness. Fill the lobster shells with the mixture, then sprinkle evenly with grated cheese. Dot the surface evenly with the remaining 2 tablespoons butter. Place the shells on a shallow baking pan side by side to keep them from wobbling. If necessary, use rock salt or pebbles in the pan to enable you to nestle the filled shells firmly in place for baking. Bake for 15 to 20 minutes, until bubbly and browned on top.

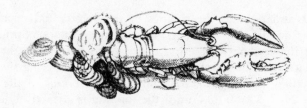

Stuffed Baked Lobster
with Crabmeat

Until we prepared good Florida lobsters at home we thought they were among the toughest and driest of shellfish. It turned out that they were not at all tough and that the meat had a delicate moist texture and a superb flavor. Overcooking them seems to be a widespread practice. Treated with respect and filled with a crabmeat stuffing or dressing, they are delicious.

FOR TWO

2 *small Florida lobsters or 1 large lobster*
½ *c. (1 stick) salt butter*

CRABMEAT STUFFING

5 *Tbs. salt butter*
½ *lb. lump crabmeat*
¾ *tsp. salt*
½ *tsp. freshly ground white pepper*
¼ *tsp. dry mustard*

⅓ *c. white bread, soaked in water and squeezed dry*
3 *Tbs. minced chives*
¼ *tsp. mace*
1 *tsp. Worcestershire sauce*
2 *tsp. lemon juice*

TOPPING

½ *c. bread crumbs*
¼ *c. melted butter*

Split and clean the lobsters as directed for Broiled Stuffed Florida Lobster. Also remove the matter above the solid segment of meat as directed. Melt the ½ cup butter and pour evenly over the meaty portions. (You will need 2 halves per portion if the lobsters are small, 1 half if they are large.) Begin preheating the oven to 425°F.

To prepare the stuffing, melt 5 tablespoons butter in a sauté pan over low heat, then add the crabmeat. Toss gently with a fork to distribute the butter evenly without breaking up the lumps. Add the remaining ingredients for the stuffing and toss again briefly. Cook over low heat for 3 minutes, stirring very gently.

Spoon the stuffing into the cavities of the lobster halves and pack down very gently with the back of a wooden spoon. Sprinkle the surface of the stuffing with bread crumbs and baste with the melted butter. Place the stuffed lobster halves on a heavy baking sheet or in a large shallow baking dish. Bake on the middle rack of the oven at 425°F. for 25 to 30 minutes, until the topping is attractively browned

The Pleasures of Seafood 198

and the lobster meat is tender when pierced with a fork. Remove from the oven and set on heated plates. Garnish with lemon wedges and serve immediately.

Crabmeat Imperial

Our favorite Crabmeat Imperial is served at O'Donnell's seafood restaurant in Washington, D.C., and this version is based on fond memories of the dish served there. The butter sauce with capers has always seemed to us more successful than the usual one with pimientos; the tartness of the capers sets off the rich buttery flavor of the crabmeat in a strikingly effective way. Mix the ingredients with a light touch so as to leave the mixture fluffy, and heap rather than pack it down when filling the shells for baking.

FOR TWO

¾ lb. backfin lump crabmeat
5 Tbs. salt butter
¾ tsp. salt
¼ tsp. freshly ground white pepper

5 Tbs. drained capers
bread crumbs for topping
3 Tbs. melted salt butter, approximately

Melt the butter in a heavy sauté pan over low heat. Shred the crabmeat very gently, using 2 forks or your fingers, then add it to the butter in the pan. Toss gently with a fork, then add the salt, pepper, and capers. Toss gently again, then remove the pan from the heat. Preheat the oven to 400°F. Heap the mixture loosely on scallop shells (or foil shells) about 5 inches across, then sprinkle lightly and evenly with bread crumbs. Sprinkle the crumb topping with melted butter. Set the shells on a small baking pan with the fluted edges resting on the shallow rim to keep them from tipping over, or place a ⅜ inch layer of rock salt in the bottom of a shallow baking dish and nestle the filled shells in the salt to keep them level. Bake at 400°F. until the topping is golden brown, about 20 to 25 minutes. To serve, set the shells on plates.

Crabmeat au Gratin

A classic combination.

FOR TWO

½ lb. lump crabmeat

¼ c. thinly sliced green onion tops

1 tsp. finely minced fresh parsley

2 Tbs. plus 2 tsp. salt butter

¼ tsp. salt

⅛ tsp. freshly ground white pepper

¼ c. heavy cream

2 Tbs. milk

½ tsp. Cognac or brandy

1 c. freshly grated sharp Cheddar cheese

Sauté the green onion tops and parsley in the 2 tablespoons butter over low heat until tender, 6 to 8 minutes, then remove the pan from the heat. Add the salt, pepper, cream, and milk and mix well. Return the pan to very low heat and warm the mixture, stirring. Again remove the pan from the heat. Mix in the Cognac, then add the lump crabmeat and mix gently but thoroughly. Put half the crabmeat and sauce mixture into each of 2 individual ramekins. Sprinkle each with ¼ cup of the grated Cheddar, then dot the top of each with 1 teaspoon butter. Bake in a preheated 375°F. oven for 12 to 15 minutes, then remove from the oven and sprinkle another ¼ cup grated Cheddar over each ramekin. Place the ramekins under a preheated broiler for 2 to 3 minutes, 3½ inches from the source of heat, until the cheese is melted and begins to glaze. Serve immediately.

Crabmeat Ravigote (Hot)

A classic crabmeat casserole, with a butter, cream, and white wine sauce heightened by the tartness of white tarragon vinegar. If you cannot obtain white tarragon vinegar, substitute a good quality white wine or champagne vinegar and add to the sauce ¼ teaspoon tarragon ground very fine with a mortar and pestle. Bake and serve in individual gratin dishes.

---

1 lb. choice lump crabmeat	¼ tsp. freshly ground white
¼ c. (½ stick) salt butter, plus	pepper
4 tsp.	a few grains of cayenne
3 Tbs. flour	¼ c. dry white wine
½ c. milk	2 Tbs. white tarragon vinegar
⅓ c. heavy cream	⅔ c. thinly sliced green onion
¾ tsp. salt	tops

In a heavy saucepan, melt ¼ cup of the butter over low heat. Gradually stir in the flour, mixing constantly with a wooden spoon or a whisk to keep the mixture smooth. Remove the pan from the heat. In a separate, smaller saucepan combine the milk and cream and heat to just short of a boil. Gradually pour the milk and cream into the pan containing the butter and flour, stirring constantly to prevent lumps from forming. Return the pan to low heat. Add the salt, pepper, and cayenne and mix in. Continue cooking over low heat until the sauce begins to thicken, then add the wine, vinegar, and green onion tops. Blend very thoroughly. Add the crabmeat and cook over low heat, stirring very gently from time to time, until the crabmeat is just heated through, about 3 minutes. Remove the pan from the heat. Preheat the oven to 375°F.

Spoon the mixure into individual gratin dishes. Cut the remaining 4 teaspoons of butter into very small pieces and dot the top of each portion with butter. Bake in 375°F. oven for 14 to 16 minutes, until the butter topping bubbles and a light brown glaze begins to form over the surface of each portion. Remove from the oven and set the gratin dishes on plates. Serve immediately.

Lump Crabmeat Hollandaise

A simple baked lump crabmeat dish transformed with a spicy, glazed hollandaise. Bake and serve in small individual gratin dishes or a single large one.

1½ lb. lump crabmeat	½ tsp. freshly ground white
1½ Tbs. salt butter,	pepper
approximately	2 c. hollandaise sauce

Rub the inside of 4 small gratin dishes or 1 large dish generously with butter. Fill with lump crabmeat and sprinkle evenly with white pepper. Set in a preheated 275°F. oven to warm while you prepare the hollandaise sauce. Prepare the sauce as directed for Broiled Redfish Hollandaise, tripling the quantities given there. Set the blender container in a basin or bowl of warm water and remove the crabmeat from the oven. Cover the crabmeat loosely with foil to keep warm. Turn on the broiler and allow to heat for about 5 to 8 minutes. Spoon ½ cup hollandaise evenly over each portion of crabmeat, or over the entire dish if you are using a single large one. Set under the broiler about 4 inches from the source of heat and heat just until the hollandaise forms a light brown glaze with a few darker specks, about 1 to 2 minutes. Remove from the broiler immediately. To serve, set individual dishes on dinner plates, or bring 4 heated plates to the table along with the single large dish of crabmeat and carefully lift the portions, glaze and all, onto them with a large serving spoon.

Savannah Baked Deviled Crab

Delicately spicy with a crunchy brown crust. Packaged cracker crumbs are too fine; it is best to make your own in a blender. Be sure to refrigerate the mixture for 30 minutes or more before shaping the cakes, for maximum flavor.

FOR THREE

½ lb. crabmeat, shredded
1 large egg, well beaten
5 Tbs. very finely chopped onion
2 tsp. Worcestershire sauce
½ tsp. dry mustard
¼ tsp. salt
1 Tbs. mayonnaise

1 Tbs. fresh lemon juice
⅛ tsp. freshly ground black pepper
¼ tsp. Tabasco
¼ c. coarse plain cracker crumbs (made in a blender)
3 Tbs. melted butter, approximately

Combine the ingredients for the deviled crab in a large bowl. Toss with a fork to mix thoroughly. Cover the bowl with plastic wrap and refrigerate for 30 to 40 minutes.

Begin preheating the oven to 375°F. Heap the crab mixture onto 3 crab or scallop shells and smooth down gently with your fingers to make a dome-shaped top. Sprinkle each one with about 1½ teaspoons cracker crumbs and then drizzle with about 1 tablespoon melted butter. Set the shells on a baking pan or cookie sheet. Bake in 375°F. oven for 18 to 20 minutes, until browned on top. To serve, set the shells on plates.

Charleston Shrimp Pie

Our favorite version of this old-time dish, made with raw shrimp, chopped vegetables, and a generous dose of seasonings, then baked slowly as a deep dish casserole. Shrimp Pie can be prepared ahead of time, refrigerated, then reheated slowly in the oven about 45 minutes before serving.

FOR FOUR

2 lb. fresh shrimp in the shell, peeled and deveined (1¼ lb., approximately, after peeling)

3 slices white bread, crusts removed and cut up, then soaked in 1 c. milk

2 large eggs, beaten

2 Tbs. butter, melted

½ c. chopped white onions

¼ c. chopped green pepper

1 Tbs. finely minced parsley

1 tsp. Worcestershire sauce

1 tsp. salt

¼ tsp. freshly ground black pepper

⅛ tsp. mace

scant 1/16 tsp. cayenne

1 Tbs. dry sherry (Manzanilla)

Combine all the ingredients in a bowl and mix gently but thoroughly with a wooden spoon, lifting from the bottom to the top as you mix. Butter thoroughly the inner surface of a 2 to 2½ quart casserole, then fill with the shrimp mixture. Bake in a preheated 375°F. oven for 40 to 45 minutes, until nicely browned on top. To serve, bring the casserole to the table and spoon the portions onto heated plates.

To serve later, allow the casserole to cool at room temperature for about 12 to 15 minutes, then cover and refrigerate. To reheat, uncover and set in a low (325°F.) oven for about 30 to 35 minutes, until thoroughly warmed through.

Norwegian Steamed Fish Pudding
with Dill and Tomato Sauce

We find this the best of the Scandinavian fish puddings. It can also be served chilled, but we much prefer it hot. You don't need a food grinder or food processor to prepare this dish, although they do help some. An ordinary blender will give you the proper texture; it just takes a little longer. Any 2 to 3 quart mold— fish mold, bundt pan, square pan—will work nicely. For steaming, set the mold in a pan with some water in it, then cover just the mold with aluminum foil. The dill and tomato sauce is a perfect complement to this delicate, delicious dish.

FOR SIX TO EIGHT

FISH PUDDING

2 to 2¼ lb. fresh cod or haddock fillets, skin removed

1½ c. heavy cream

⅓ c. milk

1 tsp. salt

¾ tsp. freshly ground white pepper

⅛ tsp. nutmeg

butter for greasing the mold

flour in a shaker for dusting the mold

DILL AND TOMATO SAUCE

MAKES 1 CUP

½ c. mayonnaise

3½ Tbs. tomato paste

3 Tbs. milk

¾ tsp. sugar

¾ tsp. salt

1 tsp. freshly ground white pepper

1 tsp. freshly gound dill weed (ground with a mortar and pestle)

1 tsp. fresh lemon juice

Cut the fish into large pieces. Put about ¼ to ⅓ pound fish into the blender container. Add 3 tablespoons cream. Cover the blender and turn on high for 2 minutes, then off. Uncover and scrape down the sides of the container. Repeat. Add several teaspoons of milk. Blend on high again. Spoon the contents of the container into a large mixing bowl. Repeat until all the fish is puréed. Add the remaining cream to the bowl. Mix with a hand electric mixer at low speed or a whisk for 4 to 5 minutes, then add the seasonings. Mix for 5 minutes longer.

Butter the inside of a 2 to 3 quart mold or bundt pan. Dust evenly with flour. (Shake out any excess flour by inverting the mold over the sink and rapping it sharply with your fingers.) Turn the pudding into the mold; distribute it evenly and pat the surface flat with a spatula. Set the mold in a large saucepan one-third filled with water. The water should come to about ¾ inch from the top of the saucepan when the mold is placed in it. Cut a piece of aluminum foil to cover the mold and overlap about 1 inch all around. Tuck down all around. Set on the middle rack of a preheated 325°F. oven and bake for 1 hour.

To make the dill and tomato sauce, combine all the ingredients in a small stainless steel or porcelain bowl. Mix with a whisk for 4 to 5 minutes, until evenly blended and very smooth. Cover the bowl and refrigerate for at least 1 hour before serving.

Remove the fish pudding from the oven. Tip the mold gently over the sink to drain off excess liquid, then set on a cake rack to cool for 5 minutes. Place a large plate over the mold and invert. The pudding will slip easily onto the plate. Soak up any additional liquid with paper towels. Serve hot in slices with dill and tomato sauce spooned to one side.

If you have any pudding left over, refrigerate it and reheat the next day as follows: put the entire piece of pudding into a small shallow baking dish. Add 2 to 3 teaspoons of water. Place the dish on a large piece of aluminum foil and fold the edges together tightly above, but not touching, the top of the pudding. Set in a 350° F. oven for 20 to 25 minutes or until heated through.

Alsatian Fish and Potato Pie

Our favorite fish and potato pie. This French version has a single thin bottom crust and an attractive nutmeg and butter glaze that forms during baking.

FOR FOUR

THIN PASTRY CRUST

1¼ c. sifted flour	¼ c. (½ stick) salt butter
½ tsp. salt	¼ c. ice water, more if necessary

FILLING

1 lb. fresh haddock or cod, filleted, skin removed, cut into 1 inch pieces

coarse salt for sprinkling

1 Tbs. salt butter, plus 2 tsp. for dotting

1 oz. slab bacon, finely chopped

1 c. chopped onions

1 Tbs. minced chives

1 lb. boiled potatoes,* peeled, sliced ¼ inch thick

¼ c. heavy cream

1 large egg

¼ c. sour cream

⅜ tsp. freshly ground white pepper

¾ tsp. nutmeg

To prepare the crust, sift the flour and salt into a large wide bowl. Cut in the butter with a knife or spatula. Blend by rubbing the flour and butter together gently with your fingertips until the butter is evenly distributed and the flour appears mealy. Add ¼ cup ice water and work the mixture with your hands until it forms a ball. If necessary, sprinkle in very small amounts of additional ice water, just until the pastry sticks together. Do not allow it to become too doughy or sticky. Wrap the ball of pastry with wax paper and refrigerate for about 25 minutes.

To roll out the pastry, flour a work surface, your rolling pin, and your hands. Press down on the ball of pastry from the center outward with the rolling pin, giving the pastry a one-quarter turn at intervals, until you have an approximately circular shape which is ⅛ inch thick and at least 10 inches in diameter. Using a sharp knife, cut the dough into a 10 inch circle. Place in a 9 inch pie pan or tart mold. It will overhang the edge about ½ inch. Fold the overhang under and pinch at ½ inch intervals all around to form a fluted edge. If desired, cover the crust with a piece of aluminum foil and fill the center space with pebbles or dried beans (this will help it keep its shape) and bake in a preheated 425°F. oven for about 7 to 9 minutes. Or place the unbaked dough in its pan in the freezer while you prepare the filling.

To prepare the filling, sprinkle the pieces of fish with coarse salt and refrigerate for about 15 to 20 minutes. Meanwhile, melt 1 table-

---

* To boil potatoes, bring approximately 2½ quarts of salted water to a rolling boil, then add the potatoes. Boil for 15 minutes or until you can pierce the potatoes with a fork using some pressure. Do not overcook them. Dump into a colander set in the sink, then rinse under cool running water for 1 minute. Allow to cool down sufficiently to be handled comfortably, about 8 to 10 minutes longer, then peel off the skin. (It will pull off easily.) Cut out any dark eyes or brown spots, then slice.

spoon of butter in a sauté pan and add the chopped slab bacon. Cook until the bacon has rendered most of its fat, about 5 minutes, then add the chopped onions. Sauté, stirring frequently, until the onions begin to turn brown, then remove the pan from the heat. Sprinkle in the chives and mix thoroughly. Remove the fish from the refrigerator, rinse off all the salt, then dry thoroughly with paper towels.

To fill the pie, arrange a layer of potato slices on the bottom, cover with a layer of fish pieces, and top with a layer of sautéed onions and some of the butter from the sauté pan. Repeat the layers one or two more times, until all the fish and sautéed onions are used up, then top with a layer of potatoes. Beat the cream and egg together in a bowl, then add the sour cream and gently mix it in with a folding motion. Add the pepper and mix, then pour the contents of the bowl over the top of the filling. Sprinkle the nutmeg evenly over the top of the pie, then dot with the remaining 2 teaspoons butter. Bake on the bottom rack of a preheated 350°F. oven for 40 to 45 minutes.

To serve, allow to cool on a rack for 4 to 5 minutes, then cut into wedges using a serrated knife or the edge of a spatula. Lift the portions carefully with a pie server or spatula onto heated plates.

Marinated Baked King Mackerel

King mackerel sliced into steaks, then marinated for at least 8 hours. An hour before serving, just stir the marinade, dot the surface with butter, and set the dish in the oven.

FOR FOUR TO SIX

4 king mackerel steaks, sliced ½ inch thick

MARINADE

¼ c. fresh lime juice
¾ tsp. freshly ground black pepper
¾ tsp. salt
2 Tbs. thinly sliced green onion tops
½ tsp. sugar

¼ tsp. mace
1 small carrot, peeled and cut into ¼ inch slices
1 small white onion, sliced, ⅛ inch thick
¼ c. dry white wine
3 Tbs. water

5 Tbs. salt butter

Place the mackerel steaks flat in an attractive sauté pan or shallow baking dish just large enough to hold them comfortably. (The pan should be stainless steel lined; any other metal will produce a strange taste in contact with a marinade. Porcelain enamel over cast iron, as in pots made by Le Creuset, is also suitable here, as well as any ceramic baking dish.) Top with the marinade ingredients and stir gently to distribute evenly over and around the mackerel steaks. Cover the pan or dish with several layers of plastic wrap and refrigerate for at least 8 hours, or overnight.

One hour before serving, begin preheating the oven to 425°F. Remove the marinated fish from the refrigerator and uncover. Gently stir the marinade with a wooden spoon. Cut the butter into small pieces and dot the contents of the pan. Bake for 40 to 45 minutes. Set the pan or baking dish on a large platter or a trivet on the dining table and serve from it onto heated plates.

Florida Red Snapper with Orange

An unusual combination, the result of imaginative use of choice local ingredients. The red snapper fillets are marinated briefly in oil, onion, and oranges, then baked. Serve the delicious marinade, including the strips of orange peel, over the fish.

FOR FOUR

4 red snapper fillets, with the skin left on	of the inner white membrane removed
3 Tbs. olive or peanut oil	1¼ tsp. salt
¼ c. fresh orange juice, strained	⅜ tsp. freshly ground white
⅓ c. finely chopped onion	pepper
2 tsp. grated orange zest	¼ tsp. nutmeg
1½ Tbs. orange peel slivers, about ¾ inch long, with all	2 Tbs. dry white wine
	2 Tbs. salt butter for dotting

Grease the inside of a large shallow porcelain baking dish (or stainless steel lined sauté pan) evenly with a small amount of butter. Add all the ingredients except the snapper fillets and the butter for dotting. Mix with a wooden spoon, then arrange the fillets, skin side up, in the mixture. Spoon some of the liquid from the dish over the tops of the fillets and cover with plastic wrap. Refrigerate for 1 to 1½ hours.

Preheat the oven to 400°F. Remove the baking dish from the refrigerator, uncover, and turn the fillets over. Baste thoroughly with the liquid in the dish, then arrange several slivers of orange peel on top of each fillet. Dot with butter. Bake for 13 to 15 minutes, basting once after 10 minutes. To serve, lift the fillets carefully onto heated plates, then spoon about 1½ teaspoons of the liquid remaining in the dish around each one. Bring to the table immediately.

Mexican Whole Striped Bass with Adobo Sauce

A handsome whole fish dish with a rich dark sauce similar to the one used in Mexican mole poblano, but without chocolate. The carefully balanced blending of spices, including dried ancho chili peppers, produces a rich smoky flavor that is intriguingly aromatic but not too hot. If you can't get powdered ancho chilies, use bottled chili powder with a dark color and a smoky aroma; it will contain a large proportion of ancho chilies. If the chili powder you find has a strong aroma of cumin, reduce the amount of cumin specified in the recipe by half. The fish is lightly pan fried, then baked with the sauce and freshly grated cheese.

FOR THREE OR FOUR

1 striped bass, 3 to 4 lb., split and cleaned, head removed	salt and freshly ground black pepper
5 Tbs. olive oil	flour in a shaker for dusting

ADOBO SAUCE

3 dried ancho chilies, soaked, cleaned, dried, and crushed or 3 tsp. dried ancho chili powder	¼ tsp. freshly ground black pepper
⅔ c. chopped onions	½ tsp. salt
1½ tsp. chopped garlic	¼ tsp. crushed red pepper
¼ tsp. cloves	2 Tbs. torn-up parsley leaves
¼ tsp. cinnamon	1½ c. ripe tomatoes, peeled and coarsely chopped (2 medium-sized tomatoes)
½ tsp. oregano	
¼ tsp. cumin	2 tsp. lime juice
½ tsp. thyme	1/16 tsp. cayenne
¾ tsp. sugar	

½ c. freshly grated Parmesan cheese
2 Tbs. butter

Rinse the fish under cold running water and dry very thoroughly with paper towels. Heat the oil in a large skillet. Sprinkle one side of the fish with salt and pepper, then dust evenly with flour. Place floured side down in the hot oil. Season and dust the upper side. Fry until golden brown on the bottom, lifting gently with a spatula to check for color. It should take about 4 minutes. Carefully turn the fish over and brown on the other side, about 3 minutes. Lift the fish out of the skillet with a slotted spatula and set in a buttered shallow baking dish that will hold it comfortably. (An oval shape is most attractive, if you've got one.) Set the dish in a 175°F. oven or on a warming tray while you prepare the sauce.

Combine all ingredients for the sauce in a blender container and mix on high speed for a few seconds, then turn off. Repeat until the mixture appears even-colored, but still rather grainy and coarse in texture. Remove all but about 2½ tablespoons of the oil remaining in the skillet, then heat for a few minutes. Pour the sauce into the skillet and bring to a simmer. Cook for 8 to 10 minutes or until the sauce is reduced a bit and appears thickened, stirring frequently and scraping across the bottom of the skillet to keep it from scorching.

Remove the baking dish from the oven and spoon the sauce over the fish evenly, then around the sides. Sprinkle the surface evenly with the grated cheese, then dot with butter. Bake in a 400°F. oven for 30 to 40 minutes or until the fish flakes easily when tested with a fork. (Test the sides, so as not to disturb the sauce coating.) Bring the dish to the table and serve onto individual heated plates, spooning generous quantities of cheese and sauce over each portion. To divide the fish into thick slices, cut downward with a sharp knife and wiggle it a bit till you find a joint in the backbone and continue cutting downward until the slice is clearly separated. Lift out of the dish with a long wide spatula.

The Pleasures of Seafood 210

Roast Eel with Fruit Mustard

Young eel marinated, then slowly roasted, and served with a marvelous Cremona fruit and mustard sauce. This unique sauce uses fresh ripe fruits of the season, Dijon mustard, honey, and a touch of lemon. An unusual Italian classic.

FOR THREE OR FOUR

2 lb. small eel (about 1 inch thick) skinned, cleaned, cut into 2 inch lengths

MARINADE

1½ tsp. salt	*4 small bay leaves, crushed*
¼ tsp. freshly ground black pepper	*½ c. white wine vinegar*
1 Tbs. finely minced garlic	*½ tsp. oregano*

FRUIT MUSTARD

1½ c. diced ripe fruit (peaches, plums, etc.)	*⅛ tsp. freshly ground white pepper*
1 Tbs. honey	*1 tsp. fresh lemon juice*
1 Tbs. Dijon mustard	*¼ tsp. salt*

Place the pieces of eel in a shallow porcelain baking dish. Combine the ingredients for the marinade in a bowl and mix very thoroughly, then pour over the eel. Turn the pieces over several times with tongs to coat well, then cover the dish with plastic wrap and marinate on the bottom shelf of the refrigerator for about 2 hours.

Preheat the oven to 350°F. Place a roasting rack (or cake rack) in a shallow roasting pan. Lift the pieces of eel out of the marinade with tongs, allowing most of the liquid to drain off, then place on the rack. Roast at 350°F. for 45 minutes, turning the eel over twice during that time. Serve with fruit mustard.

To prepare the fruit mustard, combine all the ingredients in a stainless steel or porcelain bowl and mix with a wooden spoon, mashing the pieces of ripe fruit against the sides of the bowl with the back of the spoon. Complete the mixing by beating briefly with a whisk or a fork.

Soufflé and Mousse Recipes

Shrimp Soufflé	*Lobster Mousse*
Crabmeat Soufflé	*Crabmeat Mousse*
Crabmeat Soufflé with Cheese	*Shrimp Mousse*
Oyster Soufflé	*Mousse of Pike*
Fish Soufflé	*Salmon Mousse*

10

Soufflés and Mousses

One is nearly always hot, the other nearly always cold. And yet the processes are so similar, we felt that soufflés and mousses belonged together. We love them as elegant and festive light suppers. With a bottle of chilled white wine we almost feel as if we were on a holiday in France. The soufflé and the mousse are characteristic of French cooking. And not simply because they taste so good. These dishes uniquely express the French genius for making the most out of a small quantity of ingredients. Using air beaten into egg whites or cream, soufflés and mousses are the triumph of imagination and taste over a paucity of ingredients.

The most difficult part of soufflés or mousses is learning the basic techniques. After that they are as simple as turning out good omelettes. Light, delicate, they are the most elegant of all seafood dishes; easy to serve, and awe-inspiring to eat, they seem to capture the very essence of the seafood.

Basic Soufflé Techniques

Use eggs at room temperature; if necessary, warm cold eggs in a bowl of tepid water.

Separate eggs carefully; beat whites until stiff but not dry.

Use a copper bowl or add a pinch of cream of tartar for maximum egg white volume.

Scald milk and allow to cool slightly before adding to butter and flour.

Don't add beaten whites to soufflé base all at once; add in 3 or 4 parts to maintain volume.

Use soufflé dishes of the proper size; butter inner surfaces and dust with flour.

Preheat oven.

Bake on middle rack.

Serve as soon as baking is completed.

Basic Mousse Techniques

Dissolve gelatin carefully in small amount of cold water.

Whip ingredients at low speed until blended, then at high speed for airiness and volume.

Attractive molds make mousses look better.

Chill filled molds thoroughly before turning out.

Unmold carefully, repeating loosening and warming operations as often as necessary. (Avoid too much warmth, which will destroy shape of mousse.)

Shrimp Soufflé

Few seafood dishes are more attractive to serve than soufflés. They are grand and elegant as well as light and very satisfying. Made with fresh boiled shrimp and the essence extracted from the shells, this is one of the best soufflés we know. This recipe describes all the basic techniques for making seafood soufflés. Mas-

---

tering one will enable you to prepare all the others that follow with a minimum of difficulties, as well as to create other soufflés with seafood ingredients you have on hand. The basic proportions remain the same; all that is necessary is a few minor adjustments in the seasonings. One last comment: forget all the caveats about the difficulty of preparing soufflés. Just take the time to combine the elements carefully, remember to butter and flour the soufflé dish, to fold in the beaten egg whites in three parts as indicated, and to use the correct baking temperature. You will get perfect results every time. Should you wish to double the recipe, use two soufflé dishes rather than a single larger one.

FOR THREE OR FOUR

SOUFFLÉ BASE

¾ lb. Mild Boiled Shrimp in the shell	¼ c. heavy cream
	¾ tsp. salt
reserved shells from the boiled shrimp	¼ tsp. freshly ground black pepper
1½ c. water	⅛ tsp. cayenne
1 Tbs. salt butter	½ tsp. chervil
3 Tbs. finely minced shallots	¼ tsp. nutmeg
4 tsp. brandy	5 tsp. finely minced fresh parsley

BÉCHAMEL

3 Tbs. salt butter
3 Tbs. flour
1 c. scalded milk

EGGS

4 large eggs plus 1 large egg white

---

butter for greasing soufflé dish
flour in a shaker for dusting soufflé dish

Peel the shrimp and reserve all parts of the shells. Remove any dark flecks (pieces of vein or bits of seasoning from the court bouillon) from the shrimp as you peel. Place the peeled shrimp in a bowl, cover with plastic wrap, and refrigerate while you prepare the stock base.

To prepare the stock base, crush the shells a handful at a time with a mortar and pestle, removing the crushed shells to a heavy 1½ to 2 quart saucepan. Add the water and bring to a boil over high heat. Reduce the heat slightly and boil gently for 15 minutes. Push the

---

shells down into the boiling liquid from time to time with a wooden spoon or spatula. While the shells are simmering, remove half the peeled shrimp from the refrigerator and chop them very fine. Also chop the shallots. At the end of the 15 minutes strain the contents of the pan through a fine strainer into a bowl. Discard the shells and wipe out any pieces of shell left in the pan with a paper towel. Return the liquid to the pan and cook until reduced to 2 tablespoons or less. Remove the pan from the heat.

In a medium-sized sauté pan melt 1 tablespoon of butter over medium heat and sauté the shallots until slightly soft, for 3 to 4 minutes, stirring frequently. Add the 2 tablespoons of reduced shrimp stock. (If necessary, add a bit of water to the pan containing the stock and stir well to make up 2 tablespoons.) Reduce the heat to very low and add the brandy and cream. Stir and cook over low heat for 2 minutes, then add all the remaining ingredients for the soufflé base except the parsley. Mix thoroughly, cook for 1 minute more, and remove the pan from the heat. Chop the rest of the boiled shrimp into fairly coarse pieces, about ¼ inch across. Add them to the contents of the pan along with the parsley. Mix thoroughly and set aside while you prepare the béchamel.

To prepare the béchamel, melt the butter in a heavy 2½ to 3 quart porcelain or stainless steel lined saucepan over low heat, then gradually stir in the flour. Mix constantly to keep the texture free of lumps. Add the scalded milk in a steady stream, stirring evenly with a whisk as you pour. Cook over low heat, always stirring, until the sauce thickens. Remove the pan from the heat and mix in the shrimp base with a wooden spoon. Do not beat.

Separate the eggs into 2 large mixing bowls. (A copper one for the whites is preferred if you have one. If not, add a few grains of cream of tartar to the whites before beating.) Discard the extra yolk or save it for thickening another sauce. Beat the yolks with a whisk or a fork until smooth and almost lemon-colored. Add the contents of the saucepan to the yolks and mix in gently but thoroughly. Beat the whites until quite stiff and almost dry. Add the beaten whites a third at a time to the yolk mixture. Fold the first third in thoroughly and the second a bit less thoroughly. Add the final third and fold in very, very gently.

Evenly butter the inside of an 8-cup soufflé dish, then dust with flour. Turn the dish upside down over the sink and tap it hard several times to shake out the excess flour. Pour the soufflé mixture into the dish and set it on the middle rack of a preheated 375°F. oven. Bake for 30 minutes, or until the soufflé is puffed about an inch above the top of the dish and browned on top. A cake tester inserted into the center should come out clean. If necessary, bake for 3 to 5 minutes longer. Bring the soufflé to the table as soon as it is done. To serve, gently cut down into the soufflé with a serrated knife, then lift the portions carefully out of the dish onto heated plates. (If you find that the portions tend to topple over and lie on their sides, don't worry about it; the majority of the time that is how a single large soufflé divided into portions is served.)

Crabmeat Soufflé

Just over ½ pound of lump crabmeat is used in this soufflé, with white wine, chives, and small amounts of seasonings in the base to highlight the main ingredient. The delicate pale gold color is flecked with green and the browned top of the soufflé rises almost 2 inches above the rim of the dish. Simpler to prepare than shrimp soufflé—and every bit as good.

FOR THREE OR FOUR

SOUFFLÉ BASE

1 c. coarsely chopped lump crabmeat (approximately 9 oz.)	⅛ tsp. cayenne
	¼ tsp. nutmeg
¾ tsp. salt	⅛ tsp. coriander
½ tsp. freshly ground white pepper	1½ tsp. minced chives
	1 tsp. white wine vinegar

BÉCHAMEL

3 Tbs. salt butter	¾ c. scalded milk
3 Tbs. flour	¼ c. dry white wine

EGGS

4 large eggs plus 1 large egg white

---

butter for greasing soufflé dish
flour in a shaker for dusting soufflé dish

In a small bowl combine the elements for the soufflé base. Prepare the béchamel as directed for Shrimp Soufflé, adding the wine gradually after the sauce has begun to thicken, stirring gently and evenly until

---

the béchamel is smooth and heated through. (Do not bring it to a boil.) Separate the eggs and proceed as directed for Shrimp Soufflé. Bake in a preheated 375°F. oven for 25 to 30 minutes. The top of the soufflé should rise about 1½ to 2 inches above the rim of the soufflé dish. (Test for doneness as for Shrimp Soufflé.) Serve as directed.

Crabmeat Soufflé with Cheese

This version of Crabmeat Soufflé, made with freshly grated cheese, has a markedly different flavor from the preceding one. This form is ideal for times when you have very little crabmeat—it requires only ⅓ pound. The additional density added by the cheese makes it essential to use 2 additional egg whites rather than the usual 1.

FOR THREE OR FOUR

SOUFFLÉ BASE

a scant c. finely diced crabmeat (approximately 5½ oz.)
¾ tsp. salt
½ tsp. freshly ground white pepper

⅛ tsp. cayenne
¼ tsp. nutmeg
6 Tbs. freshly grated French Gruyère or Swiss Emmenthal or American Swiss cheese

BÉCHAMEL

3 Tbs. salt butter
3 Tbs. flour

1 c. scalded milk
¼ c. dry white wine

EGGS

4 large eggs plus 2 large egg whites

---

butter for greasing soufflé dish
flour in a shaker for dusting soufflé dish

In a small bowl combine all the elements for the soufflé base except the cheese. Prepare as directed for Crabmeat Soufflé. Add the cheese to the béchamel and mix it in thoroughly before adding the remaining elements of the base. Increase the total baking time by about 5 to 10 minutes, checking for doneness first at 30 minutes.

Oyster Soufflé

Delicate and rich, with chopped oysters, bits of crisp bacon, and flecks of green onions. Drain the oysters over a bowl using a fine mesh strainer: the liquor will be strained and ready for adding to the base when you need it.

FOR THREE OR FOUR

SOUFFLÉ BASE

1¼ c. drained chopped oysters, liquor reserved (approximately ⅔ pint oysters)

¼ tsp. salt

⅜ tsp. freshly ground white pepper

⅛ tsp. cayenne

¼ tsp. nutmeg

2 Tbs. finely chopped green onion tops

2 Tbs. crumbled crisply fried breakfast bacon

BÉCHAMEL

3 Tbs. salt butter

3 Tbs. flour

¾ c. scalded milk

¼ c. strained oyster liquor

EGGS

4 large eggs plus 1 large egg white

---

butter for greasing soufflé dish
flour in a shaker for dusting soufflé dish

In a small bowl combine the elements for the soufflé base. Prepare the béchamel as directed for Shrimp Soufflé, adding the oyster liquor gradually after the sauce has begun to thicken. Separate the eggs and proceed as directed. Bake for 25 to 30 minutes in a preheated 375°F. oven. The top of the soufflé should rise about 1¼ to 1½ inches above the rim of the soufflé dish. Test for doneness as indicated. When done, serve in the same manner as for Shrimp Soufflé.

Fish Soufflé

An excellent way to serve a small quantity of poached fish fillets.
If you use fish left over from another dish, warm it briefly in a
skillet with about 1 teaspoon of water before flaking to restore the
moisture that tends to evaporate during refrigeration.

FOR THREE OR FOUR

Prepare as directed for Crabmeat Soufflé, substituting 1 cup finely
flaked poached fish (approximately 8 ounces) for the crabmeat.

Lobster Mousse

Seafood mousses make fine light supper and luncheon main dishes.
They are particularly attractive when set to chill in shaped molds
—fish molds, pâté molds, bundt pans are all suitable. Be sure to
allow at least 3 hours of refrigeration for firm setting. Electric
standing or hand-held mixers greatly simplify the mixing and
aerating needed to give mousses their characteristic creamy tex-
ture. Blenders also work, but you will have to divide the in-
gredients into several batches during the mixing phase, then whip
the batches together with a whisk before filling the mold. We have
not included recipes for hot mousses, which have always struck us
as far less successful than soufflés prepared with the same seafood
elements. Boiled Florida lobster is our favorite for this creamy,
delicately colored mousse, but any boiled lobster meat can be used.

FOR FOUR TO SIX

1¼ to 1½ c. diced cooked
    lobster meat (see Boiled
    Florida Lobster for directions)
¼ c. cold water
1 envelope unflavored gelatin
¾ c. mayonnaise
1 Tbs. fresh lemon juice
¼ c. chopped onion
¼ c. finely minced shallots

½ tsp. salt
½ tsp. freshly ground white
    pepper
¼ tsp. dry mustard
¾ tsp. marjoram
¼ tsp. mace
a few grains cayenne
⅓ c. heavy cream, whipped

Put the cold water in a small saucepan and sprinkle the gelatin over
it. Cook over low heat, stirring constantly with a wooden spoon or
spatula, until the gelatin is dissolved, about 3 minutes. In a large

mixing bowl, combine the mayonnaise, lemon juice, and dissolved gelatin. Purée the onion, shallots, and lobster meat together coarsely in a blender, food processor, food mill, or meat grinder. (Or chop together thoroughly, using a wooden chopping bowl and rounded chopper.) Do *not* make too fine a purée; the finished mousse should have a faintly and pleasantly coarse texture, with tiny bits of the lobster still distinguishable as one eats. Add the purée to the mixture in the bowl. Sprinkle in the seasonings, then whip at medium-high speed until the ingredients appear smoothly blended. Fold in the whipped cream very thoroughly. Pour the mousse into a 1 to 1½ quart mold or loaf pan. (If you use a fish-shaped mold, set it in a round or oval baking dish to keep it level, lining the dish with pebbles or rock salt if necessary to stabilize the mold.) Cover the mold with aluminum foil and set on the top shelf of the refrigerator to chill for 3 to 4 hours.

When ready to serve, remove the mousse from the refrigerator and uncover. Carefully slide a thin sharp knife around the edge between the mousse and the mold, then dip the bottom of the mold in moderately warm water for about 8 seconds. Wipe the bottom with a towel, cover the top with a serving plate that extends past the edges of the mold at all points, then invert. Rap the mold firmly. If the mousse does not slip out onto the plate, turn it upside down again and repeat the knife and warm water operations. Depending on the texture of the mousse and the type of mold you use, it may take as many as 4 repetitions. Serve at the table, slicing with the edge of a large spatula.

Crabmeat Mousse

Paler and more delicate in flavor than Lobster Mousse, this one with crabmeat is most attractive served on plates with colorful rims. Any garnish you like can be placed on the mousse after it is turned out. If you prefer to incorporate the garnish before chilling, take care to choose things dense enough to remain under the mousse while it is still liquid.

FOR FOUR TO SIX

Prepare as directed for Lobster Mousse, substituting 1½ cups lump crabmeat for the lobster meat. If desired, decorate the mousse by placing sliced olives, pimiento strips, etc., inside the mold before chilling. To keep the garnish in place first pour about ⅓ cup of

---

the mixture into the mold, just enough to barely cover the pieces of garnish, and set in the freezer for 10 minutes or until set. Then add the remainder and chill in the usual manner.

Shrimp Mousse

A mousse with shrimp can be prepared exactly like one with lobster, but our favorite version uses both finely puréed shrimp and some whole shrimp embedded so as to be at the top of the turned-out dish, and has a very light curry taste due to the use of coriander and cumin.

FOR FOUR TO SIX

1 c. puréed boiled shrimp (see Mild Boiled Shrimp)

⅓ c. whole boiled shrimp, approximately

½ c. cold water

1 envelope unflavored gelatin

10 Tbs. mayonnaise

⅓ c. heavy cream

½ tsp. salt

¼ tsp. freshly ground white pepper

¼ tsp. coriander

⅛ tsp. cumin

1/16 tsp. cayenne

⅛ tsp. mace

1 tsp. fresh lemon juice

2 tsp. sugar

2 Tbs. thinly sliced green onion tops

Put the cold water in a small saucepan and sprinkle the gelatin over it. Cook over very low heat, stirring constantly with a wooden spoon or spatula, until the gelatin is dissolved, about 3 minutes. In a large mixing bowl combine the mayonnaise, dissolved gelatin, cream, and all the remaining ingredients except the whole shrimp and the green onion tops. Whip at low speed until thoroughly blended, then at high speed until the mousse appears creamy and fluffed-up. Pour about ⅓ cup of the mousse into a mold, then place the whole boiled shrimp in a decorative pattern on the bottom of the mold. Set the mold in the freezer for 12 to 14 minutes, until it appears firmly set. Add the green onion tops to the mousse mixture remaining in the bowl and whip briefly, just long enough to distribute evenly. Remove the mold from the freezer, fill with the remainder of the mousse, then arrange on top of a baking dish to keep it level, cover, and chill as described for Lobster Mousse. Serve as directed.

Mousse of Pike

A classic fish mousse, made with puréed freshly poached fillets of pike, a béchamel for additional firmness, and heavy cream for fluffiness. Any fairly firm fish with white flesh can be prepared in this way. For variety, substitute rosemary, basil, or a smaller amount of tarragon for the chervil.

FOR FOUR

1½ lb. pike fillets, plus the head and bones

COURT BOUILLON FOR POACHING THE FISH

2 c. water	2 parsley sprigs
½ c. dry white wine	½ tsp. salt
1 medium-sized carrot, peeled and thinly sliced	¼ tsp. thyme
	½ bay leaf
½ medium-sized onion	3 whole black peppercorns

BÉCHAMEL

2 Tbs. salt butter	⅛ tsp. freshly ground white pepper
2 Tbs. flour	
1 c. scalded milk	1/16 tsp. nutmeg
the reduced poaching liquid	a few grains of cayenne

---

1 tsp. salt	½ tsp. chervil
½ tsp. freshly ground white pepper	¾ c. heavy cream, whipped

Poach the fish fillets and the head and bones in the court bouillon in a skillet for 6 to 7 minutes. Carefully remove the fillets from the liquid with a slotted spoon or spatula, allowing the excess liquid to drain back into the pan. Place the fillets on a plate to cool for a few minutes. Strain the poaching liquid through a fine mesh strainer, then pour into a small saucepan and cook over high heat until the liquid is reduced to about 2 tablespoons. Reserve. Purée the fish in a blender, food processor, grinder, or food mill until quite smooth. Put the puréed fish into a large mixing bowl. In another small saucepan, melt the butter for the béchamel over low heat, then gradually stir in the flour. Add the scalded milk and cook until thickened. Add the reduced poaching liquid and the seasonings for the béchamel and stir to mix thoroughly. Remove the pan from the heat and set aside to cool for a minute or so, then put into the refrigerator or freezer

---

just long enough to remove the last bit of heat. (This is a good time to whip the cream.)

Add the cooled béchamel, salt, pepper, and chervil to the puréed fish in the mixing bowl. Whip at medium-high speed until very smooth and slightly fluffy. Fold in the whipped cream fairly thoroughly. Pour the mousse into a mold, then stabilize and cover the mold, and chill as directed for Lobster Mousse. Serve in the same manner.

Salmon Mousse

Canned salmon, available throughout the country, is one of the few canned fish we genuinely enjoy. Red sockeye salmon, in 7¾ ounce cans, is the most flavorful. And a mousse made with red salmon, chilled in a fish mold and flecked with chervil, is beautiful to look at and a delight to eat. Be sure to whip the ingredients thoroughly for about 5 minutes (an electric mixer is a help here) to mix them properly and to incorporate enough air to give the finished mousse the desirable creamy texture. Prepare it well ahead of time as it takes 3½ to 4 hours to chill firmly.

FOR THREE OR FOUR

one 7¾-oz. can red salmon, thoroughly drained	*1 tsp. fresh lemon juice*
½ c. cold water	*2 tsp. chervil*
1 envelope unflavored gelatin	*¼ tsp. freshly ground white pepper*
9 Tbs. mayonnaise	*5 tsp. sugar*
6 Tbs. heavy cream	*¼ tsp. salt, more if necessary*

Put the thoroughly drained salmon in a large mixing bowl. Break into flakes with a fork. Put the cold water in a small saucepan, then sprinkle the gelatin over it. Warm over low heat, stirring constantly, until the gelatin is dissolved, about 3 minutes, then add the contents of the saucepan to the bowl containing the salmon. Mix. Add the remaining ingredients and whip, using a portable electric mixer, a standing electric mixer, or a wire whisk, until the mixture is thoroughly blended and slightly fluffy in texture. This should take about 4 to 5 minutes with an electric mixer at fairly high speed, about 8 to 10 minutes with a whisk. Pour the contents of the bowl into a 1 to 1½ quart mold, preferably a fish-shaped one if available. You can also use a small bundt pan, a ring mold, or a simple, fairly shallow rectangular or round dish with the proper capacity. For a fish-shaped mold, set the mold in an oval baking dish to hold it level, or put a layer of rock salt in a pie pan and nestle the mold in the salt crystals. Cover the top of the mold with aluminum foil, taking care to keep the foil *above* the level of the still-liquid mousse. Tuck the edges of the foil loosely around the edges of the mold and set on the top shelf of the refrigerator to chill. Allow 3½ to 4 hours for proper firmness to develop.

When ready to serve, take the mold out of the refrigerator, remove the foil, then slide a thin knife gently around the edge of the mousse, pressing lightly against the mold as you slide the knife. Fill the sink or a large wide bowl with medium-hot water and hold the mold, with about 1 inch submerged, in the water for about 15 to 20 seconds. Remove from the water, wipe the bottom of the mold dry with a towel, then place a serving dish larger than the mold over the top of it. Turn over. The mousse should fall onto the fish in a single, shaped piece. If necessary, repeat the loosening with the knife and the immersion in hot water one or more times until the molded mousse falls onto the serving dish. (It may take anywhere from 1 to 4 repetitions. Don't rush it, and don't attempt to gouge the mousse out of the mold or you will destroy its shape.) Bring the serving dish to the table and use a large spatula first to cut the mousse into pieces, then to carefully lift the pieces into individual plates.

Soup and Chowder Recipes

Bourride (Provençal Fish
  Stew with Garlic Sauce)
Bouillabaisse
Cioppino
Zuppa di Pesce (Italian
  Fish Soup)
Waterzooi (Belgian Fish
  Soup)
Marmite Dieppoise (Dieppe
  Fish Soup)
Matelote of Eel (Sailors'
  Stew with Red Wine)
*New England Clam
  Chowder*
Manhattan Clam Chowder
Oyster Chowder

Conch Chowder
*Old Fashioned New England
  Fish Chowder*
Turtle Soup
Creole Turtle Stew
Conch Stew
Shrimp Gumbo
Crab Gumbo
Oyster Gumbo
Seafood Gumbo
She-Crab Soup
French Shrimp Bisque
Lobster Bisque
Oyster Soup
Oyster Stew
Cádiz Fish Soup with Orange

11

Soups and Chowders

We confess that we are probably not as partial to soups and chowders as are many of our readers. Not because we don't like them, but because we don't like meals with many courses. Our favorite way of eating all of these soups, chowders, and seafood stews is as the only course in a relatively light supper. For that reason they are not nearly as central to our style of eating as they are to families that start off most dinners with a soup. We've always marveled at how people can go on with other courses after eating something as rich and as satisfying as soup. Is it habit or a genuine preference? Restaurants like soup because it fills up the customer and is relatively inexpensive to prepare. Of course, in the more complex French fish stews such as Bouillabaisse and Bourride the soup is more obviously a main course. We make a whole meal of all the soups, stews, and chowders included here. With a good bottle of wine and a fruit dessert they are eminently satisfying, easy on the waistline as well as the budget, and good enough to stand by themselves without the distraction of later courses. They also save a lot of wear and tear on the cook.

Soups, chowders, and stews are perfect mirrors of the food cultures from which they spring. You can immediately tell what is abundant in an area by what goes into the soup. You can also tell a great deal about the cooking styles. The clams and potatoes of New England Clam Chowder, the oysters and okra of New Orleans gumbo, the vast profusion of fish and garlic from Provence, the She-Crab Soup of the American Carolinas, all are miniature cultural masterpieces of ethnic and regional cooking. They are the people's dishes, very much closer to the heart of things than the formal dishes served at the public restaurants.

Because soups and chowders relate closely to the natural supply of indigenous ingredients, there has been a lot of canonical writing about authenticity. Unfortunately these writings too often concentrate on the question of ingredients rather than on what is more important, cooking techniques. All of these dishes arose out of the need to make use of ingredients that were abundant and cheap. The trick was to take what was common and cook it uncommonly, so that the people would not tire of the most accessible local food. Like the nineteenth century New England cartoon showing a small boy complaining at the dinner table, "Not lobster, again!" all of these stews show ingenuity and cooking imagination. These are far more important than the specific ingredients used. Even though the ingredients may be exotic to us, they are common in their place of origin.

Of course, New Orleans gumbo tastes different with clams rather than oysters, but it would taste even more different if the basic roux were omitted. And Bouillabaisse without *rouget* will perhaps strike a Marseillais as tragic. Without the *rouille* it will strike everyone as tragic. Sometimes corruption of style becomes institutionalized, as in Manhattan Clam Chowder, where tomatoes are substituted for cream. We share the anguish of the Yankee coming to grips with that atrocity for the first time! Try to forget about the authenticity of ingredients. Any fish will do. Any shellfish will do. Locals would be more astonished by a clam chowder with expensive clams than with cheap oysters. To be truly authentic in spirit each of these dishes should be cheap and made in the style of the region. Obviously there are exceptions to this rule of easy substitution. Eel stew calls for eel, Turtle Soup for turtle. But Cioppino, Bourride, Waterzooi, and Bouillabaisse are designed for places where seafood is abundant and where the surplus is turned from a problem into a feast. And what hearty and brilliant feasts they can be!

Basic Soup and Chowder Techniques

Use a heavy saucepan or kettle large enough to permit boiling without overflow.

Do not overcook the seafood; cook base sufficiently before adding seafood to soup.

Once added, seafood should be stirred gently to prevent breaking up pieces.

When reheating soups, do not allow them to come to a boil.

With thick soups, scrape sides and bottom of pan frequently during cooking.

Do not let chowders come to a boil after milk or cream has been added. On electric ranges remove pot from burner periodically to avoid second boil.

Before beginning a gumbo roux, have all chopping done and seasonings and herbs ready.

Bourride
Provençal Fish Stew with Garlic Sauce

Of all the great fish soups and stews, this one is our favorite. The fish retains its distinct flavor more than in many other dishes of the type, and the creamy garlic sauce is a delight: a Provençal master dish, with the aroma and flavor of fennel, orange, olive oil, bay leaves, and garlic. The delicately poached fish is perched on rounds of crisp French bread, surrounded by a rich garlicky sauce and topped with garlic mayonnaise—exciting to prepare as well as to eat.

FOR FOUR

2 lb. bass, mullet, whiting, haddock, or halibut fillets

COURT BOUILLON

1 medium-sized onion, quartered
2 small bay leaves, broken up
2 strips orange zest, 3 inches long by about ¼ inch wide
1 tsp. fresh lemon juice
1 tsp. fennel seed, crushed with a mortar and pestle

1 tsp. salt
¼ tsp. freshly ground black pepper
1½ Tbs. white wine vinegar
3 c. cold water

AÏOLI (GARLIC MAYONNAISE)
MAKES 1½ CUPS, APPROXIMATELY

4 large or 7 small garlic cloves, pounded to a paste with a mortar and pestle
2 large egg yolks
¾ tsp. salt
½ c. olive oil combined with ½ c. peanut oil

¼ tsp. freshly ground white pepper
1/16 tsp. cayenne
½ tsp. dry mustard
1½ Tbs. white wine vinegar
4 tsp. fresh lemon juice

SAUCE

6 Tbs. aïoli
2 large egg yolks
½ c. strained court bouillon

------

8 slices toasted French bread, 1 inch thick (bake on a rack in a 350°F. oven for 4 minutes on each side)

Combine the ingredients for the court bouillon in a large heavy sauté pan or skillet. Bring to a boil, then simmer for 10 minutes. Strain the court bouillon, return to the pan, then poach the fish for 8 to 10 minutes depending on size and texture. Remove the pan from the heat. Carefully lift the fillets out of the pan with a large slotted spatula, allowing the liquid to drain off. Place the fish in a shallow baking dish, cover loosely with aluminum foil, and set in a 175°F. oven to keep warm.

To prepare the aïoli, combine the garlic, egg yolks, and salt in a mixing bowl. Beat with a whisk or an electric mixer until the yolks are thick and lemon-colored. Begin adding the oil, a scant teaspoon at a time, until the aïoli begins to thicken. Add the pepper, cayenne, and dry mustard and beat to mix. Add a bit more oil, then about 1 teaspoon of the wine vinegar, beating. Repeat the addition of some oil, then some vinegar, until all the vinegar has been incorporated.

The sauce should be quite thick at this point. Increase the amount of oil being added to about 1 tablespoon at a time, followed by a scant ½ teaspoon of lemon juice. The sauce will continue to thicken. Toward the end of the mixing, when the sauce is very thick, the oil can be added in a constant slow stream. Complete the sauce by beating in any drops of lemon juice still remaining, then beat for about 20 seconds more.

To make the sauce for the Bourride, in a small stainless steel or porcelain bowl combine 6 tablespoons of the aïoli with 2 large egg yolks. Beat to mix with a whisk, then gradually pour in ½ cup of the strained, still-warm court bouillon. (If the court bouillon has cooled too much, warm it briefly.)

To serve, place 2 slices of toasted French bread side by side in the bottom of each of 4 preheated wide soup bowls. (Italian spaghetti bowls are ideal.) Pour ⅛ of the sauce over each portion of bread, then top with the pieces of poached fish. Pour the remaining sauce over the fish, then top each portion with 2 to 3 tablespoons of aïoli. Serve immediately.

Any leftover aïoli can be refrigerated, covered. It will keep for 4 to 5 days.

Bouillabaisse

Our Bouillabaisse is not authentic. We say this tongue in cheek, since discussion of authenticity in a dish that began humbly, as a way of using leftover seafood in the fishing port of Marseilles, is as amusing as it is irrelevant. Bouillabaisse disputes range from whether or not it is proper to use shellfish, to discussions of particular fish which we are told must be used. All of this is nonsense. Variety, not particularity, is the genius of this dish. One of the most attractive restaurant presentations shows the diner a platter with one each of the fish used in the Bouillabaisse. Most of the time the fish remain largely anonymous, especially in the eating. The joy of a fine Bouillabaisse comes from using a variety of ingredients, from intelligent timing (sturdier fish go in first and cook longer), a judiciously hearty hand with the seasonings, and a good rouille, *the great hot pepper and garlic sauce served with it. If you live in a coastal area, pick up the cheapest fresh fish you* can find at the market or those that most appeal to you, then enjoy making the soup and serving it. Pay no attention to anyone who lectures you on "the real thing." It's true that rouget and rascasse, used near Marseilles, are delightful in Bouillabaisse, but so is any unusual fish the family fishermen have caught over the weekend or the unfamiliar fish your fish market's other clients are too timid to try. The hallmark of a good Bouillabaisse is how you cook it and how it tastes, and the variety rather than the pedigree of its ingredients.

FOR EIGHT TO TEN

5 lb. of mixed fish, approximately, filleted and skin removed, or cut into steaks, depending on size*

⅓ c. olive oil or olive oil and butter, half and half

3 c. coarsely chopped onions

2 Tbs. minced garlic

1 celery stalk, chopped

2 carrots, peeled and chopped

3 large ripe tomatoes, peeled and coarsely chopped

2 bay leaves, broken up

2 fennel sprigs or ½ tsp. ground fennel seed

¾ tsp. ground saffron

1½ Tbs. salt

1½ tsp. freshly ground black pepper

1 tsp. finely chopped orange zest

1½ tsp. fresh lemon juice

2 qt. boiling water, approximately

2 Tbs. chopped parsley

16 to 20 slices lightly toasted French bread, ¾ inch thick

OPTIONAL SHELLFISH (ANY OF THE FOLLOWING, UP TO APPROXIMATELY 2 LB. TOTAL)

peeled raw shrimp

medium-sized squid, cleaned and cut into ½ inch strips or rounds

lump crabmeat

small soft shell crabs, cleaned

crawfish, peeled

lobster meat, cut into large pieces

ROUILLE (HOT PEPPER SAUCE)

½ tsp. cayenne and 1/16 tsp. cumin (1¾ tsp. canned or bottled hot peppers, drained, seeded, and chopped, may be substituted)

4 large or 6 small garlic cloves

2 Tbs. olive or peanut oil, more if necessary

2 Tbs. mashed potatoes or 2 Tbs. flour moistened with water or stock

½ tsp. lemon juice

* If you can get some small tender fish and also pieces of some large tougher ones, you will be able to add the fish in two stages; this gives you a more interesting broth. However, this difference is more noticeable to the cook than to the eaters. Buy what's fresh and plentiful and gauge the cooking time by poking the fish with a fork. The tougher ones should be cooked for 12 to 15 minutes, the others for 7 to 10 minutes.

Heat the oil in a heavy 7 to 10 quart saucepan, then add the onions, garlic, celery, and carrots. Reduce the heat to low and cook the vegetables, stirring frequently, until they are glazed and soft, but not brown. Add the tomatoes, bay leaves, fennel, saffron, salt, and pepper. Cook for 3 to 4 minutes, then add the firm fish, orange zest, lemon juice, and if you are using shellfish, the squid, crawfish, and lobster meat. Add just enough boiling water to cover, raise the heat, and cook at a hearty boil for 5 minutes. Add the tender fish and if used, the shrimp, crabmeat, and soft shell crabs. If necessary, add a very small amount of boiling water. Sprinkle in the parsley and boil for 7 to 9 minutes longer. Remove the pan from the heat, stir to mix, and cover very loosely. Allow to stand for a few minutes.

To prepare the *rouille*, put the cayenne and cumin (or drained, seeded, and chopped hot peppers) in a large mixing bowl. Cut up the garlic cloves and mash them to a paste with a mortar and pestle. Add the garlic paste to the pepper and mix thoroughly. Gradually pour in 1 tablespoon of the mashed potatoes or moistened flour and stir. Stir rapidly, then add the lemon juice. Stir again. Check the consistency of the sauce. It should resemble that of light sour cream. If necessary, beat in a bit more oil, then stir in a bit more potatoes or flour and water. Repeat until the desired consistency is reached.

To serve, ladle ¼ cup of the broth from the pan into each preheated wide soup bowl. Place pieces of each kind of fish in the broth along with equal portions of the shellfish, if used. Ladle a bit more broth over each portion, just enough to barely cover the fish and shellfish. Pour the remaining broth into a serving bowl; put a ladle in the bowl. Heap the pieces of toasted French bread on a plate and put the *rouille* into a small sauceboat or bowl along with a spoon. Bring the portions to the table. Set the bowl of broth in the center of the table, and pass the French bread and the *rouille* around. It is traditional to place at least 1 slice of bread in the broth. The *rouille* may be spread very lightly on the bread or dipped directly into the broth as desired. Be sure to inform the diners that the sauce is *very* hot. Each person then helps himself to additional broth, bread, and sauce.

Cioppino

We debated for some time about including Cioppino in this book. Neither of us had ever tasted a restaurant Cioppino we liked. The dish originated as a way of cooking a flexible variety of seafood found in the San Francisco area. A dish that combines seafood and tomato sauce was a natural for San Francisco, with its many good Italian cooks. But all the prose about the "tradition" of Cioppino is nonsense. Most Cioppino served these days is a commercialized, rather gross dish that stretches a little seafood further than it can successfully be stretched. This version is our own. We have substituted a gazpacho style gravy for the usual heavier tomato sauce because we like the lighter, more delicate effect.

FOR SIX TO EIGHT

3 lb. sea bass, skinned and deboned, then cut into large pieces

1 lb. fresh shrimp, peeled and deveined

the meat of a medium to large spiny lobster or several pieces of king crab, rock lobster tail, or stone crab

¼ c. olive oil

1 c. coarsely chopped onions

½ c. chopped green pepper

1 Tbs. minced garlic

4 to 5 large ripe tomatoes, peeled and coarsely chopped

3 Tbs. white wine vinegar

4 slices white bread, lightly toasted and cut into cubes

3 to 4 c. water, approximately

2 tsp. salt

½ tsp. freshly ground black pepper

⅛ tsp. cayenne

2 c. peeled and coarsely chopped cucumbers

¼ c. chopped parsley

Arrange the fish and shellfish in layers in a heavy 7 to 10 quart saucepan or kettle. In a large sauté pan or skillet, heat the oil, then add the onions, green pepper, and garlic. Cook over low heat until the vegetables are soft, then add the tomatoes. Continue cooking over medium-low heat for 5 minutes, stirring frequently. Add the vinegar, bread, 2 cups of the water, the salt, pepper, cayenne, and cucumbers. Mix very thoroughly, then remove the pan from the heat. Pour the contents of the sauté pan over the seafood in the large saucepan. Bring to a boil over high heat, cover loosely, then lower the heat to very low and simmer for 20 to 30 minutes, stirring very gently from time to time and adding a bit more water if the level of the liquid in in the pan falls more than 1 or 2 inches below the seafood. Add the parsley after about 15 minutes of simmering.

Serve in wide soup bowls, with pieces of fish and portions of the shellfish on the bottom of each bowl and about ⅓ cup of the liquid from the pan ladled over.

Zuppa di Pesce
Italian Fish Soup

Italian Fish Soup, like Bouillabaisse, is more of a stew than a soup. The broth is traditionally made with olive oil, onions, garlic, and tomatoes. Various fish are used, depending on the region, along with squid, small clams, shrimp, and small spiny lobsters. Slices of French bread toasted in the oven are the usual accompaniment.

FOR SIX TO EIGHT

3 to 4 lb. mixed fish, filleted and skin removed, or cut into steaks, depending on size

½ lb. squid, cleaned and cut into ½ inch strips or rings

1 pint small clams, scrubbed to remove the sand (optional)

½ lb. peeled and deveined shrimp

½ to 1 lb. lobtser meat, cut into large pieces

3 Tbs. olive oil

¾ c. chopped onions

2 Tbs. chopped celery leaves

2 Tbs. chopped parsley

1½ Tbs. finely minced garlic

2 c. peeled, coarsely chopped ripe tomatoes

½ c. dry white wine

½ c. water

1 tsp. freshly ground black pepper

⅛ tsp. cayenne

2 tsp. salt

6 to 8 slices French bread, ½ inch thick, lightly toasted in the oven

several cut garlic cloves for rubbing the bread

In a large heavy saucepan heat the olive oil. Add the onions and cook over medium heat until glazed and soft, but not browned; add the celery leaves, parsley, and garlic. Mix thoroughly and cook for 3 to 4 minutes longer, then add the tomatoes. Raise the heat and bring the mixture to a simmer, then cook until the tomatoes are reduced to a thick sauce. Add the wine, water, and seasonings and simmer for about 5 minutes. Add the fish and shellfish and cook until the fish are fork tender and the clams have opened, about 12 minutes. Remove the pan from the heat, cover loosely, then allow to steep while you toast the bread. Rub the slices of bread with the cut sides of the garlic cloves. To serve, place several pieces of fish and a selection of the shellfish used in wide soup bowls. Pass around a platter heaped with the seasoned toasted bread.

Waterzooi
Belgian Fish Soup

A delicate Belgian Fish Soup made with freshwater fish, butter, leeks, and white wine.

FOR FOUR

2 lb. perch or other small freshwater fish, filleted and skin removed

¼ c. (½ stick) salt butter

3 to 4 leeks, white bottom parts only, cut into thin slices or, if leeks are not available, 1 c. green onion bottoms

1 medium-sized carrot, peeled and cut into thin strips about 2½ inches long

2 celery hearts, cut into thin slivers

3 Tbs. finely minced parsley

1¼ c. dry white wine

1½ c. water

1½ tsp. salt

¼ tsp. freshly ground white pepper

⅛ tsp. nutmeg

2 tsp. fresh lemon juice

Melt the butter over medium heat in a large heavy saucepan. Add the vegetables and cook, stirring, until soft but not browned. Place the fish over the vegetables, then pour the wine and water over them. Sprinkle in the salt, pepper, and nutmeg. Raise the heat and bring to a boil, then lower the heat to very low. Cover the pan loosely and cook at a very low simmer for 20 to 25 minutes. Remove the pan from the heat. Carefully remove the fish to a platter and set the platter in a 200°F. oven to keep warm. Return the pan to the heat and bring the liquid to a boil. Add the lemon juice and cook for 8 to 10 minutes, until the vegetables are reduced to a purée. Mash the still-solid pieces of vegetables with the back of a wooden spoon as they cook. To serve, place the pieces of fish flat on the bottom of wide soup bowls, then ladle about ½ cup of the thick liquid from the pan over each portion. Buttered brown bread is the traditional accompaniment.

Marmite Dieppoise
Dieppe Fish Soup

We fell in love with this French fish soup the first time we tasted it in a casino dining room in Dieppe. It's the rare classic over which there are few arguments about authentic ingredients—sole, plenty of butter, cream, and white wine, and often some small shrimp and mussels—a beautiful and irresistible Norman dish with a rich creamy stock that deserves to be better known.

FOR SIX TO EIGHT

SOLE

3 lb. sole fillets, skin removed
1½ Tbs. salt butter
¼ tsp. freshly ground white pepper

1 c. dry white wine
½ c. water

SHELLFISH

1 lb. raw shrimp in the shell
1½ qt. well scrubbed mussels or 1 pint freshly shucked oysters and their liquor
1 qt. water

STOCK

2 Tbs. salt butter
½ c. chopped onion
2 leeks, minced, or 5 green onions, minced
the reserved fish poaching liquid
the reserved shellfish liquid
1½ Tbs. flour rubbed together with 1½ Tbs. butter (beurre manié)

1 c. heavy cream
⅛ tsp. freshly ground white pepper
2 tsp. salt
scant 1/16 tsp. cayenne
2 tsp. Calvados or applejack

Butter a large shallow baking dish, skillet, or sauté pan thoroughly with 1½ tablespoons butter. Place the sole fillets in the dish, sprinkle with pepper, then add the wine and water. Bring to a boil over a stove burner, then cover loosely and set in a preheated 350°F. oven for 12 minutes. When the fish is poached, remove from the oven, carefully lift the fillets onto a platter with a large slotted spatula, then loosely cover the platter with aluminum foil. Set in a 175°F. oven or on a warming tray. Pour all of the poaching liquid into a heavy 3 to 4 quart saucepan and reserve.

Put the shrimp and mussels into a large kettle or saucepan and add the water. Bring to a boil over high heat. Cook, loosely covered, until the mussels open, about 8 to 10 minutes. If you are using oysters in place of mussels, add the oyster liquid along with the shrimp and water; add the oysters after 5 minutes. When the shellfish are done, remove the pan from the heat and lift the shellfish out with a mesh skimmer or slotted spoon, allowing the liquid to drain back into the pan. If shrimp are used let them cool a bit, then peel them. Place the shellfish on the platter along with the poached fish fillets. Strain the shellfish liquid through a fine mesh strainer to remove all sand or shells, then return to the pan and cook over high heat until reduced by one-third. Add the reduced shellfish liquid to the pan containing the fish poaching liquid. In a sauté pan or skillet, melt 2 tablespoons of butter and sauté the onion and leeks (or green onions) until quite soft and glazed but not brown. Add the vegetables along with the butter in which they were sautéed to the pan containing the poaching and shellfish liquids.

Cook the stock over high heat for 6 to 7 minutes, just until it begins to thicken a bit. Remove the pan from the heat and stir in the flour and butter with a whisk. Add the cream very gradually, stirring constantly. Return the pan to low heat and cook for 8 or 9 minutes. Do not allow the stock to come to a boil. Sprinkle in the pepper, salt, cayenne and Calvados as the stock cooks, mixing them in thoroughly with a wooden spoon. Toward the end of cooking, taste the stock. If necessary, add about ¼ teaspoon salt, ⅛ teaspoon white pepper, and a few grains of cayenne. When you have finished cooking the stock, remove the pan from the heat and allow to stand, uncovered, for a minute or two.

To serve, place several pieces of fish and equal quantities of shellfish in each of 6 to 8 preheated wide soup bowls. Ladle about 1 cup of the stock over the fish and shellfish. Bring to the table immediately.

Matelote of Eel
Sailors' Stew with Red Wine

The great French country eel dish—a "sailors'" stew with red wine, herbs, and a touch of Cognac. It is hearty and delicious, and red wine goes very well with it. For a dramatic flaming, be sure to heat the brandy separately in a small saucepan; when it is bubbling add it to the dish and ignite immediately.

FOR FOUR

2 to 2½ lb. eel, skinned, cleaned, cut into 1 inch slices

3 Tbs. salt butter

2 c. chopped onions

1 Tbs. flour

1 c. beef stock or water

1 c. red wine

1¾ tsp. salt

½ tsp. pepper

½ tsp. thyme

3 small bay leaves, broken in half

3 Tbs. parsley

1 tsp. minced garlic

1½ Tbs. flour rubbed together with 1 Tbs. butter (beurre manié)

¼ c. Cognac or brandy

four ¼-inch slices French or white bread, fried

In a heavy 4 to 6 quart saucepan melt the butter over low heat. Add the onions and cook, stirring frequently, until they are browned. Stir in the flour and mix very thoroughly. Add half of the stock and half of the red wine. Stir to mix thoroughly, then add all the remaining ingredients except the Cognac and bread slices. Raise the heat a bit and bring to a simmer. Add the eel and simmer for 5 minutes more. Heat the Cognac in a separate small saucepan until bubbling hot, then pour it into the stew and ignite. After the flame dies out, cook over very low heat for 20 minutes more. Remove from the heat, cover the pan, and allow to steep for 5 minutes before serving. To serve, ladle the portions into preheated wide soup bowls, being sure to include plenty of eel in each one. Bring to the table immediately along with pieces of fried bread. Break the slices of fried bread into large pieces and place on top of each portion of stew.

New England Clam Chowder

A classic American regional soup, rich with onions, potatoes, cream, and butter. It's easier to steam the clams open than to shuck them for chowder. Be sure to strain the broth well to remove any sand. Larger clams should be minced before being added. Be careful not to bring the chowder to a boil after you've added the milk and cream.

3 doz. large or 4 doz. small hard shell clams

3 c. cold water

2½ oz. salt pork, finely diced, or slab bacon

1 qt. potatoes, diced ½ inch thick (approximately 3 medium-sized potatoes)

1½ c. chopped onions

¾ c. hot water

1½ c. reserved clam broth

¾ tsp. salt

½ tsp. freshly ground black pepper

⅛ tsp. nutmeg

2 c. milk plus 1 c. heavy cream, combined and scalded

2 Tbs. salt butter

an additional ½ tsp. salt, if necessary

additional butter for dotting

Wash and scrub the clams thoroughly to remove excess sand. Place them in a 6 to 8 quart saucepan or kettle along with the cold water. Bring to a boil over high heat, then cover the pan. Reduce the heat a bit and steam the clams for about 8 to 10 minutes, until they are all opened. Remove the opened clams to a large bowl, using long-handled tongs and picking each one up by the edge of its opened shell. Allow the liquid in each clam to drain back into the pan as you remove them. If a few are still unopened, steam them for 2 to 3 minutes longer. Any that still remain closed should be discarded. Line a large strainer with several layers of paper towels and set it over a bowl. Strain the broth through the towel-lined strainer and reserve. Remove the clams from their shells, cutting off the black muscle tip. Chop the clams and reserve.

In a heavy 5 to 7 quart saucepan cook the salt pork or bacon over medium-high heat until it has rendered all its fat. Remove the solids with a skimmer or slotted spoon. Add the potatoes and onions and cook over high heat for 2 minutes, stirring constantly. Add the hot water. Stir. When the liquid in the pan comes to a boil, reduce the heat to low and simmer, stirring frequently, until the potatoes begin to become tender and appear glazed, about 8 minutes. Add 1½ cups of the reserved clam broth, the chopped clams, the salt, pepper, and nutmeg. Cook until the potatoes are done, about 10 minutes more. Remove the pan from the heat. When the simmer dies down, add the scalded milk and cream mixture very gradually, stirring with a wooden spoon. Turn the heat to very low and return the pan to the heat. Warm gradually, stirring from time to time. Do not bring to a boil. Add the butter and stir until it is melted. Taste, and add a bit more salt if necessary. Serve in preheated soup bowls with a teaspoon of butter placed on the surface of each portion immediately before bringing to the table.

Manhattan Clam Chowder

This always struck us as a dubious substitute for the New England dish—until we hit upon this version which uses cream and tomatoes.

FOR FOUR TO SIX

Prepare as directed for New England Clam Chowder, adding 2 cups peeled, chopped ripe tomatoes, which have been sautéed until very soft and liquidy in 2 tablespoons butter, after the scalded milk and cream mixture is added.

Oyster Chowder

Use fresh oysters only for this variation of New England Clam Chowder designed for places where clams are less plentiful than oysters.

FOR FOUR TO SIX

Prepare as directed for New England Clam Chowder. Substitute 1½ pints freshly shucked oysters and their liquor for the clams and clam broth. Reduce the white pepper to ⅛ teaspoon and increase the nutmeg to ¼ teaspoon.

Conch Chowder

For Floridians. (Who else can get enough conch to have some left over for making soup?)

FOR FOUR TO SIX

Prepare as directed for New England Clam Chowder, substituting 1½ pints conch, diced ½ inch across, for the clams. Steam the diced conch in 1½ cups cold water and ½ cup dry white wine for 10 minutes, then proceed as directed.

Old Fashioned New England Fish Chowder

A hearty Yankee soup. Use fish fillets with the skin left on. They handle better and give the stock the rich flavor all great fish soups must have. Salt pork is traditionally used, but we prefer sugar-cured slab bacon. This chowder does not reheat well.

FOR FOUR

1 lb. fresh haddock or cod fillets, skin left on	1 c. coarsely chopped white onions
2 c. water	1½ c. milk
½ tsp. salt	1½ Tbs. salt butter
2 medium-sized potatoes, peeled and diced ¾ inch thick	½ tsp. salt
1½ oz. sugar-cured slab bacon, rind cut off and cut into ½ inch cubes, or 1½ oz. salt pork	⅜ tsp. freshly ground white pepper
	scant ⅛ tsp. mace

Rinse the fish fillets under cold running water, then place them in a heavy 3 to 4 quart saucepan. Add the water and salt and bring to a boil over high heat. Reduce the heat to low and simmer the fish for 6 to 8 minutes, just until it can be flaked off the skin with gentle pressure from a fork. Remove the pan from the heat and lift the pieces of fish out with a slotted spoon or mesh skimmer, allowing the liquid to drain back into the pan. Place the fish in a wide shallow baking dish or a pie pan in a single layer to allow it to cool down fairly quickly; set the dish aside.

Put the potatoes into the pan and return the pan to the heat. Raise the heat to bring the liquid to a boil, then reduce the heat slightly and

---

cook the potatoes for 7 minutes, or until the pieces are fork tender but not mushy. While the potatoes are cooking, fry the slab bacon in a small sauté pan or skillet over medium-high heat for 3 minutes, then add the onions. Reduce the heat a bit and sauté the onions until they are lightly browned; stir very frequently with a wooden spatula or spoon to ensure even browning. Remove the pan from the heat. Remove the skin from the fish, which will be cool enough to handle by this time. Discard the skin and add the fish and any liquid that has collected in the dish to the pan containing the potatoes. Also add the sautéed onions, slab bacon, and any fat from the sauté pan. Stir gently to mix, then place the saucepan over low heat. Add the milk, butter, and seasonings, and mix gently once again. Cook over low heat for 8 to 10 minutes. Do not allow the chowder to come to a boil; if necessary, reduce the heat still further or take the pan off the heat for a minute, then return it again. To serve, ladle into soup bowls, including plenty of potato pieces and fish and 4 or more pieces of slab bacon in each serving.

Turtle Soup

Our favorite version of Turtle Soup, made with diced ham, fresh tomatoes, rich beef stock, and very little sherry. Adding sherry to Turtle Soup at the table has always struck us as a mistake; it's all too easy to overpower the other flavors and end up with an unpleasant sherry soup. Adding the sherry an hour before the end of cooking gives you the balance and aroma a really good Turtle Soup should have. Fresh turtle meat or good quality frozen can be used. Turtle meat is very perishable, so keep it refrigerated until you add it to the soup.

FOR EIGHT OR MORE

SOUP BASE

2 lb. turtle meat, cut into ¾ inch cubes and kept refrigerated	2 large ripe tomatoes, coarsely chopped (about 1½ c.)
½ lb. lean ham, cut into ½ inch cubes	2 Tbs. chopped celery tops
	2 Tbs. finely minced parsley
1 c. chopped onions	1 Tbs. finely minced garlic

ROUX

¾ c. (1½ sticks) salt butter
½ c. flour

SEASONINGS AND LIQUID

2 tsp. salt

1 tsp. freshly ground black
pepper

⅛ tsp. cayenne

3 whole bay leaves, broken into
quarters

½ tsp. thyme

½ tsp. cloves

½ tsp. allspice

¼ tsp. mace

3 c. rich beef stock

1¼ c. water

---

1 Tbs. Worcestershire sauce
1 Tbs. fresh lemon juice
1 Tbs. dry sherry (Manzanilla)

Prepare the ingredients for the base first. Refrigerate the meats while preparing the roux.

In a large 7 to 8 quart heavy pot or kettle, melt the butter over low heat. Gradually add the flour, stirring constantly. Cook over low heat, always stirring, until a light brown roux (the color of light peanut butter) is formed. When the roux reaches the right color (after about 25 to 30 minutes) quickly add the ham, onions, tomatoes, celery tops, parsley, and garlic. Mix thoroughly and continue cooking over very low heat, still stirring, until the vegetables are browned; this should take another 20 to 30 minutes. Add the seasonings and mix well, then add the turtle meat, beef stock, and water, stirring as you do so to keep the soup smooth. Raise the heat to high, bring to a boil, then lower the heat again and simmer for 3 hours. At the end of 2 hours add the Worcestershire, lemon juice, and sherry. Stir from time to time with a wooden spoon or spatula and scrape down the sides and across the bottom of the pot to prevent scorching.

When the cooking is done, let the soup stand for 5 to 10 minutes in the pot. Stir thoroughly before you ladle out the portions to distribute the solids evenly.

Creole Turtle Stew

A rich spicy semiliquid stew served with boiled rice. This recipe can be multiplied several times over with no difficulties. Test the turtle meat for doneness after the suggested cooking time; occasionally one gets tougher turtle, and longer simmering just gives the stew a richer flavor. Better to freeze than refrigerate leftovers.

FOR FOUR TO SIX

2 lb. cleaned turtle meat, cut up

2 Tbs. salt butter

2 tsp. salt

¾ tsp. freshly ground black pepper

1½ c. chopped onions

1 Tbs. flour

½ lb. lean boiled ham, cut into ⅜ inch cubes

1 large ripe tomato, cut up

1 c. dry red wine

3 Tbs. brandy

2 c. water

2 bay leaves, crushed

1½ tsp. finely minced garlic

¼ tsp. mace

⅛ tsp. cayenne

½ tsp. fresh lemon juice

an additional ¼ tsp. salt, if necessary

BOILED RICE

MAKES APPROXIMATELY 4 CUPS COOKED RICE

2 c. long grain white rice

4 c. cold water

2 tsp. salt

2 tsp. salt butter

Melt the butter in a large heavy saucepan. Add the turtle meat, 1½ teaspoons of salt, and ½ teaspoon pepper. Cook over medium-high heat, stirring frequently, until the turtle meat is no longer red, about 8 to 12 minutes. Remove the pan from the heat and drain off the liquid that has collected. Return the pan to high heat, add ½ teaspoon salt and ¼ teaspoon black pepper, and cook, stirring constantly, until the turtle meat is browned, about 7 to 9 minutes. Add the onions and cook, stirring, until the onions are browned. Stir in the flour and mix very thoroughly. Cook for 2 minutes more, then add the ham and tomato. Continue cooking until a thick pastelike gravy begins to form at the bottom of the pan. Add the wine and brandy and mix thoroughly. When the liquid comes to a boil, add the water, bay leaves, garlic, mace, cayenne, and lemon juice. Bring to a boil again, stir to mix very thoroughly, then reduce the heat to a point where the stew simmers visibly but not too vigorously. Cover the pan loosely and cook until the turtle meat is tender, about 45 minutes. Toward the end of cooking, taste the thick liquid in the pan and, if necessary, add ¼ teaspoon salt. Prepare the rice while the stew is cooking.

To prepare the rice combine all the ingredients in a heavy 3 or 4 quart saucepan for which you have a tight-fitting cover. Bring to a boil over high heat. Stir with fork, cover the pan tightly, then reduce the heat to medium-low. (If the lid begins to pop up, lower the heat still further.) Cook covered for precisely 15 minutes, remove the pan from the heat, uncover, and fluff the rice with a fork.

This recipe can be multiplied with no difficulty. With larger quantities, you may find the rice still a bit wet at the end of 15 minutes; if so, cook for several minutes more, uncovered, to dry it out.

To serve the stew, spoon about ½ cup boiled rice to one side of each preheated dinner plate, then ladle about ⅔ cup of the stew onto the center of the plate.

Conch Stew

FOR FOUR TO SIX

Prepare as directed for Creole Turtle Stew, substituting 2 pounds conch meat, cut into large chunks, for the turtle meat. Increase the total cooking time by about 1 hour.

Shrimp Gumbo

Gumbo is one of the classic inventions of American cooking. It originated in southwestern Louisiana and remains one of the popular dishes in New Orleans. The name gumbo *is derived from the African word* gombo, *meaning okra. Okra and filé (ground dried sassafras leaves) are both used as thickening agents for this hearty soup, but the real key to Creole gumbo is the roux. The roux, made with flour and fat, gives the soup its fundamental flavor and texture. In New Orleans okra gumbo is generally preferred, while in Cajun Louisiana there is a marked preference for filé gumbo which uses no okra. Be sure to have the vegetables and sausage chopped and the shrimp peeled and deveined before starting to make the roux: they will be used to arrest the browning and must be at hand when needed—you can't leave the roux unattended.*

GUMBO BASE

2 lb. fresh shrimp, peeled and
deveined (about 4 lb. in
the shell)

2 c. chopped onions

¾ c. chopped green pepper

½ c. thinly sliced green onion
tops

2½ Tbs. finely minced parsley

1 Tbs. finely minced garlic

1½ c. coarsely chopped ripe fresh
tomatoes

⅔ c. finely chopped smoked
(Polish or French garlic)
sausage or ½ c. finely chopped
fried slab bacon

2 lb. fresh okra, sliced ¼ inch
thick, or two 10-oz. pkg. frozen
baby okra, drained and sliced
¼ inch thick

ROUX

½ c. salt butter
¼ c. bacon or sausage drippings
¾ c. flour

LIQUID AND SEASONINGS

2½ qt. cold water

2 large bay leaves, crushed

1¼ tsp. thyme

1 Tbs. salt

1¼ tsp. freshly ground black
pepper

¼ tsp. cayenne

5 tsp. fresh lemon juice

10 whole allspice

½ tsp. mace

7 whole cloves

Chop the vegetables and sausage or bacon first. Peel and devein the
shrimp, rinse them, then roll in paper towels and refrigerate until
needed. Slice the okra. To make the roux, heat the butter and bacon
drippings in a heavy 7 to 8 quart saucepan over medium heat. Add the
flour gradually, stirring constantly to keep the mixture smooth. Cook
over medium-low heat, stirring constantly, until a medium brown roux
(the color of pecan shells) is formed. This will take from 20 to 30
minutes. As soon as the roux reaches the desired color, add all the
chopped vegetables except the parsley and tomatoes to arrest the
browning. Stir vigorously, then cook for about 12 to 14 minutes more,
until the vegetables are lightly browned. Add the parsley, tomatoes,
and sausage and mix very thoroughly. Gradually add 2 quarts of the
water, stirring as you add. Add 1 pound of the shrimp, the okra, and
the seasonings. Raise the heat and bring the liquid to a boil, then
lower the heat just enough to keep a simmer going and cook for 1
hour, stirring frequently and scraping the sides and bottom of the
pot to prevent scorching. At the end of the hour, add the remaining

½ cup water. Stir to mix thoroughly. Remove the pan from the heat, cover loosely, and allow to stand at room temperature until 30 minutes before you plan to serve the gumbo.

At 30 minutes before serving, put the pan back on medium heat and bring to a boil. Add the remaining pound of shrimp. Simmer just until the shrimp turn pink, about 10 minutes. Stir thoroughly once, cover the pan, and remove from the heat. Allow to steep for 15 minutes before serving. Serve over about ½ cup boiled rice (see Creole Turtle Stew) in wide deep soup or gumbo bowls.

Crab Gumbo

FOR EIGHT OF MORE

Prepare as directed for Shrimp Gumbo, substituting 2 pounds lump crabmeat for the shrimp. Reduce the final cooking period, when the second pound of crabmeat is added, to 8 minutes.

Oyster Gumbo

A classic Louisiana filé gumbo. The roux gives it the thickness, richness, and a marvelous smoky flavor. The filé is added after cooking for flavor and for a slight additional thickening. The thickening properties of filé have been vastly exaggerated: it will not thicken a soup that is too thin; it will not disguise a poor roux. Filé is primarily used because it has a pleasant if not too pronounced flavor, a fine dark color, and because it is the traditional touch for this type of gumbo. If you omit it your gumbo will be missing something, but that something is more crucial for Louisiana natives who have grown up accustomed to the taste, smell, and above all the idea of filé. Don't heat or further cook

*the gumbo once the filé is in, or the gumbo will get ropy. It is
safest to add the filé to the individual bowls just before serving if
you are likely to save some of the gumbo for the next day or for
freezing.*

FOR EIGHT OR MORE

GUMBO BASE

2 c. chopped onions

⅔ c. chopped green pepper

½ c. thinly sliced green onion
  tops

1 Tbs. finely minced garlic

2 Tbs. finely minced parsley

1 c. finely chopped smoked
  (Polish or French garlic)
  sausage or ½ c. finely chopped
  fried slab bacon

ROUX

6 Tbs. salt butter

¼ c. vegetable oil

½ c. flour

LIQUID AND SEASONINGS

2 qt. cold water

1 Tbs. salt

1¼ tsp. freshly ground black
  pepper

⅛ tsp. cayenne

1 tsp. thyme

3 bay leaves, crushed

⅛ tsp. mace

2½ to 3 Tbs. filé powder

---

1 pint freshly shucked oysters (about 2 doz. medium) and their liquor
(about ½ c.)

Chop the vegetables and sausage or bacon first. Leave the oysters in
the refrigerator and refrigerate the chopped sausage. Heat the butter
and vegetable oil in a heavy 7 to 8 quart saucepan over medium
heat. Add the flour gradually, stirring constantly to keep the mixture
smooth. Cook over medium-low heat, stirring constantly, until a
medium brown roux (the color of pecan shells) is formed. This will
take from 20 to 30 minutes. As soon as the roux reaches the desired
color, add all the chopped vegetables except the parsley to arrest the
browning. Stir vigorously, then cook for about 12 to 14 minutes more,
until the vegetables are lightly browned. Stir thoroughly, then add ¼
cup of the water and the chopped sausage. Mix thoroughly again and
continue browning over low heat, stirring constantly, for 10 minutes
longer. Add the parsley and all the seasonings except the filé powder.
Raise the heat to medium, then gradually pour in the remaining
water. Bring the gumbo to a boil, then lower the heat and simmer

---

for 1 hour, stirring frequently. At the end of the hour add the oysters and the oyster liquor. Cook for 4 to 5 minutes longer, just until the oysters curl around the edges. Remove the pot from the heat and let the simmer die down. Add the filé powder and mix well, then allow the gumbo to steep in the pot for 5 minutes before serving. To serve, mix very thoroughly, then ladle into soup bowls over boiled rice (see Creole Turtle Stew).

Seafood Gumbo

The relative merits of okra and filé in gumbo can still provide fuel for an evening's argument in French Louisiana. We were delighted to find a Gulf Coast restaurant that sidestepped all objections by using both, with excellent results. We tried a version of our own with both. It works well and looks as good as it tastes. Just keep in mind that it's still the roux that makes a distinctive gumbo.

FOR EIGHT OR MORE

Prepare as directed for Shrimp Gumbo. Add 1 cup of shredded lump crabmeat along with the second pound of shrimp. After removing the pot from the heat, sprinkle in 5 or 6 drops of Louisiana Green Hot Sauce (or 3 drops Tabasco) and stir, then add about 3 tablespoons of filé powder. Allow to stand for 5 to 10 minutes before serving. Serve in soup bowls over boiled rice (see Creole Turtle Stew).

She-Crab Soup

Carolina's great contribution to American cooking. There's a good reason why crab lovers prefer female crabs—the delicious roe is one of the delights of this soup. If you cannot get she-crabs or the she-crabs you get have no roe, you can cheat a bit by putting a scant teaspoon of crumbled hard boiled egg yolk in the bottom of each bowl just before serving. The roe is valued primarily for its texture and if you keep a straight face, you'll probably get away with it. Be sure to use freshly grated onion and the lowest possible burner heat for the richest flavor and texture.

FOR FOUR

½ lb. crabmeat and crab roe	⅜ tsp. salt
2 Tbs. salt butter	⅛ tsp. freshly ground white pepper
2 Tbs. flour	
1½ c. milk	⅜ tsp. mace
½ c. heavy cream	a few grains cayenne
2 tsp. finely grated onion	⅜ tsp. very finely chopped lemon rind
¾ tsp. Worcestershire sauce	

1 Tbs. dry sherry (Manzanilla)

Melt the butter over low heat in a heavy 2 to 3 quart saucepan or the top of a double boiler. Stir in the flour and mix until smooth. Add the milk a bit at a time, stirring constantly with a whisk. Cook until thickened, then add the cream. Cook for about 1 minute longer, then add all the remaining ingredients except the sherry. Stir very gently with a wooden spoon and cook over the lowest possible heat for 20 minutes. If the soup appears about to boil, remove the pan from the heat for a minute or so, then put it back. Remove the pan from the heat and add the sherry. Stir to mix, then allow to steep in the pan for 3 minutes before serving.

French Shrimp Bisque

One of the grand French dishes, the distilled essence of shrimp, with a superb texture, delicate color, and a richness that lingers. A fine demonstration of what is so special about French cooking. Shrimp Bisque is not an easy dish; the whole shrimp are transformed in a number of separate steps until nothing is left of them but their taste. We prefer this as a main dish for an elegant light supper. If you serve it as an appetizer, a scant cupful per person is sufficient—it's an incredibly rich soup.

2 to 2½ lb. whole shrimp in the shell, rinsed and drained thoroughly
3 Tbs. salt butter
1 Tbs. olive oil
1 c. chopped white onions
⅓ c. finely chopped carrot
¼ tsp. thyme

1 small bay leaf, crushed
2 tsp. finely minced fresh garlic
2 c. chicken stock
½ c. dry white wine
1 medium-sized ripe tomato, peeled and cut up
2 Tbs. brandy

---

1 Tbs. salt butter worked into 2 Tbs. flour with your fingers (beurre manié)
¼ tsp. salt, or a bit more
½ tsp. freshly ground white pepper

scant ⅛ tsp. cayenne
1 c. plus 6 Tbs. heavy cream
1 tsp. brandy

In a heavy 4 to 6 quart saucepan or kettle melt the butter, then add the oil. Mix, then add the onions and carrot and cook over medium heat until the vegetables are slightly soft. Add the thyme, bay leaf, and garlic. Stir thoroughly. Add the shrimp and raise the heat to high. Stir and toss for a few seconds, then add the stock, wine, tomato, and brandy. When the liquid reaches a boil, reduce the heat to medium-low and simmer for 40 to 45 minutes. Remove the pan from the heat.

Remove the shrimp from the pan with a slotted spoon and place on a platter in a single layer to cool off. Peel, reserving the shells. Purée the shrimp along with some of the stock base, a batch at a time, in a blender, then strain first through a coarse sieve, then through a very fine one. Crush the shells in the coarse sieve with a pestle; put the strained liquid and any pastelike solid that collects on the underside of the sieve into the pan along with the strained purée. Stir, turn the heat on very low, then gradually add the remaining ingredients. Heat until warmed through. Do not allow to come to a boil. The texture should be quite smooth, the color a rather pale peach pink. Set off the bisque by serving in white bowls or cups, or bowls with a delicately decorated edge.

The preparation can be suspended after the puréeing and straining is done; then the beurre manié, etc., can be added about 20 minutes before you plan to serve.

Lobster Bisque

A variation of French Shrimp Bisque. The same process and the same result, but with the essence of lobster.

FOR TWO OR THREE AS A MAIN COURSE; FOR SIX AS A FIRST COURSE

Prepare as directed for French Shrimp Bisque, substituting 2 to 2½ pounds lobster meat in the shell for the shrimp.

Oyster Soup

A delicate light soup that does justice to the flavor of fresh oysters. Be sure to reserve all the oyster liquor for the base. Oyster Soup can be prepared in larger quantities. Don't try to keep it for more than 2 days under refrigeration. Reheat it very gently, just enough to warm it through.

FOR THREE OR FOUR

1 pt. oysters and their liquor
hot water
2 Tbs. plus 2 tsp. salt butter
2 Tbs. flour
3 Tbs. thinly sliced green onion tops

1 Tbs. finely minced parsley
¾ tsp. salt
⅜ tsp. freshly ground white pepper

Strain the oysters through a fine mesh strainer or a piece of cheesecloth, allowing the liquor to drain into a small saucepan. Remove the oysters from the strainer and with your fingers pick out any particles of shell that remain, then chop or cut the oysters into ½ inch pieces. Simmer them in the oyster liquor for 3 minutes, then strain them out again. Add sufficient hot water to the strained oyster liquor to make up 2½ cups. Measure out ½ cup of the chopped oysters to be added to the soup when it is finished. Discard the rest, or use as a garnish for another dish.

Melt 2 tablespoons of the butter in a heavy saucepan, then gradually stir in the flour, mixing constantly to keep the béchamel smooth. Cook for a minute, then slowly pour in the hot liquid. Cook over medium-low heat, stirring with a whisk to keep mixture free of any lumps, then lower the heat and add the green onion tops, parsley, salt, and pepper. Raise the heat just until the liquid begins to boil, then lower it again to just keep a gentle simmer going. Simmer for 20 minutes. About 2 to 3 minutes before the soup is done, add the reserved ½ cup of chopped oysters. To serve, ladle the liquid into bowls, then add 2 tablespoons of chopped oysters to each serving. Top each bowl with a thin sliver of butter (about ½ teaspoon) and bring to the table immediately.

Oyster Stew

Butter, cream, and freshly shucked oysters are the keys to this rich and delicious American classic.

FOR SIX TO EIGHT

3 pt. freshly shucked oysters, their liquor (about 1½ c.) reserved
3 c. milk
1 c. heavy cream
1 Tbs. salt
½ tsp. freshly ground black pepper

¼ tsp. cayenne
6 Tbs. salt butter
4 Tbs. thinly sliced green onion tops

Strain the oyster liquor into a 4 to 5 quart heavy saucepan. Add the milk and cream and warm over low heat. Add the salt, pepper, and cayenne, then raise the heat. Bring just to a boil, then quickly lower the heat and add the oysters. Cook just below a simmer for 4 to 5 minutes, just until the oysters begin to curl at the edges. Remove the pan from the heat. Add the butter and green onion tops. Stir to mix thoroughly. Ladle into preheated soup bowls, then serve immediately.

Cádiz Fish Soup with Orange

An intriguing Spanish soup combining fish and fruit, ideal for light summer dining.

2½ to 3 lb. fish with white flesh, cleaned and cut into fillets or steaks, skin left on

coarse salt for sprinkling the fish

¼ c. olive oil

4 small or 2 large garlic cloves, peeled and cut into large pieces

1 c. chopped onions

2 qt. boiling water

1 Tbs. finely minced parsley

1 bay leaf, broken into quarters

⅛ tsp. mace

⅔ c. freshly squeezed sour orange juice (add 1½ Tbs. lemon juice if the oranges you use are sweet)

½ tsp. salt, more if necessary

¼ tsp. freshly ground white pepper

Sprinkle the pieces of fish with coarse salt, place in a shallow baking dish, cover with plastic wrap, and refrigerate for 1 hour. Toward the end of the hour, heat the olive oil in a 4 to 6 quart heavy saucepan or sauté pan. Add the garlic and fry until browned. Remove the garlic with a slotted spoon and add the onions. Fry until soft and very lightly browned, then add the boiling water. Boil until the onions are very soft. Remove the fish from the refrigerator, rinse thoroughly under cold running water to remove the salt, shake dry, then add to the pan along with the parsley, bay leaf, and mace. When the liquid boils up again, cover the pan, reduce the heat a bit, and simmer for 15 to 20 minutes, until the pieces of fish are tender. Remove the pieces of fish with a slotted spoon or spatula, then strain the soup through a fine mesh strainer to remove all solids. Wipe out any sediment that clings to the inside of the pan, then pour the strained soup back into it. Put the pan back on medium-low heat and add the orange juice. Simmer for about 3 minutes, then add the fish. Sprinkle in the salt and pepper and continue cooking, below a boil, until the soup and the fish are quite hot. To serve, lift several pieces of fish into each preheated soup bowl, then ladle about ¾ to 1 cup of liquid over.

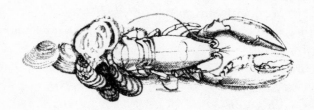

Soups and Chowders 255

One Dish Meal Recipes

Paella

Nasi Goreng (Indonesian Fried Rice)

Oyster and Sausage Jambalaya

Shrimp Jambalaya

Lobster Jambalaya

Coquilles au Riz à la Basquaise (Scallops and Rice Basque Style)

Shrimp and Yellow Rice

Harina con Camarones (Corn Meal with Shrimp)

Shrimp Creole

Crawfish Étouffée

Shrimp Étouffée

Crabmeat Étouffée

Oysters with Spaghetti

Clams with Spaghetti

Squid with Spaghetti

Snails with Green Sauce and Spaghetti

Clams and Tomato Sauce with Spaghetti

Shrimp Pansit

Bami Goreng

Shrimp Stuffed Peppers

Apalachicola Chicken and Oyster Pie

Veal Oscar

Veal with Lump Crabmeat

Bacalao con Chile (Codfish and Chili)

Oyster Omelette

Crab Omelette

12

One Dish Meals

Simplicity and satisfaction are the keynotes of the one dish meals in this chapter. What gives pot dinners their fundamental appeal is their economy. They use noodles and rice as the basic elements and achieve their ultimate taste by imaginative seasoning and a minimum use of expensive seafood. It is not true that Americans do not like one dish meals. What many Americans lack is experience in dealing with them. Poorer cultures, accustomed to stretching a meager food budget, have made rice and pasta staples of the daily diet. Through years of experience they have evolved rice and pasta dishes that are favored traditions enjoyed for their own sake as well as for cheapness. One does not have to turn to supermarket convenience foods as a change from meat and potatoes or hamburger and potatoes. All these ethnic dishes are simple to prepare and serve, and are both filling and satisfying in much the same way as a steak and potato dinner. They also make fine choices for small dinner parties. In Louisiana a dinner of Crawfish Étouffée and a bottle of wine or beer is as festive a meal as one can imagine. Spanish Paella is dramatic, attractive, and delicious; Indonesian Nasi and Bami Goreng are exotic, well seasoned, and superb eating. Pasta makes a grand complete meal prepared in some of these imaginative combinations. Being poor is no fun, but few of the rich in the world eat better than the less well off ethnic groups who regularly enjoy many of the favorites included here.

One Dish Meal Techniques

Choosing suitable and attractive cooking-serving dishes is one of the key elements. The wrong size or shape cooking vessel can radically alter texture or taste of finished dish.

Use skillets or sauté pans for dishes with little liquid.

Use large heavy saucepans for stews and jambalayas.

Use heavy casserole dishes with fitted lids for slow, long-baking dishes.

Warm leftovers very slowly, adding a small amount of water if necessary.

Paella

Another marvelous dish often beleaguered by questions of authenticity. Paella is above all an inventive dish, and will work well with a great variety of available ingredients. This is one of our favorite versions, made with chicken, squid, shrimp, a sturdy white fish, chorizos, chopped vegetables, and long grain rice. Of these ingredients the chicken, chorizos, rice, and pimientos, all readily available, are the indispensable elements. Clams, mussels, octopus, lobster tails, artichoke hearts, peas are some good additional ingredients if you happen to have them. We have found long grain rice preferable to the frequently recommended short grain rice; American long grain rice holds its texture and character better when surrounded by all the other ingredients. Paella pans are the traditional cooking vessel and are nice to use, but a good heavy large skillet will do just as well. Present the dish at the table in its cooking pan so everyone can see how attractive the Paella is, then serve directly from the pan.

½ lb. medium squid, cleaned and cut into ½ inch strips or rings

½ lb. peeled and deveined fresh shrimp (about 1 lb. in the shell)

½ lb. firm fish, cleaned and cut into large chunks

½ tsp. freshly ground black pepper

½ c. olive oil

1 small frying chicken, cut up

two 11-oz. cans Spanish chorizo* sausage, sausages rinsed, dried, then cut into ½ inch pieces

1 c. chopped onions

1½ c. chopped ripe tomatoes (2 medium-sized tomatoes)

½ tsp. paprika

1 Tbs. finely minced garlic

⅔ c. thin strips of green pepper

3 c. uncooked long grain rice

7½ c. boiling water

½ tsp. ground saffron

2 tsp. salt, more if necessary

GARNISH

3 canned pimientos, drained, dried, then cut into strips

½ c. cooked green peas (optional)

1 pint mussels, steamed open (optional)

Heat the olive oil in a 12 to 14 inch paella pan or heavy skillet until quite hot. Add the chicken and fry, turning the pieces over frequently, until very lightly browned. Add the *chorizos* and fry for about 4 minutes more, until the chicken is a medium brown color. Remove the chicken and *chorizos* to a platter with tongs or a slotted spoon, allowing the oil to drain back into the pan as you lift the pieces out. Reserve. Add the onions to the pan and fry until golden, stirring frequently, about 3 to 4 minutes. Add the tomatoes and cook over high heat until most of the tomato liquid appears dried up. Reduce the heat to low and add the paprika, garlic, and green pepper. Stir very thoroughly, raise the heat a bit, and fry until the garlic and pepper are browned. Add the rice, raise the heat to high, and cook, stirring and tossing constantly, for 5 minutes, until the grains of rice appear browned and glossy. Return the chicken and *chorizos* to the pan,

---

* Spanish *chorizo* sausage is available in fancy groceries or those specializing in ethnic items. The sausage is packed in 11 ounce cans and preserved in lard. (The "El Baturro" brand is available in most parts of the country.) Half a tin yields approximately 4 ounces of sausage once you rinse off the lard under hot running water. Drain the sausage on paper towels. The remainder of the *chorizos* can be put into a small freezer container and kept in the refrigerator for several weeks. Be sure to cover the pieces of sausage with the lard from the can.

One Dish Meals 259

then add about 4 cups of the boiling water. Stir, then add the saffron (dissolve it first in a teaspoon of boiling water) and salt. Mix very thoroughly. When the liquid in the pan once again reaches a boil, add the squid, shrimp, fish, and black pepper. Stir again very thoroughly, add 3 more cups of boiling water, then cook at medium-high heat, stirring occasionally, until the liquid in the pan is almost totally absorbed. Lower the heat, then cook for 8 to 10 minutes longer, until the rice is done. Test by tasting a few grains. If the rice is still tough and the paella appears to be too dry, add the remaining ½ cup water. When the dish is done, remove the pan from the heat and allow to stand for 4 to 5 minutes before bringing to the table. If desired, garnish the paella with pimientos, cooked green peas, and mussels. Serve from the pan, spooning the paella onto preheated plates with a large long-handled spoon.

Nasi Goreng
Indonesian Fried Rice

A staple fried rice dish of Indonesian cuisine, using shrimp, pork, a heady mixture of seasonings, and rice stir-fried together, and served with eggs cooked like a thin omelette and cut into strips. Peanut oil will give you the finest, and most characteristic, flavor, but other vegetable oils can be substituted.

FOR FOUR

½ lb. fresh shrimp, peeled and deveined (1 lb. in the shell)	1½ Tbs. finely minced garlic
3 large eggs	½ c. minced fresh pork
½ tsp. salt	1½ Tbs. dark soy sauce
¼ c. peanut oil	¼ tsp. cayenne
1½ c. chopped onions	3 c. boiled rice (see Creole Turtle Stew)

OPTIONAL GARNISH

¼ c. thin strips prosciutto or Smithfield ham
⅓ c. fried onion flakes*

* Fried onion flakes are traditionally made in Indonesian cooking from fresh onions cut into quarters, then sliced paper thin, dried thoroughly, and fried in vegetable oil until crisp and brown. After being drained and cooled, they can be put into a tightly covered jar and kept unrefrigerated for several weeks.

You can also use dehydrated onion flakes available in supermarkets; fry them for about 30 to 40 seconds in hot vegetable oil. Do not allow to brown.

Beat the eggs in a bowl along with about ¼ teaspoon salt. Heat 1 tablespoon of the oil in a large heavy skillet or sauté pan about 12 inches in diameter. Tip the pan with a rolling motion to ensure that the entire bottom surface is coated with oil. Pour in the eggs and cook until thoroughly set. If desired, turn the omelette over and cook briefly on the other side. Remove the omelette to a plate. Cut into ¾ inch squares and reserve.

Add 2 more tablespoons of the oil to the skillet and allow to heat, then add the onions and garlic. Stir-fry for about 2 minutes, until the vegetables are glazed and lightly browned. Add the pork and continue stir-frying until it is cooked. Add the shrimp, omelette squares, soy sauce, remaining ¼ teaspoon salt, cayenne, and rice. Lower the heat to medium-low and toss together thoroughly. Add the remaining tablespoon of oil. Stir-fry for about 10 minutes, until the shrimp are cooked and the grains of rice appear evenly coated with oil and seasonings.

To serve, spoon onto heated plates. If desired garnish with strips of ham and fried onion flakes.

Oyster and Sausage Jambalaya

Gonzales, a small Louisiana town between New Orleans and Baton Rouge, is the self-proclaimed Jambalaya Capital of the World. This unusual Spanish settlement in the midst of French Louisiana is the home of this great one dish meal made with rice, descended from Spanish Paella. The sad pink or red servings of Spanish rice often called jambalaya on restaurant menus have little to do with the real dish, a rich smoky amalgam of oysters, shrimp, chicken, or meat with a complex balance of seasonings and spectacularly flavored rice. Because there is always some fat present in the base from the sausage or chicken, the uncooked rice is quickly coated and sealed when added to the pot, enabling it to keep its texture during the long slow cooking while absorbing all the flavors that surround it. Take care to drain the oysters thoroughly and to stir gently so as not to demolish them or the pieces of sausage; the finished jambalaya should be as handsome to look at as it is marvelous to eat.

FOR FOUR

1 pt. freshly shucked oysters (about 2 doz. medium), drained

2 Tbs. salt butter

4 c. chopped onions

⅔ c. chopped green pepper

½ c. chopped green onions

1 Tbs. finely minced garlic

2 Tbs. finely minced parsley

1 c. finely chopped lean baked ham

1 lb. lean pork, cut into ½ inch cubes

1 lb. Polish, French garlic, or other smoked sausage, sliced ½ inch thick

1 Tbs. salt

½ tsp. freshly ground black pepper

⅛ tsp. cayenne

½ tsp. chili powder

2 bay leaves, crushed

½ tsp. thyme

¼ tsp. cloves

1½ c. long grain white rice

3 c. beef stock

¼ to ½ c. water, if necessary

In a heavy 7 to 8 quart pot or kettle, melt the butter over low heat. Add the vegetables, parsley, ham, and pork and brown over low heat, stirring constantly, for 15 minutes. Add the sausage and seasonings, mix thoroughly, and continue cooking over low heat, stirring frequently, for 20 minutes. Add the rice and raise the heat to medium. Cook for 5 minutes, or until the rice is lightly browned, stirring and scraping the sides and bottom of the pot. Add the beef stock and oysters and mix gently.

Raise the heat to high, bring to a boil, and cook, uncovered, for 5 minutes, then cover the pot, lower the heat to low, and cook for 50 minutes, removing the cover to stir every 5 minutes or so. If you notice the jambalaya getting too dry, add ¼ to ½ cup water after about 25 to 30 minutes. Uncover the pot during the last 10 minutes of cooking and raise the heat to medium to allow the rice to dry out. Stir very gently so as not to break up the oysters. Serve immediately.

Shrimp Jambalaya

Another jambalaya variation, made with peeled raw shrimp. You can easily feed eight with this recipe by increasing the amount of shrimp and sausage by half and doubling the rice and the liquid. Jambalaya has traditionally been "stretchable," served as it is in the country where one must always be prepared to feed unexpected visitors; there are few public eating places where one can send them once they've arrived.

FOR FOUR

Prepare as directed for Oyster and Sausage Jambalaya, substituting 1 pound peeled and deveined raw shrimp (about 2 pounds before peeling) for the oysters and omitting the lean pork. If desired, substitute 8 ounces of cubed slab bacon for the pound of smoked sausage and reduce the salt specified in the recipe to 1 teaspoon.

Lobster Jambalaya

Our own variation. While we were working on the lobster recipes for this book one of us remarked, "This would be great in jambalaya." It was.

FOR FOUR

Boil 1 large or 2 small Florida lobsters (see Boiled Florida Lobster) for 8 minutes, then split, clean, and shell them as directed. Cut the lobster meat into 1 inch chunks. Proceed as directed for Oyster and Sausage Jambalaya.

Coquilles au Riz à la Basquaise
Scallops and Rice Basque Style

A splendid colorful dish from the French Pyrenees, made with scallops, Spanish sausage, green pepper, and pimiento. Simple to prepare and irristible. Frozen scallops work perfectly; just be sure to defrost them quickly and drain them well before adding to the casserole.

1 lb. scallops, rinsed and drained
1 c. uncooked rice
2 c. chicken stock
1 Tbs. olive oil
4 oz. Spanish chorizo sausage, drained and cut into ⅜ inch pieces (see note under Paella)

⅓ c. pimiento, drained and cut into thin strips about 1¼ inches long
1 small green pepper, seeds and core removed, cut into thin strips

Combine the rice, chicken stock, and olive oil in a 3 to 4 quart saucepan and bring to a boil over high heat. Reduce the heat to low and simmer, stirring frequently, for 7 minutes. Remove the pan from the heat. Put the rice and all the liquid from the pan into a 3 quart casserole, preferably one that has a cover to fit. Begin preheating the oven to 350°F.

Add the *chorizo*, pimiento, and green pepper to the casserole and mix with a wooden spoon. Cut the scallops in half if they are small, into quarters if they are medium or large size. Add them to the casserole and mix thoroughly again. Set the dish over medium heat on the range and bring to a simmer; immediately cover the dish and place it in the preheated oven. Bake for 15 minutes covered, then uncover, stir very thoroughly, and bake uncovered for 30 to 35 minutes longer, or until all the liquid is absorbed and the rice is sufficiently cooked. Mix lightly with a wooden spoon several times during the last half hour. Bring the casserole to the table and serve directly from it.

Shrimp and Yellow Rice

A Florida Spanish dish, made with chicken stock and saffron. Some finely diced slab bacon heated with the olive oil gives the base a fine smoky flavor. The rice is heated in the oil and vegetables before the liquid is added to coat and seal the rice so that it holds its texture and shape during cooking.

FOR FOUR

1 lb. raw shrimp, peeled and deveined (about 2 lb. in the shell)	1 bay leaf, broken up
	¼ tsp. thyme
	¼ tsp. cumin
2 Tbs. olive oil	2 c. chicken stock
1 oz. slab bacon, chopped	¼ tsp. crushed saffron threads
¾ c. chopped onions	½ tsp. salt
½ c. chopped green pepper	¼ tsp. freshly ground black pepper
1½ tsp. finely minced garlic	
1 c. uncooked rice	scant 1/16 tsp. cayenne
1 Tbs. minced parsley	1 tsp. lemon juice

Heat the oil in a heavy sauté pan or deep skillet about 10 inches in diameter. Add the bacon and cook for about 2 minutes. Add the onions, green pepper, and garlic and cook, stirring frequently, until the onions are soft and glazed. Raise the heat to high and add the rice. Cook, stirring and scraping the bottom of the pan constantly, for 2 minutes. Add the parsley, bay leaf, thyme, and cumin. Stir to mix thoroughly, then add the shrimp and ½ cup of the chicken stock. Cover the pan loosely, lower the heat a bit, and cook for 4 minutes or until the shrimp turn pink. Uncover the saffron into the remaining 1½ cups chicken stock, then add the stock to the pan very slowly. Stir to mix. Sprinkle in the salt and pepper, then raise the heat to high. When the liquid comes to a boil, stir several times, cover the pan tightly, then reduce the heat again. Uncover briefly to add the cayenne and lemon juice. Simmer for 15 minutes, then remove the pan from the heat and uncover. Stir very thoroughly, then allow to stand uncovered for 3 to 4 minutes before serving.

Harina con Camarones
Corn Meal with Shrimp

A Cuban shrimp dish from Tampa, made with yellow corn meal, peeled raw shrimp, and a carefully measured amount of finely chopped small green hot chili peppers, widely available in jars or cans. Begin timing the dish when the corn meal is put to boil and be sure to stir and scrape frequently. A marvelous dish just as good reheated in a 400°F. oven the second day. Stone ground yellow corn meal, available at health food stores, will give you a particularly sturdy texture and nutty flavor.

1 lb. peeled and deveined raw shrimp (about 2 lb. in the shell)	1 c. chopped onions
	1 tsp. finely chopped canned chili peppers (1 or 2, depending on size)
1 c. stone ground yellow corn meal	1¼ tsp. finely minced garlic
4 c. water	2 Tbs. tomato paste
1 tsp. salt	⅛ tsp. cumin
2 Tbs. olive oil	½ tsp. salt

Combine the corn meal, water, and salt in a heavy 4 to 5 quart sauce-pan. Bring to a boil over high heat, then lower the heat to the lowest possible setting. Set the timer for 45 minutes. In a sauté pan or skillet heat the olive oil over medium heat, then add the onions, chili peppers, and garlic. Sauté, stirring, until the onions are soft and beginning to turn brown. Add the shrimp and tomato paste. Stir to mix thoroughly, then raise the heat and cook for 3 minutes, tossing the contents of the pan with a wooden spoon as you cook. Add the contents of the sauté pan to the pan of corn meal. Mix, then cook over low heat for 30 minutes more or until the corn meal is very thick, stirring from time to time. Add the cumin and salt 5 minutes after mixing the vegetables and shrimp with the corn meal.

Shrimp Creole

Creole cooking at its best is a complex and artful regional cuisine. The popular dish called Shrimp Creole on American menus generally combines shrimp, rice, tomato sauce, and celery in a watery bland stew, and has little to do with the authentic dish. The original Shrimp Creole was a rich, very peppery dish with a smoky roux base. We suspect the impostor was created to accommodate visitors and tourists. The version we include here, which we would call Shrimp Sauce Piquante, is the dish as it once was. No one serves it publicly this way any longer because in culinary matters Gresham's law frequently prevails and the bad has driven out the good; even the best restaurants keep the bad Shrimp Creole on their menus for visitors who have come all the way to New Orleans to taste it. They're actually getting a reimported dish that would be more at home in places where the mere idea of shrimp is exotic. We can't do anything about the poor ver-

*sions, but we hope that once home cooks try the real thing, they
and their families and guests will never again be content with
the ersatz.*

FOR FOUR TO SIX

*2 lb. fresh shrimp in the shell,
peeled and deveined (1¼ lb.
after peeling, approximately)*

⅔ c. vegetable oil

½ c. flour

1¾ c. thinly sliced green onions

⅓ c. chopped celery

1 c. chopped onions

½ c. chopped green pepper

4 tsp. finely minced garlic

3 Tbs. finely minced parsley

*1 can (1 lb.) Italian style whole
peeled tomatoes, drained*

1 can (8 oz.) tomato sauce

1 Tbs. minced chives

4 Tbs. dry red wine

4 bay leaves, crushed

6 whole allspice

2 whole cloves

2 tsp. salt

*¾ tsp. freshly ground black
pepper*

*¼ tsp. cayenne, ½ tsp. if you
prefer a more peppery flavor*

¼ tsp. chili powder

¼ tsp. mace

¼ tsp. basil

½ tsp. thyme

4 tsp. fresh lemon juice

2 c. water

*boiled rice (see Creole Turtle
Stew)*

In a heavy 6 to 8 quart pot or kettle, heat the oil and gradually add
the flour, stirring constantly. Cook over low heat, stirring constantly,
until a medium brown roux (the color of rich peanut butter) is
formed. Remove from the heat and add the fresh vegetables and
parsley. Mix well with the roux, then return to low heat and cook,
stirring constantly, until the vegetables begin to brown. Mix in the
canned tomatoes and tomato sauce, then add the chives, wine, seasonings, and lemon juice and mix again.

Raise the heat under the pan and bring to a low boil. Add the water
and mix thoroughly. When the mixture boils up again, reduce the
heat and simmer for 45 minutes. Add the shrimp and allow the mixture to come to a low boil again, then cover, reduce the heat slightly,
and simmer for 20 minutes. Remove the pot from the burner and
allow to stand, covered, at room temperature for about 10 minutes
before serving. Serve over boiled rice.

Crawfish Étouffée

A classic southwestern Louisiana Cajun dish, a spicy hot stew always served with rice. You will need about 2½ to 3 dozen crawfish to prepare this. If you obtain live ones, parboil them for 3 to 4 minutes to facilitate peeling them. Be sure to scoop out and save the fat that is in the heads—it's an essential part of the stock. Frozen prepicked crawfish tails and containers of frozen crawfish fat, where available, greatly simplify the preparation. If you double the recipe, do not double the amount of green pepper, celery, and green onion tops because they tend to overpower the seasonings. For the doubled recipe increase the simmering time to about 16 minutes.

FOR FOUR

1½ c. crawfish tails (about 30 tails)
½ c. crawfish fat, kept refrigerated
6 Tbs. salt butter
¼ c. flour
1 c. chopped onions
½ c. chopped green pepper
½ c. chopped celery
1 Tbs. finely minced garlic
1 tsp. salt
¼ tsp. freshly ground black pepper

¼ tsp. cayenne
scant ⅛ tsp. crushed red pepper pods
1/16 tsp. cumin
1 tsp. fresh lemon juice
⅓ c. thinly sliced green onion tops
1 Tbs. finely minced parsley
1 c. cold water
2 c. hot water, approximately
boiled rice (see Creole Turtle Stew)

In a heavy 5 to 6 quart pot or kettle, melt the butter over low heat. Gradually add the flour, stirring constantly. Cook over low heat until a medium brown roux is formed, about 15 to 20 minutes. Quickly add the onions, green pepper, celery, and garlic and continue to cook, stirring frequently, until the vegetables are glazed and tender, about 20 minutes. Add the crawfish tails, crawfish fat, salt, black pepper, cayenne, pepper pods, cumin, lemon juice, green onion tops, and parsley and mix well. Add the 1 cup cold water and bring to a boil, then lower the heat and simmer, stirring frequently, for 12 minutes, or until the crawfish tails are just tender. Shortly before serving, heat the étouffée slowly over low heat and gradually add 1 to 2 cups hot water to provide the gravy. Serve over boiled rice.

Shrimp Étouffée

A great way to try étouffée in areas where crawfish are not available.

FOR FOUR

Prepare as directed for Crawfish Étouffée, substituting 1½ cups small or medium-sized peeled and deveined raw shrimp (about 1½ pounds before peeling) for the crawfish. For a richer flavor, substitute 3 tablespoons of lard for 3 tablespoons of the butter used to make the roux and also dice ½ cup of the shrimp very fine and add to the base 10 minutes after adding the chopped onions, etc.

Crabmeat Étouffée

Crabmeat Étouffées are unusual in Louisiana. Because crabmeat is accessible to cooks in many parts of the country, we worked out this dish.

FOR FOUR

1½ lb. lump crabmeat	1/16 tsp. cumin
6 Tbs. salt butter	⅛ tsp. mace
¼ c. flour	1½ tsp. fresh lemon juice
1 c. chopped onions	½ c. thinly sliced green onion tops
½ c. chopped green pepper	
½ c. chopped celery	1 Tbs. finely minced parsley
1 Tbs. finely minced fresh garlic	1 c. cold water
1¼ tsp. salt	1 to 2 c. hot water, approximately
⅜ tsp. freshly ground white pepper	
⅛ tsp. cayenne	boiled rice (see Creole Turtle Stew)

In a heavy 5 to 7 quart pot or kettle melt the butter over low heat. Gradually add the flour, stirring constantly. Raise the heat slightly and cook, stirring constantly, until a medium dark brown roux (the color of hazelnuts) is formed, about 20 minutes. Immediately add the onions, green pepper, celery, and garlic and stir vigorously. (This will arrest the browning.) Cook, stirring frequently, over medium heat until the vegetables are lightly browned and appear glazed, about 15 minutes. Add the crabmeat, seasonings, lemon juice, green onion tops, and parsley and mix well. Keeping the heat at medium, very gradually add the cup of cold water, stirring constantly but gently to keep the mixture smooth. Lower the heat and simmer for 10 minutes. Remove the pan from the heat, cover, and allow to steep at room temperature for about 15 minutes. A few minutes before serving, put the pan back on low heat, uncover, and add ¾ cup of the hot water. Stir gently, then check the liquidity of the gravy. There should be approximately 1 quart of medium-thin liquid in the pan. Add more hot water, ¼ cup at a time, if necessary. Serve over about ½ cup boiled rice on pre-heated dinner plates.

Oysters with Spaghetti

One of the most satisfying seafood and pasta combinations we know, popular in several New Orleans restaurants and quite simple to prepare at home. Be sure not to cook the garlic too long—or it will begin to lose its flavor—and to allow the finished dish to steep in the pot for a bit before serving in order to let the flavors finish expanding.

FOR FOUR

1 quart freshly shucked oysters (about 4 doz. medium), well drained	1 tsp. basil
	2 Tbs. finely minced parsley
	1 tsp. freshly ground black pepper
½ c. (1 stick) salt butter	
½ c. plus 1 Tbs. olive oil	2 Tbs. plus ½ tsp. salt
6 large garlic cloves, peeled and cut into large pieces	6 qt. cold water
	24 oz. spaghetti

Melt the butter over low heat in a large sauté pan or saucepan. Add ½ cup olive oil and mix thoroughly. Continue cooking for 3 minutes, then raise the heat to medium and add the garlic. Cook for about 4 to 5 minutes, just until the garlic begins to turn brown. Quickly remove the garlic with a slotted spoon and discard. Add the basil, parsley, pepper, and ½ teaspoon salt to the butter and oil and simmer for about 4 minutes. Add the drained oysters and cook over low heat for about 5 minutes, just until the oysters begin to curl at the edges. Remove the pan from the heat, cover loosely, and set aside while you cook the spaghetti.

To cook the spaghetti, combine the water, 2 tablespoons salt, and 1 tablespoon olive oil in a large saucepan or kettle (8 to 10 quarts is the best size for this amount). If your pan is a bit smaller, reduce the water by a bit to prevent boiling over. Bring to a rolling boil, then add the spaghetti. When the water boils up again, cook for 8 to 10 minutes, checking for doneness after 8 minutes. When the spaghetti is cooked, dump the contents of the pan into a large colander placed in the sink. Allow the spaghetti to drain thoroughly, then return it to the large pan and add the oil and oyster mixture. Mix gently but thoroughly, using a long fork and a smooth circular motion. Cover the saucepan and allow to stand for about 8 minutes before serving. If you have a heavy pan, no additional heat is required. If you don't, set the pan on a warming tray or in a 200°F. oven.

To serve, toss the spaghetti and oysters thoroughly with the long fork in order to redistribute the sauce, which tends to settle to the bottom of the pan. Serve in preheated wide soup or spaghetti bowls, taking care to place a generous quantity of oysters on top of each portion. Spoon any sauce that remains in the pan over the portions.

Clams with Spaghetti

Our preferred way of preparing this popular dish, using the garlic, butter, and oil sauce we like for oysters. Be sure to get the smaller hard shell clams and to cut away the tougher muscle tissue. Freshly shucked uncooked clams give the best results, but if shucking is too much trouble, you can use clams that have been steamed open; they will simply be a bit chewier in the finished dish. Or you can chop the steamed clams into large pieces.

FOR FOUR

Prepare as directed for Oysters with Spaghetti, substituting 1 quart freshly shucked small hard shell clams for the oysters. If you use steamed clams, cut them up before putting them into the garlic, butter, and oil sauce.

Squid with Spaghetti

There are only two types of reactions to squid—people who love them and people who won't eat them. Lovers of squid may be a minority, but they're far from silent and certainly not oppressed. This dish may make a few more converts, but it is primarily intended for squid lovers, who are always looking for still other ways to enjoy them.

FOR FOUR

Prepare as directed for Oysters with Spaghetti, substituting 2 pounds small to medium-sized squid for the oysters. After cleaning as directed for Biscayan Squid, cook the squid in a small amount of water and chicken or beef stock combined for about 15 minutes. Drain thoroughly, then cut them into ½ inch strips or rings. Proceed as directed for the oysters, adding 1 teaspoon rosemary and reducing the basil by half.

Snails with Green Sauce and Spaghetti

It's unfortunate that snails are almost always served only as an appetizer. Most of us who like them like them a lot. One of our favorite snail main dishes is this one, made with a rich sauce containing butter, olive oil, garlic, and a modified pesto or green sauce. Sprinkle freshly grated Romano cheese over each portion before serving—the cheese is an integral part of the dish.

FOR TWO

12 giant snails, each cut in half	½ bay leaf
¼ c. dry white wine	6 whole black peppercorns
¼ c. water	¼ tsp. salt

GREEN SAUCE

¼ c. olive oil plus 2 tsp.	1 c. fresh parsley sprigs
¼ c. (½ stick) salt butter	1 tsp. oregano
1 Tbs. coarsely chopped garlic	½ tsp. basil
¾ tsp. salt	1½ tsp. coriander leaf
¼ tsp. freshly ground white pepper	(cilantro)

6 Tbs. freshly grated Romano cheese
12 oz. #4 spaghetti, cooked firm (7 to 9 minutes)

Poach the snails in a small saucepan with the wine, water, bay leaf, peppercorns, and salt for 8 to 10 minutes, then drain very thoroughly. In a 2 to 3 quart sauté pan heat ¼ cup of the olive oil and the butter over medium heat, then add the garlic, salt, and pepper. Cook over low heat for 4 minutes, then remove the pan from the heat and set aside. In a blender or food processor, purée the parsley, oregano, basil, coriander leaf, and 2 teaspoons olive oil. Spoon the purée into the sauté pan and return to low heat. Add the snails and cook, stirring frequently, for 4 to 5 minutes. Remove the pan from the heat, cover loosely, and set aside while you cook the spaghetti. Cook and drain as directed for Oysters with Spaghetti. Serve in preheated wide soup or spaghetti bowls. First heap a generous quantity of spaghetti in each bowl, then spoon the sauce and snails over it. Toss to mix with 2 forks, then sprinkle 3 tablespoons of Romano cheese over each portion. Bring to the table immediately. Also provide a bowl containing some additional cheese to be added as desired.

Clams and Tomato Sauce with Spaghetti

A delicate clam and spaghetti dish with a simple sauce containing fresh tomatoes, freshly grated Parmesan cheese, and a small amount of bread crumbs. The texture and flavor remind us of good Italian besciamellas with a touch of tomato.

FOR TWO OR THREE

5 qt. small to medium-sized hard shell clams	*½ tsp. thyme*
water for steaming clams	*½ tsp. freshly ground black pepper*
¼ c. olive oil	*¼ tsp. nutmeg*
1 c. chopped onions	*1 tsp. salt*
2 Tbs. finely minced garlic	*2 tsp. fine bread crumbs*
3 c. coarsely chopped ripe tomatoes (2 large tomatoes)	*½ c. freshly grated Parmesan cheese*
3 Tbs. minced parsley	*12 to 16 oz. spaghetti*
½ tsp. basil	

Scrub and rinse the clams, then steam them open as directed for Steamed Hard Clams. Remove the clams from their shells, trim off the connecting muscle, then chop coarsely.

In a 3 to 4 quart heavy saucepan heat the oil. Add the onions and cook, stirring frequently, until they are glazed and just beginning to brown, about 8 to 10 minutes. Add the garlic and cook, stirring, until the garlic begins to brown, about 2 minutes. Add the tomatoes, parsley, basil, thyme, pepper, nutmeg, and salt and stir to mix. Cook over medium heat, stirring frequently and mashing the chunks of tomato with the back of the spoon, until the tomato pieces have almost totally liquefied, about 15 minutes. Stir in the bread crumbs and cook for 10 minutes longer, then add the cheese. Mix thoroughly and cook for 1 minute, then turn off the heat. Add the chopped clams and stir. Cover the pan and set aside while you cook and drain the spaghetti as directed for Oysters with Spaghetti.

When the spaghetti is cooked and has been dumped into a colander to drain, turn the heat on under the pan of sauce. Stir gently and heat just until bubbles begin to appear around the sides. Do *not* bring to a boil. Fill serving plates or wide bowls with spaghetti and ladle about ¾ to 1 cup of sauce over each portion. Serve immediately.

Shrimp Pansit

Pansit, the national dish of the Philippines, is a pasta somewhere between Chinese lo mein or soft noodles and Italian spaghetti. Narrow egg noodles are a good and readily available choice for the home cook. The sauce is the key element, a mixture of sautéed vegetables, delicate seasonings, and shrimp, pork, or chicken. We became attached to Shrimp Pansit eating it in New Orleans' only Philippine restaurant, The Tahitian Room, and worked out this home version.

FOR THREE OR FOUR

1 lb. peeled and deveined raw shrimp (2 lb. in the shell)
1 lb. egg noodles (¼ inch wide)
boiling salted water
2½ Tbs. sesame or peanut oil
1 c. chopped white onions
1 Tbs. finely minced garlic
1 c. finely chopped lean pork
½ c. thinly sliced green onion tops
1⅓ c. finely shredded young white cabbage

1½ c. light beef stock or water
3 Tbs. soy sauce, more if necessary
¼ tsp. ginger
¾ tsp. salt, more if necessary
¼ tsp. freshly ground black pepper
1/16 tsp. cayenne
¼ tsp. nutmeg

Cook the noodles in boiling salted water until tender but not mushy, then place in a colander to drain. Heat the oil in a large heavy sauté pan or skillet, then cook the onions and garlic until quite soft but not browned. Add the chopped pork, green onion tops, cabbage, and shrimp. Mix very thoroughly, then add 1 cup of the beef stock or water. Simmer for 10 minutes, or until the shrimp are cooked and all the vegetables are tender. Once the simmering has begun, sprinkle in the soy sauce, ginger, salt, pepper, cayenne, and nutmeg, mixing gently after each addition. If the mixture begins to appear dry during the simmering, add a bit more beef stock. To combine the noodles and the sauce, remove the solids and one-fourth of the sauce with a large spoon and place in a small saucepan. Add the noodles to the sauté pan, toss gently with the sauce until well mixed, then heat very slowly, just enough to heat the noodles through. Cover the pan loosely and remove from the heat. Warm the reserved solids and sauce a bit.

To serve, spoon equal quantities of noodles and sauce onto preheated plates, then top each portion with equal quantities of sauce from the small saucepan. Provide additional soy sauce to be added at the table as desired.

Bami Goreng

An Indonesian dish made like Nasi Goreng with noodles used in place of rice.

FOR FIVE OR SIX

Prepare as directed for Nasi Goreng, substituting 1¼ pounds egg noodles for the rice. Cook the noodles as described in Shrimp Pansit, then add to the sauce as directed for the rice. Serve in the same manner.

Shrimp Stuffed Peppers

A Creole dish combining seafood and hearty seasonings with a readily available vegetable. Parboiling the peppers first avoids the faintly sour taste one often finds in stuffed pepper dishes. This dish can be prepared ahead, then reheated by placing the stuffed

---

peppers upright in a saucepan with a few tablespoons of water, covering the pan loosely, and warming over low heat for about 10 minutes.

FOR FOUR

4 medium to large firm green peppers
boiling salted water

———

1 lb. fresh shrimp in the shell, peeled, deveined, and cut into ½ to ¾ inch pieces
¼ lb. lean sliced bacon
1½ c. chopped onions
½ c. chopped green pepper
3 Tbs. chopped celery
1 Tbs. finely minced garlic
1 c. coarsely chopped ripe tomatoes (1 large or 2 small tomatoes)

½ c. chopped green onions
1½ tsp. salt
½ tsp. freshly ground black pepper
¾ tsp. thyme
2 bay leaves, crushed
3 Tbs. finely minced parsley
⅛ tsp. cayenne
½ c. slightly dampened crumbled white bread, crusts removed

Cut off and discard the top fourth of the green peppers (or use for the stuffing). Remove the seeds and membrane. Place the peppers upright in about ½ inch salted water in a heavy saucepan that will hold them snugly but not tightly. Bring the water to a boil, then cover the pan, reduce the heat, and cook for 5 minutes. Remove the peppers from the pan, drain thoroughly, then set aside to cool while you prepare the stuffing.

To prepare the stuffing, fry the bacon in a large heavy sauté pan or skillet until almost crisp. Add the onions, green pepper, celery, garlic, tomatoes, and green onions. Sauté just until the vegetables begin to turn soft, about 8 minutes. Add the salt, pepper, thyme, bay leaves, parsley, and cayenne. Mix well with a wooden spoon. Add the pieces of raw shrimp and cook over low heat just until the shrimp turn pink. Add the dampened crumbled bread and blend well.

Stuff the parboiled peppers and bake uncovered in a preheated 350°F. oven for 30 minutes or until lightly browned on top.

———

The Pleasures of Seafood 276

Apalachicola Chicken and Oyster Pie

Apalachicola, Florida, produces some of the most unusual oysters in the Gulf Coast region and with them an interesting regional cuisine that makes imaginative use of abundant local ingredients. Oysters go well with almost everything; they go especially well with poultry in this splendid variation of American chicken pie.

FOR THREE OR FOUR

1½ pt. freshly shucked oysters and their liquor

3 Tbs. salt butter

3 Tbs. finely minced celery

⅓ c. chopped onion

1 Tbs. finely minced parsley

½ c. dampened crumbled white bread, crusts removed

⅓ c. chicken stock

2 c. ½ inch pieces of cooked chicken

¼ tsp. mace

¼ tsp. chervil

⅜ tsp. freshly ground black pepper

½ tsp. salt, more if necessary

RICH BISCUIT DOUGH

½ c. flour

¾ tsp. double-acting baking powder

¼ tsp. salt

1 Tbs. vegetable shortening

¼ c. milk

butter for glazing the crust

Drain the oysters and strain the oyster liquor. Reserve ½ cup of strained oyster liquor for making the pie filling.

Melt the butter in a heavy medium-sized sauté pan. Add the celery, onion, and parsley and cook over medium heat, stirring frequently, until the vegetables are soft and lightly browned. Lower the heat and add the crumbled bread. Mix very thoroughly, then raise the heat to medium again and gradually pour in the oyster liquor and the chicken stock, stirring constantly. Bring to a boil, then reduce the heat just to keep a bare simmer going. Add the oysters, cooked chicken, and seasonings. Stir to mix, cover the pan loosely, and remove from the heat. Begin preheating the oven to 425°F.

To prepare the crust, sift the dry ingredients together, then combine them in a mixing bowl with the shortening and milk. Mix thoroughly with a wooden spoon. Flour a work surface, then turn the dough out of the bowl onto it. Knead for 4 to 5 minutes, then roll out to a thickness of approximately ½ inch. Using the 2 to 2½ quart casserole you will be using for baking the pie, invert the casserole over the rolled-out dough and press down to make an exact impression of the crust you will need. Cut out the crust with a sharp knife. Cut the remaining dough into biscuit rounds and set on a greased baking sheet. Fill the casserole with the chicken and oyster mixture, then cover with the biscuit dough topping. Rub the crust with butter and cut several slits about 1½ inches long in the crust in a decorative pattern. Rub the extra biscuit rounds with butter. Set the casserole and the baking sheet in the oven and bake for 20 to 25 minutes, until the crust is browned on top. If the biscuit rounds brown sooner, remove them from the oven and cover the baking sheet loosely with foil to keep them warm.

To serve, bring the casserole to the table along with warmed plates. Using a serrated knife, cut the pie into segments. Lift the portions onto the plates using a large, long-handled spoon and lifting from the bottom so that the crust remains on top. (If the crust should slide away or fall off, simply set it back where it belongs.) Be sure to spoon any liquid that remains in the casserole around the portions. Place the biscuit rounds in a napkin-lined basket and pass them around the table.

Veal Oscar

A restaurant favorite combining veal, asparagus, crabmeat, and béarnaise sauce. We've often thought there may be one ingredient too many—perhaps the asparagus—and that the dish is admired more for its layered complexity than its taste. But there's no doubt that made with fresh asparagus, the best lump crabmeat, and good white veal it's rather impressive . . . and almost as costly as a trip to Europe.

FOR FOUR

2 Tbs. salt butter	freshly ground white pepper
2 veal rounds, ¼ inch thick (about 2 lb. total weight), each cut into 2 pieces	salt

———

12 to 16 young asparagus, tougher stem ends removed
boiling salted water

———

¾ lb. lump crabmeat
1½ Tbs. salt butter

———

BÉARNAISE SAUCE

3 Tbs. finely minced green onion tops
½ tsp. finely minced garlic
4 tsp. fresh lemon juice
½ c. dry white wine
1 Tbs. tarragon
1 Tbs. chervil

¼ tsp. salt
½ tsp. freshly ground white pepper
1 c. (2 sticks) salt butter
6 large egg yolks
scant ¼ tsp. cayenne

Melt the butter in a sauté pan or skillet. Sprinkle the pieces of veal lightly with white pepper and salt on both sides, then sauté in the hot butter until tender and golden brown on both sides. Place side by side on a large platter and set in a 175°F. oven to keep warm.

Cook the asparagus in a small amount of boiling salted water, using a large skillet and a cover to fit, for about 8 minutes or until tender but not soft. Remove the asparagus from the water with tongs or a large slotted spatula and place on a plate. Set the plates in the warm oven along with the sautéed veal.

In a small sauté pan melt the butter and sauté the lump crabmeat just until warmed through, about 4 minutes, stirring very gently so as not to break up the lumps. Set the pan in the warm oven along with the other cooked ingredients.

To prepare the béarnaise sauce, combine the green onion tops, garlic, lemon juice, wine, tarragon, chervil, salt, and pepper in a small heavy saucepan. Cook over medium-high heat until the mixture is reduced to about ¼ cup; it should have almost no liquid left. Remove the pan from the heat. In another small saucepan melt the butter. Put the egg yolks and cayenne in the container of a blender. Cover and turn on high speed for a few seconds, just long enough to break the yolks. Add the glaze (the reduced herb-wine-lemon juice mixture), cover the container again, and mix on high speed for a second. Turn the blender to high speed, then leaving it on, remove the cover and gradually pour in the hot melted butter in a steady stream. Cover the container and switch the blender off. Turn on for 60 seconds, then off for 30 seconds, repeating this on-off cycle until the sauce is quite thick and barely drips from a long thin spoon.

To assemble the portions, first place a portion of sautéed veal on each preheated plate, then top each with 3 or 4 asparagus tips. Place 3 ounces of sautéed lump crabmeat over the asparagus, then pour or spoon about ½ cup béarnaise sauce over the top of each portion. Serve immediately.

***

Veal with Lump Crabmeat

An opulent combination, this veal, crabmeat, and hollandaise combination is a haute cuisine *dish that is relatively simple to prepare at home.*

FOR FOUR

Prepare 2 veal rounds and ¾ pound lump crabmeat as directed for Veal Oscar. Set in the oven to keep warm. Prepare the hollandaise sauce as directed for Broiled Redfish Hollandaise, doubling the quantities indicated. To assemble, place the sautéed veal on heated plates, top each portion with 3 ounces of sautéed lump crabmeat, then spoon about ½ cup hollandaise over. Serve immediately.

Bacalao con Chile
Codfish and Chili

A good salt cod dish from the California Mexican cuisine. You will need dried red chili peppers to prepare the sauce. Be sure to wear rubber gloves when handling them; in contact with moisture they can sting and burn your hands.

FOR THREE OR FOUR

1 lb. salt cod
1 Tbs. lard or vegetable shortening

RED CHILI SAUCE

½ lb. dried red chilies	*3 Tbs. toasted bread crumbs*
1 qt. water	*1 Tbs. finely minced garlic*
2 Tbs. vegetable oil or lard	*1 Tbs. wine vinegar*

Soak the cod overnight in cold water to cover to remove the salt. When ready to cook, rinse in clear water and press dry between several layers of paper towels. Cut the cod into large pieces suitable for serving 1 or 2 per portion. Heat the lard or shortening in a heavy skillet, then add the cod. Fry at high heat until browned on both sides, then lower the heat and cook for about 15 minutes longer or until tender. Remove the pan from the heat and set aside while you prepare the sauce.

To prepare the sauce, stem and slit the dried chilies, then remove the veins and seeds. Cook in 1 quart of water until the pulp separates easily from the hulls. Rub the pulp through a fine sieve into a bowl. Add the water in which the chilies were cooked gradually to the pulp, mixing as you add. When you have added about 3 cups, check the consistency of the purée. If it appears too thick, add some or all of the remaining water. Reserve. Heat the oil in a large skillet and fry the toasted bread crumbs and the garlic until well browned, about 4 minutes. Add the chili purée and the vinegar. Simmer for about 10 minutes, until all the ingredients appear to be thoroughly blended. Pour over the fried codfish and return the skillet to the heat. Simmer for 12 to 15 minutes longer. Serve with traditional side dishes such as *frijolitos* and hot tortillas.

Oyster Omelette

An unusual, very filling pancake style omelette made with freshly shucked oysters. We like this with a chilled white wine as a simple and festive light dinner.

FOR TWO

⅔ c. freshly shucked oysters, drained and cut into ¾ inch pieces (about 1 dozen medium-sized oysters)
4 large eggs
3 Tbs. milk

½ tsp. salt
¼ tsp. freshly ground white pepper
6 Tbs. salt butter

Put the eggs, milk, salt, and pepper in a mixing bowl and beat with a whisk until light and airy, about 2 minutes. Add the cut-up oysters and mix gently into the omelette batter with a wooden spoon.

Melt 2 tablespoons of the butter in a 10 to 12 inch omelette pan or skillet. When the butter is hot, add the omelette batter and cook, shaking the pan to keep the omelette from sticking, until it begins to set. (It will start to appear firm around the edges.) Turn the omelette over carefully with a large spatula and cook on the other side just until lightly browned, about 1 to 2 minutes. Remove the pan from the heat. Cut in half across with the edge of the spatula and slide the portions onto heated plates. Add the remaining 4 tablespoons of butter to the pan and cook over high heat until it turns a rich brown. Spoon the browned butter over the omelette portions and serve immediately.

Crab Omelette

Just over ¼ pound of lump crabmeat makes a delightful seafood omelette. It is filling and excellent as a light supper.

FOR TWO

FILLING

4½ to 5 ounces lump crabmeat	¼ tsp. salt
2 Tbs. very thinly sliced green onion tops	¼ tsp. freshly ground white pepper
1½ Tbs. salt butter	

OMELETTE BATTER

4 large eggs	½ tsp. salt
3 Tbs. milk	3 drops Tabasco

---

2 Tbs. salt butter
2 tsp. finely minced parsley

To prepare the filling, melt the butter in a sauté pan or skillet over low heat, then add the crabmeat and green onions. Sprinkle on the salt and pepper and cook, stirring very gently so as not to break up the lumps, until the crabmeat is warmed through, about 4 minutes. Set the pan in a 175°F. oven or on a warming tray while you prepare the omelette batter.

Mix the ingredients for the batter with a fork or whisk just until well blended, about 1 minute. Melt 2 tablespoons butter in a 10 inch omelette pan or skillet. When the butter is quite hot, pour in the omelette batter and tip the pan with a circular motion to spread the batter evenly over the entire bottom. Cook over medium-high heat until the omelette begins to set. Spoon the sautéed lump crabmeat across the center of the omelette in a band about 2 inches wide. When the inner side of the omelette appears almost dry, fold the edges across the filling so that they overlap about an inch. Remove the pan from the heat and cut the omelette in half with the edge of a spatula. Slide the portions onto heated plates, then sprinkle each with a teaspoon of minced parsley.

Fish Cake and Quenelle Recipes

Fish Quenelles with Nantua
  Sauce

Gefilte Fish

Fish Pirogi

Chinese Boiled Dumplings
  Filled with Crabmeat

Crab Cakes

13

Fish Cakes and Quenelles

In this chapter we have included a selection of dumpling-type seafood preparations ranging from classic French Fish Quenelles to American Crab Cakes. All of them use a ground, pounded, or flaked form of seafood in combination with eggs and sometimes flour to bind them into attractive shapes, or a simple dough shaped into a kind of edible container. These dishes are poached, fried, boiled, or steamed in the final stage of cooking and all of them can be prepared in advance and reheated. Most quenelles are traditionally served as first courses, the cakes as main courses.

The techniques used in preparing these seafood delicacies range from relatively complex in the French and Jewish quenelles to quite simple in the Crab Cakes. The more difficult culinary procedures have been enormously simplified with the proliferation of electric food grinders and food processors. Where it once took many hours to purée the raw fish, then to push it through a fine sieve, it now takes just minutes. We have indicated several ways of carrying out these operations in each applicable instance, so that you can use whichever appliance you happen to own. And of course you can always choose the old fashioned way and simply chop the fish in a wooden bowl until it's fine enough to pass through a sieve. The days of pounding the fish to a paste with a mortar and pestle are happily past (the unavailability of the enormous mortars once needed for this task is a ready index of the change).

We enjoy preparing these dishes at home and urge you to try them in your own kitchen. Once you get the hang of them, you'll enjoy making them for special dinners (they have such a professional look, simple as they are), as well as for family eating. You'll look forward to the aesthetic pleasure of bringing to the table a platter of quenelles or dumplings—small attractive symbols of your growing proficiency as a seafood cook.

Basic Fish Cake and Quenelle Techniques

Chopping or processing fish until very smooth is essential for quenelles.

If shaped quenelles appear soft, chill on top shelf of refrigerator until firm before adding to boiling liquid.

Wrap poached quenelles carefully before refrigerating to prevent moisture loss.

Chill *pirogi* dough for 45 minutes before rolling out.

Avoid overcooking boiled dumplings.

Fish Quenelles with Nantua Sauce

One of the classics of French cooking, seafood quenelles should be light as a feather and topped with a rich and piquant sauce. Since one finds quenelles on almost every French restaurant menu it would be logical to assume that the dish presents no problems. In fact, the lightness and smooth texture of fine quenelles seem to elude most restaurants. This is the version we make at home— it should satisfy the lover of quenelles—with the crawfish sauce that best sets them off. If you can't get crawfish, substitute shrimp or lobster meat.

1½ lb. pike or other white fish,   ⅛ tsp. nutmeg
   cleaned, skinned, and boned   6 Tbs. salt butter
1 c. milk or milk and water or   1¾ c. flour
   fish stock   6 large eggs
1 tsp. salt   lightly salted water for poaching

NANTUA SAUCE

1 lb. crawfish tails, parboiled for   ¼ tsp. freshly ground white
   3 minutes, then chopped very   pepper
   fine   ⅛ tsp. cayenne
6 Tbs. (¾ stick) salt butter   5 Tbs. fish stock, or strained fish
¾ c. heavy cream   poaching liquid, or water
1 Tbs. brandy   ¼ c. flour
1 tsp. salt

Pass the fish twice through the fine blade of a food grinder or process in a food processor until smooth. Combine the liquid, salt, nutmeg, and butter in a large saucepan. Bring to a boil and as soon as the butter has melted completely add the flour all at one time. Stir with a wooden spatula or spoon until the mixture begins to adhere to itself and to clear the sides of the pan. Remove the pan from the heat. Weigh the puréed fish, then put it into a large mixing bowl. Weigh out an equal quantity of the mixture—called the *panade*—in the saucepan and add it to the puréed fish. Mix thoroughly with a wooden spatula. Beat in the eggs one at a time and continue beating until the mixture is perfectly smooth and light in texture. Fill a large sauté pan with about 1½ to 2 inches of salted water and bring to a boil. Reduce the heat so that the water remains at a very low simmer. Using 2 table-spoons, shape the mixture into quenelles. They should look like short, rather plump sausages. Drop them directly from the spoons into barely simmering salted water and simmer very gently for 10 minutes. Remove the quenelles from the poaching liquid carefully with a slotted spoon and place on paper towels to drain. After they have cooled a bit, place the quenelles on a platter and cover with aluminum foil. Be sure to fold the foil over twice where the edges meet to create an air-tight covering. Refrigerate.

When you are ready to serve the quenelles, reheat them by placing in barely simmering water for about 3 to 4 minutes, just long enough to warm them through.

Prepare the Nantua sauce as directed for Poached Red Snapper with Nantua Sauce. To serve, place the quenelles on heated plates, then spoon the Nantua sauce over.

Gefilte Fish

This famous Jewish dish is actually a quenelle in carp's clothing. Heartier in flavor than the classic French quenelles and slightly firmer in texture, Gefilte Fish has all the seasonings in the mixture itself rather than in an accompanying sauce. While we are aware that Gefilte Fish is customarily made with 2 or 3 different kinds of fish, we much prefer it made with just one, carp or buffalo. Combining carp with the finer and more expensive whitefish or pike is explicable more for social reasons than for reasons of taste. Also, carp was the old country's fish and the affluence of Americanization may have called for an "upgrading." In reality, carp, with its rich distinctive flavor, tends to mask the taste of other fish almost entirely.

A meat grinder or food processor makes the initial preparation easier, but a chopping bowl and a rounded sharp chopping blade will work as well—they just take more time. The key to good Gefilte Fish is lots of onions and carrots. It tastes best chilled overnight or for several days.

FOR SIX TO EIGHT

2 to 2½ lbs. carp or buffalo, filleted and skin removed, fish head, bones, and skin reserved	1 tsp. salt
	½ tsp. freshly ground white pepper
1 medium-sized white onion	1 tsp. sugar
3 large eggs, lightly beaten	2 to 3 Tbs. water

BROTH FOR SIMMERING FISH TRIMMINGS

fish head, bones, and skin	½ tsp. freshly ground white pepper
2 qt. cold water	
1 tsp. salt	½ tsp. sugar

BROTH FOR SIMMERING FISH BALLS

strained broth from simmering fish trimmings (see above)	4 tsp. salt
	¾ tsp. freshly ground white pepper
3 medium-sized white onions, sliced	1 tsp. sugar
3 carrots, peeled and sliced ⅜ inch thick	

Grind the fish and 1 onion together twice through the fine blade of a meat grinder, or purée together in a food processor. Put the puréed fish and onion into a bowl along with the eggs, 1 teaspoon salt, ½ teaspoon white pepper, 1 teaspoon sugar, and 2 tablespoons water.

Mix very thoroughly, then check the consistency. If it appears a bit dry, add an additional tablespoon of water. With your hands shape the mixture into oval fish balls about 2½ inches long by 1½ inches across. Place the shaped fish balls on a flat platter and refrigerate while you simmer the fish trimmings.

In a 6 to 8 quart heavy saucepan combine the fish trimmings, water, salt, pepper, and sugar and bring to a boil over high heat. Lower the heat and simmer for 30 to 40 minutes. Strain the broth through a fine mesh strainer. Wipe out any sediment that clings to the inner surface of the pan. Put the sliced onions and carrots on the bottom of the pan. Carefully place the fish balls on top of the vegetables, then sprinkle on the remaining seasonings. Slowly pour in the strained broth. Bring to a boil over high heat, then reduce the heat and cook at a low simmer for 1¼ to 1½ hours, occasionally spooning some of the simmering broth over the fish balls which rise to the top.

Remove the cooked fish balls from the pan with a slotted spoon and place in 1 or 2 large casseroles or deep baking dishes. Spoon the carrot and onion slices evenly over the fish, then pour the broth carefully into the dish or dishes so that the fish balls are completely covered with liquid. Allow to cool at room temperature for 15 to 20 minutes, then cover the dish or dishes with several layers of plastic wrap or with heavy aluminum foil tucked tightly around them. (It is important to create a tight seal to prevent the aroma of the fish balls from permeating everything else in the refrigerator.) Refrigerate for at least 8 hours or overnight, until the broth has jelled.

To serve, carefully lift 2 or 3 fish balls onto each plate along with the jelly that covers it, then spoon carrot and onion slices around each serving. White or red horseradish is the traditional accompaniment.

Fish Pirogi

Classic Polish dumplings filled with flaked fish. Salmon makes a particularly attractive filling, but any firm fish will work. The filled pirogi can be steamed or baked; they're delicious either way. Our favorite pirogi dough is a simple one made with baking powder.

½ lb. salmon or other large firm fish, cut into steaks

---

12 pieces 4 inch round pirogi *dough, about ¼ inch thick*

PIROGI DOUGH
MAKES APPROXIMATELY ONE DOZEN PIROGI

1½ c. flour
½ tsp. salt
¾ tsp. baking powder

½ c. vegetable shortening
1 large egg, beaten with a fork
2 Tbs. cold water

COURT BOUILLON

½ c. water
¾ tsp. salt
1 tsp. salt butter
¼ c. dry white wine

4 whole black peppercorns
½ tsp. thyme
½ large bay leaf, broken into
2 pieces

1½ Tbs. salt butter
½ c. coarsely chopped onions
¼ tsp. salt
¼ tsp. freshly ground white
pepper

2 hard boiled eggs, finely
chopped
4 tsp. finely minced fresh parsley
⅛ tsp. allspice

Sift the flour, salt, and baking powder together twice, then put into a mixing bowl. Cut in the shortening with a pastry blender or 2 knives. Add the egg and cold water, then mix lightly with a wooden spoon or spatula until the dough begins to form a ball and to clear the sides of the bowl. Mix a bit more vigorously for a few seconds, then shape into a ball with your hands. Wrap the ball of dough in plastic wrap or aluminum foil and refrigerate for 45 minutes to 1 hour before rolling out.

To roll out, place the ball of dough on a floured surface and press down into the center of the ball with a floured rolling pin. Roll from the center outward, turning the dough every few rolls, so that the dough assumes a circular shape. Roll out to a thickness of about ¼ inch. Cut into 4 inch rounds with a sharp knife.

Poach the salmon in the court bouillon in a sauté pan or skillet until cooked, about 8 minutes. Remove from the liquid and drain thoroughly. (The poaching liquid can be strained, cooled a bit, then refrigerated for use in other dishes. If you are likely to keep it for

---

more than 2 days, freeze it.) Remove the skin and discard, then carefully flake the meat off the bones and place in a stainless steel or porcelain bowl. Set aside.

Melt the butter in a small heavy skillet and sauté the onions, stirring frequently, for 5 to 6 minutes, until soft and lightly browned. Add the sautéed vegetables, salt, pepper, chopped eggs, parsley, and allspice to the bowl containing the flaked poached salmon. Mix thoroughly but gently with a fork, keeping the mixture light and airy.

Spoon about 2 teaspoons of filling onto the center of each round of dough. Fold the edges up and toward the center, then seal tightly by pinching the edges together with your fingers. To steam, place the *pirogi* on a steaming rack (or cake rack set in a large heavy saucepan). Add about ½ inch of water, just enough to reach almost to the level of the rack. Bring to a boil over high heat, cover the pan, then reduce the heat a bit. Steam for 20 to 25 minutes, then lift out carefully. Serve hot with melted butter.

To bake, place the *pirogi* on a well-greased baking sheet, side by side but not touching. Bake in a preheated 375°F. oven for 20 minutes or until browned. Serve hot with melted butter.

Chinese Boiled Dumplings Filled with Crabmeat

These classic Chinese Boiled Dumplings Filled with Crabmeat and flavored with ginger, green onions, and sesame oil make an unusually festive and delicate first course. For a variation of dumplings with a crisper surface, they can be cooled and deep fried. The traditional condiment, a mixture of soy sauce and rice vinegar, is served in small individual bowls; the dumplings are dipped in this sauce as one eats them. They are best prepared in the large quantity given here. Cool those you do not plan to serve and refrigerate for later use.

DUMPLING DOUGH

2 c. sifted flour
¾ c. water, plus 1 or more Tbs. as needed

CRABMEAT FILLING

½ lb. lump crabmeat
¼ c. finely chopped green onions
1½ Tbs. finely chopped fresh ginger root, or a scant ½ tsp. ground ginger
½ c. bamboo shoots, drained and chopped
¼ c. chopped dried mushrooms (3 to 4 medium-sized mushrooms)

2½ tsp. soy sauce
1 Tbs. pale dry sherry
¼ tsp. sugar
¼ tsp. freshly ground white pepper
½ tsp. salt
2 Tbs. sesame oil

To make the dough, put the flour and ¾ cup water in a mixing bowl and mix with a wooden spatula until the mixture forms a ball. Sprinkle in a bit more water if necessary. Turn the ball of dough out onto a lightly floured surface and knead until very smooth. Cover with a wet cloth and allow to stand for 30 minutes. Prepare the filling by combining all the ingredients in a stainless steel or porcelain bowl and toss lightly until thoroughly mixed. Cover the bowl loosely with plastic wrap and refrigerate for 20 minutes before filling the dumplings. Shape the dough into a long thin cylinder about 1¼ inch in diameter by rolling back and forth with the palms of both hands. Cut the cylinder into ½ inch lengths. Roll each piece out with a rolling pin to form thin circles of dough 3 inches in diameter. Place 1 tablespoon of filling at the center of each round, then fold in half and seal the edges tightly by pinching with your fingers. (Each dumpling will have a fan shape viewed from the wide side.)

To boil, fill a large saucepan or kettle three-fourths full of water and bring to a boil over high heat. Drop the dumplings into the boiling water. The boiling will stop. When the water boils up again reduce the heat slightly and cook for 8 to 10 minutes. Remove the dumplings from the water with a slotted spoon or a mesh skimmer, allow to drain very briefly, then serve hot. If desired, allow the dumplings to cool, then deep fry them at 360°F. until lightly browned, about 2 minutes. Drain briefly on paper towels, then serve hot. Provide individual bowls of soy sauce mixed with rice vinegar (approximately 3 to 1) for dipping.

Crab Cakes

We've never tasted a Maryland Crab Cake we didn't like. One of the joys of living in the Baltimore area is obviously the opportunity to buy almost perfect Crab Cakes as easily as one buys a hamburger in the rest of the country. The Crab Cake we liked better than any other is the one served at O'Donnell's seafood restaurant in Washington, D.C. We have tried to duplicate the unique flavor of that version. A brilliant and original American seafood classic.

FOR FOUR

1 lb. lump crabmeat

vegetable oil and peanut oil, half and half, for deep frying

3 slices white bread, crust removed, then dampened in milk and squeezed almost dry

2 large eggs, beaten with a whisk

½ tsp. freshly ground white pepper

1 tsp. salt

½ tsp. dry mustard

2 tsp. fresh lemon juice

Begin heating the oil in a deep fryer to 375°F. Shred the crabmeat gently with 2 forks and put it into a mixing bowl. Crumble the dampened bread into very small pieces by rubbing it between your fingers. Add the eggs and toss lightly with a fork, using a folding motion and bringing the mixture from the bottom to the top. Sprinkle in the seasonings and toss to mix very thoroughly. With your hands shape the mixture into cakes about 4½ by 2½ by 1¼ inches, being careful to mold them gently so as to keep them light and airy. Set the shaped cakes on a platter side by side but not touching. Line another platter with several layers of paper towels and turn the oven to 200°F. Fry the cakes 1 or 2 at a time, depending on the capacity of your fryer, until golden brown. Do not allow them to get too dark. Remove from the fryer with a long-handled mesh skimmer, holding them over the fryer for about 30 seconds to allow the excess oil to drain off, then place them on the lined platter. Set the platter in the warm oven and continue frying in batches until they are all done. Serve on heated plates with tartar sauce in a small cup or ramekin set to the side of each portion.

Marinating, Pickling, and Smoking Recipes

Cured Herring

Brine-Cured Herring

Marinated Herring

Swedish Glassmaster's
    Herring

Pickled Herring with Sour
    Cream

Polish Pickled Fish

Smoked Herring

Smoked Bass

Smoked Mackerel

Smoked Eel

Gravlax (Swedish Salmon
    Marinated in Dill)

Marinated Bass

Marinated Lump Crabmeat

Marinated Squid

14

Marinating, Pickling, and Smoking

Marinating, pickling, and smoking are ancient arts, dating back to times when freshly caught seafood had to be preserved without refrigeration. These techniques change the texture and moisture content of seafood so that it ceases to be perishable. With the advent of excellent refrigerating and freezing equipment in much of the world, the techniques are still used, but for reasons other than preservation. We marinate seafood to modify its flavor; we cure and smoke fish to produce artful taste and texture variations, and to enjoy them for their own sake.

The basic primitive pleasures of smoking, curing, and marinating have rightly come back into favor with home cooks, as have bread baking and sausage making, because we are rediscovering the joys of working directly with the basic elements of what we eat, of controlling precisely the seasonings and degrees of change we want to effect. We omit from our home cures chemicals that give commercial products a stronger color but have nothing to do with their taste. Fish you cure and smoke yourself may not have the reddish color often associated with "kippered" fish unless you add the necessary dyes. We have not used any artificial coloring in the recipes given in this chapter. We have suggested curing or brining times sufficient to give you the drying-out and firming changes needed for attractive and flavorful smoked delicacies, rather than the much longer times usually indicated for these techniques. We have found that few people really enjoy the intensely salty flavor of much kippered herring. *That* much salt is neccessary only if one is obliged to keep the fish unrefrigerated for a very long time.

Once you become familiar with the fundamentals of these processes, you will enjoy creating variations of your own. Any seafood can be marinated or smoked; most can be pickled in an interesting way. We hope to suggest some new ideas to those already familiar with these procedures. For readers who have never tried them, we aim to provide an introduction to the basics of an endlessly fascinating area of seafood preparation.

Basic Marinating, Pickling, and Smoking Techniques

Home smokers differ widely. Test results of your own smoker and adjust intensity of smoke flavor by increasing or decreasing smoking time.

Dry cures are best carried out under refrigeration.

Hang cured fish with entire outer surface exposed to air.

Allow fish to dry completely after curing.

Wire racks in a well ventilated place are a good substitute for hanging facilities.

Use porcelain, glass, or stainless steel for marinating; other materials may add an unpleasant flavor or produce a chemical reaction.

When pickling fish in its own stock, allow enough chilling time for a jelly to form.

Cured Herring

Our favorite dry cure, good for herring you plan to smoke or broil simply with just a bit of butter.

1½ to 2 lb. fresh herring, split
and cleaned
2 to 3 c. rock salt
1 c. dark brown sugar

1 Tbs. crushed black pepper
2 tsp. dill weed, crushed
additional rock salt to cover

Combine the rock salt, brown sugar, pepper, and dill weed in a stainless steel or porcelain mixing bowl. Mix very thoroughly with a wooden spoon. Put a ⅝ inch layer of the curing mixture in the bottom of a deep porcelain or crockery container. Place as many fish on this layer as will fit comfortably when laid flat. Cover with another layer of curing mixture. Set another layer of fish on it. Continue until all the herring is sandwiched between layers of the cure. Place additional rock salt over the top. Cover the container tightly with several layers of plastic wrap. Refrigerate for at least 8 to 10 hours. (Overnight is ideal.) Remove the herring from the curing mixture and rinse quickly under cool running water. Hang the fish to dry or dry lying flat on wire racks or cake racks in a well ventilated place. Allow to dry until the entire outer surface of the fish looks shiny and slightly hard. This shiny surface is the pellicle; it indicates that the fish has absorbed a sufficient quantity of the cure and has lost enough of its moisture to facilitate handling and cooking or smoking without falling apart. Allow about 3 hours for the pellicle to form, longer if the air circulation is poor.

Brine-Cured Herring

If you prefer to cure the herring in a brine, this is a good basic fish brine we have enjoyed using.

1½ to 2 lb. fresh herring, split
and cleaned
1 gallon water
2 c. salt
¼ lb. brown sugar or 1¼ lb.
white sugar with
approximately 1½ Tbs.
molasses added

2 Tbs. crushed black pepper
2 Tbs. crushed bay leaves

Marinating, Pickling, and Smoking 297

Combine the ingredients for the brine in a large porcelain or crockery vessel and stir until the salt and sugar are completely dissolved. Immerse the herring in the solution, then cover the vessel. You may find it necessary to place a plate on top of the herring to keep them from floating to the top. Be sure to place the plate right side up to prevent an air pocket from forming under it. Allow to soak for about 4 hours at room temperature, or 6 to 8 hours refrigerated. After brining, rinse, then dry as indicated for Cured Herring.

Marinated Herring

It is easier than you think to make your own pickled herring at home and you can, by experimentation, work out a marinade precisely to your own taste. This version is one we particularly like.

FOR FOUR TO SIX AS AN APPETIZER

2¾ to 3 lb. fresh herring, split and cleaned, then cut into 1 inch slices

MARINADE

¾ c. white vinegar
½ c. water
½ c. sugar

SEASONINGS

1 c. coarsely chopped red onions
4 small bay leaves, broken in half
½ tsp. freshly ground white pepper

¼ tsp. salt
6 whole allspice
¼ tsp. whole coriander seed
¼ tsp. yellow mustard seeds

Combine the ingredients for the marinade in an enameled or stainless steel lined saucepan. Bring to a boil over high heat, then lower the heat a bit and simmer for 3 minutes, stirring to dissolve the sugar. Remove the pan from the heat and set aside to cool.

Rinse the herring slices under cold running water, then place on paper towels to drain for a few minutes. Put the herring slices in a large glass or porcelain bowl. Add the seasonings, then pour the marinade over them. Mix briefly with a wooden spoon, then pack the herring down gently with the back of the spoon. Cover the bowl with several layers of plastic wrap and refrigerate for at least 6 hours.

To serve, place 2 or 3 slices of herring on each plate, then spoon about 1 tablespoon of onions over or around the slices.

Swedish Glassmaster's Herring

One of the most delicate and visually beautiful pickled herring dishes we know. Use an attractive clear glass quart jar, so the carrot and red onion slices set off by whole allspice and mustard seeds can be admired while you wait; it's ready after 24 hours, but much better after a full 48 hours.

FOR SIX TO EIGHT

2 fresh herring, split and cleaned, then cut into 1¼ inch slices*

¾ c. white vinegar

½ c. water

½ c. sugar

1¼ c. thinly sliced red onions

¾ c. thinly sliced carrots

2½ Tbs. prepared horseradish, very well drained

½ tsp. ginger

2 tsp. whole allspice

2½ tsp. yellow mustard seeds

3 small bay leaves, broken into quarters

Combine the vinegar, water, and sugar in an enamel or stainless steel lined saucepan and bring to a boil over high heat. Stir until the sugar is thoroughly dissolved, then remove the pan from the heat and set aside to cool.

Wash the herring slices under cold running water and place on paper towels to drain. Place a thin layer of onion slices across the bottom of a 1 quart glass jar for which you have a tight-fitting cover. Next make a layer of herring and carrot slices and cover with some of the horse-radish, ginger, allspice, mustard seeds, and several pieces of bay leaf. Repeat the layers until all the ingredients are used up. You should have 3 to 5 layers, depending on the shape of the jar you use.

Pour the cooled pickling liquid from the saucepan into the jar, just to cover the ingredients. Place 2 or 3 thicknesses of plastic wrap over the mouth of the jar, then screw the top on tightly. (The plastic will keep the inner surface of the cover from corroding during marination.) Refrigerate for at least 24 hours before serving.

---

* If fresh herring is not available, substitute salted herring. To remove the salt soak the herring in cold water to cover for 12 hours, changing the water several times.

Pickled Herring with Sour Cream

Most homemade Pickled Herring with Sour Cream has a fresher and more distinctive flavor than the kind you get in a jar. Be sure to use heavy sour cream and to include plenty of red onions in each serving.

FOR FOUR TO SIX AS AN APPETIZER

Marinated Herring
½ pint heavy sour cream

Remove the herring slices from their marinade and place in a stainless steel mixing bowl. Scoop as much of the chopped onions out of the marinade as you can with a slotted spoon and add to the herring. Check the amount of liquid in the bottom of the bowl. You will need approximately 3 to 4 tablespoons. If necessary, add some of the marinade to make up the amount. Spoon ⅔ cup sour cream into the bowl, then mix very gently, using a lifting and folding motion. Taste. If necessary, add more sour cream and/or marinade, a very small amount at a time, until the desired flavor is reached. Mix again thoroughly.

To serve, place 2 or 3 slices of herring on each plate, then spoon about ¼ cup of the sour cream sauce, including the chopped onions, over each portion.

Polish Pickled Fish

A traditional Eastern European jellied fish dish. We like it best with carp or buffalo, but any large firm fish will work well. The fish is cut into thick slices and cooked with vinegar, vegetables, a bit of sugar, and an interesting combination of aromatic seasonings. Be sure to cook the head and tail along with the rest; they add flavor and give you an attractively firm jelly.

---

one 4 to 6 lb. carp or buffalo,
split, cleaned, carefully scaled,
head and tail left on

coarse salt

5 medium or 3 large onions,
sliced

5 carrots, sliced

1 celery stalk, cut in thirds across,
then into slivers

2 small ripe tomatoes, halved

2¼ c. white wine vinegar

4 to 5 c. water, approximately

1 tsp. salt

¼ tsp. freshly ground black
pepper

¼ c. sugar

3 Tbs. honey

2 pieces, 1 inch x ¼ inch, orange
zest

1 piece, 1 inch x ¼ inch,
lemon zest

⅛ tsp. cinnamon

1/16 tsp. nutmeg

2 whole cloves

4 whole allspice

Cut the fish into 1½ to 2 inch slices, or have this done at the fish market. Sprinkle the slices and the head and tail with coarse salt, then put them into a large porcelain or crockery bowl. Cover the bowl and refrigerate for about 30 minutes while you cut up the vegetables and assemble the seasonings.

Rinse the pieces of fish under cool running water to remove the salt and place them in a heavy 8 to 10 quart pot or kettle. Put the cut-up vegetables on top of the fish, then sprinkle on the vinegar. Add about 4 to 5 cups water, just enough to cover the fish. Add the remaining ingredients. Bring to a boil over high heat, then reduce the heat and simmer for 30 to 40 minutes, until the fish is thoroughly cooked but not mushy. Carefully lift the fish slices out of the pot with a long-handled spoon or a skimmer, trying not to break up the slices. Place the fish in a very large porcelain container at least 3 inches deep (or use 2 containers if you have none large enough). Strain the broth from the pot through a fine mesh strainer, then ladle it over the fish. Allow it to cool for about 25 minutes, then cover the container with several layers of plastic wrap and refrigerate for at least 5 hours or overnight, until the jelly has become quite firm.

To serve, place a slice of fish on each plate, then spoon about ⅓ cup of the jelly over and around each portion.

Marinating, Pickling, and Smoking 301

Smoked Herring

"Kippered" herring prepared at home is less salty and more flavorful than the commercial kippered herring available in many delicatessens across the country. With modern refrigeration there is no need for the heavy brine solutions generally used in commercial preparation, and the herrings freeze perfectly. A dry cure followed by about 4 hours of smoking over hickory chips produces a meaty and not too salty herring with good flavor and aroma. Inexpensive home smokers are widely available, simple to use, and give excellent results. Remember to do your smoking outdoors or, if indoors, in a chimney with a working flue or under a good range hood.

FOR 1½ TO 2 LB. FRESH HERRING

1½ to 2 lb. cured herring
approximately 3 lb. hickory chips

Cure the herring as directed in Cured Herring or Brine-Cured Herring. Rinse and hang, or place flat on a rack to dry, until the pellicle forms. Place in the smoker, using hooks for hanging or laying the fish flat on the smoker racks, and fill the smoking pan with hickory chips. Smoke according to the directions that accompany the smoker for 4 to 6 hours, depending on how strong a smoke flavor you prefer. Remember to refill the smoking pan whenever necessary. You can tell when the pan needs refilling when no more smoke is coming out of the exhaust holes at the top of the smoker. Empty the ashes remaining in the pan before refilling.

Allow the finished Smoked Herring to cool down a bit, then refrigerate if you plan to serve them within 3 to 4 days. If you plan to keep them any longer, wrap them individually and freeze them.

Smoked Bass

Home curing and smoking allow you to enjoy a wider variety of smoked fish than what is commercially available, since any fresh fish can be successfully smoked. Bass is a good example of a fish that is delicious smoked. There are just a few simple points to keep in mind. First, the fish should be cleaned as soon as possible after catching. Second, it should be kept at around 35°F. until the curing and smoking are undertaken. Smaller fish to be smoked are most attractive simply split and cleaned, with the heads left on. Medium-sized fish should be flattened out after splitting and cleaning to allow the proper penetration of both the cure and the smoking. Since most home smokers will not hold whole large fish comfortably, we have found that filleting them with the skin left on is the most practical way to proceed. For fillets, be sure to lay them flat, skin side down, during smoking; hanging them is likely to rip the fillets apart. Bass is a relatively nonoily fish and should be basted a bit during smoking.

FOR 2 TO 3 LB. WHOLE BASS, SPLIT AND CLEANED, HEAD LEFT ON
OR APPROXIMATELY 3 LB. BASS FILLETS, SKIN LEFT ON

2 to 3 lb. bass	*1 Tbs. crushed black pepper*
3 c. rock salt	*1 Tbs. dill weed, crushed*
1½ c. dark brown sugar	*additional rock salt to cover*
1 tsp. mace	*approximately ½ c. olive oil or*
3 small garlic cloves, crushed	*vegetable oil for basting*

Combine the salt, sugar, and seasonings for the dry cure and mix very thoroughly. Arrange the fish or fish fillets and curing mixture in layers as directed for Cured Herring, then top with an additional layer of rock salt. Refrigerate for about 8 hours or overnight.

Rinse the fish and hang to dry, or place on wire racks, until the pellicle forms. Smoke for about 4 hours, brushing the fish with oil several times during smoking to keep them from getting too dry.

Smoked Mackerel

Both small whole Spanish mackerel and steaks cut from king mackerel smoke beautifully. There's no need to baste mackerel during smoking since the fish has sufficient natural oil to keep it plump and tender. A bit less curing and a bit more smoking pro-duce the best results with mackerel. We find home-smoked mackerel is at least the equal of the more common Smoked Herring.

FOR 3 TO 4 LB. MACKEREL, SPLIT AND CLEANED, HEADS LEFT ON
OR CLEANED AND CUT INTO 1½ INCH STEAKS

Prepare as directed for Smoked Bass. Reduce the curing time to 4 to 6 hours under refrigeration and increase the smoking time to about 7 to 8 hours. Do not baste with oil during smoking.

Smoked Eel

One of the finest and most delicate smoked dishes we know, equally delicious with very small eel and with larger ones sliced across the grain into thin strips. A brief brine cure and 2 to 4 hours of smoking make eel one of the simplest fish for home smoking. The natural oils in eel keep them tender and moist during smoking. The skin can be removed easily after smoking and the eel refrigerated or frozen.

FOR FOUR TO SIX AS AN APPETIZER

2½ to 3 lb. eel, split and cleaned, heads left on (or removed if you prefer)

BASIC FISH BRINE

1 gal. water	*¼ c. lemon juice*
4 c. salt	*2 Tbs. crushed black pepper*
2 c. brown sugar	*2 Tbs. dill weed, crushed*

Combine the ingredients for the brine in a large crockery or porcelain vessel. Stir until the salt and sugar are dissolved. Rinse the eel quickly under running water, then place in the brine. Place a plate (right side up) on top of them to keep them submerged. Brine for 1 hour, then rinse briefly and hang to dry or lay flat on a rack. When the pellicle forms, smoke for 2 to 4 hours, depending on their size.

When the eel have cooled sufficiently to be handled with ease, remove the heads if left on during smoking. Loosen about an inch of the skin at the head end by inserting a sharp knife between it and the flesh. With one hand hold the eel, tail end down, by the fleshy part, then grab the loosened skin firmly with tongs or a plier and pull downward until all the flesh is stripped clean. It may be necessary to cut the skin loose from the flesh at the tail end with a sharp knife. Discard the skin and cut the flesh into 3 to 3½ inch lengths, wrap tightly in several layers of plastic wrap, and refrigerate. If you do not plan to serve them within 3 to 4 days, freeze them.

To serve small eel (no more than ¾ inch in diameter), cut the pieces in half lengthwise. If desired, the divided pieces may be sliced in half lengthwise to form thinner pieces. Larger eel are best served by first dividing in half lengthwise as for small ones, then slicing into thin pieces with a very sharp thin knife held at about a 35 degree angle; this will give you pieces cut across the grain of anywhere from 1¾ to 3 inches long depending on the diameter of the eel. Place several pieces on each plate and garnish with a lemon wedge.

Gravlax
Swedish Salmon Marinated in Dill

For those fortunate enough to get fresh salmon in abundance, we recommend this Swedish style of marinating it. Gravlax is more delicate and far less salty than lox, which is simply soaked in heavily salted water for up to 5 days. Coarse salt and fresh dill are traditionally used to prepare Gravlax, but you can manage very well with table salt and dried dill weed, readily found on supermarket spice shelves these days. It is excellent served with thinly sliced pumpernickel and the traditional Swedish mustard and dill sauce.

FOR EIGHT TO TEN AS A FIRST COURSE

2½ to 3 lb. center cut fresh
    salmon steak, cleaned,
    backbone and smaller bones
    removed, skin left on
⅓ c. coarse salt (or table salt)
⅓ c. sugar

1⅔ Tbs. white peppercorns,
    crushed
4 tsp. dill seed
1 large bunch fresh dill or
    2 Tbs. dried dill weed

MUSTARD AND DILL SAUCE

¼ c. German style mustard
1 Tbs. yellow mustard seeds,
    parched in the oven,* then
    ground with a mortar and
    pestle
4 tsp. sugar
1½ Tbs. white wine vinegar

3 Tbs. peanut or other vegetable
    oil
1 tsp. salt, more if necessary
¼ tsp. freshly ground white
    pepper, more if necessary
¼ c. finely chopped fresh dill or
    3 Tbs. dried dill weed

Cut the salmon steak in half along the backbone crease. Rinse the pieces under cool running water and pat dry with paper towels. Combine the salt, sugar, crushed peppercorns, dill seed, and dill in a stainless steel or porcelain bowl. Mix very thoroughly. Place one piece of fish, skin side down, in a deep round crockery or porcelain container. Rub some of the marinating mixture into the fish with your fingers, then sprinkle with a ⅜ inch layer of the mixture. Rub some of the marinating mixture into the flesh side of the remaining piece of fish and place, flesh side down, on top of the first piece. Sprinkle the remaining marinating mixture into the spaces around the fish, packing it down with your fingers. Place a plate slightly smaller then container on top of the fish and press down firmly. Weight the plate down (several other plates, several cans of food, or a plastic bag filled with stones will do the trick), then cover the container with plastic wrap and refrigerate for 48 hours. Remove from the refrigerator every 12 hours and turn the pieces of fish over, then cover with the plate and weights, cover the container, and put back in the refrigerator. Do not pour off the liquid that will gradually accumulate in the container; it is essential that the fish be allowed to soak in it.

After marination, remove the fish from the marinade, allow to drain, then scrape off any solids from the marinade which cling to it. Pat dry with paper towels. To slice, place the pieces of fish skin side down on a chopping surface and with a sharp knife cut the flesh on the diagonal into thin slices about ⅛ inch thick. Cut each slice away from the skin when the knife reaches it. Serve on salad plates, several overlapping slices to each portion, with several pieces of pumpernickel placed to one side and a generous tablespoon of mustard and dill sauce to the other.

To prepare the sauce, combine the mustard, ground mustard seed, and sugar in a deep stainless steel bowl or the bowl of a standing electric mixer. Mix thoroughly by beating at a slow speed with a whisk or

* Place the seeds on a piece of heavy aluminum foil and set in a 475°F. oven until they appear browned, about 12 to 15 minutes.

an electric mixer. Continue to beat slowly while adding the oil in small amounts or in a very thin steady stream. When the sauce begins to thicken like a mayonnaise, add the oil in slightly larger amounts, alternating each addition of oil with about 1 teaspoon of vinegar. Once all the vinegar has been added, beat in the salt and pepper. Taste, and add more salt and pepper if necessary. Gently stir in the dill. Spoon the sauce into a glass jar or a small stainless steel or porcelain bowl, cover tightly, and refrigerate for at least 3 hours. When ready to serve, beat the sauce vigorously with a whisk to remix and fluff it up. It will keep well under refrigeration for 3 to 4 days.

Marinated Bass

Bass prepared in the same way as Swedish marinated salmon is delicious and accessible in those areas of the country where fresh salmon is not to be found. It is possible to add food coloring so your bass looks much like salmon, but we frankly prefer the natural color.

FOR EIGHT TO TEN AS A FIRST COURSE

Prepare as directed for Gravlax, substituting 2½ to 3 pound bass steaks for the salmon. If very large bass is not available, smaller ones can be used; have them split, cleaned, and filleted with the skin left on, then proceed as directed.

Marinated Lump Crabmeat

An excellent way to use an amount of lump crabmeat that is too small for most cooked dishes. Marinated crabmeat will keep for 3 to 4 days in the refrigerator and actually tastes better the second and third days than it does on the first. We like this as a first course salad.

4 to 5 oz. lump crabmeat	*1½ tsp. basil*
¼ c. dry white wine	*¾ tsp. oregano*
juice of ½ large lemon	*½ tsp. sugar*
¾ tsp. salt	*scant 1/16 tsp. cayenne*
½ tsp. freshly ground black	*⅜ tsp. dry mustard*
pepper	*1 small white onion, cut in half*
¼ tsp. finely minced green onion	*and thinly sliced*
tops	

GARNISH

4 leaves of crisp romaine lettuce	*4 caper-stuffed rolled anchovy*
2 tsp. caviar (optional)	*fillets (optional)*

Combine the crabmeat and the other ingredients in a stainless steel or porcelain bowl. Mix lightly but thoroughly with a fork until the salad appears thoroughly blended. Cover the bowl with several layers of plastic wrap and refrigerate for at least 8 hours. Uncover after 4 hours and mix again, then cover again and refrigerate until served.

To serve, place a lettuce leaf on each plate, then top with one-fourth of the marinated crabmeat mixture. Be sure to spoon any liquid from the bottom of the bowl over the portions. If desired, top each portion with ½ teaspoon caviar and place a caper-stuffed rolled anchovy fillet on top of the caviar.

Marinated Squid

We worked out this marinade one day when we found some beautiful squid and couldn't resist buying a great deal more than we could possibly eat that day. The texture and flavor of the squid are enhanced rather than masked by a delicate marinade made with green onions, white wine, olive oil, lime juice, and a hint of cumin.

3 lb. small to medium-sized squid
½ c. olive oil
½ c. dry white wine
¼ c. thinly sliced green onion tops
3 Tbs. fresh lime juice

1½ tsp. salt
½ tsp. freshly ground white pepper
1 Tbs. basil
1½ tsp. sugar
⅜ tsp. cumin

Clean the squid as directed for Biscayan Squid, then slice into rounds or strips. Combine the remaining ingredients in a large stainless steel or porcelain bowl and mix vigorously with a whisk. Put the squid into the marinade and stir with a wooden spoon to distribute the seasonings evenly. Cover the bowl with several layers of plastic wrap and refrigerate for at least 8 hours or overnight. Uncover after 4 hours to stir, then cover and put back in the refrigerator.

En Croûte and Other Set Piece Recipes

Shrimp Toast

Shrimp Egg Roll

Crawfish Egg Roll

Shrimp Lafayette en Crêpe

Seafood Crêpes Mornay

Fish in a Rye Crust

Chilled Polish Christmas Eve Bass

15

En Croûte and Other Set Pieces

This chapter is devoted to dishes whose visual and aesthetic appeal is as significant as their fine taste. These are dishes for special occasions, good workable home preparations we've called set pieces, several festive Chinese dishes dating back hundreds of years, and an unusual Finnish dish in the grand manner. We have been extremely selective, convinced that a great many of the famous traditional set pieces are indeed attractive to look at but rather uninteresting to eat. These are dishes we have enjoyed serving and eating in our own home, dishes we feel will reward the home cook's labors by not only looking splendid but tasting splendid as well. Several of these dishes can be prepared well in advance, either entirely or in large part, greatly simplifying serving them at home. None of them is a staple of seafood eating, but once you become interested in the many pleasures of cooking and eating seafood you may well wish, for some particular occasion or because you're in the mood to be adventuresome, to prepare and serve some of these more elaborate dishes.

Basic Techniques for En Croûte and Other Set Pieces

Prepare time-consuming dishes such as Shrimp Toast and Egg Rolls ahead of time in large batches. Drain, cool thoroughly, then wrap securely in smaller batches and freeze for later use.

For crêpe dishes prepare crêpes in large batches ahead of time and freeze in multiples of 4 or 6 for later use. Stack freezer-wrapped crêpes flat to avoid breaking them.

To avoid overcooking when preparing seafood fillings, add oysters and lump crabmeat at end of cooking time.

Shrimp Toast

Shrimp, water chestnuts, and sesame seeds pressed into bread slices and fried to a golden brown—this delicate Chinese appetizer is extraordinary in every way. Shrimp Toast demonstrates that the French do not hold a monopoly on imaginative en croûte dishes. We've found that Shrimp Toast is most easily done in large batches. Fried for a scant minute on each side, then cooled and frozen, Shrimp Toast will keep for several months. It can be defrosted and fried to completion at the same time, in about 2 to 3 minutes. Be sure to use stale bread; it absorbs less oil.

FOR FOUR DOZEN TRIANGULAR PIECES

1 lb. peeled and deveined fresh raw shrimp, finely chopped

12 water chestnuts, drained and finely chopped

2 large eggs, lightly beaten

1½ tsp. salt

2 tsps. sugar

¼ tsp. freshly ground white pepper

¼ tsp. coriander

scant 1/16 tsp. cayenne

¼ c. sesame seeds, approximately

12 slices sandwich bread, at least 2 days old

vegetable oil for deep frying, preferably 1 part peanut oil to 2 parts corn oil, with several tablespoons sesame oil added

Combine all the ingredients except the sesame seeds, bread, and vegetable oil in a mixing bowl. Mix thoroughly. Trim the crusts off the bread slices, then spread each slice evenly with about 1 heaping tablespoon of the shrimp mixture. Sprinkle each slice evenly with 1 teaspoon of sesame seeds, then press the topping down gently with the back of a large wide spatula. Using a thin sharp knife, cut each slice into 4 triangles. Allow to dry a bit while you preheat oil in a deep fryer to 375°F.

Gently lower about 6 pieces of Shrimp Toast, shrimp side down, into the hot oil with a long-handled skimmer. Fry for about 45 seconds, then turn the pieces over and fry for about 30 seconds on the other side. Remove from the oil with the skimmer, allowing the excess oil to drain back into the pan, then place on paper towels to drain. Continue frying in batches until all the pieces are done. Allow them to cool to room temperature, then wrap tightly in freezer bags or freezer wrap about 6 to a package, then freeze.

About 20 minutes before you plan to serve, heat oil in a deep fryer to 375°F., then fry the frozen pieces of Shrimp Toast, 6 to 8 at a time, for about 1½ to 2 minutes on each side or until golden brown. Place on paper towels to drain, then on a platter lined with paper towels. Set the platter in a 200°F. oven to keep the Shrimp Toast warm until you have completed the number of pieces you plan to serve. Serve 3 or 4 pieces per portion as an appetizer.

Shrimp Egg Roll

One of the most familiar Chinese dishes in America, egg rolls are generally bland and undistinguished restaurant fare. At its best the Shrimp Egg Roll is a complex en croûte *preparation, with contrasting complementary flavors and textures representative of the best of Chinese cuisine. We enjoy preparing Shrimp Egg Rolls at home. The most practical way is cooking them in large batches just short of done, then freezing them. Frozen egg rolls will thaw at room temperature in about 30 minutes; they then require 3 minutes of deep frying. The frozen egg roll skins available in Chinese groceries throughout the country are uniform and work well. Extremely thin egg roll skins are impractical to make at home.*

FOR 16 EGG ROLLS

rendered pork fat (or packaged lard) for greasing skillet or wok, plus about 2 tsp. to be added during stir-frying

SEASONING MIXTURE

1¾ tsp. salt

1¼ tsp. sugar

1 tsp. coriander

¼ tsp. cumin

¼ tsp. ginger

⅛ tsp. freshly ground black pepper

¼ tsp. cayenne

⅛ tsp. turmeric

⅛ tsp. fenugreek

¼ tsp. freshly ground anise seed

⅛ tsp. freshly ground white pepper

EGG ROLL FILLING

1 c. diced Mild Boiled Shrimp

½ c. diced smoked Polish or French garlic sausage

1⅓ c. Special Boiled Rice,* fluffed up before measuring

1 c. crisply cooked young white or green cabbage (cooked for about 4 minutes in lightly salted boiling water)

1 c. finely chopped green onion tops

2 tsp. seasoning mixture

---

16 egg roll or spring roll skins
2 large eggs mixed with 2 Tbs. cold water for sealing egg rolls

To prepare the seasoning mixture, place the ingredients in a blender and blend at high speed for 30 seconds, then turn it off for about 10 seconds. Repeat until the seasoning mixture appears evenly distributed throughout. From time to time uncover the blender container and scrape down the sides. Spoon into a jar, cover the opening with a layer of plastic wrap, then screw the lid on tightly. The quantity given here will be more than required in the recipe. Save any leftover seasoning mixture for later use. This blend cannot be successfully mixed in batches smaller than the one given here. It will remain fresh and aromatic for several months if kept tightly covered.

To prepare the filling, heat a heavy skillet or a wok over high heat, then grease its entire inner surface lightly but evenly with some pork fat. Add all the ingredients, except the seasoning mixture, in the order given above. Immediately begin stirring the mixture with a spoon and shaking the skillet or wok from side to side. Sprinkle 2 teaspoons of the seasoning mixture evenly over the surface of the mixture. Continue to stir-fry for about 6 minutes, then quickly remove the

* Prepare as directed for boiled rice (see Creole Turtle Stew) substituting 1 teaspoon rendered pork fat for the butter.

---

pan from the heat and turn the contents out into a stainless steel or porcelain bowl. Reserve. Begin heating the oil in a deep fryer to 375°F. while you fill the egg rolls.

To fill an egg roll, heap ¼ cup of the filling mixture, loosely packed for measuring, at the center of the square. Fold 2 diagonally opposite corners of the egg roll skins over the filling so that the corners overlap about 1 inch. Roll up by folding the third corner as far as it will go over the center, then continuing to roll until the envelope is complete. Lift the remaining visible corner of the egg roll skin and brush its underside with a bit of the egg and water mixture. Press down gently with 2 fingers to seal. Place on a large platter to dry. Repeat for the remaining egg rolls.

Deep fry 2 or 3 at a time (do not crowd the fryer) for about 3 minutes or until golden brown. Remove from the fryer with a skimmer and place on a large platter covered with paper towels to drain. Set the platter in a 175°F. oven while you fry the remaining egg rolls.

If you wish to prepare these egg rolls in advance, deep fry for just 1 minute, then remove and drain as indicated above. Allow to cool to room temperature, then wrap them carefully, 2 or 3 to a package, for freezing. They will keep beautifully for several months. To serve, remove them from the freezer about 40 minutes ahead of time. Fry in preheated 375°F. oil for 2 minutes, then drain and serve.

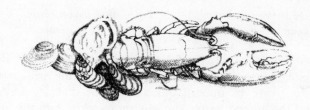

Crawfish Egg Roll

An experiment that worked out very well. It has become our favorite seafood egg roll. The flavor is richer and less polite than Shrimp Egg Roll. You will need about 2 pounds live crawfish or 1 pound frozen peeled crawfish.

FOR 16 EGG ROLLS

Prepare as directed for Shrimp Egg Rolls, substituting 1 cup diced Basic Mild Boiled Crawfish for the shrimp.

Shrimp Lafayette en Crêpe

Classic unsweetened crêpes filled with shrimp in a rich well seasoned sauce, then brushed with a simple lemon-butter glaze and browned under the broiler—a festive grand occasion dish we adapted from a Creole dish made with crawfish. Freeze the leftover crêpes for later use.

FOR FOUR AS A MAIN DISH; FOR EIGHT AS A FIRST COURSE

CRÊPES

⅞ c. flour

¼ tsp. salt

3 large eggs

2 Tbs. Cognac

2 Tbs. melted salt butter

1½ c. milk, approximately

approximately 2 Tbs. melted butter for greasing crêpe pan

FILLING

2 c. Mild Boiled Shrimp, peeled and deveined before measuring

¼ c. (½ stick) salt butter

½ c. heavy cream

¼ tsp. freshly ground black pepper

¼ tsp. freshly ground white pepper

⅜ tsp. salt

⅛ tsp. cayenne

¼ c. Cognac

⅛ tsp. nutmeg

2 large egg yolks

GLAZE

¼ c. (½ stick) salt butter

1 tsp. flour

1 tsp. fresh lemon juice

scant ⅛ tsp. cayenne

To prepare the crêpes, sift the flour and salt together twice, then put into a mixing bowl. Stir in the eggs one at a time with a wooden spoon, taking care to smooth out any lumps that form. Add the Cognac and the melted butter and mix thoroughly. Add the milk very gradually, stirring constantly with a wooden spoon or wire whisk to keep the batter very smooth. When you have added all but ¼ cup of the milk, check the consistency of the batter. It should have the texture of light cream. If necessary, add some or all of the remaining ¼ cup milk. Heat an 8 inch black iron crêpe pan until it is very hot, then rub it with a wadded-up paper towel dipped in melted butter. (The pan should be evenly but lightly greased.) If you see runny streaks of butter, wipe them up with a dry edge of the paper towel wad. Heat the pan for a few seconds longer, then spoon or ladle about 3 tablespoons of the batter into the pan. Tip the pan with a circular motion to spread the batter evenly in a thin layer over the bottom of the pan. (Any excess batter can be poured back into the bowl.) Cook the crêpe until the edges begin to turn brown. Loosen it from the pan with a thin narrow spatula or by shaking the pan, then turn the crêpe over with the spatula or with your finger. Cook on the other side for about 30 seconds. Turn the crêpe out of the pan by inverting the pan over a flat plate placed near the burner. (All the cooked crêpes will be stacked one on top of the other on this plate.) Remember to stir the batter frequently to keep it smooth, and to rub the pan with a small amount of butter every second or third crêpe to keep the crêpes from sticking. Continue until all the batter is used up. Put 8 of the crêpes on another plate and reserve. Freeze the remainder for later use.

To prepare the filling, in a large heavy sauté pan melt the ¼ cup butter over low heat. Add all the remaining ingredients for the filling except the egg yolks and cook over very low heat for about 5 minutes, then remove the pan from the heat. Beat the yolks lightly with a fork in a small bowl and add them to the shrimp mixture. Mix thoroughly, but without beating, then return the pan to low heat for about 1 minute. Fill the 8 crêpes with the shrimp mixture and fold opposite edges over so that they overlap about ¾ inch. Place the filled crêpes in a large shallow baking dish, side by side but not touching, then set in a preheated 350°F. oven for about 10 minutes, or until thoroughly warmed through.

Meanwhile, combine all the glaze ingredients in a small saucepan and heat, then remove the baking dish from the oven and brush the crêpes with the glaze mixture. Heat the broiler and place the baking dish under the source of heat at a distance of about 3 inches, just until the glaze turns light brown, about 30 to 45 seconds. Carefully lift the filled and glazed crêpes onto heated plates with a long wide spatula. Pour any of the glaze sauce from the bottom of the baking dish over the portions, then serve immediately.

Seafood Crêpes Mornay

We particularly like these seafood crêpes filled with shrimp and crabmeat, but you can vary the ingredients at will—scallops, oysters, lobster, squid, any firm-textured fish. The basic sauce remains the same, as do the crêpes. Remember not to overcook

---

the seafood elements. Some, such as oysters and lump crabmeat, require no precooking. For others, subtract a few minutes from the normal cooking time to allow for the period when they are cooked in the sauce.

FOR FOUR AS A MAIN DISH; FOR EIGHT AS A FIRST COURSE

8 unsweetened crêpes (see Shrimp Lafayette en Crêpe)

FILLING

1 c. Mild Boiled Shrimp, peeled and deveined before measuring

1 c. loosely packed lump crabmeat

6 Tbs. salt butter

3 Tbs. finely minced shallots

¼ c. sliced mushrooms (if canned are used, drain very thoroughly)

¼ tsp. freshly ground white pepper

1/16 tsp. cayenne

⅛ tsp. nutmeg

¼ tsp. thyme

¼ tsp. chervil

3 Tbs. dry white wine

MORNAY GLAZE

½ c. (1 stick) plus 1 Tbs. salt butter

6 Tbs. flour

2 c. scalded milk

¾ tsp. salt

¼ tsp. freshly ground white pepper

⅛ tsp. nutmeg

2 large egg yolks

½ c. freshly grated Parmesan cheese

heavy cream for thinning out the sauce if necessary

First prepare the crêpes, or take 8 of them out of the freezer if you have some already prepared.

To prepare the filling, melt the butter over low heat in a large heavy sauté pan. Add the shallots and sauté until soft but not browned, about 4 minutes. Add the mushrooms and seasonings, then stir with a wooden spoon to mix very thoroughly. Mix in the wine and cook over low heat for 2 minutes, then add the shrimp and crabmeat. Cook over low heat, stirring very gently so as not to break up the crabmeat lumps too much, for 4 to 5 minutes, then remove the pan from the heat and set in a 175°F. oven or on a warming tray.

To prepare the Mornay glaze, melt ½ cup of the butter in a saucepan and stir in the flour. Cook over low heat for about 3 minutes, then gradually pour in the hot milk, stirring. Sprinkle in the salt, pepper, and nutmeg. Cook over low-medium heat until the sauce thickens.

Stir almost continually to keep the sauce smooth. Remove the pan from the heat and mix in the egg yolks, stirring constantly to keep them from curdling. When the yolks are thoroughly blended in, return the pan to very low heat for a few minutes while you add the grated cheese and the remaining tablespoon butter, and mix them in thoroughly. Be careful not to let the sauce get too hot or come to a boil. Remove the pan from the heat again and check the consistency of the sauce. If it appears a bit too thick, thin it out by adding about 1 teaspoon of heavy cream at a time and mixing it in thoroughly until the desired texture is attained.

Fill the crêpes with equal quantities of the seafood mixture, then fold up the crêpes so that the edges overlap about ¾ inch. Place in a large shallow baking dish, side by side but not touching, then set in a 350°F. oven for about 5 minutes. Remove the baking dish from the oven and spoon about ¼ cup of Mornay glaze over each crêpe. Place the crêpes under the broiler for about 1 minute, just until the glaze begins to brown. Remove from the broiler immediately. Carefully lift the crêpes, including their glazed topping, onto heated plates with a long wide spatula. Spoon any sauce remaining in the baking dish decoratively around the crêpes, then serve immediately.

Fish in a Rye Crust

A traditional Finnish dish made with small fish with the bones left in, baked inside a loaf-shaped crust at low heat for 4 hours. Even the bones become edible. Allow about 2 hours for the dough to rise because of the high proportion of rye flour.

FOR SIX TO EIGHT

RYE CRUST

1 pkg. or 1 Tbs. active dry yeast
1 c. warm water
1¾ tsp. salt
1½ tsp. sugar
¼ tsp. freshly ground white pepper
2 c. rye flour (stone-ground dark rye, preferably)

1 c. white flour (hard wheat flour, "bread flour," preferably), more if necessary
¼ c. (½ stick) salt butter, softened
butter for greasing the mixing bowl

FILLING

1½ lb. small fish, split and
cleaned, heads and tails
removed
1 tsp. salt
¼ tsp. freshly ground black
pepper

½ tsp. sugar
1 Tbs. finely minced parsley
4 slices breakfast bacon, cut
into ¾ inch pieces
scant ⅛ tsp. nutmeg

To prepare the dough dissolve the yeast in ¼ cup of the warm water
in a large mixing bowl. Sprinkle in the salt, sugar, and pepper and
stir briefly with a wooden spoon. Stir in 1 cup of the rye flour and
½ cup of the white flour, then add the remainder of the water. Cut
the butter into several pieces and stir into the bowl. Add the remainder of the flour gradually, stirring as long as possible, then mixing
with your fingers. Dust a work surface lightly with flour and turn the
contents of the bowl out onto it. Knead the dough, which will be
rather stiff, until it is smooth. This will take from 5 to 8 minutes.
(If you use an electric mixer with a dough hook, mix for about 4
minutes.) Allow the dough to rest while you rinse and dry the bowl.
Rub the inside of the bowl with butter, then place the ball of dough
in it and cover the bowl with plastic wrap. Set in a warm draft-free
place, such as an unlit oven. (The pilot of a gas oven will give you
just enough warmth. With an electric oven, turn it to 150°F. for
about 3 minutes. This will give you a temperature of approximately
85°F.) Put the bowl of dough in the oven and shut the door. Allow
the dough to rise until almost doubled in bulk, about 2 hours.

Turn the dough out onto a floured surface and flatten into an oval
about ½ inch thick and 12 inches long by 10 inches wide, using the
palms of your hands or a straight heavy rolling pin. Dust the surface
of the rolled-out piece of dough evenly with flour and rub it in gently
with the palms of your hands. Allow to dry while you rinse the fish
and dry them very thoroughly with paper towels.

Fill the crust by placing the fish side by side or in layers on the dough.
Sprinkle with salt, pepper, sugar, and parsley. Top with the bacon
pieces. Sprinkle on the nutmeg. Bring the dough up over the fish to
cover it; to seal completely, wet your fingers and smooth out the top
as much as you can. If the dough happens to crack anywhere, dampen
the broken edges and reseal them. Butter the inside of a large heavy
casserole with a lid, or an enameled or stainless steel lined sauté
pan or saucepan with a lid, which will fit in your oven. Place the loaf
carefully in the casserole, then add 2 tablespoons of water and cover.

Bake in a preheated 300°F. oven for 4 hours. At the end of the first hour, uncover the casserole and brush the crust with butter, then cover again. At the end of 3 hours, remove the casserole from the oven. Remove the loaf from the casserole and wrap it in heavy-duty aluminum foil. Put it back in the casserole and bake uncovered for the last hour. At the end of 4 hours, remove the foil-wrapped loaf from the casserole and allow to cool in the foil on a cake rack for about 15 to 20 minutes. To serve, remove the foil covering and place on a large plate or, preferably, a large wooden serving board, then cut into slices at the table with a long serrated knife.

Chilled Polish Christmas Eve Bass

A spectacularly beautiful main dish—pieces of poached bass encased in a jellied sauce studded with fruit and nuts. Prepare this a day in advance and chill it in a large attractive baking or gratin dish at least 2 inches deep.

FOR FOUR TO SIX

Prepare as directed for Polish Christmas Eve Bass. After the fish is poached, carefully lift the pieces out of the poaching liquid with a slotted spatula and place them on a plate to cool while you prepare the sauce. When the sauce is done, allow it to cool for about 15 minutes. While the sauce is cooling, arrange the pieces of poached fish in a large baking or gratin dish. Group them toward the center, with some space between the pieces to allow room for the sauce to coat them all around. Carefully ladle the sauce over the pieces of fish, arranging some of the raisins and almonds decoratively on top of each piece. If the decoration moves too easily in the liquid, set the dish on the top shelf of the refrigerator for about 10 minutes to firm the sauce a bit, then remove it and rectify the decoration. Cover the dish tightly with several layers of plastic wrap and refrigerate for at least 24 hours.

To serve, uncover the dish and set it on a platter (or an attractive wooden bread board) and bring to the table. Lift several pieces of fish along with the jellied sauce covering them onto each plate. Spoon several additional tablespoons of jellied sauce from the sides of the dish around each portion.

Chilled Seafood and
Salad Recipes

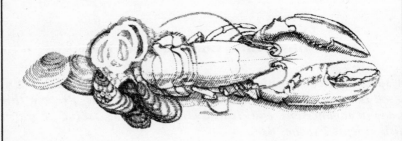

Chilled Greek Stuffed Squid

Chilled Poached Bass with
Cream Horseradish Sauce

Chilled Polish Bass with
Cold Béarnaise Sauce

Seviche

Chilled Eel in Green Sauce

Shrimp and Crabmeat Louie

Piquant Crabmeat Louie

French Shrimp Rémoulade

New Orleans Shrimp
Rémoulade

Stone Crabs with Cream
Mustard Sauce

Cold Crabmeat Ravigote

Shrimp in Aspic

Fish in Aspic

Cold Mackerel in White
Wine

Shrimp Cocktail

Crabmeat Cocktail

Oyster Cocktail

Conch Cocktail

Crabmeat Salad with
Homemade Mayonnaise

Chilled Seafood Coquilles

Cracked Crab Salad

Shrimp in Sour Cream Dill
Sauce

Herring Salad

Rock Shrimp Salad

Codfish Salad

16

Chilled Seafoods and Salads

For us nothing is as simple and elegant as a festive cold meal. Cold seafood dishes are excellent for entertaining, and they are delightful for simple home eating. Some of our favorite meals have been chilled versions of dishes we had hot the night before. And because we have preached simplicity to friends, we have been treated to lovely light cold suppers of pâté, stone crabs, and fresh fruit salad, which were satisfying and elegant.

The liberated hostess can get up her courage and simplify her entertaining. To her delight she will find that most of her friends overeat because they feel they are expected to. With fewer courses and side dishes everyone is happy. All of the dishes included here can be served as either first or main courses depending on the portion sizes; they are also eminently suitable for buffets. Some dishes require marinating time in the refrigerator; others are better with the dressing or sauce served separately or put on just before serving. Above all, this kind of eating is easy on everyone, the hostess and the guests. Few things are as delightful, pleasant, or simple to prepare and enjoy as a cold seafood supper. Just add some chilled white wine and enjoy the food and the company.

Basic Techniques for Chilled Seafoods and Salads

Cook elaborate seafood dishes intended to be served cold a day ahead; use attractive dishes and allow sufficient time for chilling.

Marinate cold fish dishes with a sauce in the refrigerator to avoid spoilage; allow at least 8 hours for full flavor development.

Refrigerate dressings for seafood salads immediately after completion; sauce chilled seafood right before serving.

Boil shellfish for salads ahead of time, cool, then peel and refrigerate.

When clarifying aspics, allow clear liquid to drip through damp cloth slowly; do not stir to hasten process.

Chill clarified aspics about 20 minutes before coating inside of mold; set coating quickly by placing mold in freezer for about 8 minutes.

Allow at least 4 hours for aspics to set properly.

To turn out aspics, proceed gently and slowly, alternating warming bottom of mold with loosening aspic around the edges with a knife; repeat as often as needed until aspic comes free.

Chill serving containers for seafood cocktails in refrigerator for 15 minutes before assembling, or use servers with an ice compartment.

Chill homemade mayonnaise for 20 to 30 minutes before dressing salads.

Chilled Greek Stuffed Squid

An unusual cold appetizer, squid in a rice and tomato sauce with currants, parsley, and pine nuts. Prepare this a day in advance and bring it to the table in a handsome oval baking dish.

FOR EIGHT TO TEN AS A FIRST COURSE

Prepare as directed for Greek Stuffed Squid, doubling the quantities given in the recipe. When the squid and sauce are cooked, carefully arrange the squid in a large oval baking dish. Spoon the sauce over and all around the squid. Allow to cool to room temperature, then cover the dish with several layers of plastic wrap and refrigerate for at least 24 hours.

To serve, remove the dish from the refrigerator, uncover, and bring to the table. Serve with a large spoon, placing several stuffed squid on each plate topped with about 3 tablespoons of sauce. If desired, carefully remove the toothpicks that hold the squid closed before bringing the dish to the table.

Chilled Poached Bass with Cream Horseradish Sauce

Small to medium-sized bass should be filleted, larger bass cut into steaks for poaching. Be sure to drain the cooked fish thoroughly and to cover it tightly before refrigerating. The sauce is served to one side of the fish.

FOR THREE OR FOUR

Poach the bass as directed for Poached Bass with Almond Curry Sauce, omitting the orange rind and ground fennel seed from the seasonings. Allow the cooked fish to cool at room temperature for 5 to 8 minutes, then place in a shallow baking dish and cover the dish tightly with plastic wrap or aluminum foil. Refrigerate for at least 6 to 7 hours before serving.

To serve, place the chilled fish on plates and spoon about ¼ cup of cream horseradish sauce to one side of each portion.

CREAM HORSERADISH SAUCE

MAKES ABOUT 1 CUP

6 Tbs. prepared white horseradish (do not use any labeled "extra hot")	⅛ tsp. cayenne
	¼ tsp. freshly ground white pepper
1 Tbs. Dijon mustard	½ tsp. freshly ground toasted yellow mustard seeds
3 Tbs. white wine vinegar	
⅛ tsp. sugar	½ c. heavy cream

Combine all the ingredients except the cream in a stainless steel or porcelain bowl. Mix thoroughly with a whisk. Allow to stand at room temperature for about 20 minutes, then very slowly add the cream, stirring constantly with a whisk. Cover the bowl and refrigerate for at least 1 hour before serving.

Chilled Poached Bass with Cold
Béarnaise Sauce

We discovered by chance that our favorite béarnaise sauce was delicious cool, and tried it on chilled poached fish—a winning combination. To make the sauce hold for a comfortable length of time, we added a slight stabilization element to it. A very attractive main dish, with the deep gold sauce flecked with green, set off by ripe tomato wedges. The quantities given here can be multiplied several times over with no difficulty.

FOR TWO

1 medium-sized (2 to 3 lb.)
striped bass, filleted

⅔ c. water

½ tsp. salt

¼ tsp. freshly ground white
pepper

¼ tsp. fresh lemon juice

½ small bay leaf

⅛ tsp. thyme

2 slices white onion

COLD BÉARNAISE SAUCE

MAKES APPROXIMATELY ¾ CUP

1½ Tbs. finely minced green
onion tops

¼ tsp. finely minced garlic

2 tsp. fresh lemon juice

¼ c. dry white wine

½ Tbs. tarragon

½ Tbs. chervil

⅛ tsp. salt

¼ tsp. freshly ground black
pepper

3 large egg yolks

scant ⅛ tsp. cayenne

½ c. (1 stick) salt butter

¾ tsp. flour

1¼ tsp. water

To poach the fish, place the fillets and the remaining ingredients in a skillet and bring to a boil over high heat. Cover the skillet loosely and reduce the heat to very low. Cook for 7 to 9 minutes, or just until the fillets break easily into flakes when poked with a cake tester or toothpick. Remove the fish from the skillet with a large slotted spatula and place on a platter. Cool to room temperature, then cover the platter with plastic wrap and refrigerate to chill.

To prepare the sauce, make the glaze by combining the first 8 ingredients in a small heavy saucepan. Boil, stirring frequently, until reduced to about 2 tablespoons. (There should be almost no liquid left.) Reserve. Put the egg yolks and cayenne in a blender container and turn on high speed for a few seconds, just to break the yolks, and mix in the pepper. Add the glaze from the saucepan and blend again

---

for a few seconds to mix. Melt the butter in a small saucepan until quite hot but not browned. Turn the blender on high speed and slowly pour in two-thirds of the hot melted butter. Leaving the blender on, add the flour and water, then the remaining butter. Blend until the sauce is quite thick and fluffy. Turn off the blender and scrape down the sides of the container several times to ensure incorporating all the herbs from the glaze. When the sauce has reached the desired consistency, set the blender container, uncovered, on the counter to cool for about 8 to 10 minutes, or until the sauce reaches room temperature, then set the container on a lower shelf of the refrigerator to chill.

To serve, place the chilled fillets on plates and top each portion with about ⅓ cup of the chilled béarnaise sauce. Garnish with ripe tomato wedges.

Seviche

This South and Central American raw fish dish exists in a number of variations. Our version uses trout and mackerel, but feel free to vary the fish with regionally available ones. The fish must be very fresh. Be sure to allow sufficient time for marination. We've found that marination in the refrigerator for at least 8 hours, or overnight, gives the best results and eliminates the possibility of spoilage.

FOR SIX

1 to 1½ lb. bass and trout fillets, skin removed, frozen for 48 hrs. (see "Sushi," p. 357)
¾ tsp. salt
½ tsp. freshly ground black pepper
⅔ c. finely chopped white onions
2 tsp. chopped canned jalapeño peppers, drained and seeded

juice of 6 limes
3 Tbs. olive oil
1 Tbs. white wine vinegar
1½ Tbs. finely minced parsley
2 small ripe tomatoes, peeled, seeded, and chopped (optional)

Cut the fish into large pieces and arrange in the bottom of a porcelain or glass bowl. Sprinkle on the salt and pepper. Cover with the chopped onions arranged in an even layer. Add the chopped jalapeño peppers, distributing them evenly over the onions. Pour the lime juice evenly over the top. Cover the bowl with plastic wrap and refrigerate for at least 8 hours or overnight. Uncover and mix gently with a wooden spoon after 6 hours, or in the morning if left overnight. Add the olive oil, vinegar, parsley, and tomatoes. Stir gently. Cover again and put back into the refrigerator for at least 1 hour or until served.

To serve, ladle into soup bowls, being sure to include some of the liquid and solids that have settled to the bottom of the bowl.

Chilled Eel in Green Sauce

Our favorite eel dish served chilled, with its beautiful creamy herb sauce jellied over and around the parboiled and sautéed eel. Small eel no more than 1¼ inches thick work best here. Allow at least 8 hours for proper chilling, and use an attractive baking dish you can bring to the table.

FOR FOUR AS A MAIN DISH; FOR EIGHT AS A FIRST COURSE

Prepare as directed for Eel in Green Sauce. When the cooking is completed, arrange the pieces of eel in an attractive shallow baking dish, then spoon the sauce from the pan over and around them. Cool to room temperature, then cover the dish with several layers of plastic wrap and refrigerate for at least 8 hours.

To serve, carefully lift the pieces of eel along with their topping of jellied sauce onto plates, then spoon the sauce remaining in the dish around each portion.

Shrimp and Crabmeat Louie

One of the best versions we've ever had of this San Francisco shellfish salad was served at Maye's Oyster House, one of San Francisco's older and less fashionable seafood restaurants. With interest we watched the waiter assemble the salad in alternating layers of shellfish and dressing. The results were superb—every bit of seafood was lightly coated with the excellent dressing. Be sure to scoop up as much of the onion juice as you can after chopping; it's essential to the flavor of the dressing. Once mixed, the dressing should be refrigerated for about 10 minutes, just long enough to assemble the salad elements.

FOR FOUR

1½ lb. Mild Boiled Shrimp in the shell, chilled

12 oz. lump crabmeat, chilled
8 crisp leaves romaine lettuce

LOUIE DRESSING

1 c. mayonnaise
¼ c. heavy cream
¼ c. chili sauce
1 tsp. Worcestershire sauce
1 tsp. fresh lemon juice

⅜ tsp. salt
⅛ tsp. cayenne
2 Tbs. very finely chopped white onion and the liquid released during chopping

Combine the ingredients for the dressing in a stainless steel or porcelain bowl and mix very thoroughly with a wire whisk. Be sure to mix in the damp pieces of chopped onion that tend to settle to the bottom of the bowl, as well as the onion juice. (The juice is essential to the flavor balance of the sauce.) Refrigerate the dressing while assembling the salad elements.

Rinse the lettuce leaves and shake off the excess moisture over the sink, then roll them loosely in a large linen towel and place in the refrigerator. Peel and devein the shrimp and place on paper towels to soak up any excess moisture. Place 2 leaves of romaine lettuce on each plate, then top with one-eighth of the crabmeat and one-eighth of the boiled shrimp. Ladle one-eighth of the dressing over the shellfish. Make a second layer of crabmeat and shrimp and top with the remaining dressing. Serve immediately.

Piquant Crabmeat Louie

Lump crabmeat with a variation on the Louie dressing. Instead of prepared chili sauce, which can vary widely from one brand to another, we use chili powder and cumin, which give the dressing a pleasant bite. Minced parsley and green pepper add a bit more flavor and set off the white crabmeat attractively.

1 lb. lump crabmeat

PIQUANT LOUIE DRESSING

½ c. mayonnaise	1 Tbs. finely minced green
2⅔ Tbs. ketchup	pepper
2 Tbs. heavy cream	¼ tsp. cayenne
⅛ tsp. dark chili powder	⅛ tsp. freshly ground white
1½ tsp. finely minced white	pepper
onion and its liquid	scant 1/16 tsp. cumin
2 tsp. finely minced fresh	½ tsp. salt
parsley	1¼ tsp. fresh lemon juice

Combine all the ingredients for the dressing in a stainless steel or porcelain bowl. Mix well with a wooden spoon, then beat with a whisk, or an electric mixer at medium speed, for 3 minutes. Cover the bowl with plastic wrap and refrigerate for at least 15 minutes.

Heap one-eighth of the crabmeat on each plate, then spoon one-eighth of the dressing over it. Repeat the layers. If desired, garnish with ripe tomato wedges and slivers of crisp cucumber. Serve immediately.

French Shrimp Rémoulade

Firm, mildly seasoned shrimp with a classic French shellfish sauce made with mayonnaise, Dijon mustard, capers, and herbs. Simple and delicious. Be sure to stir rather than beat the sauce when mixing it; it should be thick and creamy, but not fluffy.

FOR FOUR

*1¼ lb. Mild Boiled Shrimp, peeled, deveined, and chilled
(about ¾ lb. after peeling)*

FRENCH RÉMOULADE SAUCE

¾ c. mayonnaise (purchased, or see Crabmeat Salad with Homemade Mayonnaise)	¼ tsp. dried tarragon or 1½ tsp. chopped fresh tarragon
1¾ tsp. Dijon mustard	2 tsp. finely minced fresh parsley
4 tsp. drained, finely chopped capers	⅛ tsp. anchovy paste
2 Tbs. finely chopped green onions	⅛ tsp. freshly ground white pepper

---

Put the ingredients for the sauce one at a time, in the order given, in a stainless steel or porcelain bowl and combine. Stir thoroughly but gently after each addition with a whisk or a wooden spoon. Do not beat. When the sauce is thoroughly mixed, cover the bowl with plastic wrap and refrigerate for at least 30 minutes.

When ready to serve, remove the sauce from the refrigerator and stir thoroughly but gently to ensure even distribution of the ingredients. Place the portions of chilled cooked shrimp on plates, then ladle about ¼ cup of sauce over each one. Serve immediately.

New Orleans Shrimp Rémoulade

Well seasoned shrimp on chopped lettuce covered with a sea of well seasoned Creole rémoulade sauce, a New Orleans classic. This very rich, reddish colored sauce contains both puréed and chopped vegetables, and tastes best refrigerated for several hours before use. The sauce also works well with milder boiled shrimp.

FOR FOUR

1¼ lb. New Orleans Boiled Shrimp or Mild Boiled Shrimp, in the shell and chilled

1 c. coarsely chopped lettuce

CREOLE RÉMOULADE SAUCE

1 bunch green onions
2 small celery stalks
2 parsley sprigs
3 Tbs. Dijon mustard
1½ tsp. freshly ground toasted yellow mustard seeds (see note under Gravlax)
5 tsp. paprika
1¼ tsp. salt
½ tsp. freshly ground black pepper

¼ tsp. cayenne
6 Tbs. white wine vinegar
5 tsp. fresh lemon juice
½ tsp. basil
¾ c. olive oil
1 green onion, chopped
1 Tbs. chopped celery
2 tsp. finely minced fresh parsley

Put the bunch of green onions, celery stalks, and parsley sprigs into a blender or food processor and reduce to a coarse purée. Put the vegetable purée into a mixing bowl, then add the mustard, ground mustard seeds, paprika, salt, pepper, and cayenne and blend thoroughly with a wooden spoon. Add the vinegar, lemon juice, and basil and blend again. Pour in the olive oil very gradually, stirring constantly, and stir until the sauce appears evenly blended. Add the chopped green onion and celery and the minced parsley. Stir with a wooden spoon just long enough to mix them in thoroughly. Cover the bowl with plastic wrap and refrigerate for at least 2 hours.

About 30 minutes before you plan to serve, peel and devein the shrimp, then place them on paper towels. Rinse, drain, and chop the lettuce. Put ¼ cup chopped lettuce on each plate, then top with the peeled shrimp. Remove the sauce from the refrigerator, stir to mix thoroughly, then ladle about ¼ cup of sauce over each portion, making sure to completely cover the shrimp. Serve within 5 minutes of saucing.

Stone Crabs with Cream Mustard Sauce

The classic way to serve this unusual shellfish, with a simple mustard-based sauce. Marketed boiled and frozen, the huge claws require only that you thaw them before serving. We have found that the most practical way to defrost them is on the counter at room temperature. Allow 6 hours for full defrosting and check one after 4 hours by cracking a claw. If the meat appears thawed by then, simply refrigerate the claws until serving time. The sauce can be prepared just a few minutes before you plan to serve.

FOR FOUR

8 to 12 stone crab claws, defrosted and cracked with a hammer

CREAM MUSTARD SAUCE

1 c. heavy cream, well chilled
6 Tbs. Dijon mustard
1½ tsp. sugar
¼ tsp. freshly ground white pepper

Place 1 cracked crab claw on each plate and put the rest on a large attractive platter to be set at the center of the table. Put the chilled cream in a mixing bowl and mix with an electric mixer at medium-low speed until slightly frothy. Add the mustard, sugar, and pepper, then whip at high speed until the sauce is very fluffy and almost stiff. Place a small ramekin or glass dish to one side of each plate and fill with sauce. Spoon the remainder of the sauce into a bowl, set the bowl on a platter with a spoon, and bring to the table along with the platter of additional crab claws. Serve the portions with seafood forks and dinner forks. Place several nutcrackers on the table to be used if necessary.

Cold Crabmeat Ravigote

Lump crabmeat in a slightly tart butter, cream, and white wine sauce flecked with green onion slices—a casserole dish we like even better cold. Allow about 2 hours for proper chilling once the sautéing is complete. This makes a rather substantial first course, or a very satisfying main dish for an elegant cold supper.

FOR FOUR

Prepare as directed for Crabmeat Ravigote. Eliminate the additional 4 teaspoons butter and the baking stage. Once the crabmeat is heated through in the sauce, remove the pan from the heat. Allow to cool for a few minutes, then spoon into individual gratin dishes. Cool for about 5 minutes longer, then cover the dishes with aluminum foil and refrigerate for at least 2 hours.

To serve, set the chilled individual casseroles on plates and sprinkle ½ teaspoon very finely minced fresh parsley over each one before bringing to the table.

Shrimp in Aspic

A classic cold seafood dish, firm boiled shrimp in a molded salad. We like an aspic combining both chicken stock and tomato juice, with a slightly tart flavor best achieved with fresh lime juice. Clarifying the aspic gives you a finished dish that sparkles. It's

worth the small additional effort. A fish-shaped mold is attractive
for shrimp aspic, but any ¾ to 1 quart mold or shallow baking
dish can be used.

FOR THREE OR FOUR

SHRIMP

1½ to 2 lb. whole shrimp in the shell
court bouillon for Mild Boiled Shrimp

BASIC STOCK AND TOMATO ASPIC

½ c. cold water	*¼ tsp. freshly ground white*
3 envelopes unflavored gelatin	*pepper*
2½ c. chicken stock	*3 Tbs. fresh lime juice or lemon*
1 c. tomato juice	*juice, if limes are unavailable*
1 Tbs. sugar	*2 large egg whites, beaten until*
	frothy
½ tsp. salt	*2 egg shells, crushed*

SEASONINGS AND GREENS

1 tsp. brandy	*½ tsp. marjoram*
1 Tbs. dry white wine	*1 Tbs. finely minced parsley*
1/16 tsp. cayenne	*¼ c. thinly sliced green onion*
⅛ tsp. nutmeg	*tops*

Cook the shrimp as directed for Mild Boiled Shrimp. Allow to cool, then peel and devein. Place the shrimp in a bowl, cover with plastic wrap, and refrigerate to chill thoroughly.

To prepare the aspic, put the cold water in a small saucepan, then sprinkle in 2 envelopes of gelatin. Warm very slowly over low heat, stirring with a wooden or rubber spatula until the gelatin is completely dissolved. Remove the pan from the heat. In a 2 to 3 quart saucepan combine the dissolved gelatin, chicken stock, tomato juice, sugar, salt, pepper, and lime juice. Add the egg whites and egg shells. Heat slowly, stirring constantly, until the mixture boils up in the pan. Lower the heat and allow to simmer for 1 minute, then remove the pan from the heat and allow to stand at room temperature for 5 minutes. Place a large fine mesh strainer over a deep bowl. Moisten a kitchen towel with cold water, then wring it out. Line the inside of the strainer with the damp towel and pour the contents of the pan into the strainer. Allow to drip through undisturbed; do not stir or mix at all. When the dripping has stopped, remove the strainer from the bowl. Stir in the third envelope of gelatin and mix until thoroughly dissolved. Place the bowl of liquid on the top shelf of

The Pleasures of Seafood 334

the refrigerator to chill for about 20 minutes. Place the mold you intend to use in the freezer for about 15 minutes.

To fill the mold, remove it from the freezer and pour about ¾ cup of the chilled aspic mixture into it. Tip the mold with a circular motion to coat the entire inner surface, then place on a shallow baking dish or a pie pan to hold it level. If necessary, fill the dish with rock salt or pebbles to form a stabilizing surface. Place the baking dish and the mold in the freezer again for about 6 to 8 minutes, just until the aspic coating on the inside of the mold sets. Place the chilled boiled shrimp in the mold in a decorative arrangement. If desired, sprinkle some of the sliced green onion tops between the shrimp or beneath each shrimp if you prefer. Stir the remaining seasonings and the greens into the slightly chilled aspic and mix gently to distribute as evenly as possible. Slowly ladle the aspic into the mold until the level of the liquid is about ⅜ inch from the top of the mold. Carefully cover the mold with a piece of aluminum foil, making sure the center of the foil cover does not dip down into the aspic. Place on the top shelf of the refrigerator and allow to chill for at least 4 hours before serving.

To serve, remove the foil cover, then place the mold in about ½ inch of warm water in the sink or in a large dish for about 60 seconds. Remove the mold from the water, and slide the tip of a thin flexible knife around the inner edges of the mold to loosen the aspic. Wipe the bottom of the mold with a towel, then cover with an inverted platter large enough to hold the turned-out aspic comfortably. Holding the platter firmly against the mold, turn them over. Rap the top of the mold firmly. The mold should fall onto the platter in a solid piece. If it doesn't, repeat the warm water immersion and knife-sliding operation, then the turning-over motion until the mold comes free. (It may be necessary to repeat the process 4 or 5 times. Do *not* attempt to hasten the operation by soaking the mold in warm water for longer than 60 seconds at a time, or the surface of the turned-out aspic will be uneven and partially melted.) Bring the aspic to the table on its platter and cut into portions with a sharp knife, then lift the portions onto plates with a wide spatula.

Fish in Aspic

A striking way to serve chilled poached fish, in a stock and tomato aspic studded with slices of steamed carrot and pieces of cooked marinated broccoli or zucchini. With a bit of deft arrangement, you can create a multicolored fish encased in a shimmering jell. Substitute 1 cup of strained fish stock for 1 cup of the chicken stock if you prefer a more strongly flavored aspic.

FOR THREE OR FOUR

*approximately 10 oz. chilled poached fish (see any of
the recipes in Chapter 5) cut into large pieces
basic stock and tomato aspic (see Shrimp in Aspic)
½ c. chilled cooked broccoli, soaked in ¼ c. dry white wine,
2 Tbs. olive oil, and ¼ tsp. freshly ground black pepper
for 1 hour, then drained very thoroughly
1 medium-sized carrot, steamed until cooked but still firm,
then peeled and sliced about ⅛ inch thick*

Prepare and clarify the aspic as directed for Shrimp in Aspic, then chill a 1 to 1½ quart mold and the still-liquid aspic. Coat the mold and chill briefly, then arrange the pieces of fish toward the center of the mold. Outline with carrot slices, then cut the drained marinated broccoli into thin pieces and make an even layer of broccoli across the fish and carrot layer. Fill the mold with aspic, stabilize, then set to chill for at least 4 hours. Unmold and serve as directed.

Cold Mackerel in White Wine

A traditional French chilled fish dish, mackerel marinated in white wine and onions. Fillets from smaller mackerel or steaks cut from the larger king mackerel work equally well. This is an excellent way to prepare a large catch of fresh mackerel brought in by fishermen friends. It keeps under refrigeration for up to 4 days. The longer the mackerel marinates, the richer the flavor. Be sure to spoon some of the marinade and onions over and around each portion when you serve.

FOR FOUR TO SX

2 lb. mackerel fillets or steaks, skin left on

MARINADE

3 c. coarsely chopped onions	*6 whole black peppercorns*
3 c. dry white wine	*1 tsp. thyme*
¾ tsp. salt	*1 large bay leaf, broken up*

----

eight ¼-inch slices fresh lemon
¾ tsp. freshly ground coarse black pepper

Rinse the mackerel fillets under cool running water and place between several layers of paper towels to absorb the excess moisture. Combine the ingredients for the marinade in a small heavy skillet. Bring to a boil over high heat, then reduce the heat slightly and boil gently until the liquid in the pan is reduced by one-third. Remove the pan from the heat.

Put the mackerel fillets flat in the bottom of a large heavy stainless steel lined or enameled sauté pan or skillet. Arrange the lemon slices over the fish. Carefully pour the reduced marinade around and over the fish, taking care not to disturb the lemon slices. Spoon the chopped onions evenly over and around the pieces of fish. Set the pan over medium heat. Sprinkle in the coarsely ground pepper. Bring to a boil, then reduce the heat just enough to keep a simmer going. Simmer for 5 minutes, then remove the pan from the heat and allow to cool to room temperature. When sufficiently cooled, cover the pan with a tight-fitting lid or, if you have none, a piece of heavy aluminum foil tucked tightly all around the edges of the pan. Refrigerate for at least 12 hours, preferably 24 hours, before serving.

To serve, lift the fillets out of the pan carefully with a large wide spatula onto serving plates. taking care not to disturb the lemon slices and onion pieces on top of each fillet. Spoon the jellied sauce and onions remaining in the pan evenly over the portions.

Shrimp Cocktail

The simplest and still one of the best ways to serve good fresh shrimp carefully boiled. Whether you cook them in a mild or a well seasoned court bouillon, watch the timing—overcooked

----

shrimp are never more sadly apparent than when served this way. The cocktail sauce can be prepared ahead of time, but should not be put on the shrimp until you're ready to serve.

FOR FOUR

1 lb. Mild Boiled Shrimp or New Orleans Boiled Shrimp, peeled, deveined, and chilled (approximately 2 lb. in the shell)

COCKTAIL SAUCE

1 c. ketchup	6 drops Tabasco
3 Tbs. fresh lemon juice	
2 Tbs. prepared white horseradish (do not use "extra hot")	

---

8 small leaves crisp romaine lettuce or 4 large leaves, torn in half, rinsed, and dried thoroughly	4 lemon wedges coarsely cracked ice

If you have specially designed chilled seafood cocktail servers, fill the ice compartment with coarsely cracked ice. Or set a soup bowl on a salad plate and fill the bowl one-third full with ice, then nestle a small baking ramekin or glass custard cup or bowl into the ice. Line the small container with 1 or 2 pieces of lettuce. Place the chilled shrimp in the center container with the thicker ends down and the tail ends pointing outward in a circle over the edge of the container. Combine the ingredients for the cocktail sauce in a stainless steel or porcelain bowl and mix very thoroughly with a whisk. Spoon about ¼ cup of sauce onto each portion, covering only the bottom half of the shrimp. Serve immediately.

Crabmeat Cocktail

FOR FOUR

Prepare as directed for Shrimp Cocktail, substituting 1 pound lump crabmeat for the shrimp. Reduce the horseradish to 1 tablespoon when preparing the sauce; if desired, substitute 1 tablespoon dry white wine for 1 tablespoon of the lemon juice. Serve as directed.

Oyster Cocktail

A good way to serve those freshly shucked oysters that are not large enough or handsome enough to present on the half shell— for example, the tiny Olympia oysters available on the West Coast.

FOR FOUR

Prepare as directed for Shrimp Cocktail, substituting 1 pint freshly shucked drained oysters for the shrimp. Serve as directed or, if desired, omit the lettuce leaves and the icing compartment. When omitting the icing compartment, be sure to chill the serving containers for about 15 minutes on the top shelf of the refrigerator before assembling the cocktail.

Conch Cocktail

We first tasted this marinated cocktail in a restaurant in Key West. It makes an unusually attractive first course, with the small pieces of conch mixed with diced green pepper and pimiento. A delicacy limited to those few areas of the country where fresh conch is available. We don't recommend using canned for this dish—the texture is far too soft.

FOR FOUR

1 lb. parboiled, finely diced conch meat	⅓ tsp. freshly ground black pepper
⅔ c. fresh lime juice or ⅓ c. fresh lemon juice diluted with 3 Tbs. cold water	⅛ tsp. sugar
	¼ c. drained diced pimiento
3½ Tbs. olive oil	¼ c. diced green pepper
1 tsp. salt	

Put the diced conch into a deep stainless steel or porcelain bowl. Add the lime juice, olive oil, salt, pepper, and sugar and toss to mix thoroughly with a wooden spoon. Cover the bowl with plastic wrap and refrigerate for 3 to 4 hours. About 30 minutes before you plan to serve, remove the bowl from the refrigerator, uncover, and add the diced pimiento and green pepper. Cover the bowl again and refrigerate for 30 minutes more. To serve, spoon into small glass cocktail cups (or short-stemmed sherbet glasses), including in each portion about ¼ cup of the marinade from the bottom of the bowl.

Crabmeat Salad with
Homemade Mayonnaise

A classic way to serve the best lump crabmeat, with freshly made mayonnaise. We've found that putting just a few tablespoons of the mayonnaise on the crabmeat and serving the remainder in a small glass container set to one side of the plate looks best and keeps the crabmeat from getting at all soggy. Have all the ingredients for the mayonnaise at room temperature for the best results.

FOR EIGHT

1½ lb. best quality lump crabmeat

HOMEMADE MAYONNAISE

2 large egg yolks
1 tsp. salt
¼ tsp. freshly ground white pepper
scant ⅛ tsp. cayenne

1 tsp. dry mustard
1 Tbs. fresh lemon juice
1½ c. olive oil or ¾ c. olive oil and ¾ c. vegetable oil
1½ Tbs. white wine vinegar

Warm a large stainless steel or porcelain bowl just until it feels slightly warm to the touch. Put the egg yolks, salt, pepper, cayenne, mustard, and lemon juice into the bowl. Beat rapidly with a wire whisk. Begin adding the oil, a few drops at a time, beating constantly as you add. When the sauce begins to thicken, increase the amounts of oil you are adding to about 2 teaspoons. Continue to beat with the whisk after each addition, and do not add the next bit of oil until the one just added appears thoroughly incorporated. When the sauce is quite thick, begin adding the wine vinegar, about ½ teaspoon at a time, alternately with the oil. After you have added 1 tablespoon of the wine vinegar, taste the mayonnaise. Add as much of the remaining ½ tablespoon as desired. Cover the bowl with plastic wrap and refrigerate for about 20 to 30 minutes before serving. When you are ready to serve, remove the bowl from the refrigerator, uncover, and beat the mayonnaise quickly with a whisk for a few seconds before using.

To serve the salad, heap the portions of lump crabmeat at the center of attractive salad plates, then top each one with about 1½ tablespoons of mayonnaise. Put the remaining mayonnaise into small glass containers and set one on each plate to one side of the crabmeat. Serve immediately. Provide seafood forks.

Chilled Seafood Coquilles

An unusually attractive main dish seafood salad with shrimp, crabmeat, scallops, and pieces of poached fish tossed with home-made mayonnaise and served on scallop shells. All the elements can be prepared ahead of time, then assembled in just a few minutes. Do not attempt to sauce the salad in advance or the seafood will get soggy.

FOR FOUR

½ c. peeled, deveined, and chilled Mild Boiled Shrimp

½ c. chilled lump crabmeat

½ c. chilled poached scallops (see directions in Coquilles Saint-Jacques)

½ c. chilled poached fish (see directions in Poached Red Snapper with Nantua Sauce), cut into large pieces

about 2¼ c. homemade mayonnaise (see Crabmeat Salad with Homemade Mayonnaise)

4 leaves romaine lettuce, rinsed, dried, and crisped in the refrigerator

2 tsp. finely minced parsley

four ⅛-inch thick slices lemon

Put the seafood into a stainless steel or porcelain bowl, then add ¾ cup of the mayonnaise. Toss gently but thoroughly, using 2 forks or 2 soupspoons, until the mayonnaise is evenly distributed. Place 4 large scallop shells on salad or luncheon plates, then place a lettuce leaf on each shell. Heap about ½ cup of the seafood salad on each lettuce leaf, then top each portion with about 1½ tablespoons mayonnaise. Sprinkle ½ teaspoon minced parsley over each portion, then place a slice of lemon to one side of each coquille, on the serving plate. Bring to the table immediately.

Cracked Crab Salad

Steamed hard shell crabs marinated in olive oil, vinegar, and lime juice. Serve this salad in wide shallow soup bowls and provide sea-food forks and nutcrackers for breaking open the smaller pieces

---

of crab. Since the crabs need to marinate for several hours, we find it most practical to prepare this dish in the morning. By dinnertime, the flavors have had sufficient time to permeate the crabmeat, Delightfully messy to eat.

FOR THREE OR FOUR

3 or 4 small to medium-sized Steamed Crabs, chilled for about 1 hour

1 c. coarsely chopped white onions

2 tsp. finely minced garlic

1/3 c. white wine vinegar

1/4 c. olive oil

2 1/2 tsp. salt

1 tsp. freshly ground coarse black pepper

1/8 tsp. cayenne

3 Tbs. fresh lime juice

1/4 c. thinly sliced green onion tops

3/4 tsp. sugar

1 1/2 Tbs. finely minced parsley

1/2 tsp. oregano

1/2 tsp. coriander

1 qt. mixed greens, rinsed, dried, and crisped in the refrigerator

Break the chilled steamed crabs into large pieces and place in a large stainless steel or porcelain bowl. Add all the remaining ingredients except the greens. Toss very thoroughly to distribute the seasonings and liquids evenly, then cover the bowl with several layers of plastic wrap. Refrigerate for at least 3 1/2 hours.

About 15 minutes before you plan to serve, put the salad, including all the liquid and any seasonings that have settled to the bottom of the bowl, into a very large salad or serving bowl. Tear the crisped greens into small pieces and add them to the salad. Toss lightly but thoroughly with a long fork and spoon. Put the bowl back into the refrigerator for about 10 minutes, uncovered. To serve, bring the bowl to the table and serve by putting several pieces of crab and several tablespoons of greens on each plate. Spoon some of the liquid from the bottom of the serving bowl over each portion.

Shrimp in Sour Cream Dill Sauce

A simple and attractive way to serve chilled boiled shrimp, with a sour cream sauce flecked with dill, celery, and green onions. Mix the sauce at least 1 hour before serving.

FOR TWO OR THREE

1 lb. peeled, deveined, and chilled Mild Boiled Shrimp

SOUR CREAM DILL SAUCE

2½ Tbs. sour cream

1 Tbs. mayonnaise

4 tsp. chopped fresh dill or ½
  tsp. dried dill weed

1½ Tbs. finely minced celery

1/16 tsp. freshly ground white
  pepper

¼ tsp. salt

1½ tsp. very finely chopped
  fresh onion

2 tsp. very finely chopped green
  onion tops

½ tsp. fresh lemon juice

⅛ tsp. sugar

OPTIONAL GARNISH

6 to 8 ripe cherry tomatoes

6 to 8 slivers crisp cucumber

Combine the ingredients for the sauce in a stainless steel or porcelain bowl and beat vigorously with a whisk for 30 seconds. Cover the bowl with plastic wrap and refrigerate for at least 1 hour before serving.

To serve, arrange the chilled boiled shrimp on salad or luncheon plates. Remove the sauce from the refrigerator and stir gently with a wooden spoon to distribute the greens evenly, then top each portion with a generous tablespoon of sauce. If desired, garnish with cherry tomatoes and cucumber slivers placed around two-thirds of the outer edge of the portions of shrimp.

Herring Salad

Based on a Finnish dish that combines soaked salt herring, apples, and sour cream, this salad of marinated herring, sliced boiled potatoes, and apples makes a striking first course. Use a mild champagne mustard if available; if not, Dijon mustard diluted with a small amount of sweetened acidulated water will work quite well. This salad requires only about 10 minutes of marination; longer marinating time tends to make both the potatoes and apple wedges soggy.

FOR FOUR TO SIX

1½ c. drained Marinated Herring

1 lb. boiled potatoes, peeled, chilled, and sliced ⅓ inch thick

1 medium-sized firm red apple, peel, cored, and cut into thin wedges

1½ c. heavy sour cream

1 Tbs. mild pale mustard (champagne mustard preferred)

3 Tbs. sugar

¼ tsp. salt

¼ tsp. freshly ground black pepper

GARNISH

hard boiled egg slices or *thin cucumber slices (skin left on)* or *thin strips of crisp green pepper*

Combine all the ingredients for the salad in a large stainless steel or porcelain bowl and toss very gently with 2 wooden spoons to mix. Refrigerate uncovered for about 10 minutes. To serve, heap the portions on small plates, spooning some of the dressing that settles to the bottom of the bowl over each one. If desired, decorate with one of the suggested garnishes before serving.

Rock Shrimp Salad

When we began to experiment with rock shrimp, one of their most useful characteristics came to light—they can be sauced and refrigerated for several hours without losing their pleasantly firm texture. For this dish rock shrimp in the shell (with or without heads) are the best choice.

FOR TWO OR THREE

approximately 1⅓ lb. frozen rock shrimp in the shell, boiled (see Rock Shrimp Boiled in the Shell)

DRESSING

½ c. mayonnaise

2 Tbs. yogurt

4 tsp. finely chopped green onion tops

½ tsp. salt

⅛ tsp. freshly ground black pepper

1/16 tsp. mace

The Pleasures of Seafood 344

Peel and devein the rock shrimp, then cut into large pieces. Put the pieces of shrimp into a large stainless steel or porcelain bowl. Add the remaining ingredients and toss thoroughly with 2 large spoons. Cover the bowl with several layers of plastic wrap and refrigerate for at least 2 hours before serving.

To serve, place several pieces of crisp lettuce on each plate, then top with portions of the salad. Garnish with tomato wedges and several thin slices of fresh lime, if available.

Codfish Salad

Soaked salt cod boiled with potatoes, then sauced with a simple vinaigrette dressing and chilled. A pleasantly hearty fish salad based on a dish prepared by some of the first settlers in California, for whom salt cod was a diet staple.

FOR FOUR

½ lb. salt cod	*2 Tbs. white wine vinegar*
2 large potatoes	*½ tsp. freshly ground black*
2 green onions, finely chopped	*pepper*
3 Tbs. olive oil	

Soak the codfish in cold water to cover overnight. In the morning, remove the fish from the water and rinse thoroughly under cool running water. Press out the remaining salty water by rolling the fish in several layers of paper towels and patting firmly with the palms of your hands. Discard the paper towels and cut the fish into large pieces. Place in a large saucepan along with the potatoes and bring to a boil. Lower the heat slightly and boil until the potatoes are cooked, about 20 minutes. Dump the contents of the pan into a colander set in the sink

and allow to drain and to cool until you can handle the potatoes. Peel the potatoes and cut into ½ to ¾ inch cubes. Shred the pieces of cooked cod with 2 forks. Put the potatoes and shredded fish into a stainless steel or porcelain mixing bowl. Sprinkle in the chopped green onions. In a small bowl combine the oil, vinegar, and pepper. Beat rapidly with a whisk for about 60 seconds, then pour over the fish and potatoes. Mix thoroughly with a wooden spoon, then cover the bowl with plastic wrap and refrigerate. Serve well chilled.

17

Useful Information

In the Fish Market

For the urban fish lover the first rule of thumb is to find a good fish market. Every large city has a number of them and you can find at least one that is dependable. Fish merchants are knowledgeable people; their livelihood depends on their knowledge. We have found them as a group to be some of the easiest businessmen to deal with. It is not a business that attracts the person out for a quick dollar. Once your fish merchant knows what your tastes are he can help you. Let him know that you are interested in the freshest possible fish. If you want a specific fish from another region he may be able to obtain it for you. And if he suggests you buy it frozen take his advice. (See p. 348.)

His most useful advice is on what is the most desirable fish in the market on any given day. Ask him how he himself would clean and cook it; from what he says you can easily find several applicable cooking procedures in this book. If you want to you can yourself devise some tests for freshness, but looking into a fish's eyes and pressing the flesh to see if it springs back are poor substitutes for a friendly relation with a fish merchant. Most of us are not equipped to assess proper aging of meat; we rely on a good butcher. Most of us are just as ill equipped to look squarely into a fish's eyes and tell when he was caught. Trust the fish merchant. He will more than repay your respect for his professional advice.

Fresh and Frozen

The standard advice that any fresh fish is preferable to any frozen fish is nonsense. The freshest possible fish is that which is eaten as soon as it is caught or which has been flash frozen immediately. Quickly frozen fish properly stored is always preferable to fresh fish that has been on ice a day or two. We first left the rank of the frozen fish doubters one day in Baltimore's legendary old seafood restaurant, Miller Brothers. We saw pompano on the menu and knowing full well that it was out of season and scarce, asked the waiter how fresh it was. He replied that it was frozen and if we could tell the difference in taste he'd eat it himself. He didn't have to. It was delicious. We have been using locally frozen soft shell crabs with consistently excellent results for years. And we find local crawfish elements frozen at the source more useful and of better quality than the same elements slowly hand picked by us here in New Orleans.

We still object to restaurant practices of flying in foreign fish and presenting them as fresh when they have been on ice several days. Or featuring frozen fish when locally caught fresh fish is available. Most of the sins of frozen fish do not involve carefully frozen specimen fish but mass marketed fish such as perch and Icelandic cod which suffer from poor storage at supermarkets. So you must be sure the place where you buy frozen fish is dependable; then rely on their judgment. In a perfect world all fish would be perfectly fresh. In a perfect technological world all frozen fish would be perfectly frozen and stored. Our object in an imperfect world is to get as close to a perfect situation as possible. But by accepting good frozen fish one adds that many more options to the pleasures of seafood.

Certain seafood does not freeze well: oysters are very tricky, though some friends have reported a degree of success. Alaska crabmeat freezes well; New Orleans and Chesapeake crabmeat do not. Shrimp freeze exceptionally well both peeled and unpeeled, cooked and uncooked. Whether it is the cooking, freezing, or storing process that is at fault, the hard shell Dungeness crabs served at San Francisco's Fisherman's Wharf are vastly inferior. Frozen trout served in restaurants vary widely. Some frozen farm trout tastes good although different from fresh cutthroat, some does not. Frequently loss of taste and texture comes as much from poor cooking as poor freezing. Whatever the case, freezing is not a permanent process. Only 3 to 4 months is the maximum for storing frozen fish and shellfish; 2 months is optimal. Significant flavor deterioration sets in after longer periods.

Defrosting Frozen Seafood

The rule of thumb is to defrost as quickly as possible. The best way is in a basin of cool tap water with the fish still in its freezer wrapping. Depending on the size of the fish, this will take from 40 minutes to 2 hours. If you plan to cook a thawed fish some time after the thawing, dry off the wrapping and place the still-wrapped fish in the coolest part of the refrigerator (generally the top shelf). We have not liked the results of overnight gradual thawing in the refrigerator. This slower process results in too much loss of texture and in an undeniable soaking of the fish in its own juices. The single exception we have found is Florida stone crabs, which must be defrosted relatively slowly. If you are going to soak a fish as part of its cooking, for instance, in milk prior to dipping and frying, it is actually better to begin the soaking process while there are still a few ice crystals left.

Air and Ice

You can fly in your favorite fish and shellfish from anywhere in the country. Wholesalers to the restaurant trade do it all the time and are expert at it. In the preparation of this book we flew in herring from Chicago, clams from Boston, scrod from New England, and have shipped Louisiana crawfish to all parts of

America. The additional cost for air freight is surprisingly low. Your own fish merchant can make most or all of the arrangements; your local restaurateur can suggest additional sources. We have listed some of our sources at the back of the book.

Storing Seafood

The freshest fish should be cooked within 24 hours after catching. If they are iced down, keep them cold from the start at a temperature below the usual 40°F. of home refrigerators. In cool weather fish can keep on ice for 2 or 3 days. But the fresher they are the less chance for flavor or texture deterioration. If fish can't be used immediately they should be frozen as soon as possible. Of a large catch of fish that will be consumed in a week, part should be frozen. Keep enough for the first 2 days on ice and freeze the rest. Soft shell crabs are best frozen live; pompano is best frozen whole and uncleaned; most fish should be split, cleaned, then frozen in fillets with or without the skin, wrapped in quantities to be used at any single given time. *Never refreeze thawed frozen seafood.* It's not necessarily dangerous, except to your palate which will rebel at the deterioration of taste and texture. Most fish with the "fishy taste" is refrozen thawed fish, or fish that has been too long out of the water. Don't cook over-the-hill fish. It is not worth the effort and no culinary magic can save it.

Some Fish We Have Known

Anchovy: One of these days we'll meet a fresh anchovy. The best canned ones we've had are from Spain.

Bass: We've never tasted a bass we didn't like. Striped bass is the perfect all-around fish, good for anything from broiling to saucing. Sea bass works as well. The choicest sea bass are the small black bass, which are plentiful and equally delicious broiled simply or served under the most elegant sauce. Our favorite New Orleans redfish and drum are varieties of bass and we love them fixed any way. You can cook fresh bass using any recipe in this book. A great fish.

Bluefish: The best bluefish we've ever had comes from Gage & Tollner's Brooklyn seafood restaurant, where it's grilled over anthracite coal and is perfect. (See Grilled Bluefish for a home version.) We treat bluefish as a high class relative of mackerel and consider it a fish well suited to almost any recipe in the book. A fine all-around fish.

Buffalo: See *Carp.*

Carp: One of the world's most striking fish and a central element in Chinese and Middle European cuisines. Beautiful looking, large freshwater fish, carp and buffalo, which resembles it closely, have almost as many bones as shad and like shad more than repay the effort of boning them. We have included some of our favorite carp recipes including several *tours de force* such as Chinese whole carp and our favorite all-carp version of Gefilte Fish.

Catfish: The most popular fish in America, probably because it is the most plentiful, the cheapest, and the most accessible in inland waters. Catfish symbolizes the differences in American life styles. Most urban dwellers have never tasted good catfish and most rural fish lovers literally dote on its sweet flavor. Urbanites tend to scorn it as a fish of lowly social status. But catfish, which is truly an ugly fish to look at, has a delightful taste and is in fact a great American classic, especially thinly sliced and fried (see Fried Catfish) .

Cobia: Many of our fishermen friends swear by cobia, but we have yet to bring one in; a cobia we tasted in a Florida restaurant was unlovely, to say the least.

Cod: One of the indispensable American fish. Young cod, called scrod in New England, is an extremely delicate, very flavorful fish with beautiful spotted skin and pure white meat. If you've never tasted fresh scrod try it, broiled simply like the magnificent version at Boston's Durgin Park restaurant. We flew in a batch of fresh young cod from Boston for the recipes in this book and liked it so much, we are going to make it an annual event.

Croaker: A delicacy generally eaten by fishermen. Sweet and delicious fried, especially filleted, with the tail and backbone piece also fried as an extra treat.

Dolphin: Found under a variety of pseudonyms such as Hawaiian *mahi mahi* or French *daurade,* Florida dolphin in fishable sizes is a delicious and very special fish. Strictly regional and a real delicacy broiled, grilled, or poached and sauced.

Drum: A lovely freshwater fish resembling bass.

Eel: We have described our joy at getting some local eel while cooking our way through this book and tasting them for the first time outside a restaurant. Eel are delicious prepared any way. An extremely versatile fish, eel is the basis for an unusual French red wine stew (see Matelote of Eel) and is marvelous simply grilled or smoked. Skinning an eel is no more difficult than filleting a fish, but because the eel looks much like a snake it gives some fish markets the jitters. The French adore eel and so do the Japanese. In America eel appear to be an acquired taste that's hard to acquire because no one serves them. Pity.

Flounder: A delightful Gulf and Atlantic flatfish that is inexpensive because it is plentiful, but whose taste belies its humble cost. Our favorite Gulf flounder are the small ones, about 1 pound or 1½ pounds. We love them broiled with a simple butter sauce or New Orleans meunière sauce. The best flounder cooking anywhere is concentrated in Mobile, Alabama, where nearly every restaurant broils flounder beautifully. Broiled is our favorite style. We also find flounder an ideal substitute for more expensive sole. Because flounder is so plentiful many persons like to stuff them in an attempt to make them more impressive. You are invited to join our society, which protests the unnecessary stuffing of flounder.

Garfish: An ugly fish with jaws like an alligator, popular in Louisiana because it is cheap. Gar has some vocal defenders and many non-defenders. We are probably in the latter group, although a recent serving of garfish patties in a Cajun restaurant gives us pause.

Grouper: Our favorite grouper are small fish, delicious fried or broiled.

Haddock: Not as delicate as young cod, but an estimable and plentiful fish that can be fixed in a number of ways. One of the cheapest and most useful of fish which, while generally not a first choice, is a fine substitute.

Halibut: A huge fish with some of the qualities of flounder, but not as pretty, and less delicate because of its size. Halibut would be a perfect choice for using in any of the sauced dishes in place of sole; its sturdiness is ideal for use under a sauce, and its slight lack of delicacy is masked by the elaborate preparation of the dish. Broil the sole or flounder and sauce the halibut.

Herring: Growing up on pickled herring and smoked herring we were not prepared for the taste of untreated fresh herring. Our first venture with fresh herring was in Amsterdam at a herring stand where the vendor cut it up raw for us and we ate it on the spot, and became addicted. Later in a seaside resort, Scheveningen, we spotted a herring stand and eagerly awaited our treat. We were surprised to be served a whole unsliced herring. When the vendor saw our puzzlement, his eyes lit up, and he remarked, "You must be from Amsterdam," and he proceeded to cut up the herring. American herring are not as sturdy as the Dutch ones and are not good raw. Though most seafood books describe the small herring as an easily handled fish, we found it is actually one of the most difficult to work with. When cleaned and broiled whole it tends to fall apart. Removing the bones is a painstaking process that generally causes the small herring to self-destruct on the spot. We realized why most American herring is smoked or pickled; it tastes good that way and it's the only practical way of treating this good but very difficult fish. Smaller mackerel can do what cookbooks claim herring do, broil and fry nicely, and they're plentiful and easier to use.

Jewfish: A very large fish plentiful in the Florida Keys that failed to convince us of its indispensable place in the pleasures of seafood.

John Dory: A splendid fish we enjoyed in England and in France under its name of Saint Pierre. Walleyed pike is a fairly close American substitute.

Kippers: One of us has very English parents who emigrated to America, married in 1929, and lovingly raised their son on Gilbert and Sullivan and kippers. That's our permanent English heritage, along perhaps with tea. (Quite properly rejected were shepherd's pie, Brussels sprouts, and all the other atrocities of English cooking. Inexplicably English fish and chips were not a home favorite; what "Mum" made more resembled the handiwork of American greasy spoons.) Kippers are still a favorite with one of us—and not with the other. The non-English one generally makes scurrilous remarks, especially on Sundays when Gilbert and Sullivan replace Mozart as the breakfast opera. One of the reasons we wrote a section on home kippering is the experience we had in London several years ago searching for the perfect kipper. We thought London could at least match what we were convinced were inferior Canadian or Nova Scotia kippers. We found that our hotel and even a place like the Savoy took kippers too much for granted to do them well. The best we could find, we admit shamefacedly, were at the London Hilton where the American management had not been informed that preparing kippers well was no longer a social necessity in London. Perhaps nothing better symbolizes England's decline as a great power than the decline of English kippers. But make no mistake: it's not the herring that's salty in an

imperfect kipper, it's the amount of salting and smoking meant to preserve it longer. The lightest cures are still the best, and it may well be
that the only place to get a good kipper is in a home kitchen. You've
probably got to have a little English in you to even give them a try.
The Mikado, anyone?

Mackerel: Common in numbers, uncommon in taste, mackerel is a
lovely fish. Boston mackerel and Spanish mackerel are smaller fish and
are equally good. To describe mackerel as an oily fish, as many food
writers do, is the same as calling a sunrise an orange blob. Both
descriptions are true and both descriptions miss the point. Fresh
mackerel has almost unlimited uses. If the richness bothers you, a
little marination will reduce it. Larger king mackerel, generally cut
into steaks, needs some marination.

Mahi Mahi: See *Dolphin.*

Mullet: Another rich fish, inexpensive, and particularly delicious in the
pan sizes, cooked simply and as soon as possible after catching. Not
frequently seen in fish markets, but plentiful in fishermen's hauls.

Perch: One of the most common of fish; also a name used for a large
variety of small ocean fish. In spite of its commonness, perch is an
excellent all-purpose fish, good simply broiled or fried, capable of
holding its own under the grandest sauce. Generally very inexpensive.

Petrale: A West Coast sole generally served grilled. Following the
rule of thumb that the more respected the fish, the better it is cooked,
petrale is nearly always treated with respect and well cooked in California. But not with enough respect to supplant Dover sole on the
menus of fancy restaurants. A lovely fish.

Pickerel: See *Pike.*

Pike: An excellent though bony freshwater fish well prepared in the
Midwest. It's best to let the fish market do a complete job of cleaning
pike or pickerel. Once boned they are delicious fish, either simply prepared or with elaborate sauces. One of the best all-purpose fish.

Pike Perch: See *Walleyed Pike.*

Plaice: A delicious lower class English fish despised by food writers
and epicures and revered by Englishmen who consume huge quantities
of fried plaice. Plaice is a victim of the class struggle. The rich eat sole,
the poor know their plaice. Judging from the relative merits of sole
served in fancy London restaurants and plaice eaten out of newspapers

with hot chips, the poor come off at least as well. We enjoy fried plaice in England—both for its legendary inferiority and its marvelous taste.

Pompano: A Gulf fish of great delicacy and superb flavor. Our favorite form is broiled with a little brown butter, but pompano is good amandine style or just about any way that's simple. Still best prepared in Gulf Coast restaurants, because of its reputation, pompano is often pampered in dishes such as pompano *en papillote.* Agreeable because the sauce is so good, pompano doesn't really improve with the paper bag. There is no substitute for the special taste of pompano.

Redfish: Actually a channel bass, New Orleans redfish is our favorite local fish, especially in the smaller sizes. Used in the same way as bass, and one of the most delicious all-purpose fish.

Red Snapper: One of the most common and also most prized of Gulf fish. Snapper's reputation had always seemed a little exaggerated to us until we had a perfectly fried version in a Florida Gulf Coast restaurant. Since then we have come to like it better and to find it eminently adaptable. While not quite, for us, the equal of redfish or flounder, snapper is a good fish with enough character for most of the recipes in the book. Its sturdy texture makes it an excellent choice for fish stews as well as for elaborate sauced dishes.

Rex Sole: A delightful California fish, in San Francisco served cut into thin strips and sauced with melted butter. A delicate and distinctive fish that struck us as having many unexplored possibilities.

Salmon: Fresh salmon is one of the few legendary fish that surpass their elevated reputation. Our finest fresh salmon was beautifully cooked over an open grill in San Francisco's Vanessi's restaurant. There is no substitute for fresh salmon simply prepared. Smoked salmon is a luxury almost as compelling as fine Beluga caviar. What a world of difference in the various cures and smokes! One of the best salmon we ever tasted was a delightful lightly cured fish from the Loire River at Barrier's restaurant. Scotch and Irish salmon are enough to rescue those respective cuisines from the often justified charges of barbarity. In America Nova Scotia lox with cream cheese and bagels, originating in New York City, has become a universal dish. The other irresistible cured salmon is Swedish Gravlax, a dish that allows the Swedes to make the most of their unbelievable bounty of fresh salmon and fresh dill. Canned salmon, widely available, can be quite good, especially the red variety. We especially like it served with some homemade mayonnaise as a light summer meal rounded out with fresh fruit.

Sand Dabs: Dabs are of the flounder family; the tiny delicate West Coast sand dabs we've had are delicious.

Saint Pierre: See *John Dory* or *Walleyed Pike.*

Sardines: Fresh sardines are actually very small herring. Of the canned types, the skinless and boneless Portuguese variety are quite good.

Shad and Shad Roe: Shad is a delicious fish that must be boned by specialists unless you have a lifetime to give to a fish dinner. Properly boned shad is magnificent and not to be passed up. Shad roe is one of the wonders of the world of seafood. This absolutely delicious cluster of eggs should be cooked briefly and simply. Eight minutes is the maximum cooking time for any size of shad roe. We get no shad roe at all in New Orleans and every so often when we're in the East during the late spring we find this delicacy on a restaurant menu. One of us always orders it—and it almost always is overcooked. And not just by minutes. One seafood place in Philadelphia managed after our many pleas to overcook the shad roe by only 20 minutes, a vast improvement over the usual 45 minutes too much. So please, cook the roe gently, oh so gently, in just a little butter. One of the easiest and most memorable of seafood dishes.

Shark: We don't know how much of what used to be sold as swordfish was actually shark, which closely resembles it. We know from personal experience that this fish is now openly marketed and is excellent. It is cheap; it broils well; it poaches well; it sauces well. These medium-large fish cut into steaks surpass all our memories of dried-up and tasteless swordfish. Shark under a grand French sauce will pleasantly surprise you.

Smelts: Whatever happened to our childhood favorite, crisp pan fried smelts? Not as delicate as European whitebait which are even smaller, smelts were tiny fish fried whole and reminiscent of the smallest European herring. They were absolutely delicious as an informal fun dinner.

Sole: Sole in all of its versions is a delicious and legendary fish. Dover sole has the best press and it is an impressive fish although, as we have pointed out throughout this book, probably not as impressive as the reputation most food writers have given it. It deserves to be admired, but then so do most of the non-English sole and the more common flounder. A marvelous fish to eat as plainly as possible—or in the grandest *haute cuisine* preparations.

Sushi and Sashimi: We had originally thought to include procedures for preparing these remarkable Japanese dishes made with raw fish and shellfish, but the rigid demands of preparation almost preclude eating them elsewhere than in a restaurant that specializes in them. Sushi is artfully cut up raw fish. Sashimi generally includes raw fish in combination with vinegared rice. Both are delicious. Both are also, it has been discovered, dangerous. Parasites often present in raw fish make cooking or freezing imperative. (Doctors have found that freezing raw fish at 14°F. or below for 24 to 48 hours effectively destroys the parasites.) We will continue to work on techniques for preparing sushi and sashimi using fish that has been frozen, but until an antidote for the dangerous illnesses that may follow eating raw fish is found, we will forbear from eating sushi in its traditional form, even though it has long been one of our favorite seafoods.

Swordfish: Probably no fish we ever ate when we were very young was subjected to more unimaginative preparation than swordfish. It was generally broiled dried-out and served with an air of reverence, so that neither of us felt badly when the great mercury scare of the 1970s removed swordfish from the market. We've never mourned its passing.

Trout: We've never had a bad trout; we've never had enough trout; we're always eager to try a new trout. They're all good—Rocky Mountain trout, the original cutthroats as well as the commercially marketed varieties; Colorado brook trout; rainbow trout; and New Orleans speckled trout. It's true that the farm varieties are not as special as the freshly caught uncultivated trout, but they are good. When restaurant trout is tasteless it's because it has been poorly frozen and overcooked. The best trout are the freshest trout and the best ways to prepare them are the simplest ones. A pan fried whole trout is as much of a joy to see as it is to eat. One of the great fish.

Tuna: One of the intriguing things about tuna is how different it is fresh from canned. Yes, it's different, but perhaps not in the way you expect. Except for Japanese sashimi (which can include raw fresh tuna), cooked fresh tuna is not one of the world's great gustatory experiences. It's sort of reddish and a little goes a long way, possibly because tuna are very large fish and the most flavorful table fish are small. What gives canned tuna a bad name are those horrible tuna casseroles whose chief virtue is that they can feed a large family cheaply. Since we do not have a large family we have happily been spared tuna casseroles and are pleased not to include them in this book. Tuna from a can is okay, but we both prefer salmon. We can think of hundreds of alternatives to tuna casseroles that are just as cheap. Many are included in this book. If we were given a choice we'd probably choose a bad franchise hamburger over the "best" tuna casserole. It's dishes like those that give seafood a bad name.

Turbot: A fine French–European fish in the sole-flounder family that has benefited from its association with French cuisine. The French like turbot because it is mild and won't upstage the chef's sauce. There is lots of non-French turbot around and it is no more or less interesting than halibut, which it somewhat resembles. A nice fish but not of championship caliber.

Walleyed Pike: This is a fish of championship caliber. Lovely to eat, difficult to bone, walleye is, like the French Saint Pierre and the English John Dory, an unforgettable fish with lots of character.

Whitebait: Tiny little fish fried whole and crisp and one of the treasures of English cuisine.

Whitefish: With salmon, trout, bass, sole, and pompano, one of the great and indispensable fish of the world. Planked whitefish at Karl Ratsch's magnificent Milwaukee restaurant, pan fried whitefish at Berghoff's great Chicago restaurant, will introduce you admirably to this remarkable American classic from Lake Superior.

Whiting: A good cheap, plentiful small fish, easy to cook and suitable for eating simply or sauced. Often overlooked in fish markets, where it is always a best buy.

Yellowtail: A delicious local Florida fish resembling a flounder, with a distinctive flavor, as pleasurable to look at as to eat.

Shellfish and Other Seafoods

Clams: The first thing we do when visting the East in clam season is to find the nearest clam bar and load up on clams on the half shell. We confess to not having strong feelings over the differences between raw cherrystones and raw littlenecks, but eating equal amounts of each is a pleasant way to try to pretend we're making a decision. As with oysters, we find it hard to fathom why there are such strong passions over different kinds of clams. We've never passed up a good clam yet and we never will. Until recently, we had always assumed that clams were as versatile as oysters in cooking. They are not. They toughen more quickly and the big ones have to be used in chowders. If you use even a small amount of fresh clams you should invest in a good shucking device, sold in many cookware shops. Clams are much harder to shuck than oysters, and for cooking, steaming them open is a great deal easier.

Conch: A regional delicacy found in Florida and only occasionally in other outposts such as Vincent's Clam Bar in New York (see Fried Conch).

Crabs, Soft Shell Atlantic Blue Claw: These will always be, for us, the aristocrats of the crab world. Along with poor boys and red beans, soft shell crabs are the New Orleans national dish. Soft crabs are hard crabs that have molted their shells. They begin to grow new ones immediately so one has to catch them before they completely change their cover. One way of catching soft crabs is to get them when they're hard and wait for the shell to molt. At one time fanatics in Louisiana would make distinctions between regular soft crabs and busters, which had just "busted" their shells. There were also "peelers" whose shells could easily be taken off. Now all very small crabs are called busters. Soft crabs are best deep fried. In many regions of the country they suffer from being cooked too gingerly. Sautéed crabs tend to be rather mushy, and broiled crabs are okay but not the equal of good fried crabs. It is the one food that expatriate New Orleanians universally miss and one of the few seafoods that completely elude the French. Some expatriate New Orleanians have set up a Creole restaurant at Orly Airport with soft crabs flown in daily from New Orleans.

Crabs, Hard Shell Atlantic Blue Claw: The same crab as soft shell but with the hard shell, which makes them suitable for boiling. Baltimoreans and New Orleanians have different styles of cooking and eating them and frequently think that the differences are in the crabs. They're not, they're all in the cooking. Because New Orleans' waters are warmer the crabs may be a bit fatter, but boiling and steaming make the differences. Some rural Louisianians claim they can tell from which lake the crabs come just from their taste. But with the kind of spices added as a matter of course, we're skeptical. Be that as it may, it's almost as much fun to talk about crabs as to eat them. Even better is to talk about them *while* eating them.

Crabs, Dungeness: One of these days we may taste a fresh hard Dungeness crab. The ones we've had a chance to sample are all precooked and frozen; they are cooked unseasoned. What an interesting experiment it would be to take a fresh Dungeness crab and cook it first in the

Chesapeake style and then in the New Orleans style. Come on, West Coast, use a little pepper and salt!

Crabs, Stone: Florida stone crabs are very good, and while Floridians don't use much, if any, seasoning in the cooking, they're not bashful with the accompanying mustard sauce. A real treat.

Crabs, Alaska: Alaskan king crabs are one of the wonders of the seafood world. They freeze extremely well and are delicious broiled and served with warm butter like Maine lobster. Alaska king crabmeat is somewhat sweeter than Louisiana–Chesapeake crabmeat, and in some dishes its slightly different texture and taste work out even better. Alaska snow crab is less expensive and, while different in texture from first rate lump crabmeat, is readily available and quite good.

Crabmeat, Lump: The best crabmeat is the white backfin meat and the most expensive is that which comes in the biggest lumps. If appearance is not essential the smaller lumps offer the same taste at a lower price. The claw meat and the gray crabmeat are the cheapest. For most cooking we use the cheaper varieties of backfin. The best lump crabmeat is essential for use in salads. Atlantic blue claw crabmeat, commonly available in the Gulf Coast and Chesapeake areas, is extremely perishable and has a shelf life of about 3 days. It suffers a considerable deterioration when frozen, in taste and even more in texture. If you can only get frozen crabmeat, use the Alaska varieties; they hold up better.

Crawfish or Crayfish: Louisiana Frenchmen were introduced to *crawfish* by the Houma Indians and to this day crawfish are consumed in prodigious quantities in southwestern Louisiana. Frenchmen and Scandinavians are also wild about *crayfish,* but eat them in much smaller quantities and with only a fraction of the normal Cajun seasoning. The spelling variations come from local usage. In Louisiana they are spelled the way they are pronounced, *crawfish,* except in some polite circles which hold to the usual spelling, *crayfish.* It's the same crustacean. They grow in many other areas but are generally ignored except where they are cherished as food. Farm raised crawfish are being used to supplement the natural variety, since no Louisianian can get enough of the "mudbug" to satisfy his appetite. Picking small crawfish is painstaking and backbreaking work, especially if you don't have the help of a large Cajun family. Excellent results can be achieved with the separated frozen elements picked and packed in Henderson, Louisiana, the heart of the crawfish country (see "Some Suggested Seafood Markets").

Frogs' Legs: The best are the smallest, and the largest supply of small frogs' legs seems to come from Japan. Almost never seen fresh, frogs' legs freeze perfectly. Big ones tend to be much chewier and are only decent fried. The best of the big ones lack the delicacy of the tiny ones. And frogs' legs do not taste good in gross tomato and garlic sauces, no matter what size they are.

Langoustines (Rock Shrimp): A French delicacy recently fished in quantity by Gulf fishermen and marketed in America as Rock Shrimp.

Langoustes: Spiny lobsters somewhat like Florida lobsters found throughout Europe.

Lobster, Maine: The king of shellfish, once so plentiful in America that families ate them the way hamburgers are eaten today. We like Maine lobsters boiled, steamed, or broiled and refuse to believe in the life-and-death differences claimed by fanatics. Maine lobsters are worth whatever they cost, must not be overcooked, and taste delicious with simple drawn butter. We would no more put a sauce on a Maine lobster than we would put ketchup on a prime steak.

Lobster, Florida: Like the spiny European lobsters and stellar shellfish in their own right, Florida lobsters are too often overcooked in restaurants and then served with a drab dressing. Treated with respect they are delicious, with a bit less delicacy of flavor and texture than Maine lobsters but with a lot of character.

Oysters: We have never tasted an oyster that was less than great. We've had some very great oysters and some extraordinarily great oysters and some that have reached the heights. The arguments about relative merits strike us as nonsensical. *Belons?* By all means, great French oysters. *Portugaises?* Oysters with color and character. *Plaquemines* Louisiana oysters? The most abundant and the equal of any other oysters. Blue points? As many as you offer us we'll eat. Oysters are irresistible. The only thing better is more oysters. The great advantage of French Louisiana over France is the abundance of oysters, which permits us to eat them raw as well as cooked. Oysters Rockefeller are indeed a celebration of the brave New World of America, for only in America are there enough oysters to spare from half shell duties. The other endless argument is what to put on raw oysters. Many writers assume that because the Louisianian dips his oysters in a sauce made of ketchup, horseradish, lemon, and Tabasco, the oysters are inferior. Nonsense. They're just as good as the Frenchmen's with merely a squeeze of lemon, and delicious without anything at all. We like to have a dozen plain, a dozen with lemon, and a dozen in the local style—we have no preference. Nor can we choose a favorite among the various kinds of oysters we have met. We like them all. One thing is certain. We'll never taste—it doesn't exist—a less than great, freshly shucked oyster on the half shell.

Shrimp: The most accessible of American seafood, delicious in cocktails, broiled, and in a great variety of dishes. We tend to prefer the bigger shrimp although there are many fanciers of the small or tiny shrimp which seldom leave the local area. Most of the better shrimp cocktails served in restaurants around the country are made with giant Gulf shrimp. It's fun to watch someone who has eaten only peeled shrimp being served a New Orleans whole shrimp dish and see him face, for the first time, the whole creature, head, tail, eyes and all. In some seasons all of the shrimp is edible, including the shell.

Snails: The only thing wrong with snails is that they are always served as a first course. We have included several recipes suitable for a snail orgy. Fresh snails are of course excellent, but canned ones will do very nicely, since the snail is best in combination with the sauce. Smaller snails are preferred, but big ones can be divided.

Squid: We belong to the local chapter of the Squid Lovers of the World. You can join by eating some squid at least once a year. We have never really understood why Americans are apprehensive about these creatures. As fanciers of Italian *calamari* will tell you, they are delicious prepared in a number of ways.

Turtle: Bad news: turtles are becoming extinct. A number of varieties have been placed on the endangered species list. Good news: several Caribbean islands are now farming turtles and restocking the waters as well as providing turtles for market. Varieties such as the green sea turtle should be in ample supply in the near future.

The ranks of turtle lovers are diminishing. Turtle soup is being replaced by mock turtle soup, and even in New Orleans, where old Creole cookbooks had recipes beginning "Catch a nice medium-sized turtle . . . ," turtles are not found on restaurant menus. Florida is turtle country and the last bastion of good turtle cooking. Turtle meat is highly perishable, so be sure the market you buy it from has an adequate turnover or knows its freezing.

INDEX

PILOT YOUR LIFE

RON SHAW

with Richard Krevolin

Prentice
Hall Press

Library of Congress Cataloging-in-Publication Data

Shaw, Ronald G.
 Pilot your life : comedian turned CEO helps you star in your
career / by Ron Shaw, Richard Krevolin.
    p. cm.
 ISBN 0–7352–0290–7
    1. Chief executive officers—Anecdotes. 2. Success in
business—Anecdotes. I. Krevolin, Richard W. II. Title.
 HD38.2 .S487 2001

 658.4'09—dc21   2001032740

Acquisitions Editor: *Tom Power*
Senior Production Editor: *Eve Mossman*
Interior Design/Page Layout: *Dimitra Coroneos*

© *2001 by* Prentice Hall

ISBN 0–7352–0290–7

 Paramus, NJ 07652

http://www.phdirect.com

For Phissy . . .

*My inspiration
since August 2, 1958*

CONTENTS

FOREWORD

Given that you are reading this foreword you probably fall into one of two categories: browser or purchaser. Let me explain: The browser is a person who goes to the local bookstore, sometimes with the intention of possibly buying a book and sometimes just to look around or "browse." I frequently fall into this category. I love to read and have been blessed with the good fortune of having a job that allows me to meet and interact with many prolific authors. In the end, many different things affect whether or not I remain a "browser" or become a "purchaser." For instance, I may be drawn to a particular book by something on the book cover. In some cases, it is the title of the book that has garnered my attention; in yet others, it is the author. When I pull the book off of the shelf I may read the inside jacket cover, the foreword of the book, or the opening lines of the first chapter. Maybe you are doing exactly that right now.

You may have been drawn to this book because you recognized the author on the cover from his humorous commercials for Pilot Pen. Perhaps you heard about the book during a recent television interview or read a favorable review. Regardless of how you may have gotten here, you can now consider yourself to be very lucky. Why? Well, first I need to provide you with a bit of background information:

It's hard to believe but earlier this year, I celebrated my 44th anniversary on the air. That means I have now broadcasted on television and radio in six different decades. I broke into the business by starting at a small radio station in Miami Beach on May 1, 1957. I was this little Jewish kid from Brooklyn who dreamed of following in the footsteps of Arthur Godfrey and Red Barber—such giant imprints. I wound up working with both of them at the tail end of their brilliant careers. Early in my career I actually did radio broadcasts from the window of a delicatessen in Miami Beach (I would tell you more about that here, but the details are contained inside). It was in Miami Beach that I was lucky enough to meet and interview a rising comedian who happened to be a Jewish kid from Philadelphia. Hardly did I know that this aspiring comic would change the path of his life to become the President and CEO of a major pen company. Of course, I am speaking of my friend of over thirty years, Ron Shaw.

When I hear the name Ron Shaw, several adjectives come to mind: honest, compassionate, generous, intelligent, loyal, and, of course, successful. All of these attributes have contributed to Ron becoming one of America's most successful and well-known corporate leaders. Ron is also held in very high regard for his philanthropic goodwill. Ron remains a strong supporter of numerous charitable organizations, including serving as a member of the Board of Trustees of the charity that I started to help underprivileged individuals pay for life-saving cardiac care: The Larry King Cardiac Foundation. It is in the context of the Board meetings of the foundation that I have had the opportunity to observe firsthand and fully appreciate many of the unique and effective methods utilized by Ron in interacting with people. This book will now help you to glean and develop those very same skills.

Pilot Your Life is a delightful journey that offers the reader personal insight into everyday living. This is not an ordinary "how to succeed" guide. This book is what I call a "thoroughly enjoyable read." As you traverse the pages, you will empathize with the various problems and situations that Ron has encountered over the years. You will smile as you read about how he resolves various personal and business dilemmas. The lessons contained in this book are subtle and effective; incidentally, these are two other adjectives that are aptly used to describe the author.

In this day and age we frequently hear about what some people refer to as the "ruthless corporate ethic" in American business. That type of perception seems to support the old cliché that "nice guys finish last." In this book Ron Shaw completely debunks that theory. He proves that with hard work, your own initiative, and the common sense plainly laid out in the following pages, you can not only succeed in your personal and professional life, but that you can enjoy yourself, family, and friends while in the process of doing so.

At this point, if you are still a "browser," you have now come to the time to make an important decision: Do I put the book back on the shelf or do I buy it? If you make the right choice, I am confident that you will have absolutely no regrets. If you have already purchased *Pilot Your Life,* congratulations. You are about to embark upon a fun and hopefully life-changing flight.

Larry King
May 2001

ACKNOWLEDGMENTS

As a CEO appearing in TV commercials and media interviews, I sometimes find myself in the awkward position of getting undeserved credit for single-handedly building Pilot Pen Corporation of America's operation; in fact, there are hundreds of people who have been responsible for Pilot Pen's past and present success. I cannot list all of them here, but I strongly believe that any executive who has been made to "look good" must, of necessity, have an excellent top management team reporting to him or her, and I am no exception.

Those who deserve special recognition and thanks for having been essential to our company are: Dennis Burleigh, Laurie Faulkner, Joe Kiewlen, Sallie Mitchell, Jim Plunkett, Tom Restivo, Bob Silberman, Larry Silberman, and Patty Skarupa.

None of the work would have any satisfaction if it weren't for my family. Special thanks to my wife, Phyllis Shaw, and children, Steve Shaw, Susan Shaw Santoro and Alan Shaw, for their tolerance of my travel schedule and late hours over the years, as well as their support and encouragement for my writing this book.

My deep appreciation also goes to Richard Krevolin, whose vision, tenacity and talent brought this book to life. In addition, I thank the following for their immeasurable help in putting this book together: Irwin Helford, Larry King, Sherman Krevolin, Murray and Marvin Lender,

Harvey Mackay, Jack Paige, Peter Rubie, Michael Santoro, Carrie Shaw, Nancy Shaw, Shana Smith, Tom Stemberg, tireless agent June Rifkin Clark, and sage editor Tom Power.

Finally, special thanks go to Phil Ehrenkranz, one of my boyhood buddies throughout my childhood in Miami. When we were kids, Phil wanted to be a reporter while I was already working in show business. He made me promise that when we grew up, he'd be the one to write the book about my exciting climb to comedic fame. My show business career never met his high expectations, however, and Phil became an attorney instead of a reporter. Nevertheless, he has been a tremendous help in shaping these words.

INTRODUCTION

I'm into the home stretch of my comedy act and the audience is with me all the way, leaning toward me in their seats, laughing and erupting into applause so often that I need to allow extra time before I tell my next joke. It's one of the greatest feelings in the world; a rush I experienced onstage for eleven years, from the time I was a kid of eleven to a newly married twenty-two-year-old man.

However, as a new husband with responsibilities, I suddenly needed to get a steady job. Yet my only training was as a comedian. Little could I know that my onstage education would help me beat the odds and become a successful CEO.

At the time I had no idea spending my youth in the spotlight had any applications beyond the stage, but now I see in retrospect that comedy and business have a great deal in common. Many of the lessons I learned as a comedian have been instrumental to my success over the course of my business career (and even saved my behind a few times). In addition I came to realize that the seemingly innocuous jokes I used to tell onstage are metaphors for what's important in business and in life.

Is there a secret to success? After working as a comedian, then a salesman, and ultimately the president and CEO of Pilot Pen Corporation of America, I have learned there is one essential secret to success in business and in life. This secret applies to just about every successful CEO, gutsy entrepreneur, and each fulfilled person I've met.

The secret is: Never wait for someone else to give you permission to pursue your dreams.

Just as the sun doesn't wait for permission to rise and the stars appear without waiting for their cue, you can go after the life you want without needing permission.

Follow your passions! Allow yourself to be bold! Of course, you must act within the law and uphold moral and ethical standards. But knowing this secret is the first step in seizing the controls of your life.

Once you accept that you're the one who's in charge of making the most of your life, you're on your way. If the direction you want to go is starting your own company or running a business, you'll need to add vision, goals, strategy, focus, hard work, concern for other people, attention to detail and quality, delegation of responsibility, resilience, and then a little more hard work. You'll need to recognize the difference between risky and reckless. Most of all, you'll have to pay attention to the lessons life throws in your path, then apply that hard-won knowledge to the next challenge.

When my adult children learned about the idea for this book, they said "Great!" and "We want to tell your readers that following your advice leads to success." So that I can continue to be included in family gatherings, here are their comments to you.

■

During our family dinners (when Dad wasn't traveling), we'd hear about his day at work intermingled with jokes and general fun. It was a great way to learn of the world and business in general. As a family where everyone had something to say, I learned when to speak my thoughts and when to hold back. I also learned to listen and to respect others. Now I realize that I was learning to be a successful person, a successful husband and bread-winner, and most importantly a successful dad. Some of the key business traits I learned from my father are:

✍ To appreciate, from a very young age, the value of money and how it affects (positively and negatively) so many people.

✍ To think of the mental, physical, and financial benefits of working for yourself.

✍ To understand how people view you by the way you comb your hair, wear your clothes, tie your tie, and polish your shoes.

✍ To learn the power of language, good grammar and written and verbal communication.

✍ To learn that self-confidence is one of the easiest and important traits to acquire.

✍ To sell yourself.

✍ To help your children create their own meaning or success in business and life.

—*Alan Shaw*

■

Dad taught me that no star is out of reach; that if I want something, I should go after it. His encouragement gave me the daring to think big and reach for those stars. As a real estate agent, I work by "if you want the order, ask for it" every day. Dad's stories about working with customers at Bic and Pilot, and how he learned to listen to them instead of jumping into a sales pitch, taught me to focus on making friends instead of just getting customers.

—*Susan Shaw Santoro*

■

My father is a guy who says what he's going to do, then does what he says. I guess that reads as planning your work, and working your plan. About the only word of advice he ever gave me that he didn't follow himself was, "Go into business for yourself." I did. He didn't. One time a reporter asked me, "Who is your hero?" Without hesitation (and never having given a thought to personal heroes) I said, "My dad." The reasons why are in this book.

—*Steve Shaw*

■

This book isn't filled with hype and hyperbole. It's a series of personal stories and humorous tales from my years in show business and the pen business, each intended to provide lessons and instructive insights so you can be spared some of the anguish and embarrassment I endured. I hope that you'll experience much of the exhilaration without a good deal of the exasperation as you successfully *pilot your life*.

—*Ron Shaw*
President and CEO
Pilot Pen Corporation of America
Trumbull, Connecticut

Chapter 1

SAVED
BY
SLIPPING

One evening when I was on the road, I was staying at the Concord Hotel in the Catskill Mountains. It was late at night and I was desperately trying to get some sleep before my big show the next day. I was in bed about to nod off when suddenly I heard this conversation coming from the next room.

A man was saying, "Darling, you've got an incredible face. When we get back to Philadelphia, I'm going to hire one of those chiseler guys to chisel your face in stone."

I tried not to listen and turned over in bed. Then I heard, "And you've got the most beautiful body I've ever seen. When we get back to Philadelphia, I'm going to have that chiseler guy chisel your body in stone, too."

Things were starting to sound interesting now, so I put my ear up against the wall to listen in. "Oh honey, you've got the most perfect, beautiful breasts in the world. When we get back to Philadelphia, I'm going to have them chiseled in stone."

I couldn't take it anymore, so I put on my robe, went out in the hall, and knocked on my neighbor's door. The guy inside yelled, "Who's there?"

I answered, "The chiseler from Philadelphia!"

That was one of my favorite jokes. It never failed to get a laugh, and I have told it hundreds of times over the years. But let me explain how I went from professional teenage joke teller to "slightly" older man making his living as president of a leading pen company. There is no better place to begin than the beginning.

■

It all started on September 17, 1938, in the city of brotherly love, the birthplace of our nation, Philadelphia, Pennsylvania, where I was born to Herb and Babe Schurowitz. Two and a half years later, my little sister, Rachel, was born, and our family was complete. My father was a driver/salesman for the Baldwin Uniform Company. In our apartment in the Mayfair section of Philadelphia, we had an old upright piano that my mother loved to play. She was quite a talented classical pianist. As a child, I always loved to listen to her play.

Then one day when I was six, I heard the song "Don't Fence Me In" on the radio. I liked the way it sounded so much, I sat down at the piano, my feet swinging above the floor, and started picking out my own rendition of the melody with one finger—pretty poorly, mind you, but I could replay it fairly well. When my mother realized what I had just done, she screamed with delight and was instantly convinced that she had given birth to the next Mozart or at least George Gershwin. Immediately she decided to invest what little extra money our family had in piano lessons to foster my burgeoning musical talent.

But nobody in Philadelphia wanted to give piano lessons to a six-year-old kid. They all assumed that within a few months I would, like most other young boys, move on to other interests and drop my lessons. Fortunately, my mother wouldn't give up and finally found a wonderful teacher by the name of Earl Moyer. Mr. Moyer led an orchestra at the Adelphi Hotel by night and gave piano lessons during the day. Like all the other teachers, he too was reluctant, but my mother's relentless entreating finally compelled him to take me on. Mr. Moyer turned out to be my only music teacher, and I've enjoyed playing piano ever since.

Looking back, I realize I would never have been able to enter show business if my mother hadn't persisted in finding a piano teacher for me. Even though everyone told her that she'd never find someone willing to instruct a six-year-old, she refused to listen and kept pushing. My mom provided me with piano instruction—and my first lesson in the value of perseverance.

Besides our piano, the other thing I remember most clearly about Philadelphia was the frigid winters, the hard black ice on the streets, and the brutal, freezing winds.

Let me take you back to the streets of Philly during the winter of 1947. The war had been over for two years. We were knee-deep in the American Century and the United States had proven itself the new leader of the world. Things were looking up. There was a sense of potential and expectation in the air. Anything could happen.

We had moved from the Mayfair section of Philadelphia to the Germantown section because, during a driver's strike in 1946 at the company where my dad worked, my mother convinced him to get out of the uniform delivery business and buy a candy store. They used their life savings to buy a little shop on the corner of Chelton Avenue and Anderson Street in Germantown. Our store had a soda fountain and a big glass candy counter. We also sold over-the-counter medicines like aspirin and cough syrup.

I was literally a kid in a candy store. Our family lived in an apartment above the store. My father also worked out of the store as the local bookie. He was able to make a nice living and things were looking up for our family. But that was about to change. We were one of a few Jewish families in our section of Germantown. Late one night, bricks and rocks crashed through our plate glass window with notes attached that read "Jews not welcome!" and "Jew go home!" The midnight "hate mail" continued on and off for months.

My mother came down with a nervous skin condition because of the onslaught of anti-Semitism. It was hard on all of us. As a scrawny little Jewish kid trying to get home from school in one piece, occasionally I had to fight larger boys who bullied me and pushed me around. One afternoon a gang of rowdies threw me down into an open sewer.

A few months later, on a day permanently etched in my memory, I was walking quickly and silently down Chelton Avenue, trying to avoid trouble. In a way, it was a serene and beautiful winter day; the streets were quiet and almost devoid of people or cars since the roads were so icy. But I was a Jewish kid walking through a predominantly gentile neighborhood in the late 1940s—even on this quiet winter day I felt anything but safe and serene. Yet I had no choice: It was getting late and I had to get home. So I walked as fast as I could, and I almost made it. Just a few blocks from our store, the silence was shattered by the words "Rotten Jew! Kike! Dirty Jew bastard!" The toughs who had thrown me down the sewer suddenly reappeared. I was surrounded by four boys, all of them bigger. I desperately looked around, hoping that someone might recognize what was about to happen and come to my aid, but unfortunately the weather was so bad that all the good-hearted, sane people were safe and warm indoors.

I was no coward. Sure, I was scared, but I was one of those skinny boys who wanted the world to believe that I was a lot more physically intimidating than I looked. Of course, no one ever fell for my bluffing, but I kept it up all the same. You see, in those days in our neighborhood, you couldn't easily back down from a fight. Well, to be honest, I'm not really sure if you could or not; my tormentors and I never really paused to discuss street fight protocol. What mattered was that I was a Jewish kid, and since these were not politically correct gentile boys, I was in for a hell of a beating.

I tried my best to fight back, managing to stay on my feet long enough to withstand a few blows to my stomach and a right hook to the eye. I even got a few good punches in myself, but before I knew it, I was down on the sidewalk. Suddenly, a hand grabbed me by the neck and lifted me up. I was going to be saved. Hallelujah! Unfortunately, the hand belonged to one of the bigger kids, who cursed at me and held me with my arms behind my back as a trolley car sped towards us. At the very last second, he spun me out onto the street and pushed me in front of the trolley.

I hit the ground with a thud. I instantly looked up and saw the huge steel streetcar heading straight toward me. I tried to move, to get out of the way, to get onto my feet, but I couldn't. I was skidding across the ice too quickly and slid all the way across a slick patch of black ice on the street, just as the trolley car whizzed past my head.

It missed me by inches, literally inches. Talk about your life-altering incidents. I'll never be able to forget that moment. I don't know if God meant for me to live because there was work he wanted me to do or if it was just a fluke that a patch of black ice happened to be on the street at that spot, but somehow, for whatever reason, I survived.

As I skidded across Chelton Avenue, I had a revelation of the gift of life I had been given. Since then, I have grasped the irony that I was saved by slipping: I hated cold and ice, but if it hadn't been for those cold, icy conditions that winter day in Germantown, I'd be dead instead of writing this book.

■

I've learned to take the bad with the good—even to find the good *in* the bad. So when you find yourself in difficult circumstances, remember that, though your environment may not seem to suit you, don't give up. Stay positive because what you don't like may well turn out to save your hide.

Chapter 2

HELLO, MIAMI!

$\mathcal{S}$oon after the trolley car incident, my mother's skin condition started to become unbearable. Her rashes grew so bad on her hands and feet that she thought she had skin cancer. Her condition was exacerbated by the cold weather and her close proximity to the ice cream freezers in our store. She was suffering and something had to change.

Her doctor recommended that we move to a warmer climate. "Either Arizona or Florida," he suggested. In those days, there were very few Jews in Arizona, so we opted for Florida. My father sold the store and we took a train down to Miami. We arrived on Mother's Day, 1948, and my cold Philly days gave way to warm Miami nights. I was nine and a half.

My father decided to open a dry-cleaning store in Miami with a man named Harry, who happened to be a total stranger recommended to us by a distant relative. Since my dad's name is Herb and his partner's was Harry, they decided to call themselves H&H Cleaners. Soon after they opened their store, however, cash started disappearing, and then Harry disappeared.

Only six months after arriving in Miami, my dad had lost his store and his life savings, and he was forced to support us by selling peanuts and popcorn in the grandstands of the Orange Bowl. It was a tough time for all of us. My mother, who was a registered nurse, helped out by working in doctors' offices and the Miami Jewish Home for the Aged. Fortunately, in a few months my father was able to get a job driving a laundry truck just like he had years earlier in Philadelphia. But my father's dream of succeeding with his own business was gone with Harry.

In retrospect, it's easy to say that Harry was no good, but at the time, it seemed reasonable to rely on our relative's favorable recommendation of Harry and on Harry's trustworthy appearance. Unfortunately, by the time my father discovered who and what Harry really was, he had departed with all of my father's money. This left a lasting impression on me: Don't accept something on face value; find out the background and credentials of all parties involved before committing yourself.

■

Even though things were rough for our family when we first moved south, Miami was my kind of town and I took to it very quickly. No snow; palm trees everywhere; clean, sandy beaches and lots of great restaurants and theaters—what was not to like?

Thanks to Harry, though, our family had little money. So, I did what any good-hearted, red-blooded American kid would do—I applied for a paper route. There were only two requirements for having a paper route. You had to be twelve years old, and you had to have your own bike. I didn't have a bike, so my father went down to the police auction and got a beat-up bicycle for me for only five dollars. I was ready for my first job.

Now that I had a bike, I felt confident that I could get the job—even though I was only ten. When I got down to the office to apply, there was one other kid applying to be a paperboy, Arnie Swedler. He also was only ten. Arnie and I discussed our predicament. We both decided to become two years older that day, and as a result, we both were awarded routes in our neighborhoods. The ambition Arnie and I showed in that office was to characterize both our business careers. As an adult, Arnie moved from Florida to Montreal. Learning that there was pent-up demand in Ottawa for deli foods like pickled herring, pastrami, and corned beef, he opened a wholesale food business there catering to supermarkets. He has since opened Arnie's, a wholesale food company serving restaurants and take-out delis. He has done extremely well for himself.

Every day, I got on my beat-up bike and delivered my papers. I knew that if I worked hard all week and conscientiously delivered every single copy of *The Miami Daily News* entrusted to me, I would be able to make about twelve dollars a week. This seemed like a lot of money to me then and would have kept me happy if I didn't happen to walk past the storefront window of Harry's Bike Shop (no relation to the Harry on the lam). You see, featured in Harry's window was a thing of rare beauty. Yep, I was smitten, not by a girl but a Schwinn Black Phantom bicycle. Cushy leather seat, sleek black and red frame, wide handlebars—I had to have it, especially before any of the other kids got one.

The only problem was that the new bicycle cost eighty-six dollars that I didn't have. I tried not to think about it, but all day long all I could think about was riding my route atop that beautiful Black Phantom. I would be the envy of every kid in Miami. But with my paper route income, I knew it would be months before I'd be able to afford that bike.

Still, I couldn't wait. I had to have it—right then and there! So, I decided to try negotiating with Harry and went down to the bike shop. No one had told me how to talk to Harry or offered me advice on how to negotiate a deal. I just thought I'd give it a shot and see what I could do. I walked into the shop and approached Harry with a proposal. I told him that I had six dollars in my pocket that I would give him as a down payment, and I would sign a piece of paper guaranteeing him five dollars a week until the bike was paid in full.

Harry chuckled at first, presumably at my audacity, but soon my serious demeanor made him consider my proposal. I was adamant, and even though I was only ten, he could tell I meant business. And wouldn't you know it, Harry accepted my proposal and handed me my very own Schwinn Black Phantom bicycle. I was in heaven riding it home from the shop. And for the next sixteen weeks, I made every five-dollar payment to Harry until my debt was paid off—interest-free at that. Just as my mom wouldn't accept failing to find a piano teacher for me, so I wouldn't accept not riding that Black Phantom out of that store that day. It was one of many lessons I've learned about the persuasive power of conviction and passion—and a strong offer.

(*Quick note:* In the mid-1990s Schwinn released a limited-edition remake of the Black Phantom, and again, I felt like I had to have one. Though the price was a few thousand dollars, this time I was able to purchase one without negotiating an installment plan. And so today, more than fifty years later, I am once again the proud owner of a beautiful Schwinn Black Phantom bicycle.)

Chapter 3

STEPPING
INTO
THE SPOTLIGHT

$\mathcal{M}$y paper route was a great way to make money, but it wasn't enough for me. I wanted more. I wanted to be in the spotlight, making music, performing.

At the time, south Florida was *the* place to be for an aspiring performer. You have to understand that Miami in the late forties and early fifties was like Las Vegas or Atlantic City today—where all the great performers and musicians wanted to be. The city had fantastic nightclubs, both free-standing and inside the numerous luxury hotels. Performing was in the air.

Each day several paperboys and I would sit on a curb in front of an empty lot to fold and rubber band our papers for delivery. We'd race to see who could complete his route first, but I'd always lose on Fridays. I'd stay behind to read the "Youth Round-Up" section, two pages of articles from local junior high and high schools, plus a story about a weekly radio show also called "Youth Round-Up."

Owned by *The Miami Daily News,* the radio show was taped every Saturday afternoon downtown in the Daily News Tower (now known as the Freedom Tower) and aired during prime time on Monday nights by the NBC affiliate WIOD. It was sponsored by Coca-Cola and featured teenage talent. In every show young singers and musicians performed, young people discussed problems they faced in life, and then one of the teenage cast members interviewed a major star of the day, like Clark Gable, Eddie Cantor, Patti Page, Jimmy Durante, and Nat King Cole.

I listened to the show each Monday evening, then eagerly read about it in the Friday paper. It seemed like the kids on the show had a lot of fun and I began wondering if I could get on it by playing the piano.

In July 1950, after a year-and-a-half of fantasizing about performing on the show, I took a bus to the station and asked if I could audition. I was eleven-and-a-half. I played the tango song "La Cumparsita." I was praying just to be one of the guest musicians when the producer, Dave Rabinowitz, told me that he liked my piano playing. When I thanked him, he also said it sounded like my voice was right for radio and he offered me a role as a regular member of the cast. I was overjoyed. I had walked in hoping to get on the show once, for just a few minutes, and I left as a regular cast member who appeared weekly for the next thirty-six months.

On the show each week, I went out into the studio audience and picked contestants at random for the "Quizeroo." Players had to identify either the name or composer of certain musical interludes.

During this time, after my thirteenth birthday, I was fortunate to watch the incredible performances of two then-new musical talents, Buddy Rich and Rosemary Clooney, on stage at the Olympia Theater. Buddy was already a famous jazz drummer, but Rosemary was still a relatively unknown vocalist who had just been signed by

Columbia Records. Rosemary came to our radio station for an interview, and she and I struck up a conversation. With her singing talent, personality, and beauty, I knew she was something special. I was only thirteen, Jewish, and still waiting for my growth spurt, and Rosemary was twenty-three, Irish-Catholic, and on the brink of fame, but we formed a friendship that continues to this day. I became her most ardent fan, formed a Rosemary Clooney fan club, and thereby received a stack of her records. Every night, I would visit disk jockeys at radio stations all over Miami and beg, plead, and cajole them to play her newest single.

Rosemary had no idea what I was doing and, when she found out, urged me to stop. I agreed, but I was so passionate about her singing that I wanted to share it with the world. Rosemary has since said I was the "most outgoing kid that she ever met." But I never saw myself as really outgoing. In essence, I guess I've always had the sales gene. Whether it was pushing Rosemary Clooney records or jokes, I couldn't help myself. When I believe in a product, I do everything I can to make it succeed.

In 1953, when I was fourteen, I was still working on "Youth Round-Up." Our ratings took a nosedive because television shows were drawing off the radio audience. The show's coordinator, Betty Ward, pushed to repackage us as a television program, and we were picked up for broadcast by a local TV station. Unfortunately, what was fantastic on radio turned out to be horrible on TV, and we were canceled after only thirteen weeks.

But Betty still believed in us and put us together as a performing unit for military personnel stationed throughout Florida. We were known as the "Youth Round-Up Stars on Parade." Basically, she took all of the regular teenage cast members from our show and put us on stage as a sort of USO (United Service Organizations) type of show that could play for servicemen anywhere around the state. It was a great thrill for us kids to have a chance to perform for appreciative military audiences in those spacious, well-equipped military-base theaters.

At this point in my career, I only played piano. However, after awhile, Betty asked me to introduce the acts because she thought my radio experience would lend itself to being a master of ceremony. I enjoyed emceeing and tickling the ivories, but found that what I loved most was watching our group's comedian perform. I was fascinated by the way he moved his hands when he told jokes, how he held the microphone, how he walked, and how he timed his punch lines. I wanted to know everything about the way he worked.

After a couple of months, I'd seen him do his routine so many times I knew every one of his lines by heart. It wasn't exactly a conscious thing; it was more like osmosis. His act seeped into me, and I never really thought about it until one night when he didn't show up to perform.

It was five minutes before we were supposed to start, and Betty was terribly upset. Hundreds of GIs had come to see our show and we didn't have a comic. She pulled me aside and said, "Okay, Ronnie, can you do it?"

I didn't want to let Betty down, and since I knew his act cold, I agreed. Thank God I knew his whole routine so well, because when I stepped out on that stage, I could not think. Hell, I could barely move! There I was, a fifteen-year-old kid in the spotlight in front of hundreds of GIs, trying to make them laugh. I was a nervous wreck!

I remember that long walk up to the mike with that white-hot spotlight on me, the whole time convinced that my legs were going to buckle or I'd have a heart attack. I'd played piano for lots of different people and never got nervous, but comedy, I found that night, is a different ballgame altogether. It's like being naked up there. And if you don't hook the audience quickly, you're dead. Even if you do grab them, you can lose them in any given second with one bad punch line. It's a tenuous thing and you've got to hold on tight, which is hard as hell when you're suffering from a horrible case of stage fright.

I didn't know what to do. So, I cleared my throat and just started blabbering. . . . I told all the jokes I'd heard the regular comic say show after show and, miraculously, the GIs erupted into uncontrollable laughter. Every laugh made it that much easier. Soon I relaxed and was loving it. In comedy, momentum is everything.

That night I learned that even if you're scared to death, you can't show weakness or vulnerability. Your audience will sense it and be uneasy with you. Fortunately, I had studied the details of our comedian's performances so thoroughly, I could not only deliver his jokes, I unconsciously mimicked his confident stance and mannerisms. Like an emergency service worker or soldier, I responded the way I was trained—even though I never realized I was training myself.

When you are in the spotlight, you have to make it appear as if you're relaxed, even if you're not, so that your audience can relax in your presence. It's a reciprocal thing. And then, when both the audience and you feel comfortable, wondrous things can happen. Laughter pours forth, and it's one of the greatest rushes in the world. You have power. Control. Immortality, it seems. You are the life of the party. No other feeling is quite like it.

■

It was years later that I recognized how profoundly this period of my life shaped my future. That kid who got around an age requirement to get a paper route, convinced a store owner to accept a payment plan on a new bicycle, won a three-year role on a radio show, promoted Rosemary Clooney records to nightshift DJs, and walked onstage to tell borrowed jokes in front of hundreds of servicemen taught me the value of taking risks, being innovative and inventive, following passions, and, most of all, not waiting for someone else to give me permission to pursue what I wanted. That kid taught me about recognizing and seizing opportunities to improve skills, expand talent, and foster the ability to sell myself, and about how relaxing and enjoying myself helps an audience (or customers) relax and enjoy themselves. That kid taught me the importance of momentum in the process of selling jokes, ideas, myself—and pens.

Chapter 4

REINVENT YOURSELF

$\mathcal{T}$hat first night I stood on stage as a comedian was a second unforgettable moment in my life. There I was, a mere fifteen-year-old, doing my first comedy performance, and I had those GIs convinced I was the funniest guy they'd ever met. Now let me tell you, for a teenager from Philadelphia, this was heady stuff. I'm talking a standing ovation, the whole nine yards. Betty was elated with my performance, and I never played piano for her again. I was now officially a comedian!

Obviously I loved comedy. My parents, on the other hand, weren't so sure about it, but I used the money I was making to help pay for my college education. You have to understand that my parents were not showbiz people. Second-generation American children of immigrants, they wanted the best for me. There was little precedent for this kind of strange behavior in my family. Neither my mother nor father had ever been on stage. True, I had one cousin, Arne Sultan, who was a record mimic (he did a form of lip-synching to records which is rarely seen today) and who went on to become a TV producer and writer for "The Judy Garland Show" and "Get Smart." But in general we were not a family of entertainers. Yet, for whatever reason, I was always drawn to performing. For eleven years, being on stage was my life. I think there's something to the adage that once stage performing gets in your blood, it never goes away. I guess that's why I still enjoy talking about it, and maybe that's why I still pay my dues to two theatrical unions—the AGVA (American Guild of Variety Artists, the nightclub performer's union) and the Musician's Federation.

When I was sixteen and had been doing comedy for about a year, I thought I might jump-start my career by changing my name from Ronald Schurowitz to something that would be a little easier to pronounce. The only hitch was that I had received a small fourteen-karat gold ring from my parents for my Bar Mitzvah with the initials *RS* on it. I didn't want to have to stop wearing it on stage; so I limited myself to picking a new last name that started with *S*. My great-uncle Sam Bernstein suggested *Shaw,* and I liked the way it sounded.

"SHAW!"

It rolls off the tongue with grace and ease. So, that's how I became—Ronnie Shaw!

■

A few years later, I had to change my name once again—but this time it was only for three weeks. Here's what happened.

In the thirties and forties, there was a famous night-club in New York City on 52nd Street called Leon and Eddie's. It was a launching pad for many of the greatest comedians of that time. Jackie Gleason, Phil Silvers, Alan King, and many others played there. When one of the owners, Leon Enken, retired to Florida in the 1950s, he opened a strip joint in what is now called the South Beach part of Miami Beach. Leon's new club was a direct descendant of the old-time burlesque houses that featured five strippers, a comedian, a novelty act, and a three-piece band. It was a large club, and anything but a classy place.

One day I got a call from Leon's club. They offered me $125 to perform as a comedian for one week. At that time, I wasn't working and I couldn't afford to say no, though I really didn't want to be associated with that type of establishment. Although $125 sounds like a lot of money for back then, it wasn't exactly an easy payday to make: Leon expected me to perform in three shows a night, seven nights a week.

I agreed to work Leon's club on condition that I perform under a name other than Ronnie Shaw. In keeping with this request, I stipulated that Leon wasn't allowed to use my picture in any ads that might run in the papers or on any signs outside the front of the club. Leon didn't have any problem with that, so I signed a contract.

As I approached the club the first night, I was taken aback. A big sign out in front of the club announced, "America's newest comedy sensation—Rod Roberts."

Yep, Leon had kept his part of the bargain and kept my name and photo off the marquee, and instead, he had renamed me—Rod Roberts. Not the most distinctive name in the world (apologies to all the real Rod Robertses), but it would work. I laughed and went inside.

I worked hard all week doing my twenty-one shows, and on closing night, big Leon walked over to me. I looked at him. Weighing in at over two hundred fifty pounds, a long stogie hanging from his lower lip, he sat down next to me and said, in his distinctively low husky growl, "Kid, you're great. We want to hold you over."

Now, to a novice in the comedy world, this might sound fantastic. But if you've been around a little, you know that as soon as you hear those words you are about to be suckered into a ploy used by club owners who don't have enough money to pay you. I called him on it. "So basically what you're saying to me, Leon, is you don't have my one hundred twenty-five dollars, right?"

Leon blew some cigar smoke in my face and said, "Nahh. That's not it at all. You're great. GREAT!" He slipped me fifty dollars. "Here's fifty bucks against the one-twenty-five I owe you."

I reluctantly took the fifty. I needed it and I knew that I could continue to argue with him all night, but I wasn't going to get another red cent out of him. I nodded and grunted, "All right, Leon, one more week, and at the end of that, I want all my money for both weeks, okay?"

"Sure kid. Anything you say."

He blew another puff of smoke in my face and lumbered away. Of course, at the end of the next week, Leon only paid me the balance of the first week, and nothing for the second week. So, now, I'd worked for him for two weeks—forty-two shows—and I only had $125 to show for it.

Of course, when I confronted Leon about it, he smiled and said, "Kid, you're the best. I like you." He should have liked me, since he was hardly paying me. Then he said, "I don't normally do this, but I'm gonna bring you back for another week. How 'bout that?"

"Okay, Leon. FINE! One more week. But I want all my money by the end of the week, okay? That's two hundred fifty dollars next week. OKAY?"

"Sure, you got it. All of it. I promise." I knew the game he was playing with me, but I reluctantly agreed. I really wanted to get my money from him.

And so, one week later, after twenty-one consecutive nights and sixty-three shows, when I walked up to Leon and asked for my money, wouldn't you know it, he looked at me and said, "Kid, you're the king of comedy. Unfortunately, I'm a little low on funds right now. How 'bout you work just one more week and I promise, I'll definitely have all your money by then. I swear!"

"That's it! No thanks!" I said as I quit and walked out of that crummy place. The next morning, I went to the union, told them my story, and showed them the contract. They went after Leon, and within a week, I received all of my money.

And that, my friends, was the beginning and the end of the career of America's newest comedy sensation, Rod Roberts.

Did I learn anything from this incarnation? I sure did. I learned:

- ✍ Get your agreement in writing.

- ✍ When you need the money but don't want to risk your reputation, you may want to reinvent yourself with a new name.

- ✍ Stand up for yourself, even when you think you don't have much leverage; but use what leverage you do have when more polite means of resolving a dispute have been exhausted.

Chapter 5

FIRST IMPRESSIONS CAN BE DECEIVING:

The Larry King Story

I was very fortunate to play in many clubs and hotels in Miami that featured some of the hottest comedians and singers in the country. I even had a tiny role in the Jerry Lewis film *The Bellboy,* but unfortunately my scene was cut.

After I started making some headway as a comedian, I was asked to do a radio interview. I agreed until I found out I was to be interviewed in a deli—which meant the interview was for the late-night "Larry King Show."

I'd heard Larry's show before and didn't really know what to make of it. So I told the press agent, "I'm not sure. Anyone who does his radio show from a deli is going nowhere in show business!"

Reluctantly, I finally agreed to do the interview and went over to Pumpernik's. Maybe at least I'd get a free pastrami sandwich out of it.

When Larry interviewed me, I had to sit on a little stage near the front window. I remember thinking to myself that he seemed like a nice guy, but with that gravelly voice, how could he expect to make it in radio? It just goes to show (again) that first impressions can be highly deceiving.

As most everyone knows, Larry went on to do incredibly well in a very competitive industry. Larry came from humble origins, and his success story is wonderfully instructive. As a boy named Larry Zeiger growing up in New York, he became fascinated by radio at age five. He remembers spending much of his youth pretending to be a radio announcer. He was a good student and a happy kid until his father, a Russian immigrant who worked in a defense plant building ships, died of a heart attack when Larry was just nine. Larry took his father's death hard and lost interest in school. Without his father's income to help support their family, his mother, a seamstress, had to apply for relief—what we now call welfare.

Larry never went to college and instead started working for United Parcel Service. At age twenty-three, he moved down to Florida to pursue his dream of being in radio. After a year or two in Miami, he convinced WAHR radio's general manager to let him hang around the station. Larry hardly ever left the station, learning how to rip newswire and watching the announcers work. Finally, in 1959, at age twenty-five, Larry got his first big break on air. He was told on a Friday that on the following Monday morning he would have his own show from 9:00 to 12:00 every morning and would do the news in the afternoon. For doing the morning show and afternoon news, WAHR would pay him a salary of fifty dollars a week.

Larry was so thrilled he was going to be on the air that he couldn't sleep all weekend. When he arrived at the station Monday morning, he was exhausted and scared to death. Ten minutes before 9:00, the general manager turned to Larry and asked, "So, Mr. Zeiger, what name do you want to use on air?"

Larry hadn't even thought about it and had no answer for him. Desperate, the general manager looked down at an open copy of *The Miami Herald* that happened to be flipped open to an ad for King's Wholesale Liquors. He asked, "Hey, how about Larry King?"

"Sounds fine to me," Larry answered, and Larry King was born. Larry then went into the studio to go on air for the first time. When he got his cue, he froze. His new show's opening music kept playing, and Larry turned the volume down to speak, but no words came out. He turned the music level back up, collected himself, and then flipped the level back down again. Still not a word. Larry envisioned his whole career ending before it even started. Suddenly, the general manager burst through the door and screamed, "Larry, this is a communications business, so communicate!"

And just as my mouth saved me on my first night of comedy, Larry's mouth saved him that morning. He cranked the music back down, parted his lips, and let the words pour out, "Hello. I'm Larry King. This is my first day and I've never done this before. I'm very nervous, but I'm going to talk to you and I hope you will listen."

Larry hasn't stopped talking since. One of the cardinal rules of broadcasting is, "If in doubt, leave it out." However, Larry has always been one to break this rule. If his gut instinct tells him to follow a line of questioning, even if he is unsure where it will take him, he will pursue it. Larry loves the whole world of broadcasting—being live, the happening of the moment, the sense of unrehearsed spontaneity, communicating with his guests and his audience. He doesn't use a different voice when he's on the air and doesn't pretend to be an intellectual. He just sees himself as an inordinately curious guy who's had the great fortune to get to learn about himself, other people, and the world by asking interesting people questions about their lives while millions are listening.

Two years after Larry's big debut, the owner of Pumpernik's approached him about doing a coffee-klatch radio show for WIOD in the deli. Larry loved the idea of working without any safety net in an off-the-wall, totally unrehearsed atmosphere and accepted the offer. Every day, different local people and celebrities, like Bobby Darin or Jimmy Hoffa, who happened to be in Miami, dropped in to chat on air live with Larry. This was a time before the advent of talk radio, so Larry's show in Pumpernik's was groundbreaking in that it was pure conversation, no music. Every broadcast was an exciting adventure because nobody knew exactly what was going to happen.

Soon Larry was doing a show called "Saturdays with Sinatra," announcing sports on Sundays, and working as a columnist for *The Miami Herald.* By the late 1960s, Larry was known as Mr. Miami. Then in 1977, Larry moved to Washington, D.C., to do the first national all-night network-radio talk show. Initially carried by twenty-seven stations, this show was a nationwide forerunner of what we now know as talk radio. Shortly thereafter, he got his own D.C. TV show. When *USA Today* first appeared, Larry got his own weekly column, and then, in 1985, he was offered his own talk show every night from 9:00 to 10:00 on CNN.

By the time Larry retired from radio in 1997, his show was carried by 485 stations.

Even though Larry has climbed to the top of the broadcasting world, he'll be the first to tell you that his life hasn't been without setbacks. He has lost his job twice, buried himself in debt, and filed for bankruptcy. Despite the personal and financial problems he's faced over the course of his life, he has never had an on-air problem, nor has any general manager he worked for ever frowned on anything on his shows.

I think the key to Larry's, and most prosperous people's, success is that he loves what he does. Larry sees broadcasting as a clean, wonderful way to make a living. He feels very fortunate to do what he always dreamed about doing and get paid for it. In fact, he'll tell you he hasn't worked a day in his life since he was twenty-one and delivering packages for UPS. This from a man who did a TV show, a newspaper column, and an all-night radio show every day of the week for decades.

■

The parallels between Larry's path to success and my own are rather striking: We started out broke, yet never felt poor. We realized that we could achieve success by doing what we loved to do. We followed our passions, played to our strengths, and stayed open to opportunity.

Chapter 6

PERFECTION CAN BE REHEARSED

One of my most exciting evenings as a performer was the night I opened for Dean Martin and Liberace at a benefit at the Fontainbleau Hotel in Miami Beach.

Dean Martin was an extraordinary man. I'll never forget the first time I met him. As I watched him perform on stage, I was struck by the attention he paid to every detail of his performance. While Dean always had the image of the swaggering, tipsy playboy, the truth is he was always a consummate professional. The glass of whiskey he held while he sang was usually tea. Dean was extremely serious and thorough about every aspect of his performance. He did long hours of rehearsals and sound checks. Every beat in his act, down to when he would sip his drink and slur his words, was practiced. He took every opportunity to better his presentation to the audience and never stopped trying to improve. In fact, the most important thing I learned from opening for Dean Martin was that successful professionals stay at the peaks of their fields not due to luck, but simply because they are more obsessed than anyone else with growing and perpetually improving what they do.

Martin wasn't the only one who was obsessed with being his best. Many of the comedians I saw had a real sense of how to work a crowd. Red Buttons, Milton Berle,

Bobby Byron, Henny Youngman, Alan King, Buddy Hackett, Sammy Shore, Shecky Green—these were the masters at whose feet I sat night after night learning my craft. Nightclubs might sound like a strange place for a kid to grow up, but at that time I never saw any drugs, and the clubs were really pretty safe places for a teenager to hang out and to try to work on new jokes.

■

When I wasn't playing clubs, I loved to go to the movies. My favorite old-time movie palace was the Olympia Theater in downtown Miami. I went there just about every Saturday for seven years, from 1948 to 1955. For twenty-five cents, you could see a movie and a one-hour stage show featuring a ten-piece orchestra and five different acts. The star attraction would be a major name of the day, usually a singer but many times a comedian. I would sit in the fifteenth row until the movie was over, then I'd run up and grab a seat in the front row to watch the live performers. I loved to watch all the old pros because these comedians spent years and years honing their acts, so they knew exactly how to tell each joke and just how long to wait after the punch line. Vocal intonation, accent, timing, they had mastered it all.

As soon as they walked on stage, you knew you were watching polished professionals. They could connect with the audience immediately. Every little detail of the act that followed was fine-tuned for the appropriate audience reaction. They knew exactly how to dress, how to walk, how to make an entrance and an exit. For example, many of these vaudevillians, when their acts were introduced, would wait for three beats before walking onstage. In adapting this technique to my own entrances, I would always look behind me as I walked onstage, as if I was talking to someone, thus creating a certain mystique and theatricality. If you watch tapes of Johnny Carson on the old "Tonight Show," you will see he did the same thing.

I think I learned more about how to walk into a meeting or work a roomful of people from great stage performers than from any classroom or other experience in my life.

■

In commercial business, as in show business, it is not enough to simply continue to do well those things you have mastered; success is bred by a constant quest to improve every detail of your performance.

Chapter 7

HOW TO SURVIVE A TOUGH AUDIENCE

In comedy, as in the business world, I've had to face many tough crowds, and I've come to realize that standing on stage is really selling yourself.

Many times when I performed, people had purchased high-dollar tickets to see Connie Francis or Liberace, not to see me. I was just the guy they had to deal with until the real star came out. It was almost as if they were daring me to make them laugh. So I had to win them over to my side, or I was dead and so was my career. Ever since then, I knew that if I could win over an uninterested, impatient crowd, then I could win over anybody.

But exactly how did I manage to sway them to my side? Well, I saw myself as having a choice: I could panic, which would inevitably destroy my performance, or I could focus on relaxing and just doing my job as I'd done it so many nights before. Though I was incredibly nervous, I came out *looking* relaxed and always opened with my strongest material. As soon as the laughs started rolling in, I would get more comfortable and loosen up. Yet, no matter how well things were going, I knew I could never afford to totally relax, because a single misdelivered line could blow the whole thing.

Throughout my entire routine, I slowed down every time I started to speak too quickly, and I stayed focused on the material and the audience. Fortunately, my efforts paid off in steady work up and down the East Coast, including engagements in the Catskill Mountains in upstate New York.

During the fifties, that area was still known as the Borscht Belt, the famed string of hotels and bungalow colonies popular among Jewish families looking for mountain air, kosher food, and entertainment as a summer retreat from New York City. For the ten weeks between Memorial Day and Labor Day, comedians, musicians, and singers could count on six or seven performances a week. For the most part, the million vacationers who summered in the Catskills were a relaxed, convivial group. It was an ideal place to try out new material and different ways to win over an audience.

Despite all of the fine tuning of my act, however, I encountered audiences that defied my efforts to win them over. One of the most difficult I ever faced was in a veterans hospital theater. But let me first give you a little history of this hospital.

During the booming 1920s, the ultraswank Biltmore Hotel was built in Coral Gables, Florida, by Coral Gables founder George Merrick and hotel magnate John Bowman. It opened in 1926 and was an immediate hit. Celebrity guests included the Roosevelts, the Vanderbilts, the Duke and Duchess of Windsor, Bing Crosby, and Babe Ruth. Gangster Al Capone even moved into one of the suites.

And no wonder. The Biltmore was resplendent with its landmark 315-foot central tower, beautifully appointed vaulted lobby, lavishly equipped theater, lush central courtyard, and massive swimming pool (still the largest hotel pool in the continental United States).

But the Biltmore's high times ended during the depression-ridden thirties. In the 1940s the hotel was seized by the U.S. government and converted into a hospital for the Army Air Force and eventually the Veterans Administration. The once glorious sanctuary for the rich and famous became a linoleum-covered, antiseptic-smelling way station for injured soldiers.

The U.S. government realized that those troops needed entertainment as a diversion from their injuries. Since the hotel's theater remained intact, the Veterans Administration hired entertainers to perform at what had become a veterans' hospital. By the time I was performing in south Florida, the patients were veterans of the Korean War.

Some of the biggest names in show business played that veteran's hospital theater. By this night in 1957, I had been hired to do my act numerous times and took a lot of pleasure in getting this audience laughing. God knows they needed it.

However, this one particular night turned out to be one of the biggest challenges of my whole show business career. My good friend Mike Osman and I had plans that night for a double date after my performance. We agreed that I'd pick him up on my way to the hospital, he'd watch my show, and then we'd pick up our dates.

Mike and I walked past the hospital guardhouse and made our way to the theater. When we got there, the place was dark and deserted. We retreated to the information desk where the staff member found my name on the clearance list. He said my show wasn't going to be in the theater and that someone would escort us to where I was to perform.

A uniformed staff member appeared and led the way, pulling out a huge key ring like the jailer carries in Westerns. He opened a metal, prisonlike door, which he then locked behind us. He led us down a long, windowless hallway, opened a second metal door, and locked that one behind us as well.

I was booked to perform my comedy act in the psychiatric ward. Heaven only knows what these men had been through in Korea for their minds to be so ravaged and unhinged. Clearly, I thought, a tuxedo-clad, fresh-faced comic was not going to penetrate the void they now lived in. But I had been hired to perform, and, as the saying goes, the show must go on. Mike stood in the back of the room, valiantly laughing and applauding as I did my thirty-minute act before 150 vacant-eyed patients who had no idea what was going on around them.

Over the years since that performance, I've come to appreciate what a valuable lesson that night taught me. Despite thorough preparation, I've occasionally walked into situations that were much worse than what I had anticipated. Each time, the temptation to cut my losses and escape was enormous. But I resolved to protect my reputation and salvage what I could. I've never suffered more than discomfort taking this approach, and I'm convinced that it has trained me for tackling the sort of highly uncomfortable situations every CEO has to face.

For example, as president and CEO of Pilot Pen, I was recently asked to become the chairman of a new nonprofit citizen's action group in New Haven, Connecticut, near our corporate headquarters. This group's sole purpose is to advocate improving Tweed–New Haven Regional Airport so small jets can connect New Haven by air to the rest of the nation. I used to be able to fly to Tokyo from Tweed with a connection in Chicago. That airline pulled out of Tweed years ago, forcing tens of thousands of travelers in southern Connecticut to drive to more distant and congested airports on overcrowded highways. Attracting a national carrier back to New Haven would not only give individual travelers back some valuable time but enhance the region's prospects for economic growth.

As you can imagine, airport expansion appeals to business and pleasure travelers but enrages nearby property owners. As part of its community outreach, this citizens' group scheduled a meeting with homeowners and an antiexpansion organization. I was asked to attend this evening meeting, say a few words about the necessity for expansion, then be free to go home. I was told that while many opponents would be present, there would be a civil, open discussion.

I discovered on entering the meeting room that I was to occupy the center seat at a horseshoe-shaped table, facing several rows of chairs. A few of my fellow members in the proexpansion group joined me at the table, along with leaders of those opposed. Twenty-four people took seats in the rows, crossed their arms over their chests, and glared at me. It quickly became apparent that I was to conduct the meeting and that these homeowners weren't there to politely discuss economic vitality. They didn't want commercial jets landing and taking off in their backyards, period. They were upset and came to vent their frustration.

Did I want to walk out? You bet. But I resolved to salvage what I could and began to build rapport. I calmly explained why I was there and why I believed expansion was necessary. I told them that I wouldn't want to live near an airport either. I asked why they purchased houses in this neighborhood when they knew that an airport was nearby, and listened as identical answers were voiced. In 1983, they said, the mayors of the two towns that govern the airport signed an airport master plan. These homeowners had been led to believe that the plan prohibited any airport expansion. However, the plan had been written in deliberately vague language that allowed broad interpretation. They bought houses thinking they were protected by a document that was now betraying them. No wonder they were incensed! Once the core of their outrage was out in the open and acknowledged, we proceeded with a discussion about property values, business growth, noise pollution, and so on. When the meeting ended, many of them walked up to me to shake my hand.

It had been many decades since the performance at the Coral Gables veterans' hospital, but that long-ago night put me on a path that enabled me to convert what promised to be a hostile situation into a candid exchange of opinions. We didn't change the world or even our little corner of

Connecticut that night, but by the end of the evening, everyone had developed a mutual respect for each other, and we
all had learned a great deal about each other's situation.

■

I think the most important thing I learned as a comedian
was how to connect with others. Whether I had to win over
a thousand people in a cavernous auditorium or just sway a
single individual in a small lounge to my side, I developed
the ability to sell myself—which just may be the most significant factor in any sales pitch.

So whether you are selling jokes, pens, a point of view,
or anything else, sales success is about first endowing people with confidence in yourself.

Chapter 8

YOU CAN'T JUGGLE WITHOUT FOCUSING

A salesman takes his wife along on a business trip to Las Vegas. On their first night in town, before going out to dinner, he finishes dressing before her. He tells his wife that he's going to go wander around the casino and that he'll meet her there in twenty minutes.

So the salesman's in the casino hanging around the craps table when this beautiful hooker walks up to him and says, "Hey there, mister, you want to have a party?"

Curious to know the going rates, he answers, "Well, maybe. How much?"

She looks at him and says, "One hundred fifty dollars."

He laughs. "That's a little more than I wanted to spend."

"How much did you want to spend?"

"Five bucks," he says, trying to get rid of her.

She calls him every name under the sun and storms away.

A few minutes later, his wife finally comes down to the casino and as they're leaving the hotel to get a cab, he sees the same hooker standing by the front door. As he walks by her, she shakes her finger at him and says, "Uh-huh, see what you get for five bucks?"

I loved telling jokes and getting big laughs. However, there were nights when I didn't connect well with the audience and the big laughs never came. On those nights, it seemed I didn't have what it takes to make it in comedy. In a way, I think having my very first night as a comedian go so well was a mixed blessing. Getting all those laughs at the military base that night sucked me into the limelight, but from then on, I compared every performance to the perfection of that first time. And in the end, how could any other night compare?

On those nights that I bombed as a comic, I'd go home and feel sorry for myself. But when I woke up the next morning, I'd force myself to think about all the little victories I had achieved the night before, the jokes that *had* worked, the new things I did that were getting laughs, and I'd start to feel a whole lot better.

Since I started performing at age eleven, I learned intuitively that life in show business was a constant struggle. Performing while attending the University of Miami as a full-time student wasn't easy, but college education was important to my father and I didn't want to disappoint him. I would play the Miami clubs at night during the semester and do the Catskills or tour the East Coast clubs in the summer. It was a tough schedule, but I was young and my enthusiasm kept me going.

My ability to connect with an audience on stage helped me juggle my academic, personal, and professional lives. The only way to keep so many balls in the air, I learned, was to be extremely disciplined. When I was with friends or family, I had to focus exclusively on them and not think about new jokes for my act. When I was in the classroom or doing homework, I had to clear my mind of everything but the academic material.

■

I was still a young fella, but somehow I learned that, no matter how full my plate was, the most important thing I could do was to make sure that the person I was talking to felt that I was with him or her in spirit as well as body. I employ this principle every day. This respectful approach helps me build rapport with the other person and encourage deeper levels of communication. I may have a million other things on my mind or may not have gotten any sleep the night before. No matter: I have to make it appear that whatever it is the two of us are talking about at that moment is the most important thing in the world to me. I make direct eye contact, listen carefully to what the person's saying, and always remember that he or she wants my full attention. This is one way people you encounter feel respected; and unless they do, what you say matters little.

Chapter 9

FALLING FOR PHISSY

*T*he most extraordinary of all the many accomplished and interesting people I met during those eleven years I worked in show business has to be a girl by the name of Phyllis Hollander. Her real name is Phyllis but her family and close friends call her Phissy.

I met Phissy when she was fifteen and I was seventeen. She was pledging a high school sorority that was putting on a dance called "The Matzo Ball." The members had written a skit entitled "Time Matzos On," which featured my band. Dances in those days, no matter who put them on, always had live music. There was no such thing as an "in person" disc jockey. DJs were only on the radio. The skit was a minstrel show; Phissy had to sing "Sweet Georgia Brown" and I would accompany her. The part called for her to intentionally sing it badly. It was obvious she didn't have to try very hard. She can still sing in a number of different keys—only it's all at the same time!

After that, we saw each other in school, working on various plays. I was the stage manager and she was in the thespian society. We became friends from working on those projects together and through her sorority and my fraternity. By her senior year she started dating Barry Zimbler, who played the saxophone in my dance band. I was already attending the University of Miami, but quite often I would visit Miami Senior High School during the last period of the day, when the thespians had their class. Sylvia Furlong, the drama teacher, had been my favorite. She had always shown a sincere interest in me and my career.

During one of those visits, I had heard of Phissy and Barry's serious romance. I remember commenting to her, "Barry promised I could be best man at the wedding." What irony!

It was after returning home from a three-month comedy tour of the northeast in 1958 that I discovered their romance was over. Neither of us was dating anyone at the time, and we became better friends. At an "open house" party her sorority threw we danced to records and talked. When we had spoken earlier about going to this open house, I agreed to take her home. I later learned that this was a ploy on her part to avoid driving that night. I have officially proclaimed that to be our "first date." It was August 2, 1958.

We had a great time that evening, going for coffee and dessert with two other couples after the party. In those days, the cars we drove were all big enough to easily hold six people. All night the laughter never stopped. We discussed everything under the sun, including how to politely spit out watermelon seeds.

When I took Phissy home that night and gave her a brotherly kiss on the forehead, wishing her sweet dreams, I thought about how much fun we had together. In fact, to this day, Phissy still insists it wasn't her putting on any charm, but just our having a great time with the group. To me, though, it was all her, and I was falling in love.

As I started to fall for Phissy, I knew that I had to make some big life decisions. It would be immensely difficult to support a family as a comedian. I kept thinking back to something that Georgie Jessel had told me backstage at the Fontainbleau two years earlier. Today, only a few may recognize Jessel's name, but in those days he was still a big star. He had headlined on Broadway in the original stage version of *The Jazz Singer*, before Al Jolson did the film version. Franklin Delano Roosevelt gave Jessel the unofficial title of "Toastmaster General of the U.S." Jessel was a beloved entertainer who had performed all over the world, married four times, and seen it all.

Picture this: I am seventeen years old, a fresh-faced innocent. I had just gotten off the stage at the Fontainbleau and was relaxing in the wings when Georgie Jessel grabs me and starts chatting with me about life. At first, I didn't know what to make of him, but then I started to realize he was a little tipsy and a little lonely. He had a good heart and he really wanted to give me some advice. He was an old man now who wore a crooked wig and reeked of booze, but what he said to me has stayed with me for many decades as a great truth. Jessel looked deeply into my eyes and said, "Kid, if you ever fall in love and decide to get married before you make it to the big time, get out of the business—because it ain't gonna work!"

Sure, Jessel had been drinking a little too much that evening; yet, I've never been able to shake what he said. There was authentic wisdom in his words, and maybe some prophecy. Four years after my backstage encounter with Jessel, I had to decide between show business and Phissy

Hollander. Do I marry her and get out of the business, or do I try to be the exception and stay with it?

I didn't really have to think about it for very long. I loved comedy, but I loved Phissy more, and I knew I didn't want to let her get away. So, as soon as I could save up a little dough, I bought her an engagement watch (didn't have enough money for a ring), and asked her to marry me. She said yes and we were wed on November 29, 1959. We have been happily married ever since.

■

The financial insecurity of a career in entertainment, combined with my desire to marry Phissy, led me to say good-bye to the comedy stage. I was twenty-one and knew I had to get off the economic roller-coaster ride known as show business and find a more stable way to support me and my new wife. I had to get a "real" job, but to be honest, I didn't have a clue as to what I would do for the rest of my life.

I tried selling weekly newspaper cartoon-advertising packages to small businesses, but it didn't suit me. I even tried selling insurance for six months with Mutual of New York, but that didn't work out either. And in an incident I'll tell you more about later on, I asked my dad to get me a job driving a truck for the company he worked for, but he declined. My son Steven was born on September 22, 1960, and I wanted him to have the best of everything. But that would require money that I didn't have.

For eleven years, my passion had been show business. After exiting the stage, I knew that my "new vehicle" had to be something I could be equally passionate about. What was it?

Soon enough, I found my answer: selling pens.

Chapter 10

GETTING
A "REAL" JOB

*W*hen I was twenty-two and between jobs, I was so broke that I regularly visited construction sites to find empty soda bottles to trade in for their two-cent deposit value. How's that for a contrast to performing on stage clad in a tuxedo?

I was tired of dead-end sales jobs. My car was getting run-down from all the miles I was putting on it, and to be honest, I felt as if I was getting run-down, too. But I had a family to support, and I was never a quitter, so I spent the next six weeks looking seriously for a job. I woke up every morning, put on a suit and tie, and made it my job to find gainful employment. Firmly believing that looking for a job *is* a full-time job, I pounded the pavement and pursued every lead I could.

Yet, the longer I remained jobless, the more I felt I was failing as a provider for my wife and son. In fact, Phissy's mother started to feel the same way and asked her daughter if she was starting to get worried about me.

"No, Mom," Phissy replied, "Ronnie wants too much out of life, and he knows that there's no one that can give it to him but himself."

Phissy still believed in me. In fact, she seemed to have more confidence in me than I had in myself. From the first time I met her, I had always come across with great self-confidence, but now my confidence was draining fast.

Just a few days later, Phissy saw a blind job ad for "The World's Largest Pen Company" in *The Miami Herald* classifieds. It turned out that the company that placed that ad was Bic, which actually was not so big then, but I appreciated the fact that they thought big. The ad required the applicant to send a letter to a box number at the newspaper. I applied and was granted an interview. When I showed up for the meeting, I was interviewed by Bill Clune, a Bic employee based in Philadelphia. He asked me how old I was. "Twenty-two," I replied. Bill closed his folder as he announced that the minimum age for the job was twenty-four.

Drawing on my sense of timing and remembering how as a ten-year-old I had "become" twelve to land my paperboy job, I reinvented myself again. Waiting half a beat, I shot back, "Okay, I'm twenty-four."

Once we agreed that I was the required age, we hit it off really well, and I thought I had the job. My stomach dropped when he said that while he'd like to hire me, he needed to interview some other candidates and would call me. Thinking of my nonexistent finances and very existent wife and baby, I told Bill that I couldn't wait long. We agreed that he would call me in three days.

He didn't call. My desperation increased. My cousin Jack Sherwood had been asking me for weeks to come work with him at his insurance brokerage firm, but I had resisted. Now I decided to relent and called him. Instead of meeting at his office on Monday morning, he asked me to join him on an 8:00 A.M. call to an elderly client.

We knocked on her door at 7:55 A.M. sharp. She cracked the door open a couple of inches, clearly not prepared for guests. She had forgotten the appointment. She asked if we could go to the nearby coffee shop and come back in forty-five minutes to give her time to dress.

Since Jack was buying, we sat at a booth and ordered breakfast. Just as I finished my scrambled eggs, Bill Clune walked over to my table. He had been sitting at the counter and saw us in the mirror that reflected all the booths.

Bill reintroduced himself as the guy who interviewed me at Bic. I am embarrassed to admit that I was rude. Behaving as though my financial disaster was his fault, I nearly snarled when I said, "I thought you were going to call me."

"Sorry, but I've been really busy," he said. "But, can I talk with you for a moment now?"

"It's too late," I snapped, then motioned to Jack. "I'm working with Jack Sherwood now."

Bill didn't budge. He asked, "Well then, can I meet you at one o'clock?"

I dug in my heels and said, "No! I'm with Jack now, and we have things to do! If I meet with you, you have to give me the job. I can't mess around anymore. I have a family to support."

We agreed that we'd meet at 1:00. By 1:05, I had the job.

I am a very pragmatic guy who doesn't usually speak in spiritual terms like "destiny" or "God's will," but in this case, who knows what cosmic forces were conspiring for my benefit and why? If Jack's client hadn't forgotten our appointment, we wouldn't have gone to the coffee shop. If

Bill's home had been Miami, he wouldn't have stayed in a motel around the corner from the coffee shop. And if none of us had been hungry, I might be selling insurance today.

Sometimes we come to crossroads without even realizing it. To paraphrase Yogi Berra: I came to the fork in the road and took it, but it had to stab me in the leg first to get my complete attention!

■

When I got the job at Bic, I beat out sixty-five other applicants and received $90 a week, which to me at that time was all the money in the world. My wife and I were thrilled, and I finally felt confident that I would be able to support my new family.

Now let me give a little background on Bic Pen. What is now the Bic Pen Company was launched in the United States after the French company Societe Bic S.A. acquired control of the Waterman Pen Company in 1958. Waterman was known as the inventor of the original fountain pen, in 1875. In 1960, following an extensive marketing test in Connecticut, the Bic ballpoint pen was introduced throughout the Northeast with tremendous success. In 1961 sales and distribution coverage were expanded to the Southeast when I joined the sales staff in Miami.

Thus, I joined Bic just as it was poised for rapid expansion. While today the Bic brand has become a household name, it wasn't always so well-known. In the early 1960s, the low-cost ballpoint pen market in North America was dominated by two brands—Scripto and Lindy.

Both Scripto and Lindy were selling an inexpensive pen in all distribution channels. Neither brand, however, did very much in the way of marketing. In this crowded field, Bic believed it could open new markets best through television advertising. First, a sales organization had to be hired. Bic told its salespeople to reach consumers wherever they shopped. Instead of using one blanket sales approach for all outlets, therefore, the company emphasized a variety of approaches. Though a consumer could purchase the same pen whether in a supermarket grocery chain or a national variety chain, the sales techniques used to persuade him or her to buy that pen in these different types of stores had to be very different.

As a result of this diverse sales philosophy, Bic chose not to hire salespeople with experience in selling pens. It is clear to me now that I was a good candidate to work for them.

Ironically, once I got hired, I assured my friends and family that this would only be a temporary thing, that soon I would have even a better job, since "everyone knows you can't make much money in the pen business." Little did I know that I would spend the rest of my life in that business.

■

Now that I had a "real" job, I was determined to run with it. On my second day at Bic, I stumbled.

I went to visit a small stationery store. I launched into an impassioned sales pitch to the owner. I did everything in the world I could possibly think of to get him to put up a display of Bic pens in his store. When it seemed as though I had finally won him over, he looked at me and said, "Okay, what kind of terms do you people have?"

I didn't know what he was talking about. I'd never heard the word *terms* used in this context before. Quite frankly, I'd never even been trained. The day before, Bill Clune had just given me a bag of samples and told me to go out and sell, sell, sell. And now, I didn't know what to do. I did know that I wanted to close this deal, and I didn't want to appear stupid.

So I looked him right in the eye and said, "Terms? We get along with everyone."

He burst out laughing. "Kid, you wouldn't by any chance be new at this, would you?"

I nodded and shrugged. This dealer was a nice man, and he felt sorry for me. So he gave me a little lesson.

"When I ask you," he said, "what kind of terms you have, I mean what kind of dating can you give me?"

"Oh, it really doesn't matter. Today's date, yesterday, tomorrow. Whatever you want."

He laughed again, and then he sat me down and taught me the meaning of dating and terms.

And the best part of it all was that he didn't cancel the order. I've always believed that if you want the order, you need to ask for it, and so, even though I was a novice salesperson, I didn't lose that order.

I'll admit I got lucky that time. As a salesperson I should have known my dating and terms. But I can assure you of this: From then on, I always knew the definition of all of my terms.

Chapter 11

TO STAND OUT, STAND UP

$\mathcal{T}$here was a priest I once knew by the name of Father Donnelly. His church desperately needed funds to renovate their old building. The church was in a poor part of town, however, and none of its members could afford to give any money.

So Father Donnelly turned to God. "Lord, please let me win the lottery this week, and I promise I will use all the money to renovate this house of yours."

But Father Donnelly did not win the lottery that week. So the next week, he turned to the Lord again: "Dear Lord, please, this week, let me win the lottery and I promise I will use the funds to glorify your name."

And again, Father Donnelly lost. Now desperate, he decided to try one last time. "LORD, PLEASE! I promise you, if you let me win the lottery this week, we will turn your church into one of the most beautiful places in the whole world."

Suddenly, thunder crashed, lightning struck across the sky, and God appeared to Father Donnelly, saying, "Father Donnelly, I'd love to help, but please, meet me halfway. Buy a ticket!"

■

At my first sales meeting at Bic, I was an ambitious young (twenty-two, posing as twenty-four) salesman. The credit manager, Moe Maloney, found out I used to be a comedian, so at the end of our big sales conference, he urged me to get on stage.

Now, I wouldn't recommend this to anyone else, but after so many years in show business I was very comfortable on stage, and I figured being in the spotlight might help jump-start my career. So, I grabbed the microphone. The company president, Bob Adler, was sitting right in front of me, and this was my big chance to make sure he knew who I was when our meeting was over that evening. There were a lot of new, young employees there, and I wanted to leave a lasting impression. So, I "bought a ticket" and started making jokes about him.

For example, though Bob is brilliant, he can sometimes be a bit caustic. I mentioned how his idea of a compliment is walking up to a young lady in the office and saying, "Oh, I see your face has cleared up!"

Everybody roared with laughter and I knew I was going to either lose my job right then and there, or be seen as a hot new up-and-comer.

Thankfully, Bob had a great sense of humor, and that night started me on a quick rise through the company. Bob sensed, I think, that if I had the confidence to stand in front of a large crowd and make jokes about everyone, including the head of the company, I had the confidence to sell Bic pens to anybody and everybody. And I did.

■

Starting out as assistant zone manager in Miami, I was soon winning sales contests and making a name for myself in the company. Shortly thereafter, I was promoted to Florida zone manager. Then, I was shifted to Atlanta to be zone manager for a region that encompassed parts of seven states. It was while we were living in Atlanta that our daughter, Susie, was born, May 27, 1962.

We'd been in Atlanta only eleven months when Bic started opening new regions. I am a nester and hate moving, but I understood that relocating was necessary for success in the corporate world. When I was offered the plum zone of Chicago, even though it meant another move, I knew I had to seize this opportunity. Chicago was a great territory because it was so densely populated. Instead of having to drive across seven southeastern states, now I'd never have to leave Cook County, Illinois.

We lived in Chicago for three years, until I was promoted to sales manager of the new North Central region in Detroit, Michigan. After three and a half years in Detroit, I was named national sales manager, and we moved to New Haven, Connecticut. One month later, on March 28, 1969, our third child, Alan, was born.

I attribute my ascendancy at Bic to several factors. I had a strong mentor in my immediate boss, Jack Paige, vice president of sales and marketing. Besides being a terrific boss, Jack was a bright, shining star in the Bic universe. His glow encompassed me and helped lift me through the ranks. I also made sure I remained visible in the company. I aggressively pursued every lead I was given, and I was always willing to pay my dues.

■

Looking back, though, I believe the single greatest factor was that I had a supportive wife who was always willing to endure one more geographic relocation and make one more personal sacrifice to help me on my way.

Chapter 12

IRWIN HELFORD'S FANATICAL CUSTOMER SERVICE

*A*n old friend of mine, Irwin Helford, went through a similar series of promotions and one geographic move to achieve great success as the CEO of Viking Office Products. As a young man in 1956, Irwin fell into the office supply industry right out of the Navy, joining a company in Chicago called Wilson Jones, then a manufacturer of many best-selling office products. At Wilson Jones, Irwin worked in shipping, customer service, and sales.

In 1960 the Reliable Stationery Company hired him as general manager to develop a new catalog and direct its mail-marketing program. He was also responsible for operations, the sales force, and telephone sales. At this time, Reliable's revenues were $700,000 a year. As Reliable's catalog sales started to take off, Irwin was promoted to VP of Marketing.

Twenty-three years later, under Irwin's leadership, Reliable's annual revenues were up to $40 million. In 1983 he was recruited away from Chicago by Los Angeles-based Viking Office Products. At the time, Viking's sales were stagnant at $15 million a year. Irwin had been living all his life in Chicago and never planned on moving. For years Reliable and Viking had been friendly competitors, but when Viking offered him complete authority to run the company, Irwin couldn't resist the challenge. So, he pulled up roots and moved to California.

Irwin joined Viking as president and later became CEO and chairman. He created all new merchandising, catalogs, distribution systems, and a radically innovative "Fanatical Customer Service" concept. Working with a great Viking team, Irwin pushed sales to $1.4 billion in 1997. In August 1998 Viking merged with Office Depot to form the world's largest distributor of office products, with combined revenues of $9 billion in nineteen countries. By the year 2000, Office Depot generated nearly $12 billion in revenues, including about $2 billion from its Viking subsidiary.

Irwin attributes Viking's phenomenal success to no single grand vision, but he can isolate three crucial factors. First, Viking committed to "Fanatical Customer Service," which did not exist in the office supply business before. "Fanatical Customer Service" simply means always doing more than the customer expects: no back orders, no substitutions, no mistakes, no misleading promises, and free same-day delivery for every order in twenty-one major U.S. and eleven overseas cities, and overnight delivery anywhere else. Viking's goal is to impress customers so much that they want to buy from Viking again. In other words, Viking aims to shock customers with its high level of service. As a result, Viking might not have the lowest prices in the industry, but they have the highest customer retention of any office supply company. And now with the rise of Internet sales, Viking is reaching even more customers.

The second key factor is Viking's extraordinary catalogs. The company now has no salesmen and no retail stores. Sales are generated purely by catalog marketing. At any given time, Viking offers dozens of different catalogs targeted at different market segments. Since 1984 its marketing team has developed databases that capture everything about its customers, including brand preferences, the equipment they use, how many times a year they order, and so on. Thanks to inkjet imaging, digital technology, and full-color printing, Viking can now custom print most of its catalogs. The buyer's name is incorporated directly into the copy, and the customized catalog features products Viking believes that customer will want at prices designed to trigger an order. As a result, even though it mails millions of catalogs, Viking still focuses on one customer at a time. That's what I call "Fanatical Customer Service."

The final element Irwin finds essential is the people he hires. He ensured that the company hired only particular kinds of people. If prospective hires couldn't demonstrate a deep caring for the customer, they were not Viking material. The company has no personnel or human resource department—the division in charge of hiring and firing is called the People Department. And once it hires someone, no matter at what level, the company shows great devotion to him or her. Employees are given special treatment, such as stock options, profit sharing, Thanksgiving turkeys, year-end bonuses, and more.

Viking has added branches in nine European countries, Australia, and Japan. International operations produce over two-thirds of Viking's total revenues, with greater returns and profitability than most major competitors. These principles of "fanatical service" to their customers and employees as well as highly advanced catalog marketing had never been seen in Europe before Viking introduced them. As a result, in recent years, growth and profitability have been even greater in Europe than in the

United States. And Irwin Helford is happy to report that Viking now has over two million loyal customers worldwide.

■

If you're not going to make a commitment to your customers and employees, you'll never achieve success.

Chapter 13

"IT'LL NEVER WORK"

*A*n old friend once went to a big business conference in Miami Beach. He was staying at a lovely, small beach hotel. He knew he was going to be in seminars all day, so he decided to get in a little exercise before the conference started.

Arriving at the swimming pool bright and early, he was delighted to find it empty; he would have the pool all to himself. As he walked to the edge, he noticed a little old man sitting on a chaise lounge.

"How's the water?" he asked him.

"Luke varm," replied the man in a Jewish accent.

He shrugged, threw off his towel, and dove into the pool. The water was freezing! He screamed and jumped out. He ran shivering over to the old man and said, through chattering teeth, "You call that lukewarm?! That water's like ice!"

The old man shrugged his shoulders at him. "Mister, I didn't even go in, but to me, it *luked varm.*"

■

It's important to be able to trust other people's opinions, but always be aware of who you're talking to and what their agendas are.

In 1972, it was my job at Bic to help introduce the Bic lighter to North America at the low price of $1.49. At that time, the number-one disposable lighter in the country was the Gillette Cricket. We were just a little pen company that had a share of the writing instrument market and no share of the disposable lighter industry. In fact, this lighter was the first nonpen product Bic introduced. We viewed the lighter as a logical extension of our current product line since it was inexpensive, disposable, and of high quality. Moreover, it could be easily marketed through most of the trade channels we had already established for our writing instruments. It really differed from our pens only in that it had twenty-one rather than seven basic assembly parts and, as a flammable object, was subject to government standards.

I'm proud to say that within a few years of the introduction of what would become known as the Bic Butane, we put the Cricket out of business. How did we do it? Well, obviously, launching any new product is a highly complex and risky mix of procedures, and a multitude of factors influence that product's success. But I heartily believe that the launch was what got the Bic Butane into people's hands across the country. Once we did that, the lighter started to sell itself.

In planning our launch, Jack Paige and I decided that we could not afford to let others tell us if the waters "looked warm." We had a limited budget at a time when the general consensus in the industry was that you needed a huge budget to market a new item. We understood this line of reasoning, but believed we had to dive into the market and check it out for ourselves. Thus, we initiated a thirteen-cities-in-fifteen-nights promotional tour around the country. Everybody told us it was crazy. "Too many cities in too short a time," they said again and again. "It'll never work."

We believed otherwise. In every city, we set up invitation-only cocktail/dinner parties for our best Bic Pen customers. I would warm up the crowd with a few jokes and a little shtick, then Jack would do a pitch for the Bic Butane. Customers were encouraged to bring their spouses. We invited the press and served everyone a fabulous free meal. Sure, it cost the company a pretty penny, but it was still a lot cheaper than a big ad campaign—and it was a lot more personal. We received tremendous press and did lots of interviews. Instead of an impersonal national media campaign, we were right there face-to-face with our buyers. We didn't take any orders at the cocktail parties; it was soft sell. We just wanted to create awareness and good will. Later on, we had our salesmen pursue the leads. Let me tell you, it wasn't hard for them, because all of our customers were already sold on the Bic Butane.

■

Conventional wisdom in a given industry needs to be tested, for if every player always heeded consensus thinking, the industry would stagnate. The prize goes to those whose actions *change* conventional wisdom.

Chapter 14

STARTING OVER

A group of businessmen go to Alaska to hunt moose. When they get to Juneau, they hire a young pilot with a Piper Cub to take them to the tundra where all the moose hang out. The pilot flies them a hundred miles into the tundra, and as soon as the businessmen get out, they see a huge moose standing right in front of them.

They take out their guns, and Bam! Bam! Bam! they bag their moose. The hunters are overjoyed, but the pilot is not happy. He tells them that his little plane won't be able to make it back with such a large, heavy moose. He suggests they just cut off the antlers and bring them back as souvenirs. But the businessmen want the whole moose. The pilot argues with them some more, but the hunters insist and slip the pilot an extra hundred bucks.

So they pack the moose into the little plane, and miracle of miracles, they are able to take off. Forty miles from Juneau, however, the plane gives out and nose-dives. The pilot executes a crash landing without anyone getting a scratch. They all get out of the plane, but only the pilot is scared and distraught. He looks up and sees the businessmen hugging and dancing with each other. "Guys, why are

you so happy?" the pilot asks. "It'll take us days to reach civ-
ilization now."

And one of the businessmen answers, "Yeah, but we
crashed twenty miles closer to Juneau this year than we did
last year!"

■

When you're faced with a challenge, you should embrace it
but also understand that each challenge comes with the
possibility of failure. When failure happens, as it will, never
allow it to get the best of you. Accept it, figure out why you
failed, and make sure it doesn't happen again.

The right attitude toward success and failure will ensure
your persistent efforts pay off. After many years of working
very hard at Bic and earning five promotions, for example, I
was suddenly and inexplicably let go. Well, I soon discovered
that my firing wasn't exactly inexplicable. There are a lot of
factors involved in the running of a large company. In my
case, the chairman, Marcel Bich, wanted to appoint his son
national sales manager to be in position to take over the company. Since that was my job, I had to be terminated.

So there I was, driving home Friday afternoon,
January 3, 1975, not knowing what I was going to do. My
daughter, Susie, was having a slumber party with a bunch of
other girls at our house that night, and I had promised to
take my older son, Steve, to a hockey game. I couldn't imagine how I would face or what I would say to either of them,
not to mention Phissy.

When I got home, I kept my mouth shut, sat at the dinner table with the family, wished the slumber party girls well, and went to the hockey game with Steve. When I returned home, I said goodnight to the kids and joined my wife in bed. I couldn't hold out any longer. Finally, I blurted out, "Bic fired me. I don't have a job. They gave me seven months' severance and when that runs out, I don't know how I am going to make the mortgage payments or what we are going to do."

Phissy was upset, but more for the anguish I was feeling than over me being out of a job. Her confidence in me gave her a very different point of view. She saw opportunity where I could only see despair.

"This is the chance you've waited your whole life for," she told me. "You've got seven paid months to fulfill your dream of finally having your own business. Think about it. Without a boss breathing down your neck, you are finally free to take risks."

She was right. For years, I had dreamt of running my own business. I always felt deep down that if I had come from a more affluent background or didn't have family obligations, I would have started my own company. Sure, when you're in your own business, there are no guarantees that you'll make it, but if things go bad, you know you'll be the last person to walk out the door. A person running his or her own business is in charge of his or her own destiny.

The more I thought about it, the more my sadness lifted. My wife was right. I had just been too wrapped up in my own ego and the shock of being fired for the first time to see for myself the vast opportunity that was now open to me.

I tried to envision opening my own company, but I felt the responsibilities of a mortgage, three children, and two orthodontist payments precluded such a risk. I knew I needed to find a new job.

Though I'd been fired from Bic, the Fates weren't quite done weaving pens into my professional life. Just as some cosmic force propelled me to Bic in 1961, I was nudged back toward the world of writing instruments. And I was just as stubborn in resisting destiny's nudges in 1975 as I had been in refusing Bill Clune's request for a meeting in that Miami coffee shop fourteen years earlier.

■

In the late sixties and early seventies, Pilot pens were sold in the United States by a franchised agent, a company in the South Bronx named Elta Industries. By 1972, their sales rose to $1 million a year, then hit a plateau.

In 1969, four months after Phissy, the kids, and I moved to Connecticut so I could take my fifth promotion at Bic, I met Bob Grodd. Bob was a roofer and owned Premiere Roofing Company with his brother. They eventually built that business into one of the biggest roofing companies east of the Mississippi. At any rate, Bob became one of my closest friends over the years.

About a year before Bic let me go, Bob and his wife went to a resort in Puerto Rico for a respite from the cold. While sitting by the pool, they met Harold Rosenberg, a fellow vacationer. Harold was one of three partners who owned Elta Industries. The Grodds and Rosenbergs exchanged the usual where-are-you-from, what-do-you-do niceties. When Bob discovered that Harold was from New York and in the pen business, he naturally asked, "Do you know Ron Shaw at Bic?" Harold said that we had met (although I have no recollection of meeting him). They exchanged business cards. Once home, Bob put Harold's card in his desk and forgot about it.

Despite Phissy's belief that my being fired was an opportunity instead of a tragedy, I still felt wretched. I called Bob that first weekend and told him the bad news. Bob showed up at our door to lend his support and throw in his indignant "How could they! They're fools!" and a couple of other phrases best not to print. He also said that when he was in Puerto Rico the previous year he met a guy in the pen business. He volunteered to give him a call if I wanted. I may have just had the wind knocked out of me, but I found my show-business chutzpa quickly enough. While moving up at Bic I had met a lot of people in top positions at strong companies, I told Bob. I was pretty certain that with a few phone calls and interviews I'd land on my feet. I told Bob, thanks but no thanks. I'd be fine.

Soon after Bic let me go, a small story appeared in *The Wall Street Journal* and the business section of *The New York Times*. Bic was publicly held then, and certain activities had to be reported. The company had distributed a news release announcing my departure and diplomatically reporting that I was "pursuing other interests." That same day I received a phone call from Mr. Ryouhei Yamada, the president of Pilot Corporation of America, makers of fountain and other pens. He said Pilot wanted to reclaim the rights to sell their pens directly in the United States, doing away with the franchise arrangement. He asked if we could meet. I had interviews lined up with a few large companies and didn't want to waste time with some obscure pen outfit. I politely told Mr. Yamada that I wasn't interested.

A couple of weeks and several interviews later, Mr. Yamada called again. Pilot needed a sales and marketing director, and he asked if we could meet. I had new interviews scheduled with major corporations and was confident I'd find a big job with one of them. For the second time, I told Mr. Yamada that I wasn't interested.

By the end of February, I had no written job offers from any of the large companies I liked. Though I had five months of severance remaining, I was getting anxious. Plus, I like to work and was restless. Bob came over for a social visit and said he had found that pen guy's business card, then handed it to me. I noted that Harold Rosenberg's company represented Pilot pens and told Bob about Mr. Yamada's phone calls. Bob convinced me to let him call Harold.

By the time of Bob's call, Elta Industries and Pilot Corporation had reached an agreement that would return all rights to sell Pilot pens in the United States to Pilot Corporation of America. According to the terms, Elta's three partners would do very well as long as Pilot did well. Harold now had greater incentive to make Pilot sales break that $1 million plateau. After Bob talked with Harold, Harold called Mr. Yamada to tell him about this great pen salesman who was available. Mr. Yamada told Harold that he had already called me twice and couldn't get a meeting. Harold called me and pressed me to at least meet him and

Mr. Yamada in Manhattan for lunch. Since I had no job offers and my prospects were narrowing, I agreed. They launched a hard sell during our meal. I agreed to a second meeting at Pilot's facility in Long Island City in Queens.

A stage set designer creating a dingy work environment could have used this place as the model. Pilot's entire operation in America occupied a windowless five-thousand-square-foot former taxi garage. The neighborhood was grimy, the building was gloomy, and it was a two-and-a-half-hour trip from our house in Connecticut. However, I knew the pen business and became intrigued by the challenge of taking this little-known company stuck at $1 million in sales and building it into something much larger. I wouldn't have Jack Paige or anyone else to mentor me; I'd have to go the distance on my own. I wasn't thrilled about the commute and didn't want to move again, but Mr. Yamada agreed that if I could lift sales up to $10 million, Pilot would move to Connecticut.

■

Fourteen months after Bob Grodd sat beside a pool in Puerto Rico and exchanged business cards with a stranger, I was back in the pen business.

Chapter 15

TAKING RISKS
IN ADVERTISING

Sitting on the side of the highway waiting to catch speeding drivers, a state highway patrol officer sees a car puttering along at twenty-two miles an hour. He thinks to himself, "This driver is just as dangerous as a speeder!" He turns on his flashing lights and pulls the driver over.

Approaching the car, he notices there are five old ladies inside—two in the front seat, and three in the back—all wide-eyed and white as ghosts. The driver, obviously confused, says to him, "Officer, I don't understand. I was going exactly the speed limit! What seems to be the problem?"

"Ma'am," the officer replies, "you weren't speeding, but you should know that driving slower than the speed limit can also be a danger to other drivers."

"Slower than the speed limit? No, Sir, I was doing the speed limit exactly—twenty-two miles an hour!" she says proudly as she points to a sign beside the road.

The highway patrol officer, trying to contain a chuckle, explains to her that "22" was the route number, not the speed limit.

A bit embarrassed, the woman grins and thanks the officer for pointing out her error.

"But before I let you go, Ma'am, I have to ask—is everyone in this car okay? Those women in the back seat seem awfully shaken, and they haven't uttered a peep the whole time."

"Oh, they'll be all right in a minute, Officer," she answers. "We just got off Route 116."

■

It's easy to get caught up in your own mindset, to rely too heavily on the "we're right, they're wrong" mentality. You must always be aware that just because people don't interpret things the way you do, their alternative ideas are still worth considering. Hell, *you* might be wrong. And once you give credence to other notions, those new concepts just might help you speed past the competition.

During my business life I've seen this phenomenon many times. When I first joined Pilot Pen, for example, I wanted to run a national advertising campaign. I say "national" in that I wanted to put a few small ads here and there in national magazines. Keep in mind, Pilot had hit a $1 million sales plateau in the United States, and we had no advertising budget. So I went to Japan to ask the chairman of the board to free up $75,000 to buy ads in regional editions of magazines like *Time* and *Newsweek* for our new ad campaign.

Picture this: I'm in the chairman's office in Tokyo making my pitch. The head of the company is nodding and smiling at everything I say; he can't look more pleased with my presentation. Having never been to Japan, I assume I'm doing great and will definitely close the deal.

Then, at the end of the presentation, the chairman stands up, expresses profuse admiration for my intentions, and says, "Shaw-San, this is a wonderful plan. Now, go back to America and sell enough pens so that you have enough profits to afford to do this advertising!"

Needless to say, I was very disappointed. I returned to the United States, borrowed the $75,000 we needed, and launched the company's first ad campaign. Borrowing money from a bank for an ad campaign is very risky, and I wouldn't recommend it to anyone. However, I believed in the campaign so deeply that I went forward. I always advise businesspeople that, if they believe so deeply in the concept or product they're pushing that they would spend their own money on marketing it, then, in these extreme cases, they should just go for it.

And so we did. But what was it that made me believe so deeply in Pilot pens? That first "national" ad campaign I so desperately wanted would sell Pilot's Razor Point pen. When I first joined the company, the Razor Point was our second-best seller, but that wasn't really saying much since overall sales were so low. Our problem was that the average consumer saw the Razor Point as a niche pen used only by architects and other design specialists, a technical writing instrument. I saw the Razor Point as a truly unique product that should be enjoyed by a wide array of consumers, and so we started to market it across the board.

Now, to be honest, at this point Pilot was struggling to gain a foothold in North America. The company was an industry leader in Japan, but its American division was near bankruptcy. We were a small company that hardly anybody knew about in the American pen market, and my mandate was to grab as much market share as possible. I spent much of my time and energy in those first years with Pilot on advertising, public relations, and marketing. After a concerted promotional push, we were able to make the Razor Point a huge seller that appealed to consumers engaged in all different professions. We convinced the public that anyone can write with an extra fine point pen. And within a year or two the massive sales of Razor Points proved to be the key factor that saved Pilot from extinction in North America.

Sure, it was a risky proposition to try to market a so-called specialty product beyond its known market. In the end, though, my intuition proved correct. There really was a market beyond engineers for the Razor Point, but that market had to be educated. That's what our marketing campaign did, and that's how the Razor Point and Pilot grabbed its fair share of the American pen business. Sometimes the key to making your company a success is already in the company.

■

When I started at Pilot I had many years' experience selling pens and over a decade of experience in show business. So when we created that first advertising campaign, I opted to use humor. At that time, many companies shied away from humor in their advertising, but I knew how powerful it is when done properly. We had this niche pen, the Razor Point, and humor might just be the key to make it known and accepted by all consumers.

I knew that if we could use humor, not comedy, we could sell a lot of pens. That is, rather than go for the big laugh that would obscure the product, we promoted our pens by making the reader or viewer smile and think. From day one, my goal with advertising has always been to create consumer recall and retention, and I knew that the key to both was making the consumer feel good.

We entered the print advertising arena with something a bit unconventional. We bought a full-page ad, with half of the page devoted to the headline, "Is it sick to love a pen?" The other half showed a woman lying on a couch in a psychiatrist's office, telling the doctor seated behind her that she fears she's gone out of her mind over love for her pen. Her doctor assures her that there is nothing abnormal with her as long as the pen she has fallen in love with is a Pilot.

■

Using humor as we did in this campaign is always risky, because people respond to it in different ways. But we believed the benefits far outweighed any potential downside. And the results proved our instincts correct. This campaign, developed by ad executives Don Aaronson and Stan Pearlman, owners of AMS Advertising, was wildly successful. The comedic take we employed really helped Pilot get good product attention and retention.

It wasn't a campaign intended to produce belly laughs, nor did it, but it was cute, and it allowed us to take a little-known product, the Razor Point, and turn it into a best-seller. In addition, it helped us take a relatively unknown company in America—Pilot—and turn it into a recognized brand name.

∎

When you're driving on the highway, it's important to pay attention to the speed limit. In business and life, however, it's often necessary to break the rules and take risks to move forward.

Chapter 16

TO SELL TO THE HEAD, SPEAK TO THE HEART

*A*n old friend was doing fund-raising and had been given a list of wealthy people and the charities, if any, they'd contributed to. He was encouraged to call those who were not currently supporting any specific cause. One of the people he called was particularly rude and grumpy on the phone. The records showed that this grumpy man had done very little for charitable causes. When my friend pointed this out to him, the grump got very angry.

"Well," the grump shouted, "do your records also show that I've got an old feeble mother? Do your records show that I have a brother who is out of work and that I have a sister with two kids who was abandoned by her husband? And if I don't help them, why should I help you?"

■

Some people are by nature generous while others are by nature stingy. Some are moved by their feelings while others appear to lack them. The older I get, the more convinced I am that we can't change others' natures. Whether working as a comedian, salesman, or CEO, however, I have tried to *understand* human nature. My livelihood has depended on developing deep insight into how people think, work, and behave. The better that understanding, the better my choices are and the more I can do to build our company.

I learned one of my most valuable lessons about human nature when I was at Bic. At that time, we were selling the Bic fine-point stick pen with a yellow barrel for twenty-nine cents. In an effort to stimulate sales, we started making it in white plastic in addition to the yellow. We used the same molds, added a little metal clip that probably cost one-tenth of a cent more and charged forty-nine cents for what was the identical pen. And it sold like crazy!

A close friend liked the white pen better than the yellow one. It got to the point where she'd write only with the white one, not the yellow one anymore. She believed the white one was better. I tried to explain they were identical pens, but there was no use. What can you do?

Nothing, except sell more pens! I came to understand that people respond to the way a pen looks, feels, and writes as well as its point size, ink color, and type of ink. It's quite common for people to pick out a pen for logical reasons, then "fall in love" with it for purely emotional reasons. Let's face it, out of all of the everyday office supplies—paperclips, scissors, staplers—pens are personal. They are held in our hands for great lengths of time, placed in our pockets, carried in our purses and briefcases, laid on our desks, and placed within reach of our phones. Pens are presented as gifts, used with flourish in ceremonial signings, and some are even passed down from generation to generation. With pens we write love letters, make lists of baby names, and sketch plans for dream houses. Pens are fundamental tools for satisfying the human need to express ourselves personally and be understood. Once someone discovers a pen that feels good in the hand and writes smoothly, a sort of zealous loyalty is born.

■

Many people will write with only their favorite brand of pen. That's why in the large office supply stores brand names dominate the pen aisle. Most of the tens of thousands of items in these stores—paper, folders, toner, tape—consumers view as commodities. Brand has little impact on purchasing decisions. But for pens, brand matters. For that reason, in our advertising we strive to appeal to the heart as well as the head. Emotions and logic are interwoven. That's human nature.

Chapter 17

THE BIG PICTURE
INCLUDES
DETAILS

*O*ne afternoon when I had a few hours to kill before a performance in Miami, I went to the beach to get some sun. Pretty soon, a woman with a beautiful little boy set up an umbrella and spread out a blanket. She rubbed sunscreen on the boy, placed a hat on his head, and told him to stay within sight of Mommy. She stretched out on her blanket and watched her son run to the water's edge. Suddenly, a huge wave came out of nowhere and swept the child away.

The woman screamed in horror and ran into the water after him, but it was too late. The little boy was gone, carried beneath the waves. She sank to her knees, threw her head back, and pleaded to the heavens, "Please, God. He was my only child. My pride and joy. Bring him back to me and I'll be forever indebted to you. I'll go to church every Sunday. I'll do anything if I can just have my baby back."

And then, suddenly, lightning bolted, thunder boomed, and a gigantic wave crashed onto the shore, depositing the child, unharmed, at her feet.

The woman picked up her boy, glanced down at him for a second, and then stared up at the heavens and said, "Um, excuse me, Lord . . . HE HAD A HAT!"

Of course it's crucial to pay attention to the big picture, but in business, you also have to be insistent about the details. When I worked as a comedian, I learned from the masters to hone my act to perfection, or at least try to get as close to it as possible. After I left show business, I learned to apply that discipline offstage, too.

Let me give you an example. While at Bic Pen, I went into the office of my boss, Jack Paige. Jack played a major role in increasing Bic's sales volume from $1.3 million in 1960 to $120 million in 1976. Jack received many awards for his business acumen, including Outstanding Corporate Marketing Executive of the Year by the Gallagher Poll and New England Marketing Executive of the Year.

Jack had an open-door policy, and I had a great idea that I wanted to share with him. "Jackson (we used nicknames for each other), why don't we put out a red and green Bic pen Christmas-stocking-stuffer blister pack featuring a smiling Santa on the package?"

I was convinced this would sell big-time during the Christmas season. Now, you have to understand that at this time in the business, pens were all sold individually, so there was no precedent for a multipack of pens.

Jack looked at me, smiled, and said, "Sorry, Buddy Boy. It's not gonna fly. Forget it. What are all the stores going to do with all the multipacks left over on December 26th?"

He was right. I left his office, disgruntled and depressed. But only a few hours later, he called me back in and said, "Ron, what if the Santa was perforated?"

"Excuse me?" I didn't know what he was talking about.

"Think about it, Buddy Boy. If we perforate the Santas on the multipack, then the day after Christmas, the dealers can just rip Santa off the card and they can continue to sell their stock of our multipacks instead of sending them back to us."

I smiled and looked at him. Of course, he was right. And, the perforated-Santa Christmas stocking stuffer multipack went on to become a huge seller. I had a good idea, but I still had not spent enough time thinking through the details. Fortunately, I was working with Jack, who had the vision to custom tailor what I was trying to do and make it into a real winner. Jack's marketing brilliance was one of the biggest factors in Bic's meteoric success in America.

■

Another great example of paying attention to the details in the big picture comes from Bob Adler, former president of Bic Pen. Bob deserves tremendous credit for what he did with Bic in North America. Bob helped Bic emerge from the residue of a deficit-ridden company, and over a short period of time in the extremely competitive low-priced sector of the pen industry, he helped make Bic number one. Bob attributed his success to "numerous and good management decisions based on forty percent science and sixty percent intuition."

Bob's story is a great American success story. Following his graduation from the Wharton School of Business in 1955, he reported for his first day of work as a junior accountant at the old Waterman Pen Company. The day before, the Naugatuck River had flooded the plant and when Bob showed up, instead of being shown to his desk, he was handed a shovel and told to help clean out the mud that had collected on the floor of the plant. Nine years later at the age of thirty-one, Bob Adler was named president of Bic.

He immersed himself in every aspect of the company and became conversant with every detail. He regularly walked around the plant, always remaining visible and accessible to the employees. He referred to statistics, but always valued human instinct above numbers.

In keeping with those values, when Bob hired new managers, he always seemed to accord more weight to aggressiveness and instinct than academic credentials. In fact, I think he preferred hiring people like me who were unfamiliar with the industry so that he could help influence us. A new hire who has never worked in your specific industry is a clean slate that you can imprint and mold with the company's values without interference from preconceptions.

■

In terms of leadership, Bob stressed to me that a leader gets paid to make decisions. In many instances, there is really only one way to go. In these cases, making the decision is the easy part. The hard part happens after the decision is made. What's important then is that a leader be present to insure that the decision turns out right. The decision is not so important as the outcome. Many people fail to understand this concept. At Bic, Bob followed up his hiring decisions with training that enhanced the employee's opportunity to succeed with the company. He had a clear vision of the big picture yet kept his eyes on the details.

Chapter 18

THE POWER OF GOALS

A guy who was crazy about golf was having trouble with his game and went all over the city looking for a course that suited him. One day, he showed up at a brand new public course. There was a big line to get on the course, and he was in a rush. So, he introduced himself to a group of three Baptist ministers who needed a fourth. The ministers were happy to include him, and onto the course they went.

Three hours later, this guy was shocked and amazed. The three ministers had shot 69, 70, and 71, while he had shot 109. He had to ask, "Excuse me, but what's your secret?"

One of the ministers walked over to him and said, "We are very religious men, son, and since we lead such pure and simple lives, God rewards us with great golf games."

The golf fiend took what the minister said to heart and joined the church. He got baptized and went religiously, obeying all the precepts and praying fervently.

A year later, he bumped into the three ministers again at the same course. They agreed to shoot another round of eighteen with him.

Three hours later, the results were the same as the year before. The ministers shot 69, 70, and 71, while the golf fiend shot another 109.

He was exasperated and said to one of the ministers, "I don't understand it. I got baptized and went to church religiously, and still I've gotten no better."

The minister looked at him and said, "May I ask, son, what church did you get baptized in?"

"Trinity Baptist Church."

All the ministers nodded and laughed. Then, one of them put his arm around the golf fiend and said, "Sorry to tell you this, son, but Trinity Baptist is for tennis."

■

It's important to define goals for yourself as well as for the people in your company. If you don't, you might end up with a lot of people working very hard and still achieving very little. Avoid this type of frustrating situation by always making sure that the organization's goals are clearly delineated to all.

In the early 1960s the Bic Pen Corporation was an unknown French firm trying to sell an unknown brand of pens in North America. By 1974, Bic had almost 70 percent of the U.S. market, distributing more than 2 million writing instruments per day through more than 200,000 retailers. When I was assistant zone manager in 1961, Bic was selling 8 million units a year. By 1974, Bic was selling 2.5 million units a day. Everyone had said that:

A. Bic couldn't sell 5,000 feet of writing in one unit and succeed ("5,000 feet of writing in one unit" means that one pen contains enough ink to write a line that is 5,000 feet long).

B. Bic couldn't have the biggest sales force in the writing instrument industry and make money.

C. Bic couldn't advertise a nineteen-cent pen on TV and turn a profit.

The naysayers were wrong. Bic achieved all of those goals and was on top. There were many reasons for its success, including the leadership of President Bob Adler, VP of Marketing Jack Paige, and Treasurer Alex Alexiades. I'd like to think that I also had a small hand in Bic's success. I believe that one thing I did well during my Bic years was clearly articulating and emphasizing the branding of Bic pens through the power of personal selling efforts, backed up by sales promotion activities. Our sales force was the largest in the industry. As I mentioned earlier, when Bic initially developed its sales force, management avoided hiring people with experience in pen sales because they did not want salespeople to start out with preconceived ideas about how to sell pens. Rather than allowing each salesperson in a territory to call on all types of customers, Bic's sales force was organized so that each salesperson specialized in selling to only certain types of institutions in a specific marketing channel. For example, in the New York metropolitan area, Bic had one or more salesmen who specialized in selling to only one of the following types of customers:

✍ Wholesalers for independent retail drug and sundry outlets

✍ Drug and variety chain stores

✍ Food wholesalers and retailers

✍ Commercial users and office suppliers

✍ Premium and specialty advertising suppliers

Although this degree of specialization is unorthodox for selling a one-product line, we believed that our specialized selling efforts were a major element in achieving our large market share. To augment our personal selling efforts, Jack Paige also instituted the use of premiums as a sales promotion method to entice both trade and commercial buyers to purchase in large quantities. Each of these tactics was part of the company's overall strategy to achieve specific goals.

When I joined Pilot, I used a goal-setting management style to lift sales above the $1.2 million plateau. It's still effective and today reaches beyond the sales and marketing teams to each of our employees.

■

In addition to setting goals, you need to create plans of action. They will help you achieve your goals without missing steps or jeopardizing the company. One plan I hope you'll never need is a crisis management plan. When a crisis hits, as it may, turning to a prepared plan will insure that you know what to do, how to do it, and when to do it—knowledge especially valuable when you're under attack. We are judged not by how we handle simple and easy situations, but how we manage under fire. Setting goals and establishing plans for the best is good leadership; preparing for the worst is smart leadership.

Chapter 19

LISTEN TO YOUR INSTINCTS

A friend of mine recently retired and finally fulfilled his dream of running a sheep ranch. One day he was overseeing his grazing flock when a new, fancy sport utility vehicle crested the hill and stopped beside him in a cloud of dust. Out climbed an impeccably dressed man in a perfectly tailored suit who walked up to my friend.

"Shepherd," the stranger said, addressing my friend, "if I can guess how many sheep you have grazing on this hillside, will you give me one of your animals?"

Stunned by his bravado, my friend said yes.

The stranger opened the passenger door, set up a laptop and portable printer, aimed an antennae skyward and hooked up to a satellite that beamed down on the flock. He worked the keyboard and within a few moments printed out a 27-page report with color charts. The stranger placed the report in a folder, presented it to my friend, and announced, "Shepherd, you have 1,638 sheep grazing in your flock today."

My friend looked at him in astonishment and said that was precisely correct! Whereupon the stranger swept up one of the animals and put it in the back of his vehicle. As he was about to drive off, my friend called out "Sir, I have a proposition for you. If I can guess your occupation, may I have my animal back?"

Stunned himself, the stranger replied, "All right."

Without hesitation my friend announced, "You're a consultant." The stranger's jaw dropped, then he asked, "How did you know?"

My friend said, "There are three reasons. First, you stuck your nose into my business uninvited. Second, it's clear that you know nothing about me or my business. Third, you better take my dog out of your truck!"

■

It's tempting to turn to outside professionals who promise they can provide insights into your business. Sometimes their fresh perspectives can uncover overlooked opportunities. However, examples abound of companies that relied on "experts" to expand their business in places where they did not belong. So that I will never forget this, I carry three famous market research reports with me: the report on the Edsel, New Coke, and Real cigarettes. For each of these products more research was done in their respective product categories than had ever before been done. Ford invested a record amount of money in research to bring us the Edsel, which failed miserably. Coke, the leader in the soft drink world, spent a fortune on research for New Coke— and what happened? It was instantly rejected. R.J. Reynolds spent millions on researching why the so-called "healthy" cigarette—the Real cigarette—couldn't fail and yet, IT FLOPPED!

In the end, the only people who made money from each of these new products were the research companies who convinced a few insecure CEOs that they had to be armed with piles of papers and statistics before they walked into their boardrooms and pitched their new product ideas to their boards. Sure, sometimes research is helpful, but in general I believe it is a CEO's job to rely on feel-and-touch instinct. There is always the chance of a flop, and nobody can have a perfect track record with every product; but businesspeople must never get so caught up in their research that they lose touch with their own instincts. Scan the research if you feel so compelled, but in the end, go with your instincts—they put you where you are.

Indeed, any truly honest businessman will admit that no matter what the research says, nobody can know for sure how any product will sell. In 1973, for example, Xerox Corporation had the ALTO personal computer with user interface complete with windows and icons. It even had a primitive plug-in mouse. Xerox also had developed software that allowed the user to do word processing, spreadsheets, and desktop publishing.

But the people at Xerox failed to see the value of these products and didn't pursue them. Instead, they stayed focused on copying machines. Meanwhile, Apple's Steve Jobs made a fortune by capitalizing on the icon and window concepts and incorporating them into Apple products. Bill Gates's Microsoft Corporation ended up with all the word-processing software rights incorporated now into Microsoft Word.

It's simple to look at Xerox in retrospect and wonder how they could have fumbled so badly. It's easy to say they mismanaged or should have marketed their products differently. But in 1973 they saw their future in copying machines and not personal computers, and thus, they thought it would be more financially viable to pursue that portion of the industry.

Most companies are like Xerox in that regard. There is only a limited amount of money available for marketing. Corporate leaders and bean counters must determine where to push those funds and ad dollars, and all the while, everyone is praying they've made the right choices and pushed in the right direction.

At Pilot, we are in the same situation. Now take our Razor Point pens—please! (My apologies to the great comedian Henny Youngman.) They are huge sellers in America, but were a big flop in Canada. How do you explain that? To be honest, we can't. We have just accepted these market realities and we acted accordingly.

■

So, if you have the opportunity to make marketing decisions, remember that regardless of any market research and statistics, it's your job that is on the line, and you have to obey your gut instincts to either forge ahead or sit tight. If you know your industry, go with what you know and fight for what you believe in.

■

Another realm where instincts come into play is personnel, otherwise known as human resources. I personally interview and make the final decision to hire those executives in our company who report directly to me. After years of experience, I've noticed a few things. First, there are inevitably certain people who interview well but, once they start working, prove to be very different from the image they projected in their interview. In order to keep this from happening to us, I used to be able to call as references people who previously supervised or employed the applicant. Now, however, in our highly litigious age, a court can hold one liable for giving a positive or a negative reference; so I find that personal references are suspect because many people are scared to give frank opinions. In fact, our attorneys have instructed us to give only specific dates of employment when we are called as references and not to offer any opinion about the former employee's performance—good or bad—in order to avoid a potential lawsuit.

So then, in the last analysis, I hire by instinct. As a salesman I had to be able to read people, and I think over the years I've proven to be a pretty good judge of character. An MBA has value, but I prefer to look for more important attributes like common sense, the way applicants handle themselves, and their attention span (for example, during the interview, at what point does it seem like their minds start to wander?). Also, I always consider physical appearance. This might seem a little old-fashioned, but I've found that, especially for marketing people, there is a definite correlation between the way people look and their marketing ability. It's a simple matter of pride in appearance that translates into confidence.

The final "trick" I have learned to use over the years is, if the candidates make it to the third meeting, I will frequently ask them to bring their spouses along for a dinner interview. At first some people are taken aback by this request. I am not interested in interviewing the spouse, but I've found that the spouse is a wonderful barometer of who the applicant is. I intuitively feel that choice of a life partner reflects a person's nature in a fundamental way. I am the first to admit that hiring still has a lot of mystery to it. I can do everything right and yet not have a person who fits into the company. But at least by employing these tools and rules, I feel that the majority of the people I hire are those who are best suited for working for us.

Firing people, on the other hand, is the hardest thing I have to do. One specific incident comes to mind from my days as national sales manager at Bic. This is a hard-to-believe but true story. One of Bic's own salespeople was sending anti-Semitic letters to the company with his signature on them. Bob Adler, the president and CEO, happened to be Jewish and was very disturbed by these letters. It's bad enough to receive anonymous anti-Semitic threats from the public, let alone signed notes from an employee.

Bob called me into his office and we devised a strategy. Bob believed that as sales manager, I should act on this matter but not act too rashly or harshly. I felt this employee could be reformed, so I took charge and spent time meeting with him, trying to tell him that this kind of activity was simply unacceptable. I went out of my way to do everything possible to squelch his intolerance, but as one might expect, the letters kept coming.

Finally, after weeks of meeting with this salesman, I felt that we had no recourse and couldn't afford to wait any longer; this guy's employment had to be terminated. Upon being informed of his firing, our disgruntled salesman took off in his company car. Now, technically, this made his car stolen property. He had to give the car back to us, and turn in his samples, which were still in the vehicle. Fortunately, he drove straight to his house, where the police were able to find him and get our property back.

We thought that was the end of the matter, but the following Sunday morning our former salesman went to church with his family. During the service, he excused himself to go to the men's room. Instead of going to the men's room, however, he walked behind the church and put a bullet through his head.

It was naturally very difficult for his family and friends to deal with his suicide. For a long time I wondered if I could have handled his situation differently and thereby helped avert this tragedy. In the end, I've come to realize that we had no alternative and acted appropriately. If he had stayed at the company any longer as his mental health deteriorated, he may have harmed employees or even members of his family.

While telling someone that he or she is no longer employed is the worst part of being a boss, this incident has caused me to bring even more sensitivity to these meetings. For example, when I or one of our managers have to let someone go, we tell that person on a Monday or Tuesday. This gives the person the balance of the week to start looking for a new job and some feeling of control over his or her work life. We never fire employees on a Friday, because we don't want them anguishing over their misfortune over the weekend.

In all but a few states, there is no such thing as firing at will anymore. Any job termination must be accompanied by a long paper trail documenting all the employee's work deficiencies that led to his or her termination. In my experience, when I recognize someone needs to go, I usually give the employee another chance, and invariably, I am stung by this inclination. So, no matter how hard I try to safeguard their jobs; soon enough I have to let them go anyway.

■

Since I was abruptly fired at Bic, I have had a sensitivity to the havoc an unforeseen termination can inflict on an individual and his or her family, emotionally as well as financially. As a result, if a job termination must take place, it must be done in the most sensitive and humane way possible.

Chapter 20

YOUR GREATEST ASSETS

$\mathcal{T}$here once was an old Pakistani woman who worked as a water carrier for a rich man. She had two large pots that she carried on a pole. One of the pots was in perfect condition, the other had a crack in it.

Every day the water carrier went to the well, filled her pots, and carried them back to the master's house. However, along the way, water would leak out of the cracked pot so that by the time she reached her master's house it was only half-full.

This went on for many years until one day the cracked pot said to her miserably, "I'm so ashamed of myself. For years you have been carrying water in me and when we arrive at your master's house only half the water remains. You have only one-and-a-half pots of water, though you started out with two full pots. I'm just not very good at what I do."

The water carrier told the pot to cheer up and to look at the flowers on the side of the road the next time they went to the well.

The cracked pot did as she said and noticed that there were beautiful flowers all along the side of the road. He expressed his admiration to the water carrier, but said, "The flowers are beautiful, but they still don't make me feel better about being able only to deliver half a pot of water."

"But look at the other side of the road," said the water carrier. The cracked pot looked and saw that there were no flowers on that side. "You see," said the water carrier, "I took advantage of the water leaking out of you and planted seeds down your side of the road. Every day you have watered them, and I have been able to pick them and put fresh flowers on my master's table. If you had not been just the way you are, he would not have these beautiful flowers in his house."

■

Many of us are quick to see our shortcomings, yet we're often reluctant to recognize the importance of our strengths. I spend a great deal of my time paying attention to the morale and well-being of those whose strengths contribute to our company every day, our employees. They truly are our greatest assets, and I think of them not just as members of our company, but as people with families, needs, and dreams. I want Pilot to be a pleasant, safe, and happy place to work because when our employees thrive, the company prospers.

For this reason, we work a thirty-five-hour week, either 7:30 to 3:30 or 8:30 to 4:30, with an hour off for lunch. Really! Instead of offering meditation rooms, foosball, or chair massages, I recognize that our employees have lives away from their jobs and should have the time and energy to live them. When they are at work, I want them to be comfortable. For example, when I was the number-two person at Pilot and we were building our Trumbull,

Connecticut facility, I had the architect add air conditioning to the warehouse, even though the costs of installation and operation were daunting. I could not ask our employees to labor in a sweat box during the summer while the rest of us worked in air-conditioned offices.

When you treat your employees well, there is no limit to the contribution they can make to your company. Day after day it becomes more apparent that you cannot have tunnel vision about the roles employees—and customers— have in your business. Many of them have valuable ideas they will share with you if you will only listen. Your business can't help but profit.

For instance, we have an employee suggestion box and any suggestion that we put into practice means an extra $100 for the person who offered the idea. I also like to read the letters we receive from customers so I can be attuned to their requests and frustrations. One customer gave me a strong reminder of how attached people become to our pens. Though our Razor Point pen is no longer our bestseller, we continue to manufacture it because it has such strong brand loyalty. However, we decided to limit distribution of the red ink version. Before too long, I received a scathing letter from a customer who used a red ink Razor Point every day to do *The New York Times* crossword puzzle. I immediately sent him a dozen red-ink Razor Points and was reminded of the loyalty our pens command.

Everybody wants to be a CEO, but the decisions you make once you are in a position of authority can have long-term ramifications that affect the lives of many people for years to come.

Much of life is a function of perspective and attitude. It's easy to get down on yourself and your company when things aren't going well, but it's more valuable to look around, regroup, and take definitive steps to make things work better. Let me illustrate this concept with a specific story about our sales force. For decades, we had relied on manufacturer's reps to sell our pens to all our outlets. The sales reps had done a great job for us, but I sensed it was time for a change. I knew we could do better with our own sales force.

So in 1988, when our sales reached $57 million, we decided to give up our sales reps. The reps were growing older and wealthier and were losing the energy and drive of earlier years. We figured we were getting about one-eighth of their selling time, and very few of the reps were willing to handle extra sales-building chores such as making personal consumer calls. In other words, it was time for a change.

Consequently, we decided to replace our one hundred reps with a forty-person in-house sales force to gain increased control over our sales effort. I have always believed that control is the key to managing one's future, and so we actively pursued taking back *control.*

However, this type of large transition always comes with many possible disastrous ramifications. We opted to move very carefully. We started not with an abrupt change but a full six-month transitional period. We were also very concerned about the potential backlash from the sales reps. We didn't want the company to have to suffer any economic recriminations. In addition, we didn't want these people to feel they were being replaced because of their failures and, as a result, believe we were doing damage to their reputations. Our sales reps had been a major contributor to our growth and we wanted to make sure everybody knew that. And lastly, I was sensitive to the fact that angry ex-sales reps can do tremendous damage to a company's reputation. Simply put, we were extremely careful to avoid giving anyone a good reason to badmouth us, especially to our key accounts.

We implemented the transitional strategy accordingly.

1. We sent letters to all customers announcing the change, explaining the reasons for it, and emphasizing that Pilot Pen could improve its service under the new program.

2. We made sure that this transition occurred across the whole country at the same time, thus minimizing any adverse effects on individual customers.

3. We devised severance packages to soften the economic blow to our reps. More specifically, in return for their agreement not to compete with Pilot for six months, we offered them full commission for the first month, gradually declining sums for the next four months, and then full commission again for the final month.

4. We divided the country into five sales regions, each with a field sales manager to oversee the new sales force. We authorized those sales managers to start recruiting the best sales candidates for each region. We developed selection criteria to evaluate the new recruits. These criteria were selected based upon our mission to be not the biggest but the best company in

the pen business. Among other things, we sought people with substantial office-supply sales experience who were highly motivated self-starters, had a professional appearance and demeanor, and had a stable work history.

5. Recruiting was done by placing identical ads in local papers across the country. Of the hundreds of applicants, we chose at least ten in each region and subjected them to lengthy personal interviews and a battery of tests to evaluate them.

6. We developed company policy and training manuals for the new recruits. The regional sales managers then used those manuals as a guide during a week-long classroom training program that concentrated on product knowledge, company policies, reporting and operating procedures, and presentational skills. Then we had our field managers accompany our new recruits on all their customer calls the first week and on a diminishing proportion of calls during the next month.

7. To lure the high-caliber candidates our strategy demanded, Pilot offered an attractive combination of salary, benefits, bonuses, and travel incentive contests offering trips to such locales as Monte Carlo and Japan.

When we completed our six-month transitional period, we finally had the control over our sales force that we always wanted. We could direct the sales team to focus on projects with longer-term, and potentially larger, payoffs. For example, one new task we implemented required the sales force to set aside at least one day a month to deliver new product samples. In addition, we also had them calling on smaller customers to promote the product, even though they don't in fact sell directly to such customers. Any orders resulting from these relationships would occur through our wholesalers, thus strengthening our relations with those dealers.

Two years after we had let our reps go, we had cut sales costs by $500,000 annually and sent sales revenues soaring, by close to 50 percent.

■

Recently, market conditions have changed so rapidly that we have needed to go back to sales reps in certain markets. Let me explain exactly how this has happened and why it is a good example of how one must constantly adjust to changing times.

We dropped our sales reps in 1988, coincidentally the year the big three office supply superstores—Office Depot, Staples, and Office Max—got started. To be honest, at first they were looked upon by the industry as a joke. We all thought that no one would want to walk into a huge "warehouse" store to buy office supplies.

HOW WRONG COULD WE HAVE BEEN?

We had no idea of the great impact these superstores would have on the sale of office products. In a matter of a few years, the big three ended up putting 8,000 small office supply stores out of business. As we rolled through the nineties, the small mom-and-pop stationery stores couldn't compete with the superstores' prices.

With the loss of the mom-and-pop stores, we also found that fewer direct salespeople were needed. Currently, we have one salesman who works only with the big three customers. He is forever traveling between the Delray Beach headquarters of Office Depot in Florida, greater Boston to meet with Staples, and the Office Max people in greater Cleveland.

Today, we have a combination: We use some direct in-house salespeople, and we have reemployed several manufacturer's representatives. The direct salespeople we have serve an important function, and we plan to keep them, but it has become clear that we also need sales reps.

■

Adapt and change the structure of your sales force to fit changes in your markets, but whether your salespeople are in-house or outside, treat them well.

Chapter 21

WHEN SAVING MONEY IS A LOUSY INVESTMENT

*W*hen I was visiting a new account one day, I heard this story about an elderly couple in Kansas, Stumpy and Esther. Stumpy got his nickname because he was built like a fireplug. He was a sweet, quiet man who was constantly henpecked by his wife, Esther. Every year, they'd go to the Kansas State Fair, and every year Stumpy would say, "Esther, I'd like to ride in that there airplane."

And every year Esther would say, "I know, Stumpy, but that airplane ride costs ten dollars, and ten dollars is ten dollars."

One year, Stumpy and Esther went to the fair and Stumpy said, "Esther, I'm eighty-one years old. If I don't ride that airplane this year, I may never get another chance."

Esther replied, "Stumpy, that there airplane ride costs ten dollars, and ten dollars is ten dollars."

The pilot overheard them and said, "Folks, look. For years I've been hearing you argue, so let me make you a deal. I'll take you both up for a ride. If you can stay quiet for the entire ride and not say one word, I promise I won't charge you, but if you say even *one word,* it's gonna cost you ten dollars!"

Stumpy and Esther agreed and up they went. The pilot did all kinds of twists and turns, rolls and dives, but not a word was spoken by either of them.

So then, he did all his tricks over again, but still, Stumpy or Esther uttered not a word

When they landed, the pilot turned to Stumpy, "By golly, I did everything I could think of to get you to yell out, but you didn't even say one word, so I guess your ride'll be free."

Stumpy replied, "Well, I was gonna say something when Esther fell out, but ten dollars is ten dollars."

■

As a CEO, I know how important it is to contain costs, but I'm also the first to remind my fellow board members that you have to spend money to make money. The vision of a company must be broad based and longsighted. You can't get so absorbed in saving ten dollars that you lose sight of your employees, customers, and the millions of other dollars that could be coming in.

To illustrate this point, I love to tell the story of Thomas G. Stemberg, a true business visionary. Fresh out of Harvard Business School, Tom joined Jewel's Star Market corporate training program in 1973. He rose to vice president of sales and merchandising by 1980. He moved to Connecticut-based First National Supermarkets, where he held various senior management positions and was promoted to president of the company's Edwards-Finast division. At Edwards-Finast, he devised a revolutionary plan of cost-cutting warehouse stores, buying in volume and slashing prices. After working so hard, Tom asked to be rewarded appropriately. The company's response was to let him go.

On the Friday afternoon of a Fourth of July weekend a short while after he was fired, Tom was working at home in West Hartford, Connecticut, when his printer ribbon ran out. He went to a series of stationery stores in search of a replacement ribbon, only to find that none was open. When he finally found a wholesale club store that was open, it didn't carry the ribbon he needed. Unable to print without a ribbon, Tom saw an opportunity in his predicament. He believed there was an untapped market of frustrated consumers and small business owners who couldn't easily find the office supplies they needed and, when they could, were overpaying because they couldn't buy in volume. Tom envisioned millions of them patronizing an office products superstore stocked with thousands of items at discount prices.

To test his theory, he called a very large paper products company and tried to order a direct shipment of paper for what he claimed to be a small company of twenty employees. The best deal the company would give him was a 20 percent discount. Shortly thereafter, he called back, claiming he was with a large company of over one hundred employees, and this time he got more than a 50 percent discount. Tom was thrilled. His instincts were right. The average consumer and small business owner were not able to get the discounts they wanted and deserved. It was at that moment that Tom became certain he was onto something big and quickly moved forward on his office supply superstore concept.

To turn his concept into reality, Tom got together with a retired former competitor he greatly respected from the supermarket industry who wanted to get back into business and had access to capital. Together, they put together a business plan and management team. After a few months of long days and nights, the first Staples store opened its doors in Massachusetts in 1986. By developing Staples into a retail outlet designed to slash the cost and eliminate the hassle of purchasing office supplies, Tom created a company that now does $7 billion a year in business. Under his leadership, Staples became one of only six companies to ever reach $5 billion in sales within ten years.

Tom's success resulted from his objective to meet the increasingly sophisticated needs of small business customers by providing low-cost products and fast, efficient, convenient service while creating growth vehicles for the future. Tom has propelled Staples to 33 percent earnings per share compounded annual growth over the last five years. This growth has been fueled by an aggressive store expansion program, a profitable office products delivery business, a growing international presence, strategic acquisitions such as mail order marketer Quill Corporation, and the recently launched e-commerce site Staples.com.

■

Clearly, Tom is a brilliant businessman, and First National would have been well served by rewarding his service to their company instead of firing him. But Tom believes that if he hadn't been fired, he might still be with First National today and Staples would have never been born.

Chapter 22

VISIONS
OF BAGELS

$\mathcal{B}$esides being home to Pilot Pen of America, greater New Haven is also the original home of Lender's Bagel Bakery. For many years, I've been fortunate to be friends, and work closely on several charitable and community committees, with the brains behind Lender's Bagels, Murray and Marvin Lender. Their success story is a prime example of two individuals having extraordinary foresight and the passion to act upon their vision.

In the 1930s and 1940s, Murray and Marvin Lender's parents literally had a backyard business baking bagels in the garage behind their small house. From this inauspicious beginning, baking an ethnic specialty food generally consumed mainly on Sunday mornings by Jewish people, evolved a huge business where billions of bagels are consumed every year by all kinds of people worldwide.

Things really started to change in 1955 when Murray and Marvin put their first bagels into polyethylene bags and took their product to supermarkets around New England. Because the bagels still had a short shelf life, however, further innovations were necessary if sales were to expand. In 1962, two dramatic advances occurred. First, the Lenders worked with a company to produce the first automated bagel-baking machine. Now, instead of having to train bakers for six months on the specialized techniques of making bagels, machines working twenty-four hours a day could produce hundreds of thousands of bagels a month.

Second, the Lenders started freezing sliced bagels, thus locking in their freshness and providing their product with a practically unlimited shelf life. This was probably the single most important innovation in allowing Lender's Bagels to go beyond the local area and to have a national presence. The Lenders chose to use a sales force of frozen food brokers (120 different brokerage firms), who pushed for years until they succeeded in getting Lender's frozen bagels into virtually every frozen food aisle in North America. Meanwhile, as the brokers pushed to help them penetrate the country's markets, the Lenders built the first automated bagel-baking plant.

By 1977 Lender's Bagels had reached nationwide distribution, and they started spending more money on advertising and sales incentives for their brokers. By 1984 Lender's was grossing $60 million a year and, that year, sold to Kraft Foods for $90 million. At the time of the Kraft purchase, Lender's Bagels was employing six hundred people and had three plants in the United States. As a consequence, the Lenders felt that they could no longer keep a personal touch in their day-to-day operations. Murray and Marvin were working fifteen hours a day, seven days a week. What started out as a family business was losing that personalized, family touch. Meanwhile, they had already been doing some co-promotion deals with Kraft Foods, which at that time had no frozen-food products. The buyout seemed a marriage made in heaven.

But there was a problem. The Lenders feared that after the buyout their brokers might lose faith in their product. To reassure their brokers, the Lenders came up with a brilliant idea. At the national sales meeting, they staged a huge fancy wedding ceremony that included dinner, drinks, and dancing. The Lenders called it the Wedding of the Century, and they had actors dressed in costumes designed to look like the major Kraft and Lender's products. A two-legged bag of Lender's Bagels and huge canister of Philadelphia Cream Cheese walked down the aisle just as in a wedding. Then they exchanged vows and were betrothed. The brokers cheered and cried and ate and drank and everybody had a great time.

Murray and Marvin stayed on with Kraft for a few years to ease the company's transition, and by 1992 1.5 billion Lender's Bagels were sold a year. Every person who owns a corner bagel store today owes a small debt to the Lender brothers for making the bagel not just another ethnic treat but part of American culture.

After Murray had stopped working at the company, he was still acting as its TV spokesperson. One day I invited him to have lunch so that I could convince him to allow us to honor him with a dinner for his work with the Anti-Defamation League. Murray has always been a huge philanthropist, and I thought to have a dinner honoring him would be the natural thing to do. However, he came to that lunch with his own agenda. He wanted to try to convince me to appear in TV commercials for Pilot pens. Murray believed that the success Lender's had with him doing their commercials could be equaled by the success Pilot could have with me in our commercials. Murray felt that my personality would lend itself to commercials, and he pressed me to do them. He argued that in many ways my entire life experiences in performing and sales were perfect training for me to do this.

This wasn't the first time that someone I respected lobbied me to appear in our TV ads. For years, Don Aaronson and Stan Pearlman from our ad agency had also tried to persuade me to step in front of the camera. Looking back at that lunch, I think we both succeeded that day. I was able to get Murray to agree to be the honoree for our fund-raising dinner, and I began appearing in our TV commercials.

■

The Lenders are a truly great American business success story. And it all really started with the Lenders' ability to stand back and see the market potential of a product that others ignored. So, whether you are selling Dr. Grip pens, frozen bagels, or any other product, your marketing mandate is to have a vision that extends beyond the ordinary. And if that vision is clear and true, you will reap huge financial benefits for the rest of your life.

Chapter 23

SHOW BUSINESS SECRETS FOR PRESENTATIONS

*W*hen I was in Paris many years ago, I thought I spotted Picasso at an outdoor café, drinking coffee and reading the paper. An older woman approached him and asked in an American accent, "Excuse me, you're Picasso, aren't you?"

He put down his paper, looked over the top of his reading glasses, and said, "Yes, Madam, I am."

She held out a piece of paper and said, "I thought so! Would you draw a picture?"

He obliged her request and sketched something while she watched. She was delighted with the result and asked if she could have it.

"Of course, Madam," replied Picasso. "That will be five thousand dollars."

"Five thousand dollars!" she exclaimed. "Why, that drawing only took you a few seconds!"

"No, Madam," he replied. "That drawing took fifty-two years."

■

This emphasis on perceived value reminds me of a story that concerns my son Steve when he was about twelve years old and on his summer vacation. I thought this would be a perfect opportunity for us to spend some time together, so I invited him to travel with me to Philadelphia where I was scheduled to speak to a large sales and marketing association. Steve agreed and we drove from Connecticut to Pennsylvania together.

When we arrived at the hotel where the conference was taking place, Steve and I found a ballroom filled to capacity with businesspeople anxious to hear what I had to say. As we walked in, I remember Steve looking over at me and saying, "Jeez, Dad, are all these people really here to listen to you?"

I laughed and nodded yes.

Then he added, "I hope you tell them some jokes that are better than the ones you use at home."

Filled with confidence from my son's big pep talk, I ascended to the podium and began by telling one of my favorite jokes. However, I didn't tell the audience that I was telling them a joke. I let them discover that for themselves as I went along, and I was soon rewarded for my choice when the ballroom filled with laughter.

The next day, we were back in the car driving home. Steve looked over at me and said, "Dad, I can't believe there were people there who actually paid twenty-five dollars to listen to you tell the same stories you tell us around the dinner table for free."

I laughed again. "Yep. I guess I'm going to have to charge you guys for dinnertime conversation from now on."

Steve laughed, "Dad, there's one other thing I want to ask you."

"Shoot."

"These people just paid money to hear all about the secrets to your success, and you spoke for forty minutes, but still, it seemed like all you did was just tell a few jokes and a bunch of stories."

I looked over at him and said, "Yes, but the important thing is, those few jokes and stories might be all they needed to hear to succeed!"

Just as Picasso was paid for a lifetime of work even if what he drew only took him a few minutes, I was being received as a speaker for a lifetime of knowledge accumulated in the business world. People will always come to hear speakers who they think have something of value to impart that might be directly helpful to them. And if value can be a function of perception, then that perception starts from how one values him- or herself. In turn, that value is a quality that will be evident in any speech you give or public presentation you make.

■

Thinking back to all the speaking engagements I have accepted, there are a host of techniques and lessons I've learned from masterful performers in show business. The key is that memorable presentations blend great content with great theater. Anyone can become a polished performer by following these same principles and investing time in rehearsal.

YOUR STAGING

If you will be on a theatrical-style stage, with lighting and offstage wings, you'll have the best resources available to you. If you'll be speaking from a tabletop podium in a banquet room as people eat lunch, you can still employ aspects of these techniques for a powerful presentation.

No matter what type of staging you'll encounter, the lighting and sound system are critical. After years of working in nightclubs, I noticed that the major performers have very strong opinions about how they should be lit. You should be just as detail oriented. If you'll be presenting in a banquet hall or conference room, you can build drama with a fixed floodlight attached to the ceiling and directed at you (there are portable floods with clamps that are ideal for temporary lighting). Check if the room lighting can be dimmed. If you'll be referring to notes, make sure the podium light works.

Check the sound system and any audio-visual equipment a few hours before your audience arrives. Test your microphone. How close to your mouth does it need to be? If it's handheld, that frees you to move around during your presentation and gives your hands a prop.

QUICK TIP. Listen to the microphone's amplification of your first few words once you start your presentation. Despite thorough sound checks, the sound system may need readjustment once the room is filled.

Theater-Style Stage. Think drama and mystique. You want the house lights down, leaving the audience sitting in darkness and focusing on you in the spotlight. Position your podium in the center, within inches of the front of the stage. You want to build intimacy with your audience and your proximity to them is essential. Work with the lighting technician to follow your entrance, presentation, and exit with a spotlight.

Conference Hall or Banquet Room. If you'll be speaking while your audience is eating a meal, make sure that the tables are set up so close to the stage or speaker's podium that there is only enough room for the waiters to squeeze through. The tables in the room should be just as close to each other. Again, you want to create a warm, friendly atmosphere where intimacy is possible. This closeness has a huge impact on the way your presentation is perceived. If moving the tables forward and near each other leaves an intolerable amount of bare space in the room, ask the facility manager to disguise it with plants, screens, or some other visual fillers. When your audience will be sitting in chairs and not at tables, apply the same philosophy. Move the chairs close to you.

CROWD-CONTROL TIP

The easiest way to get an audience quiet is to turn out the lights and put a spotlight on the person speaking. If a theatrical spotlight is not available, at the very least make sure there is some type of light to illuminate the speaker while the room is in darkness.

YOUR INTRODUCTION

Write your own introduction and give it to the person who will be introducing you. Keep it short and relevant to your audience (no lengthy résumé!). Reserve the mention of your name until the very end. In show business, the masters know to build anticipation to create audience excitement. Just as a stripper doesn't begin her act naked and a comedian doesn't lead with a punch line, your introduction should stimulate your audience's imagination.

Think of the thrill of being in a room as someone stands and says, "Tonight's speaker has enjoyed unrivaled access to the leaders of countries and industries around the globe. This evening our guest will talk about his [her] primary concerns and hopes for our country over the next four years, and what those mean to each of you. Ladies and gentleman, may I present the President of the United States."

I actually had the privilege of introducing former President Gerald Ford, and a definite shiver of excitement flashed through the room when I ended my introduction with his name. When composing your introduction, build audience anticipation with your credentials and what your topic means to members of your audience, saving your name until the end.

YOUR ENTRANCE

Of course, you are impeccably groomed and dressed appropriately for your audience. If you're presenting from a theatrical stage, use it for a theatrical entrance from the wings. Otherwise, simply move into position at the podium after you've been introduced.

Once you've made your entrance, launch straight into what you have to say. Don't dilute the impact of your opening with thanking your hosts or remarking how great it is to be in that city. Think of the first few seconds of a film. Would James Bond look into the camera and say, "Good evening. Thanks for buying a movie ticket!"?

If you're a panelist on a dais, don't feel compelled to introduce everyone, especially if they will eventually speak and be introduced later. The only people you could introduce are those who are not speaking and would otherwise not be mentioned. If you must introduce the people on the dais, avoid the cliché "From my right and your left . . ." As with other introductions, reserve the speaker's name until the end.

YOUR PRESENTATION

Opening. As a comedian, I learned to open with my strongest material. It was a sure way to connect with the audience, reassure them that they could relax with me, and help me relax into my act. The audience was prepared for comedy and that's what I delivered. Your audience is anticipating your message, so please don't feel obliged to begin your presentation with a joke. If you're exceptionally skilled at telling jokes, then pick an appropriate one and have fun. But learn from the pros, as I did. When you are going to tell a joke, don't let people know it's a joke before you tell it. If you don't feel comfortable about telling a joke, then don't! Trust me, it's better not to even attempt to tell a joke than to tell one poorly and launch your presentation with a giant thud.

Every comedian, every actor, and every speaker is nervous when walking onstage. That adrenaline rush can make relaxing impossible. That's why the pros have learned *to act* as if they're relaxed. To help you pretend to be at ease, prepare like the pros do. Do your homework. Make sure you know your subject and you've rehearsed. When you appear to be at ease and begin with your strongest material, your audience will respond favorably. This chain reaction results in your genuinely relaxing and having a great time.

Notes. Whenever I speak in public presentations, I write brief notes on the back of an envelope. I've seen other speakers use index cards. I like to work with key words and phrases so that one glance will trigger a section of my speech. If you work with notes, allow ample time for rehearsal—not to memorize your speech word-for-word but to imprint the sequence of your presentation's stories, facts, and insights into your mind. Select key words or phrases to represent each section and rehearse some more, referring only to your key words. By the time you give your speech, you may not need to refer to your notes at all. (I refer to my notes up to the time of my introduction, and then tuck them in the breast pocket of my jacket right before I am about to speak.) Your audience will respond to you as if you are speaking extemporaneously, even though you are presenting pre-pared and rehearsed material. After your speech, if some special phrasing or powerful concept came up during your talk that got a good response, write it down so you can include it in your next presentation.

Audience Connection. You don't need to make eye contact with various people in your audience. Instead, slowly pan the room, turning your face and attention to address those areas where people are seated. When it's appropriate to what you're saying, smile. Relax your facial muscles. Gesture naturally. Be yourself. Remember, you are talking to an ideal audience—a roomful of people who want you to succeed!

Closing. Just as you started with your strongest material, end with strong material. Never close by saying "And in conclusion . . ." This is a sure way of telling the audience you were boring. Close with a great line or a memorable point that sums up the essence of your message.

YOUR EXIT

Before you get onstage or step up to the podium, know where your exit is. When you've finished your presentation, accept the applause. Stand tall, smile, and bask in that wave of appreciation. You've earned it! If there is no question-and-answer session following your speech, make your exit before the applause dies down. If there is a Q&A session, make sure everyone hears the question (repeat it for the audience or use a roving handheld mike) and make sure you understand it before answering. Keep your answers thoughtful and succinct, and don't be embarrassed to say you don't know the answer.

MEDIA INTERVIEWS

When doing any media interview, you want to combine sounding and looking confident with being relaxed.

Concentrate on the reporter. For broadcast interviews, don't be concerned about the microphone or camera. Strive to be the same person you are when you're talking with your best friend. Be upbeat, use the reporter's name, and smile (if appropriate to the nature of the interview). If you use humor, use the self-deprecating kind. Tell stories that show your humanity or reveal a valuable lesson you've learned.

Come into the interview prepared. Know the angle of the story, some background information on the reporter, and who the readers, listeners, or viewers are. You'll find that when you're interviewed, different reporters will often ask you the same questions. Prepare succinct, clearly thought-out answers. Don't attempt to come up with fresh responses to the same questions when you already have good answers at your command.

Even though the reporter asks the questions, always include your message in your answers (you see some politicians doing this to the point that they completely ignore the question). If you have a key point you want to make about your company, product, or cause, weave it into your answers.

Characterize your responses with attention getters such as "The biggest mistake," "The most interesting aspect," or "The three most important points are . . ." Use dramatic action verbs and, instead of generalities, specific facts and figures. Include anecdotes to illustrate a point. If you don't know the answer to a question, admit it instead of faking it. And it is always better to pause for a second than to say, "Um" or "Well . . ."

Take every interview seriously, no matter how small the publication or program may be. You never know who may be reading, listening, or watching. If media interviews are a regular part of your job, work with a media trainer so you can take maximum advantage of these opportunities.

■

Even when you're not speaking before a group or being interviewed on TV, you are still presenting yourself every time you step out of your house.

I've always emphasized to my children and my employees that no matter what they do in life, they should never do it halfway. Recently when I was speaking to my son Steve, who now is a successful video director/producer, he reminded me of when he was growing up and we were having financial difficulties. He remembers how I tried to drive a nice car, dress in good clothes, and always be impeccably groomed. He remembers me telling him that, "If you look the part, doors would open that might otherwise remain closed. After that, it would be up to you to prove you deserved to stay there."

Call me old-fashioned, but I've always been a firm believer in the adage: Clothes make the woman or man. Let's face it: First impressions count. And inevitably, you will be judged not on how well you make your presentation but on how you look. So, please, don't overlook wardrobe. I am partial to a crisp appearance. For men in business, shirts need to be the proper collar size, and about one-quarter inch of cuff should show past the jacket sleeve. Suits should be properly tailored, and trousers shouldn't bunch up around the ankles. Ties should be properly knotted. For women, skirts should not be too short. For men and women, nails should be manicured and hair should be neatly trimmed. Shoes should always be shined.

If you have a regional accent, you may want to go so far as to replace it with a "neutral" way of speaking. Growing up in Philadelphia and Miami in the forties and fifties, I spoke with a Philly-southern accent—an unusual combination with no redeeming value in show business! I diligently worked to rid myself of those regional pronunciations and inflections so I could move forward as a comedian.

■

If you want to be taken seriously, let people know you take yourself seriously by presenting yourself with care. Especially with the rise of dress-down days, casual Fridays, and differing dress codes, appearance can be the key to how people perceive you. Give it your all. Make the effort to look good and speak well. You won't be sorry you did.

Chapter 24

PAY ATTENTION
TO THE
BIG ROCKS

I was in a time-management course once where I learned a valuable lesson. The instructor used an illustration to open the seminar that I will never forget. He stood in front of the class and put a huge glass jar on the table in front of him. He then took a bag of rocks from under his desk and started filling the jar with them. When he could fit no more rocks in, he stood back and asked the class, "Is the jar full?"

"Yes!" we all answered immediately. He shook his head and reached under his desk and pulled out a bag of gravel. He poured the gravel into the jar and it began to slip down and fill the spaces between the rocks. "Now is the jar full?" he asked. Aware that this was another trick question, most of us remained silent.

Someone spoke up from the back row. "Probably not," he said.

"Good!" the instructor exclaimed. He now produced a bucket of sand from under his desk and proceeded to pour sand into the jar, which took up the tiny spaces between the pieces of gravel and the rocks. "Is it full now?" he asked.

"No!" we all replied, having caught on to his game. He nodded his head, picked up the pitcher of water on his desk and poured it into the jar until it spilled over the brim. He then looked up at us and said, "Now the jar is full. What is the point of this illustration?"

I raised my hand and said with admiration for his little demonstration, "You're illustrating that no matter how full your schedule is, there's always room to fit more in if you try."

I sat back smugly, expecting to be congratulated for my interpretation. But the instructor shook his head. "No," he said. "The illustration shows us that if you don't put the big rocks in first, you'll never get them all in."

■

What are the big rocks in your life? Your family? Your health? Your education? Your dreams? Your favorite causes? What makes you happy?

Whatever your big rocks are, make sure you put them into your life first. If you fill your life with the smaller stuff of lesser importance (like the sand and the gravel), you'll never fit in the more important things. Besides working on a personal level, this lesson can also be applied on a corporate, and even global, level. In fact, in the eighties, I saw how America seemed to be putting its little rocks in first, and I spoke up about it.

If you remember, the 1980s marked a moment in history when a wave of protectionism against foreign products swept across the nation. Also at this time it seemed as if Japan had finally eclipsed the United States in economic wealth and manufacturing power. In an effort to combat this new "foreign threat," the U.S. government decided to try to step in and "protect" its economy. I was then COO of Pilot—the American subsidiary of a Japanese corporation. I had divided loyalties and was a bit uncertain exactly how I should proceed.

But I did know this for sure: As a loyal American, I want the freedom of choice to buy the best product, wherever it is made, and I do not like the idea of being told what I can and cannot sell here in the United States. The whole concept of curtailing free trade always had bothered me. I also thought these new protectionist threats did not serve America's economy, but in fact were counterproductive. The one thing I did know was that we couldn't afford to wait and see which direction the American economic and political winds would blow.

Yet, all the threats against so-called foreign products seemed vague until one day, a member of the U.S. Congress wandered into the office-supply store in the basement of the House of Representatives in Washington. This congressman was appalled by all the non-American-made products on display. In a huff, he ran to the floor of Congress where he delivered a fervent speech about the evils of foreign-made products. Now, needless to say, Pilot had quite a presence in this stationery store, and so I was personally affronted by this attack.

In fact, just a week before his tirade, there was a photo in *Time* magazine of First Lady Rosalynn Carter holding a Pilot pen in her hand, and things were really starting to look up for us. So the idea of our product being banished from U.S. soil because a single member of Congress didn't like the fact that there were more "Japanese" pens being sold in his stationery store than "American" pens was very scary to me. It was true that at that time, every Pilot pen sold in America was made in Japan. Yet, we were a U.S.-based company, and I didn't believe that the point of origin of any product for which the designated customs tariff had been paid justified a ban against the product.

By this time, we had moved our headquarters to Port Chester, New York, and I got in touch with our congressman. I told him how upset I was and how I wanted a chance to give my side of the story. He agreed to meet with me, and I flew to Washington, D.C. Without getting too emotional, I went into a diatribe that went something like this: "There really isn't a funnel that runs under the Pacific Ocean from Japan and comes up in the stationery store in the basement of the House of Representatives. Even though our Pilot pens are manufactured in Japan, we ship them to the United States by boat where we pay U.S. customs duties. Then, our pens are taken off the boats by American longshoremen, and the containers are placed on flatbed trucks driven by American Teamsters Union drivers. Then, they are brought to our American warehouse where we employ only American workers, and then they are packaged and shipped around the country on American trucks to American stores with American salespeople, and sold by advertisements written by American admen to be published in American magazines."

My entire speech clearly demonstrated to him that any easy delineation of the evils of foreign-made products being sold in the United States was a vast oversimplification.

And it worked.

Our representative took the floor and convinced Congress to back off. The U.S. government didn't carry out its threat to ban the importation of Japanese-made products. But we at Pilot Pen Corporation of America were able to read the writing on the wall. This threat was a good kick in the pants to accelerate plans we'd already been making to open manufacturing facilities in North America.

In 1985, for the first time in the sixty-seven-year history of Pilot, we started assembling Japanese ballpoint pens in the United States. We had determined that making pens in the United States allowed us to respond more quickly to changing market needs. Also, without the import fees, we could offer our products at lower prices over the long run, which more than justified the initial capital costs of building additional facilities.

■

In the end, this chain of events was fortuitous. We are now able to control our own destiny, and we no longer have, literally, to wait for the boat to come in. The importation-ban threat, which could have badly hurt business, instead aided us. It forced me to confront a new bully. Instead of getting cuts and bruises, we opened our manufacturing facilities here in North America and released Pilot America from total dependency on foreign shipments.

Chapter 25

PROTECT
YOUR NAME

$\mathcal{G}$ood businesspeople are marriage brokers of sorts. It is their job to shepherd their products into the hands of retailers and consumers who might not necessarily think they need or want that product. However, lack of consumer enthusiasm should never stop a good salesperson; it should merely serve as an incentive to try to prove to customers why they do in fact need it.

A good businessperson must also be protective of the product once it has been distributed and has become part of the consumer's life. Pilot Pen, like other companies with nationwide product distribution, is very conscious of insuring that its name is not used by other commercial enterprises. When 3Com (which used to be U.S. Robotics and is now Palm, Inc.), came out with the Palm Pilot, I knew this could be quite confusing to consumers; so I decided that some sort of action needed to be taken.

We did not go after them because of the name *Pilot*. There are a great many companies that use that name. There is a chain of Pilot gas stations, a Pilot Trucking Company, Pilot Life Insurance, Pilot Electronics. And there's nothing we can or really want to do about them. They sell different products than we. However, U.S. Robotics was selling a pocket organizer or PDA (personal digital assistant) that incorporated a writing instrument—a stylus.

We are in the stylus business and we have the necessary trademarks worldwide to insure that we are the only company that markets writing instruments under the name *Pilot*. On this basis, we wanted to prevent another company from marketing a stylus under our name.

We filed suit in a U.S. court, but the case really ended up being won in a courtroom in France, where they are stricter about using copyrighted names. A judge in Paris ruled that Palm, Inc. couldn't sell its PDA in France with the Pilot name on it, and this decision had a profound impact on the American case. After the French ruling, the Palm, Inc. people decided that if they couldn't sell their product under the name *Palm Pilot* in the large market of France, they might as well change the name globally.

The management at Palm, Inc. changed about two years ago, and soon after, I received a call from their new CEO. He said. "Ron, I'd like to see you."

"For what purpose?" I asked.

"Well," he said, "we'd like to find out how much you would charge us for permission to use the name *Palm Pilot* for our PDA."

I couldn't believe it. We had spent a great deal of money, time, and energy to secure the Pilot name, and here he was trying to get it back.

He went on. "You see, Ron. We've done lots of market research, and it seems like the consumers all agree that the name *Palm Pilot* is the best."

I answered, "Sorry, but I can't help you."

"C'mon, Ron, you must have a price. Everybody has a price."

"Not me. There isn't a dollar amount in the world you can offer me. We will not prostitute our good company name."

Taking this trademark dispute to court cost us a good deal in legal fees, but I was adamant about not giving in or changing our tune a few years later. We had worked hard to make the name *Pilot* synonymous with quality writing instruments, and I was willing to fight to protect it.

■

Today Palm, Inc. purchases Pilot stylus products from us for their Palm handheld organizers, proving the old adage that the best way to get even with a customer is to take his order! Protect your name. It is one of the most important commodities you have.

chapter 26

PUBLICIZE
YOUR NAME

A long time ago, the King of Spain had a personal servant who had the annoying habit of exclaiming "This is wonderful!" after every event.

One day, the King was on a hunting expedition in Africa. His servant was loading and preparing the guns for him. At one point, the servant handed the King a gun that he must have loaded wrong, because when the King fired it, it backfired and blew his thumb off.

The servant observed the situation and, as was his habit, declared, "This is wonderful!"

The King was furious. "No! This is NOT good!" he yelled at his servant and immediately had him locked up in jail for his transgression.

Six months later, the King was on another hunting expedition in Africa when he was ambushed and captured by a group of cannibals. They dragged him off to their village and proceeded to tie him up and prepare a fire and boiling pot. As they were lifting him into the pot, they noticed that he was missing a thumb. In their culture, it was forbidden to eat anyone who was less than whole because they believed it would bring extreme bad luck to the tribe, so they quickly untied the King and set him free.

On his return to Spain, the King ordered the release of his old servant. When the servant returned to the castle, the King apologized to him and explained what had happened.

"So you were right," he said. "It was wonderful that my thumb was blown off, and I'm sorry for sending you to jail for so long. I feel badly for doing that."

"No," the servant replied. "This is wonderful!"

"What do you mean, 'this is wonderful'?" asked the King. "How can it be wonderful to sit in jail for six months?"

"Because if I had not been in jail," replied the servant, "I would have been with you."

■

The success or failure of a company lies in the ways management deals with the unforeseen occurrences of everyday business. It's easy to deal with success, but when things don't go the company's way, that's when a manager's skills are truly tested.

For example, when we heard about the upcoming signing of the peace treaty between Israel and the PLO in 1993, we were curious to learn if Yitzhak Rabin or Yasser Arafat would use a Pilot pen. However, when asked by a reporter about the pen that would be used, Yitzhak Rabin replied that as a representative of the common people, he did not want to use a fancy pen, but instead whatever ordinary plastic pen was in his pocket at the time. So, we realized all we could do was wait and see if he would go with Papermate, Bic, or Pilot.

And wouldn't you know it? At the moment of the signing, Rabin pulled a blue Pilot V5 out of his pocket and used it to sign the accord.

I witnessed this on CNN and was ecstatic. I immediately called our head marketing guy and asked him what he thought we could do with this. He answered blandly, "Well, we should probably get a copy of the videotape and enter it into our archives!"

Wrong answer! This was not just an archival moment; it was a great marketing opportunity, and I decided to handle it personally. I got on the phone with our advertising agency and we generated an immediate full-page newspaper ad campaign with a close-up photo of our pen being used to sign the accord. My son Steve wrote the headline, which read, "There's a line between war and peace. This one was written with a Pilot pen." We believed this ad merited going into every paper in the country, but happily settled for the top twenty-five markets and thereby avoided busting our advertising budget.

For many people this would have been the end of the peace pen, but as soon as the ad campaign was placed in the papers, we had another brainstorm. Maybe we could get our peace pen ad story picked up as a news item. I called our gung-ho public relations firm, PR News, headed by Jim Plunkett, and he pitched the story to a contact at the Associated Press.

Before we knew it, besides the twenty-five papers, we also had a news story about our peace-pen ad campaign in almost every paper in the world. What a coup! We were able to take a half-million-dollar ad campaign and get $20 million worth of positive publicity out of it. Now that's what

I call taking advantage of an opportunity and capitalizing on it. Clearly, a company's success depends on how it creatively deals with unforeseen circumstances.

■

Public relations is a huge part of business these days. I don't know a CEO who wouldn't rather have articles written about his company (as long as they are positive) than spend money on advertisements.

This brings me to a story about a special CEO. Thousands of years ago, Moses had a PR guy who followed him everywhere he went. The guy's name was Sam. Moses paid Sam a good deal of money to make sure he was highly publicized throughout the land, and to ensure that everyone knew where to find him.

When Moses and the Israelites got to the Red Sea, Moses asked Sam, "Where are the boats?"

"I'm sorry, Moses," Sam said, "I was so busy with all the press releases, I forgot to order the boats. Boat ordering isn't exactly in my job description anyway."

Moses was extremely angry. "Sam! You've really messed up here. What do you expect me to do now? Raise my staff and ask God to part the Red Sea?"

"Hey, boss," Sam said, "if you can do that, I bet I could get you two pages in the Old Testament!"

■

If you've hired people to do your public relations (or, for that matter, to do any work for you), don't expect them to know they have to order boats if you've forgotten to tell them to do so. Hire the right people to do the right jobs and don't assume that anyone will take on extra responsibilities without being expressly asked.

This brings to mind the Silly Putty story. In the 1940s, the U.S. War Production Board asked General Electric to make a cheap substitute for rubber that could help with the war effort. James Wright, a GE engineer, produced a synthetic compound he called "nutty putty." In 1949, Paul Hodgson, a former ad copywriter running a toy store, saw a demonstration of the product at a party. Hodgson bought twenty-one pounds of the stuff and hired a Yale student to cut the putty into small balls and place them in small plastic eggs. He called it Silly Putty, and soon it outsold everything else in his little store.

The real stroke of genius here, though, was getting a piece about the Silly Putty in the "Talk of the Town" section of *The New Yorker* magazine, which almost single-handedly launched the huge success of the product in the fifties and sixties.

■

So, whether you're selling Rollerball pens and using the Israeli Peace Accord as a springboard or you're selling Silly Putty and using magazine articles and word-of-mouth, it is up to your company's PR agency to generate the sizzle necessary to sell your product.

Chapter 27

ARE YOU SAYING WHAT THEY'RE HEARING?

A few years back, one of my older friends began to lose his hearing. We were all telling him he had to get a hearing aid. For awhile, he didn't want to hear it, but eventually, we were able to persuade him to see his doctor and get fitted with a great hi-tech hearing aid.

A few days later, we were having dinner and he loved his hearing aid so much, he started boasting about it: "This hearing aid is the best ever made. Top of the line, the most advanced model there is. And not cheap either. Very expensive. But it's worth it—I can hear a pin drop!"

"That's great!" I told him looking at the tiny contraption in his ear. "What kind is it?"

My friend looked at his watch and said, "Oh, about six-thirty."

■

That story speaks loudly about the need for clear communication and the ease with which misunderstanding can creep into conversation. This issue of communication and miscommunication became very significant to me when I became the sixth American in history to be elected to the board of directors of a Japanese public company—Pilot Corporation. This couldn't have happened without a mentor at Pilot in Japan, Mr. Akira Tsuneto. Just as Jack Paige was a terrific mentor to me at Bic, I was very fortunate to have someone at our parent company in Tokyo take interest in me.

I've had the pleasure of visiting Japan more than fifty times during my time with Pilot. The Japanese have earned their reputation for being gracious hosts and exceptionally polite people. Unlike let-it-all-hang-out Americans, the Japanese prefer to avoid confrontation and seek agreement.

That is, except for Akira Tsuneto, the president of Pilot Corporation and the man responsible for my being named a board member. Mr. Tsuneto is direct and to the point. He speaks his mind about what he believes is good for the company.

Japan's centuries of tradition and homogenous population have led to a strong image of what it means to be Japanese. It is highly unusual to meet a Japanese businessman who deviates from what have become cultural characteristics, particularly one over the age of fifty. But Mr. Tsuneto is most unusual. In addition to being candid, he is passionate about hot dogs, Big Band music, and vacationing in France. He doesn't smoke. He has lived in Europe. He is proudly Japanese yet he is also a maverick.

For instance, many Japanese companies operate subsidiaries in the United States. Most of them have a Japanese national as the CEO. In 1986, when I was promoted to president, the company's board of directors made the remarkable decision that Pilot Pen Corporation of America would be under my sole leadership. Eventually, that approach was extended to include our subsidiaries around the world. Today the Pilot operations in England, France,

Germany, Hong Kong, Indonesia, Israel, Italy, Malaysia, Russia, and Singapore are run by citizens of those countries, locals who understand the national culture, customs, and market. That autonomy is due to Mr. Tsuneto's willingness to do things differently and to battle for what he believes is right.

Mr. Tsuneto faced some opposition when he stated that he wanted me to serve on the Pilot Corporation board of directors. Publicly-held Japanese companies rarely have foreigners serve on their boards. But Mr. Tsuneto was convinced that to be a competitive global company, Pilot must diversify its board. He pushed until it happened: I was elected to the board of directors in March 1992.

Our steadfast public relations man, Jim Plunkett, invested hours poring over the Japan Company Datafile to put my appointment in the context of Americans in leadership roles in Japanese companies. He wrote a news release that the Associated Press picked up and the story shot around the world.

Of course I was thrilled about joining the board of directors and knew it was a great honor. Prepared for my first board of directors' meeting, I flew to Tokyo assuming the Pilot shareholders meeting in Tokyo would be like an annual meeting in America. When I walked into the corporate headquarters, I saw a battery of reporters and photographers but thought nothing of it. They were there to cover the meeting. However, as I walked by them, I heard one yell, "There he is!"

Suddenly, as in the movies, this horde of journalists and cameramen from ABC, CNN, and CBS as well as numerous

Japanese stations ran after me. It was a little scary, let me tell you. (Later on, I found out that reporters are not allowed into our shareholders meetings, so they had to try to interview me outside the meeting room.)

I've studied the Japanese language, but even after years of lessons I have a very limited vocabulary. For that first meeting, I didn't have a translator and had to sit for many hours without really understanding what was being said. Occasionally one of the other directors who was bilingual whispered tidbits of information into my ear.

Since then, I now receive instant translations from two professionals who provide nearly perfect English translations with an eight- to nine-second delay. As a result, I am now able to participate fully.

I'd like to claim that I was elected to the board because of our performance in the United States. By 1992, we'd gone from $1.2 million in sales to $86 million, evidence that I could make some contribution to our global operations. However, I know that despite our performance none of this would have happened if Mr. Tsuneto's style were less candid. I admire him tremendously for the risks he takes to keep Pilot Corporation innovative and competitive in a global market. He shows remarkable courage in his leadership and I am proud to have him as my friend.

Mr. Tsuneto, Jack Paige, and many show-business pros went out of their way to help me further my two careers. It's important to me to pass along that generosity. At Pilot Pen, we look first within our company for people to promote rather than immediately hire outside. We offer education reimbursement so our employees can advance their knowledge and skills. When employees are promoted, we work closely with them to help them succeed and do well. And we delineate the scope of responsibilities and what is expected.

∎

Clear and unambiguous communication is essential to conducting corporate business, particularly when different languages and cultures are involved. A single mishandled word can change the entire substance of a message.

Chapter 28

MARKETING HIDDEN TREASURES

A professional golfer was sitting in the bar at his club one day, when a blind man came up to sit next to him. He was puzzled to see the man in the bar. He seemed to be on his own, so the pro golfer, feeling sorry for him, bought him a drink. "Are you waiting for someone?"

"No," replied the man, "I'm a member here."

The pro golfer couldn't hide his disbelief and rudely exclaimed, "But how can you play golf? You're blind!"

The man smiled and explained, "I get my caddie to walk down the fairway and call to me. Then I hit the ball in the direction of his voice."

"That's amazing!" said the pro. "But how do you putt?"

"Easy," replied the blind man, "I get my caddie to lie down behind the hole with his head on the ground and I just play the ball towards his voice."

The golfer was overwhelmed by all of this and asked the blind man if he had a handicap. "Actually," the man said, "I'm a scratch golfer."

The golfer couldn't contain his curiosity. "I'd love to see you play," he said. "Perhaps you'd like to play a round with me sometime."

"I only play for money," warned the blind man. "And it's got to be a thousand dollars a hole!"

The golf pro laughed, but he could also see the blind man was serious. In the end, not really wanting to offend the man, the pro agreed.

"Great!" said the blind man. "What night would you like to play?"

■

Don't rush into judging other people or products. You can never be too sure of anything. Sometimes you just have to have the flexibility to reevaluate what the best business applications really are for a product. Many times a great product or employee may already be part of your company; you just have to see how to apply and market them. Silly Putty and the Razor Point pen exemplify this principle, as does a Pilot product called Magna Doodle, the world's most popular drawing toy. Even though Magna Doodle is sold by Fisher-Price Toys, Pilot Pen produces it and it has sold over 80 million units.

Magna Doodle was invented in 1974 by a group of engineers working for our parent company. They were assigned to design a dustless chalkboard for business applications. When a member of the Takara Toy Company was visiting Pilot and accidentally saw the prototype, he asked if he could place an order. He was told that the prototype he was looking at was no toy. It was a business tool with a cost per unit of more than $25, which was much too expensive for a toy. The Takara Toy employee soon left, but his idea for a magnetic-screen toy took hold. Our company immediately formed a project team to develop a means to mass-produce the product at a much more affordable level, and soon the Magna Doodle was born.

The product was first marketed in Japan and almost instantly became a big hit. In the mid-1980s, we wanted to bring it to America, but we realized we needed the trade connections of a strong toy company to bring it into the homes of American families nationwide. So in 1986 we chose View-Master to launch the market line.

Tyco Toys acquired View-Master in 1989 and launched Magna Doodle's first television advertising campaign in the spring of 1990. Under Tyco's direction Magna Doodle achieved one sales record after another despite stiff competition. Five years later, Tyco and Pilot celebrated the manufacturing of our 40 millionth Magna Doodle. Magna Doodle, with its emphasis on ease of use, imagination, creativity, and fun, now outsells Etch-A-Sketch™ four to one and consistently outsells every other toy in the mechanical design category. Almost half of the households in America with children under seven years of age own a Magna Doodle.

In 1997, Mattel, Inc. acquired Tyco Toys, and Magna Doodle moved to Mattel's Fisher-Price division. Soon after, Fisher-Price began to restyle the entire Magna Doodle line to assure its continued success into the twenty-first century. The new styles incorporate handles and clips for conveniently taking Magna Doodle from place to place. Today's versions include the regular, deluxe, travel, and pocket clip-on Magna Doodle. Even with Magna Doodle's great success, we haven't sat on our laurels. Other products that incorporate the magnetic screen technology include the QUEST,™ a device that allows divers to communicate underwater; the Clean Mag, that allows for use in sterile business environments; and the Mag Media, for use in stadiums, schools, and other public places.

■

Ever since I sat atop my first Schwinn Black Phantom bicycle, I've been drawn to and felt the power of doing things right, of going all out. Treat yourself like the best, and you will become the best. Cut corners, and it shows. These truisms became apparent to me when we first started considering the marketing of Pilot's high-end writing instruments that are now known as Namiki. These pens range from the $125 Vanishing Point, the world's only one-click retractable fountain pen, to our top-of-the-line Namiki, which costs $6,500. Usually this pen is purchased not for writing but by collectors to be kept under glass as a work of art. Many of these high-end pens are finished with a special Japanese process known as *Maki-é* (pronounced MOCK-ee-ay). This process endows the most expensive Namiki writing instruments with a gorgeous, highly lacquered artistic finish. All illustrations on the bodies of these pens are done by hand by artists with brushes so small that some have only two rat-hair bristles.

Back in the 1970s, our high-end writing instruments were not called Namikis; they were just very expensive Pilot pens. This, however, eventually resulted in some problems. For example, imagine two big business executives who are about to sign an important agreement that they've spent months negotiating. One of the executives whips out his

$3,000 Pilot fountain pen he's purchased for just such a special occasion. Then his counterpart pulls out his black 79¢ Pilot disposable pen. At this point, one would tend to believe that the businessman who had just spent $3,000 on a Pilot pen might feel a little foolish.

When you are dealing with high-end products like very expensive pens, there is a distinct snob appeal that must be taken into consideration. Thus, I determined that we needed to shut down Pilot's high-end pen distribution in North America in the late seventies, and I promised our Japanese parent company that we would reopen it in a year or two once we had made some very specific marketing decisions.

My time estimate was off the mark by only a decade; we ended up taking eleven years before bringing our high-end writing instruments back into the North American market. And when we did, we knew the most important thing was that these pens must not be known as Pilot. They had to have a name that rang with distinction—something that would carry the same prestige as a name like Tiffany. As luck would have it, a fascinating cultural occurrence took place during the intervening eleven years. America had shifted 180 degrees in how Japanese products were regarded.

In other words, during the seventies some Japanese products were still seen as lacking good quality, but by the late eighties, Japanese products had become known as the epitome of good quality.

So we decided to lean towards a Japanese name—but what would it be? Many possibilities were bandied about the office until somebody in our marketing department suggested going with the original name of our company in

1918—Namiki. It sounded great, so we did an investigation into the Namiki name only to find out that over the years another company had bought the rights. So we bought back the name. Once we finally secured the legal rights to the Namiki name, we spent a great deal of time designing a logo and attractive gift boxes to present the pens. Every eighteen months, we sell a specially designed model as a signed and numbered limited edition of only seven hundred pens worldwide. Today, collectors and true pen lovers can purchase Namiki pens all across America, wherever fine pens are sold.

■

Aesthetics matter, whether the subject is a pen, a Black Phantom bicycle, or you. If you want to write, you don't need to spend hundreds or thousands of dollars for a pen. You can buy our Better Grip ballpoint for seventy-nine cents. There are many people who purchase our Namiki pens, however, simply because they are beautiful. In addition to being fine writing instruments, they are an accessory, like a fine watch or expensive jewelry. They let you express yourself by what you write and by the artistry of the pen itself. Sure, physical appearance isn't everything; the pens must write well—there must be substance beneath the surface. But in the end, any retailer will tell you, most sales usually result from customers being drawn to physical appearances first. Customers come back because, after being hooked by appearances, they are then pleased with performance; but remember, it was the appearance that hooked them initially.

Chapter 29

MY FAVORITE
FAILURES

*T*here were once two very successful businessmen who were brothers. They attended church regularly, pretending to be good, honest Christians. The truth was, however, they were evil to the core. They were extremely rich but hoarded their money and then put it to ill use.

One day the pastor of the church retired and a new one was appointed. He soon saw right through these two brothers but kept quiet. He was an inspiring pastor, and the church membership grew and grew. He even started a fund-raising campaign to fix the church roof.

Then one of the brothers died suddenly in a car accident. Before the funeral, the other brother handed the pastor a check for the full amount needed to fix the roof. He said to the pastor, "You can have this on one condition. At the funeral you must say that my brother was a saint."

The pastor promised to do so and cashed the check.

The next day, at the funeral, the pastor stood up and told the truth but kept his word, saying, "He was an evil man. He cheated on his wife, abused his family, and was cruel to others. But compared to his brother—he was a saint."

■

It's easy to pull the wool over people's eyes. It's easy to lie and to paint a more saintly picture of yourself, especially when you have a public relations machine behind you, as many companies do today.

But always be careful; one day, the truth may be exposed. Remember what James E. Burke, former chairman and CEO of Johnson & Johnson, did when the Extra-Strength Tylenol poison scare struck the country in 1982 (Tylenol is a product of Johnson & Johnson's McNeil Consumer Products Company). He did not try to evade responsibility. He did not try to hide. He immediately took full responsibility and recalled the product nationwide. Johnson & Johnson suffered short-term financial losses, but as a result of his actions, people never lost faith in the product, and Tylenol soon was selling better than ever. Deception will catch up to you, but truth and acceptance of responsibility will build consumer confidence.

■

So far, I've related a series of business success stories, but I would be presenting a false picture of myself and Pilot Pen Corporation of America if I didn't also share with you a few stories of some of the products we've been associated with that have really BOMBED!

My favorite failure anecdote has to be the tale of the Pilot Brougham pen. Never heard of the Pilot Brougham? Well, there's a very good reason for that—the Brougham came and went really fast. Let me tell you exactly what happened.

In North America, Pilot has always been known for fine-point or extra-fine-point pens. In fact, we are the only large manufacturer of ballpoint pens that sells more fine-point than medium-point pens. And even though the fine point put us on the map, we still wanted to get a larger share of the medium-point market. So, we decided to go in the opposite direction and make a broad-point pen. In other words, if the average medium-point pen has a 0.7 millimeter ball, we opted to go with a larger, 1.0 millimeter ball. We were excited about the possibilities, especially since the larger ball allows for a smoother line.

So we jumped into manufacturing this new broad-point pen. The new pen was going to be my baby, and I really wanted to make it a classy-looking writing instrument. We chose a beautiful charcoal gray color for the pen body and a shiny silver clip on the cap.

We designed it in-house with a little help from a design company. I knew it had to have an imposing name. We played with lots of titles, but none seemed to click. I was driving an Oldsmobile Regency Brougham at the time, so I thought—what a perfect name for a pen, the Regency. But this name was already taken. So, we settled for the name *Brougham*, which means a high-class carriage. In fact, it was a name used by Cadillac. So, there it was. Our new broad-point pen—the new Pilot Brougham. I thought it couldn't miss.

Unfortunately, we laid a horrible egg and lost millions. The Brougham didn't write so smoothly as it was supposed to. The name *Brougham* was hard to pronounce and hard to remember for most Americans. After a year, when we knew we had a real flop on our hands, we sold our inventory at cost and took the loss. It was my fault. It was my pet project, and there was nobody else I could blame for its failure. So, I stood naked in the spotlight and took the blame.

A few years later, we invested in a great office product that we were sure would be a huge seller. It was called the Grippa—in honor of the way it really gripped paper! The Grippa was a plastic paper holder that attached to the side of any desktop computer monitor to hold a piece of paper at eye level, thus making it much easier for people working at a keyboard to enter information. I fell in love with this product when I saw how cleverly it was bent and curved to beautifully hold a piece of paper without ever allowing it to fold over.

The Grippa was designed by a man in England. We made a deal for the rights to sell the Grippa in North America at a retail price of $17.95. In this case our parent company in Japan was not involved. Again, this was my baby. When we first demonstrated the Grippa to our wholesalers, they flipped over it. They all said they'd never seen anything like it. Since we were receiving such great support from them, we eagerly moved forward. We designed a special Grippa box and packaged it beautifully. Unbeknownst to us and our wholesalers, however, at this same time another similar product to hold paper was about to be released by one of our competitors at a price of $10.99. As soon as we learned this, we realized we were virtually dead in the water at the outset. Again, we took a big financial hit.

In both of these cases, I was saddened by our inability to make the Grippa and the Brougham into viable business successes, but I didn't allow our company to dwell on our losses. Instead, we focused on our growing sales of other products and learned whatever we could from our mistakes.

■

If you ever find yourself backing a product or idea that can't take off, get out quickly and move on.

Chapter 30

MY FAVORITE RECOVERIES

Though I play golf, my passion is tennis, especially since Pilot Pen has gotten involved in one of the top women's tennis tournaments in the country. But I'm getting ahead of myself. Here's a suspenseful tale of a business situation that could have become a catastrophe but ended up a victory.

It was a winter day in 1982. I was getting a haircut at Vinny's Barber Shop in New Haven. As Vinny did his magic, Larry Hoffman walked in. Larry was an active member of the local Probus Club, a charitable organization whose main goal is to raise funds for handicapped and autistic children. Larry told me that the club had been approved to do a little Challenger Series tennis event in New Haven, but they had limited funds and needed to find a title sponsor.

The previous year, Bic Pen had sponsored the event, which took place in August at Southern Connecticut State University. Bic decided not to renew their sponsorship, however, throwing the Probus Club's tournament and primary fund-raiser in jeopardy. Right there in the barbershop, Larry offered Pilot the chance to take over the title sponsorship. I expected it would cost around $75,000, but like any good businessperson in a negotiation, I kept my mouth shut and asked, "Larry, how much?"

He looked at me and said, "It's only going to cost you five thousand dollars."

I wasn't sure if I heard him right and asked, "Larry, excuse me, but would you repeat that?"

"Just five thousand bucks."

"Okay," I said, "we might be able to do that. But the name of the tournament has to be only three words long and two of the words have to be Pilot Pen."

Larry agreed, we shook hands, and the Pilot Pen Open was born in the barbershop. The first day of the tournament, only twelve people showed up, and I was a friend with eleven of them. I panicked. What a horrible waste of money! I was mortified. I went home depressed and embarrassed. However, as I was reading the paper the next morning, I noticed how many times Pilot was mentioned and realized, "Hey, wait a second! Maybe our little tournament wasn't such a failure after all."

The truth was, we received a tremendous amount of favorable publicity for sponsoring the tournament, much more than we could have received spending $5,000 on ordinary advertising. We continued to sponsor the event each August, and in 1984, during the third Pilot Pen Open, an idea began fidgeting in my imagination. What would happen if we became the title sponsor of a *major* tournament with really big name players? I studied the demographics of people who play tennis recreationally and saw a huge correlation with Pilot pen users. I contacted our ad agency, which made an introduction to a sports management company. Our timing was perfect. The title sponsor of a major tennis tournament wanted out, and the tournament director was talking with potential sponsors.

Within two weeks of hatching this idea, I met with the tournament director, Charlie Pasarell, at the U.S. Open in nearby Flushing, New York. Charlie made his presentation, and I liked what I heard. He also said one of the major automotive companies was very interested in taking over the title sponsorship. I knew that big corporations meant many layers of approval, and I had a window of opportunity. I asked Charlie whether, if I made a decision on the spot, we'd have a deal. Charlie said we would. That's how, in addition to sponsoring the little Pilot Pen Open, we became the sponsor of the Pilot Pen Classic, held each February in Palm Springs, California.

For the next three years, from 1985 through 1987, Pilot Pen received a great deal of positive publicity across the country. Before it was time to renew our option to continue sponsoring the classic, I learned that the tournament organizers were trying to raise more money from another sponsor. We quickly renewed our contract to lock us in for the next three years at the same fee we had been paying. The organizers of the event were now in a bind. They were contractually obligated to work with us, but they had interest from a larger corporation with more financial clout. In the end, we worked out a deal that we felt was very fair and economically advantageous to us. We decided to withdraw as title sponsor of the classic.

Meanwhile, the Pilot Pen Open in New Haven kept going, finally ending in 1991 after a ten-year run. At the same time, the Volvo International Tennis Tournament, a major Association of Tennis Professionals (ATP) men's event, moved to New Haven in 1990 and was doing well. In 1994, however, Volvo notified the owner of the tournament that it was no longer interested in being title sponsor, and the owner had two years to find a replacement. The tournament owner talked to many companies that are bigger than Pilot and came up empty. Finally, he came to see me. I gave him a price. He laughed at our offer and was not interested. For the next two years, he kept talking to other companies but unsuccessfully. Finally, he became so desperate that he returned to us and agreed to the original price he'd laughed at two years earlier. In 1996 we became the title sponsor of the newly named Pilot Pen International.

We were thrilled to be involved with another large, prestigious tournament that featured the top men players in the world and one of the country's finest facilities. A few years earlier, the state of Connecticut had built a 15,000-seat, $18 million-facility on the grounds of Yale University, in New Haven. At the time, it was the second largest outdoor tennis stadium in the United States. Only the Stadium Court at the USTA National Tennis Center in Flushing, home of the U.S. Open, was bigger. Since the tournament is held in late August—the week before the U.S. Open—we looked forward to crowds of fans, ideal weather, and considerable media coverage. We envisioned the Pilot Pen International as a natural lead-in for the U.S. Open. Because of the timing and since Connecticut is one of the most affluent states in the country, our tournament's potential seemed unlimited. In fact, the purse had been raised from $675,000 to $1,040,000 to take advantage of the combination of the money, the market, the stadium, and the time of year. In doing so, the hope was that Connecticut would grow to have an irresistible draw as host to the pre-U.S. Open tournament.

But our euphoria was quickly deflated. Within five months of becoming the title sponsor, we faced a crisis. In January 1997 we discovered that the tournament owner was in serious financial trouble, and it was very possible there would not be a tournament that summer. The 1996 tournament had a terribly disappointing attendance. The crowds weren't coming because many of the high-profile players chose the ATP tournament in Indianapolis instead of coming to New Haven. The tournament owner was in debt somewhere between $2 million and $4 million.

Linda Lorimer, Yale University vice president responsible for relations with the city of New Haven, met with the owner in January. He opened his books to Yale, revealing that the money brought in for the upcoming tournament had already been spent. He suggested that an investor be found. Immediately after their meeting, Linda called me to express her alarm. I was aware of the tournament's recent history of dwindling attendance and the diminished promotion for the upcoming event, so her call came as no surprise. The loss of the tournament would be a huge black eye for Yale, New Haven, and of course Pilot. No one wanted to lose this event. Serious action had to be taken, and quickly.

I was motivated by visions of angry ticket holders protesting outside our headquarters and demanding refunds—and the media picking up the story that would discredit Pilot across the country. Even though we were just the title sponsor and had nothing to do with the administration of the tournament, it was our name that was associated with the event, and thus it was our corporate reputation that was on the line. Yale and New Haven held large stakes in this tournament's success, as well. Although Yale is one of the top universities, it competes for students. Parents consider the totality of a university's offerings and this high-level tournament enhanced Yale's appeal. The city of New Haven rec-

ognized the tourism and economic benefits from the tournament, as well as the prestige of being the hosting city.
Compounding the problems of losing the tournament was
the chance the press would discover the fiscal crisis. With
such juicy bait as Yale, Pilot, and the city of New Haven,
if reporters uncovered this story, it would be like blood in
the water.

Linda discretely arranged a private meeting among
Yale president Rick Levin, the mayor of New Haven, herself, and me. After much discussion, we agreed that we had
to immediately search for a way to bring in someone new.
Rick and Linda said they'd search among Yale graduates for
tennis promoters and tournament directors. I agreed to
meet with the owner to assess the situation.

The owner and I met. Because of his monetary dis-
tress, the 1997 tournament itself and its promotion were
being severely cut back. At the next Yale-New Haven-Pilot
meeting, I reported the worsening news. Linda and Rick
produced their list of candidates to rescue the tournament.
They asked if I had a list. I gave them a piece of paper with
one name written five times: Butch Buchholz.

Butch was a top tennis player in the 1960s, touring and
competing with champions such as Jack Kramer, Frank
Sedgman, Pancho Gonzalez, and Pancho Segura. Butch
competed until he was forced to retire from injuries in
1970. But he didn't leave tennis. He went on to become one
of the country's most successful tournament promoters and
owners, including founding the Lipton Championships in
1985 (now named the Ericsson Open).

Over the years I had watched Butch's Lipton
Championships in Key Biscayne, Florida grow into one of

the world's top tennis events. It was well run and brilliantly promoted, consistently attracted the world's top men and women players, and brought in sellout crowds. In fact, box seats to the Lipton were so hard to come by they were bequeathed in wills. I absolutely believed that bringing in Butch was our only shot at salvaging the Pilot Pen International and turning it into a successful event. Rick, Linda, and the mayor agreed that Butch was our strongest option, and since I had met him once at a cocktail party, I was elected to contact him at his office in Miami.

I called. Butch was aware that our tournament was in trouble. The current owner had already contacted him about becoming his partner and infusing the event with new cash. However, Butch had no interest in becoming a partner; he needed to be in charge. I talked with him about the problems we faced but also pointed out the potential, particularly since our tournament was the week before the U.S. Open. I confessed my concerns about ticket holders losing their money and Pilot's reputation being damaged. Butch said he'd come to New Haven to meet with the owner and look at the numbers.

He did, and he still wasn't interested in a partnership. But I hadn't lost interest in Butch. He agreed to meet me in Miami so we could talk face-to-face. When I arrived, I was shocked to see that the Pilot Pen tournament owner was there for the meeting! Naturally, his presence inhibited what I could discuss. After I returned home, I phoned Butch and told him what I had wanted to say in person. Pilot, Yale, and New Haven would agree to bring him in as the sole owner, not as a partner. Butch was intrigued but pragmatic. In addition to the Lipton, he was creating a new tournament in Latin America. He didn't need the business and his family was unwilling to lose even more of his time.

After eleven years of reading audiences and three decades of reading customers, I sensed that Butch was attracted to the challenge and that his only reluctance was displeasing his family. I persevered in my campaign until Butch said he'd meet with his family to discuss his taking over our tournament. A few days later Butch phoned and with great enthusiasm said he'd take us on. He'd buy out the tournament owner, accept the debt that had been incurred, put his own money into our event, and run it as a top tennis tournament. I was thrilled! I called Rick and Linda at Yale and the mayor with the good news. We rejoiced that the tournament had been saved and the story had been kept out of the papers.

However, this bout of euphoria was also short-lived. Butch called me five days later to say his involvement was off. He just couldn't take on one more project. He told me that this was a very tough call for him. Since it was the end of February and our tournament was less than six months away, the call was even tougher for me. I pleaded with Butch to reconsider, and probed for any new reasons for his sudden turnabout. Butch brought up an obstacle that he felt was the deal breaker. He initially thought he could get around it but realized he could not. I assured him we could take care of it, and again asked him to reconsider. He agreed to let me know in a week. Six days later, he called to say we were on again.

It was now March. Phissy and I were in Washington, D.C., to attend a fund-raiser at the Kennedy Center. While we were dressing in our hotel room, the phone rang. Butch had tracked me down. My stomach clenched and my heart sank as I heard him say, "Ron, this is the most difficult phone call of my life. It's final. I can't do it." By the end of the call we were late for our event so we hurried to the Kennedy Center. I was so distraught that Phissy and I went to the wrong cocktail reception, nibbling someone else's refreshments for half an hour before we figured out why we didn't recognize anyone. We ducked out and I found a pay phone to call the mayor with the bad news. He agreed to set up an early morning meeting in New Haven the next day with Rick, Linda, himself, and me.

The four of us knew we had to find a solution in record time. We discussed who else we could approach. However, I remained convinced that Butch was our man and that he really wanted to take a swipe at this challenge. I felt confident that if I could sit with him face-to-face one more time, I could sell him. I suggested that we ask Butch if he would accept a meeting with the four of us. I thought that if he accepted, we were halfway there. The others agreed and began comparing their availability while consulting their schedules. I interrupted to say that we had to go *today*. Every hour that passed worked against us. There were protests about the impossibility of getting a flight to Miami that day, but I would not accept impossibility. If Butch said he would meet us, I said we'd charter a plane. The expense would be negligible compared to the cost of losing the tournament.

Since it was still early in the morning, I called Butch at home. He said he would meet with us and that he'd pick us up at the airport. I told him we could get there by 3:00. We chartered a small jet and landed at five minutes before 3:00.

(Rick Levin was the only one who could not make the trip, since he was meeting several world dignitaries at Yale that day.) Butch had just arrived at the airport as well. Since the Lipton was opening in a few days, he drove us to the stadium and gave us a tour before we sat down for an early dinner. We didn't have much time: Our jet had to be back in the air before 9:00 for our pilots to be legal to fly.

Once our meals were served, it was my time to be on. I never sold so hard in my life. I pitched my heart out to Butch. Linda and the mayor stepped in to add information and answer questions. Butch brought up his list of concerns. One by one, the mayor and Linda said that each would be addressed. Anything that Butch needed, they said they'd handle. The three of us came up with ways for him to get everything he wanted. It was close to 8:30, and the sky was thick with rain clouds; lightning and thunder bolted through the heavy air. Butch rushed us back to the airport. At ten minutes before 9:00, Butch and I stood in the rain beside the jet, facing each other. I asked when I should call him. He said that he'd call me the next day, one way or the other. We shook hands, I boarded, and we took off.

The next morning I told Patty Skarupa, my assistant, that when Butch Buchholz called she should track me down no matter where I might be in the building. Though I had plenty to do, the day dragged by. Even though I believed that Butch wanted to take over the tournament, we'd gone back and forth so many times that I didn't know what his final decision would be. I was deeply concerned about what we would do if Butch said no. Finally, at 3:15 Butch called. The deal was on!

With less than five months before the tournament's opening day, Butch officially agreed to take the reins. The Pilot Pen International was saved! Needless to say, we were ecstatic. Butch was our white knight who galloped in at the last minute.

In the first two years, he lost $2.2 million but he stayed with it. In 1999, for the first time, the event turned a profit. Furthermore, Mike Davies, a former tennis star from the U.K., moved to New Haven and became president of the tournament. Working with him is tournament director Anne Worcester, who previously served as CEO of the Women's Tennis Association (WTA). Butch continues as the chairman of the event.

Today, the tournament is called Pilot Pen Tennis and features professional women exclusively, attracting the top players in the world. It has grown into the tournament we envisioned and continues to get even better. And we've adhered to the requirement I gave Larry Hoffman in Vinny's Barber Shop on that long-ago winter day—the name is three words long, with two of them being Pilot Pen.

Getting involved in a small, basically unknown tennis tournament in 1982 has led to many significant dividends for us to this day. It also reinforced three valuable lessons:

1. Develop a vision for any major endeavor.
2. Hold on to that vision with tenacity.
3. Identify and recruit the best talent.

I also learned a lesson that may have helped save someone's life.

■

Howard and Sandie Taubin have been very close friends to Phissy and me for years. Howard is a doctor, a gastroenterologist, and Sandie works in a law firm. Every year they attend the Pilot Pen Tennis tournament. One year, following the day's matches they drove to Cape May Courthouse in New Jersey, about 225 miles away, a solid five-hour drive with traffic.

Not long after they arrived at their destination, Howard complained he wasn't feeling well. He developed a fever, chills, and severe muscle aches. Six hours later, he was transported to the local hospital by ambulance. His condition deteriorated so quickly that he was lapsing in and out of consciousness.

After an examination and a few blood tests, he was given a diagnosis of flu. However, Howard's condition worsened. His coloring turned gray, and his vital signs became unstable. Sandie grew frantic and called Howard's medical partner, Dr. Greg Soloway, in Stratford, Connecticut, relaying the symptoms. Dr. Soloway said to have Howard tested for meningitis and demanded that he be started on the appropriate medication.

Sure enough, meningitis was the correct diagnosis, and Howard had contracted the deadly meningococcal meningitis. Sandie telephoned us at home and we knew from the fright in her voice that it was serious. We dropped everything, rushed to the car, defied speed limits, and arrived at the hospital within five hours of Sandie's call.

It was worse than we feared. Howard was in the intensive care unit in isolation and could have only one visitor at a time. I suited up in that blue sterile hospital garb and was heartsick to hear Howard quietly say "Ronnie, I think this is the big one." His doctors seemed to agree.

It made me nuts to know that if this had happened while Howard was at home, he'd be cared for like royalty in his own hospital in Bridgeport and have a better chance at pulling through. I plunged into finding a way to get him medically evacuated in an airplane. While transporting him in his condition was extremely risky, he didn't seem to have any options if he stayed where he was. Sandie was understandably distraught. I couldn't ask her to make a decision that might save her husband or kill him.

We tracked down Howard's brother Joel, also a doctor, but he was traveling and couldn't get to Cape May Courthouse until the next morning. Howard hung on while we waited. I had a medical evacuation team on standby. Finally Joel arrived and examined Howard. Joel told me that his brother had a fifty-fifty chance of surviving a flight home. I persuaded him to go for it and we put Operation Howard in motion.

A medical evacuation plane comes with a pilot, co-pilot, and nurse. Joel accompanied Howard on the flight to Connecticut, which was met by ambulance at the Bridgeport airport. Howard was rushed to the hospital, where a medical A-team of his colleagues was waiting to meet him. In the meantime, Phissy, Sandie, and I drove home, checking on Howard's progress by phone and struggling to prevent fear from overtaking us.

Howard survived the medical evacuation and spent weeks in the hospital recovering. Today he is healthy, fit, and practicing medicine full time. He credits me and many others with saving his life. I believe a higher power is responsible for getting him through that flight; however,

I am deeply grateful that I was able to be there for my friend.

■

Experiences like this are kicks in the head for remembering what is truly important. I also relearned the value of creating options when there appear to be none, and to summon the courage to push forward and make things happen when the result would be worth the risk.

Chapter 31

DRESS REHEARSAL FOR A RETIREMENT DREAM

$\mathcal{E}$ver since I was a youngster, standing on stage in a big glowing white spotlight, I've always dreamed that someday I would open my own theater.

In the late 1980s, as passing thoughts of retirement started to creep into my head, in an effort to find out if I really would like being in the theater administration business, I got involved with the legendary Shubert Theater in downtown New Haven, Connecticut.

It all started out rather innocently. I was tapped to chair a big fund-raiser for the New Haven Jewish Home for the Aged. Not sure what we would do for the fund-raiser, I decided, as Mickey Rooney and Judy Garland would have, that we should put on a show. First, we booked a big-name performer, and in order to really make it an exceptional event, I insisted that we do it at a special venue, someplace with cachet, with history. There's no place in Connecticut with more ties to the legends of Broadway than the Shubert Theater, frequently the "tryout" stop for a new show headed for Broadway.

We arranged to get Neil Sedaka to headline. After he was booked, my close friend ever since my Miami days, the talented Rosemary Clooney, gave me a call and said she was going to be in Massachusetts around the time of the fundraiser. On her way back to New York, she agreed to stop by and sing a few songs—for no pay, mind you—just to help. I opened with a few minutes of my shtick, and then I introduced Rosemary as a surprise guest. The audience was thrilled. Rosie sang a few songs, and then she introduced Neil. I didn't know it at the time, but that night while I was doing some of my old act, the president of the Shubert was sitting in the audience, and then and there she decided that I was exactly the kind of person she wanted on their board of directors.

She enrolled a mutual friend, Lindy Gold, to draft me, and I readily agreed. I regularly attended board meetings for the next few years, but as a board member I felt like I wasn't really contributing very much. And so, after my fourth year, I went to the chairman of the board, Cheever Tyler, and told him that I was ready to step down.

He looked at me and laughed, saying, "No, you can't. I'm retiring and you're going to take my place. You're stepping up!"

So in the span of less than ten seconds, I went from an exiting low-level board member to chairman of the board for the next five years. And it was during those five years that the Shubert hit a huge fiscal roadblock and almost went under. We had to embark on a major campaign to raise money to pay off the Shubert's mortgage and keep the theater's doors open.

The new president of the Shubert, Caroline Werth, and I had a major problem on our hands. New Haven was facing its own fiscal crisis, and there were not a lot of funds floating around the city. We decided to start by asking Rick Levin, the president of Yale University, for money. Like every university, Yale is a hard sell since they are constantly in the process of raising funds for the school and their own endowment. So, although Yale University was not the most logical choice, I trusted that if we could convey to Rick a sense of what the downtown area would look like with the Shubert dark, I could win him over. Caroline and I went to his office and stressed that if the whole block around the Shubert—which is less than a block from Yale's old campus—was boarded up, wouldn't this convey to prospective Yale students and their parents a bad impression of our city? Rick nodded in agreement and came up with an ingenious idea. Every year, Yale paid $50,000 to sponsor a dance series. So Levin arranged to forward us a half-million dollars as a ten-year advance, and in doing so, he helped to keep the arts alive in New Haven.

Yet that still wasn't enough to pay off our mortgage; we needed more money. Carolyn and I went to private foundations, arts councils, even the governor of Connecticut and clearly articulated to each of them how we can't have a viable community without the arts. Over and over again, we emphasized what the Shubert meant on nights that the theater is open in downtown New Haven. We even utilized statistics from restaurants, bars, and parking lots, demonstrating the substantial influx of money that came in on nights that the theater was lit. Through our efforts, we conclusively proved the significant economic impact that the Shubert has on the city. Our campaign started working, but the money we received was still not enough. Two days before we were going to have to close, we had yet to reach our goal. Something like panic set in. The theater was in big trouble and despite our efforts, we were still unsure if we were going to be able to keep its doors open.

Ultimately, May 6, 1996, was our D-Day. Would the Shubert survive or die? Caroline and I called a press conference to take place at the theater. I walked out onto a bare stage with a single spotlight; it was all very dramatic. I looked very somber and serious. I started by speaking about the perilous condition that the Shubert was in. Then, I raised my voice and exclaimed, "And I'm here to say we have saved the Shubert!"

The key had been getting rid of the mortgage. The monies that we raised through all the different channels allowed us to pay off the mortgage and become solvent. We had structured a new, five-year plan with the city of New Haven that would let us operate the theater with an annual subsidy. And so, with that announcement, show tunes blasted through the sound system and colorful sets dropped down from the fly space above my head and moved in from the wings. By the time I had finished my speech, the entire stage was dressed. It was pure theater and everybody loved it.

Since my five-year stint as chairman of the board elapsed, I have remained a board member and still go to see all the shows. I feel lucky to have had the experience and been able to do something that directly impacted the New Haven community in a most favorable way.

■

Working in the nonprofit world has given me a true appreciation for what people in the arts have to go through to stay afloat and also taught me that despite my childhood dreams, I made the right choice in my life. I was not meant to be a theater owner!

Chapter 32

PILOT YOUR LIFE

I'm now sixty-two years old. I've worked hard for a long time and sold a lot of pens, but over the course of my life some things have stayed with me and profoundly affected me. For example, I still remember when our family moved to Florida in 1948 and I saw segregation for the first time in my life. People of color could not drink from the same water fountains as white people, or sit beside them in movie theaters, or ride in the front section of buses. Even when a headline performer like Sammy Davis, Jr. came to Miami to do a show, he was relegated to "colored hotels." I might have been young, and it was many years ago, but the injustice of this type of racism has stayed with me to this day.

In fact, one day in a store when I was ten, my mother tried on a dress. It didn't fit, so she didn't buy it. At the same time, an African-American woman tried on a similar dress, and she was told that she had to buy it because she had tried it on. Ever since then, I've spent a great deal of my time and energy fighting against bigotry. Once I retire, I hope to be able to spend even more time working with some of the charitable organizations I am now involved with.

Also, I'm happy to report that I have four beautiful grandchildren—Stephanie Santoro, Lauren Shaw, Bryan

Shaw, and Jacob Shaw—and I'm looking forward to having more time to spend with them.

In fact, one of my biggest regrets in life is being so caught up in the business world that I feel like I probably did not get enough time with my own children in their formative years. There were many weeks when I was away two, three, four, or even five days of the week. I really became a weekend father; fortunately, my wife did a phenomenal job of playing both mother and father during the week. However, I cannot stress enough the value of making time for one's own family. When my kids were young and I did come home from a business trip, I would always make a special effort to spend time with each of them, carefully listening and getting up-to-date on everything they had done while I was away. I also tried to schedule my trips around their Little League games and dance recitals.

Speaking of family, there's one last story that is very dear to my heart that I promised at the beginning of this book I would like to share with you. When I was a young man with a new wife and a baby, I approached my father and asked him to help get me a job at his company as a truck driver. I was flat-out broke and really needed the money. I knew my father was well liked at his company and had a little influence, so I thought the chances of his getting me hired were really good.

He looked over at me and said, "You know, Ron, I think I could get you a job. But if I do, you'll stay at that company, drive a truck every day for the next forty years, collect your pension, and never achieve anything close to what you are capable of."

"But, Dad, it's a good salary. $125 a week. We could really use the—"

"Ron, listen to me. I'm sorry, but I won't do it. I want you to do more. I know you can do better. Trust me, you can do better!"

I was angry with him at the time, but now I see how right he was.

So thanks, Dad. Thank you for not getting me that job and instead urging me on to do more with my life and stretch all the way until I fulfilled my potential. I've come to see how great a gift you gave me on that day. It is this very same gift that I want to give to *you*, my reader. I hope this book has helped inspire you and stretch a little fruther and dare to achieve your potential.

Remember, we are all blessed with certain gifts and it is your job in life to find them, exploit them, and, don't forget, along the way try to give something back.

■

Looking back over my career, there seems to be one great irony that rises above the rest. Even though I have spent the past forty years of my life in the pen business working for others, I have always emphasized to my children and all young people the significance and advantages of working for yourself. There are so many rewards that come from being in business for yourself. There's nothing that can beat the freedom and independence of it. In fact, I'm happy to say that all three of my children and their spouses have their own companies, and I believe they are all better off for it.

In fact, whenever I deliver college commencement addresses, I always ask the graduates to take this little test:

"Think for a moment of the five wealthiest people you personally know. I am not talking about Donald Trump or Bill Gates. I am talking about friends and family members."

When they have thought for a few seconds, I go on to say, "Without even knowing any of those five people, I would bet you that at least four of them are in business for themselves." Inevitably, I see the mass of students nodding their heads. It never fails.

In fact, I was told that when one of the fathers of a graduate in the audience heard my speech, he ran home to fulfill his lifelong dream of finally starting his own business. God bless him, and I hope he makes it; yet, even if he doesn't, at least he will know that he tried and will not have to live with the awful specter of "What if?" hanging over his head for the rest of his life.

It has always seemed to me that there are just two kinds of people in this world: those who want and need a steady job and are happy to follow the crowd, and those who need to lead, to take chances, to get ahead. And it is those filled with the great entrepreneurial spirit who should and must go into business for themselves.

■

Though I may have started my career on stage, I've spent the vast majority of my life as a salesperson and a businessman. I love what I do and have no regrets about the choices I've made. I feel very fortunate to have worked with so many great people along the way, and even more fortunate to have each of my setbacks produce something better.

And so, to everyone who's ever had to work for a living or dreamt of being a little more successful, I hope this book has taught you a few things, given you a few laughs, and maybe helped you pilot your life and your career.

INDEX